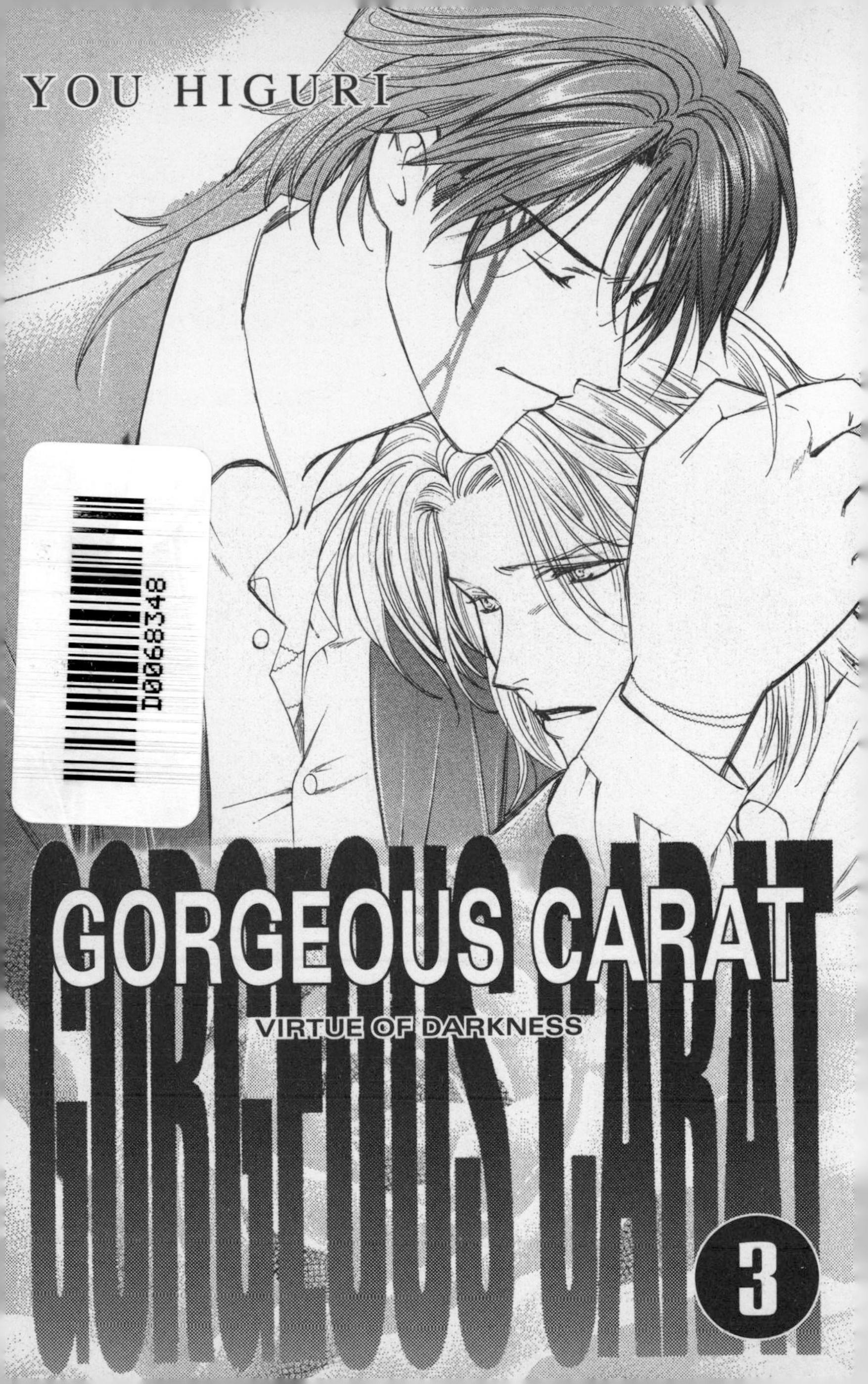

YOU HIGURI

GORGEOUS CARAT

VIRTUE OF DARKNESS

3

GORGEOUS CARAT

Virtue of Darkness

GORGEOUS CARAT

Character Introductions

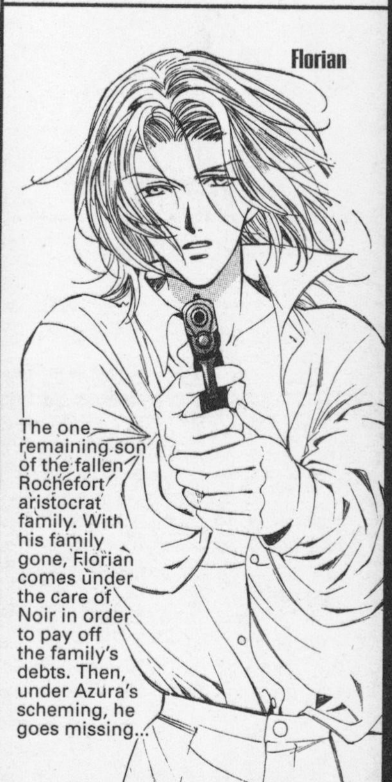
Florian
The one remaining son of the fallen Rochefort aristocrat family. With his family gone, Florian comes under the care of Noir in order to pay off the family's debts. Then, under Azura's scheming, he goes missing...

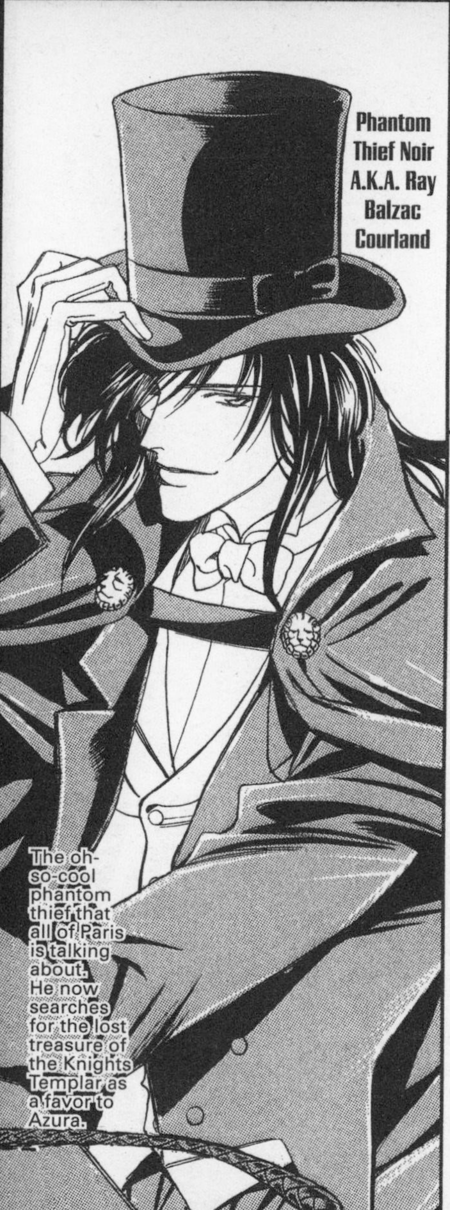
Phantom Thief Noir A.K.A. Ray Balzac Courland
The oh-so-cool phantom thief that all of Paris is talking about. He now searches for the lost treasure of the Knights Templar as a favor to Azura.

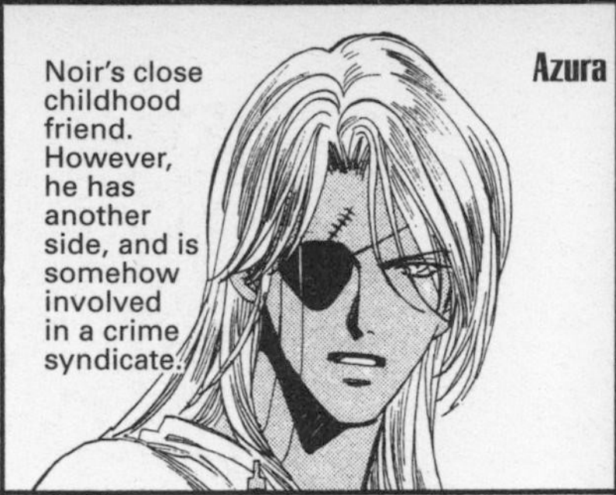
Azura
Noir's close childhood friend. However, he has another side, and is somehow involved in a crime syndicate.
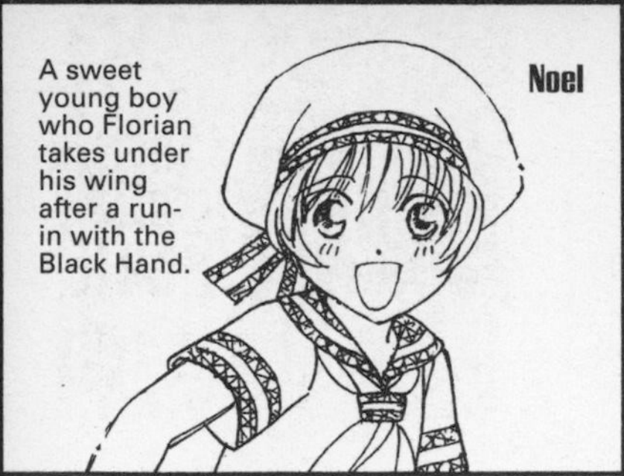
Noel
A sweet young boy who Florian takes under his wing after a run-in with the Black Hand.
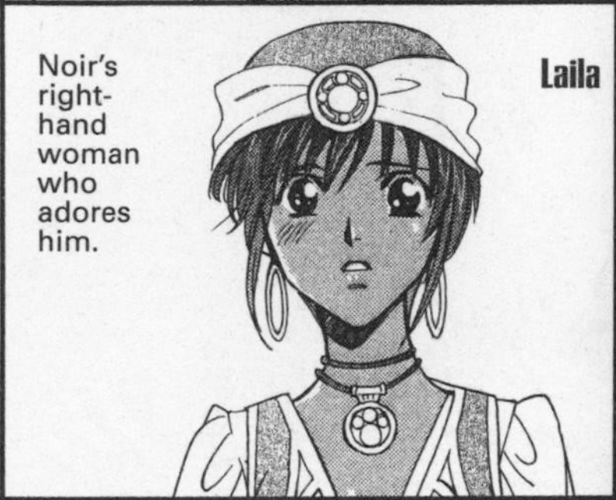
Laila
Noir's right-hand woman who adores him.
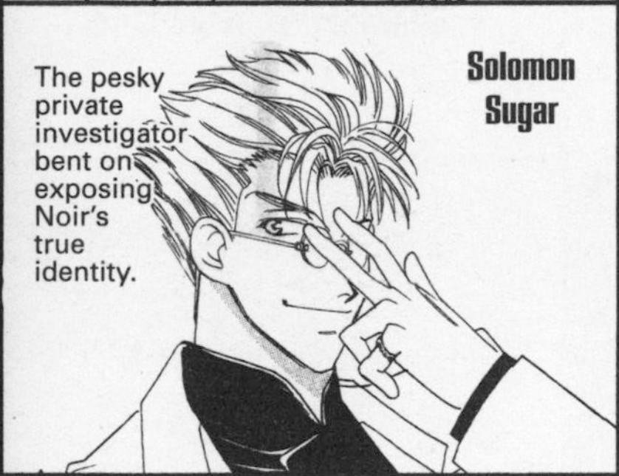
Solomon Sugar
The pesky private investigator bent on exposing Noir's true identity.

Our story so far...

As Phantom Thief Noir continues to cause trouble for the city of Paris, he suddenly receives an invitation from his long-lost childhood friend, Azura, to come to Morocco. Noir has been disguising himself as a sharp loan shark, but Azura knows his true identity and asks him to crack the mystery of the treasure of the Knights Templar.

One night, Florian has the misfortunate of accidentally eavesdropping on an argument gone bad between Azura and the female boss of the crime syndicate branch of Paris. Having discovered that Azura is lying to Noir, Florian is forced to smoke opium, or risk putting his friends in danger.

It is only after noticing Florian's odd behavior in the following days that Noir finally realizes his once most-trusted friend, Azura, has betrayed him. However, it's too late, as Florian, now hooked on opium, escapes from the mansion, and Noir is taken captive and at the mercy of Azura's whip...

GORGEOUS CARAT
Virtue of Darkness

3

CONTENTS

Third Curtain: The Blue Devil of Maghreb

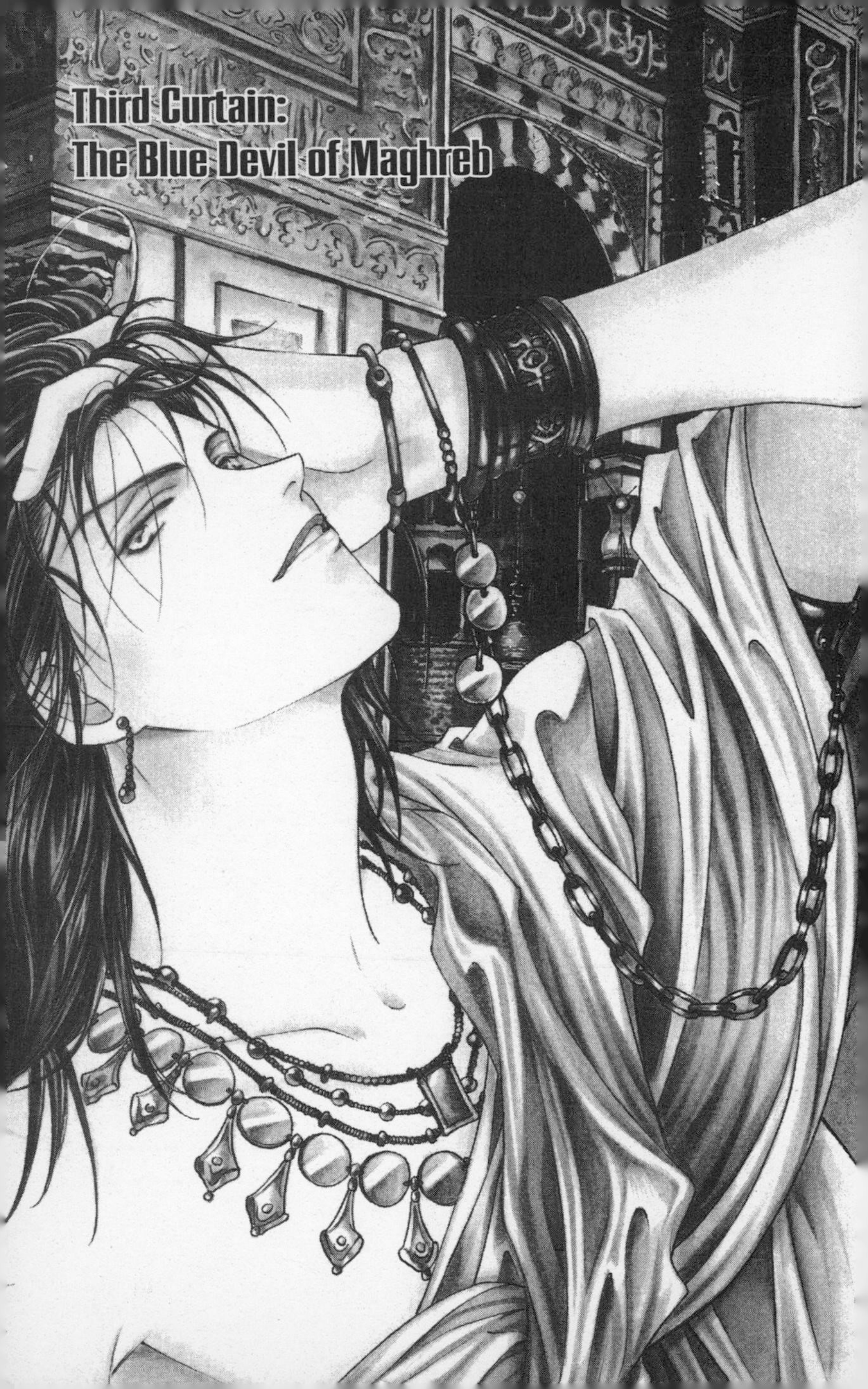

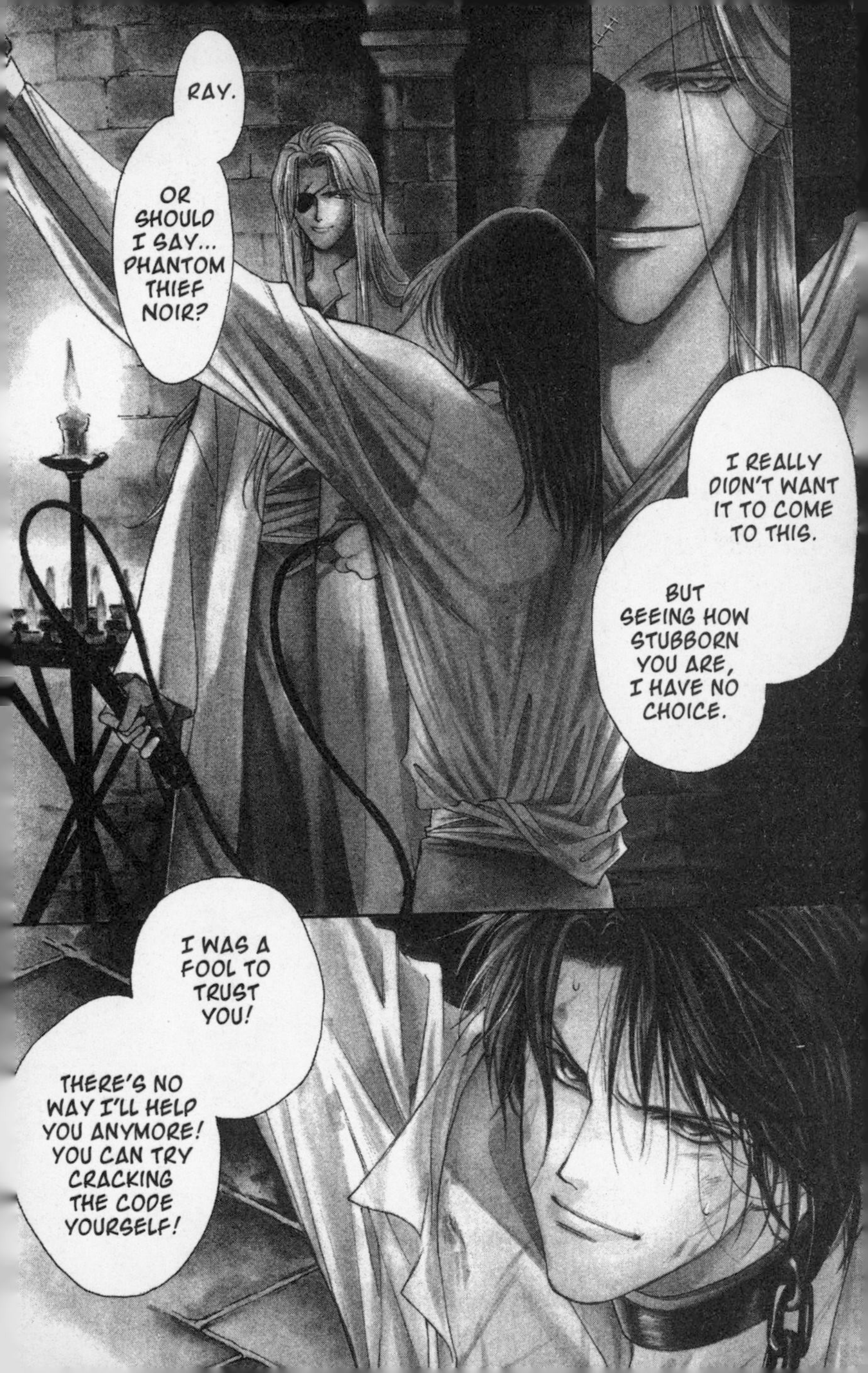
RAY.
OR SHOULD I SAY... PHANTOM THIEF NOIR?
I REALLY DIDN'T WANT IT TO COME TO THIS.
BUT SEEING HOW STUBBORN YOU ARE, I HAVE NO CHOICE.
I WAS A FOOL TO TRUST YOU!
THERE'S NO WAY I'LL HELP YOU ANYMORE! YOU CAN TRY CRACKING THE CODE YOURSELF!

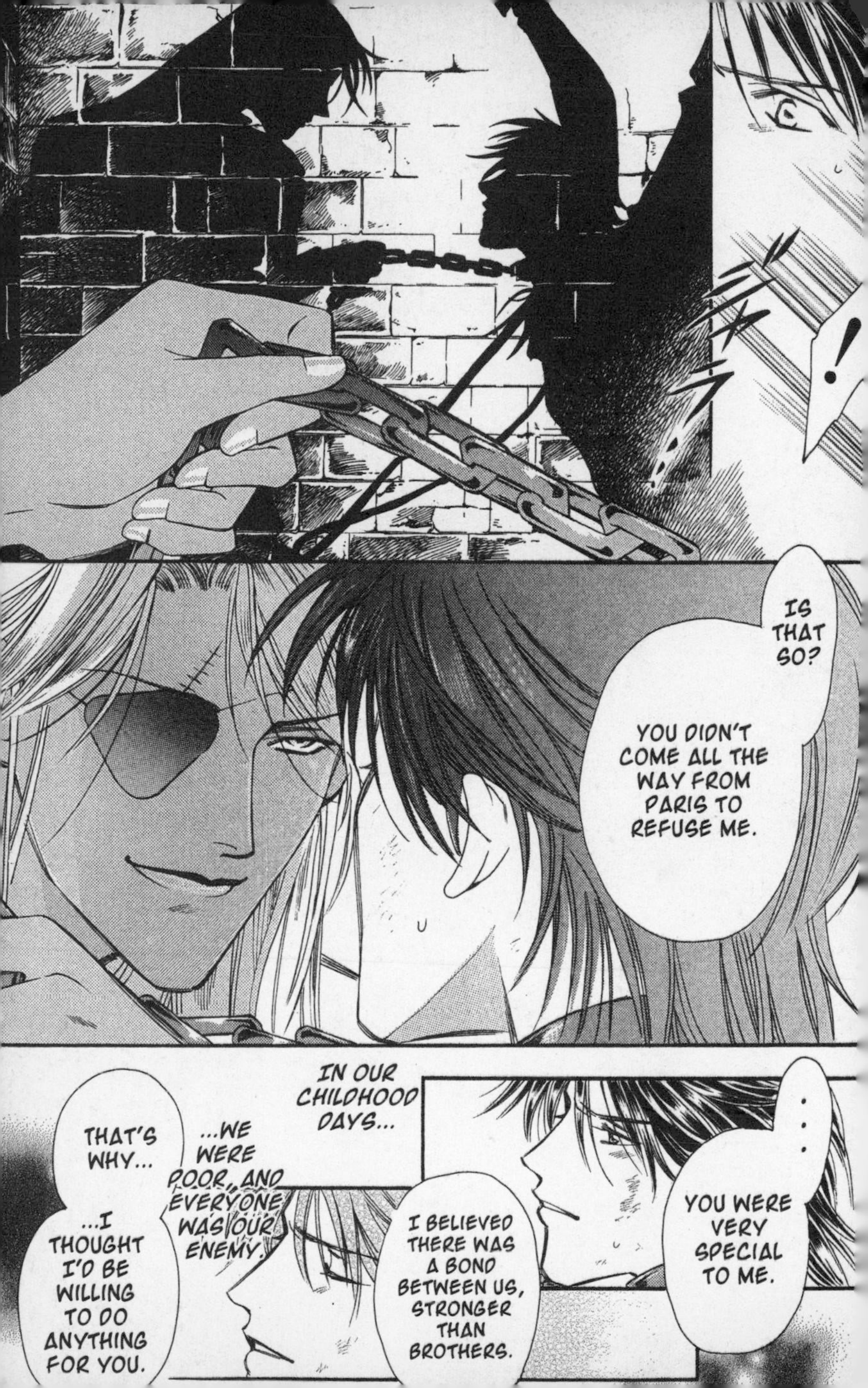
!
IS THAT SO?
YOU DIDN'T COME ALL THE WAY FROM PARIS TO REFUSE ME.
...
YOU WERE VERY SPECIAL TO ME.
IN OUR CHILDHOOD DAYS...
...WE WERE POOR, AND EVERYONE WAS OUR ENEMY.
I BELIEVED THERE WAS A BOND BETWEEN US, STRONGER THAN BROTHERS.
THAT'S WHY...
...I THOUGHT I'D BE WILLING TO DO ANYTHING FOR YOU.

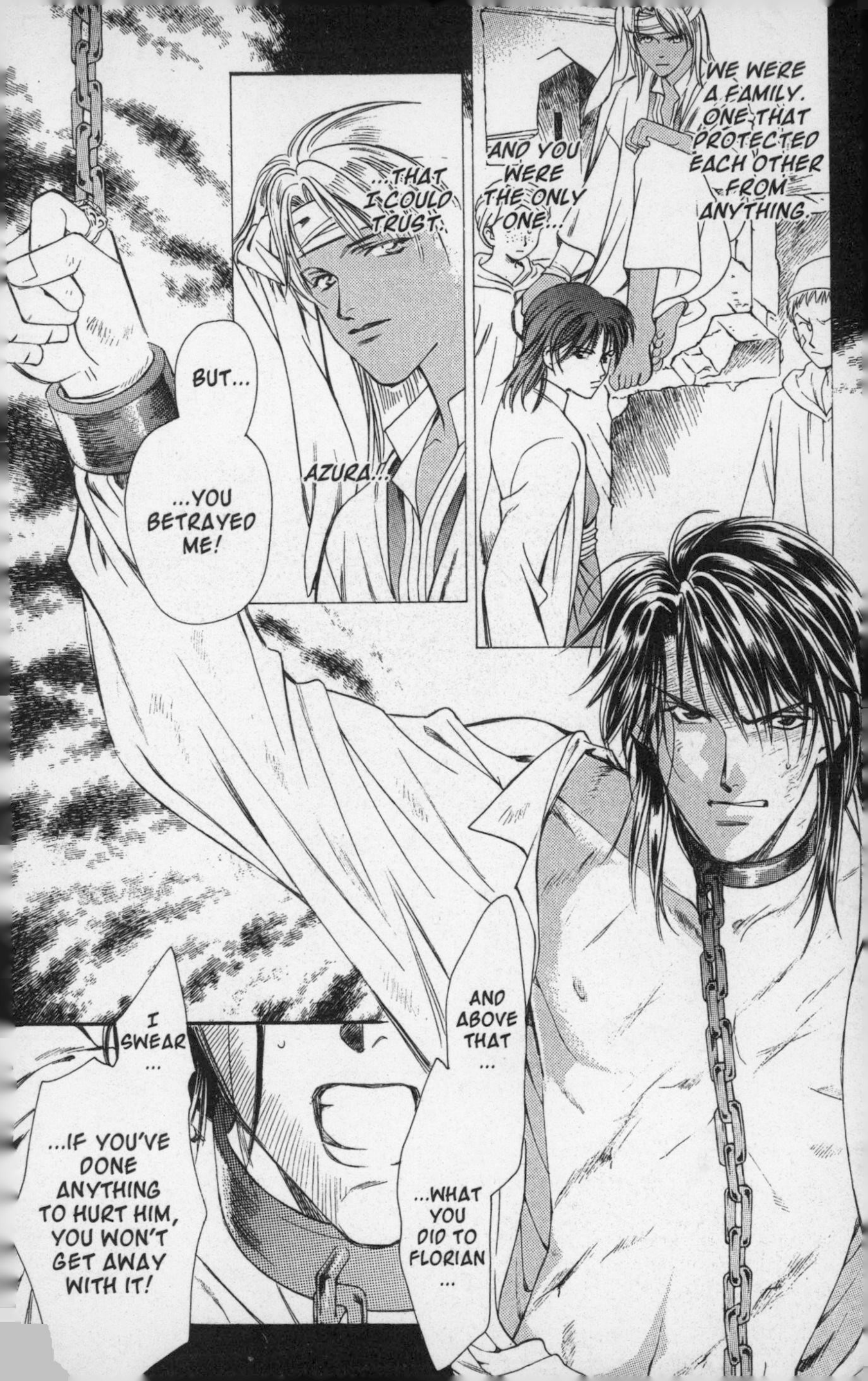
WE WERE A FAMILY. ONE THAT PROTECTED EACH OTHER FROM ANYTHING.
AND YOU WERE THE ONLY ONE...
...THAT I COULD TRUST...
AZURA..!!
BUT...
...YOU BETRAYED ME!
AND ABOVE THAT...
...WHAT YOU DID TO FLORIAN...
I SWEAR...
...IF YOU'VE DONE ANYTHING TO HURT HIM, YOU WON'T GET AWAY WITH IT!

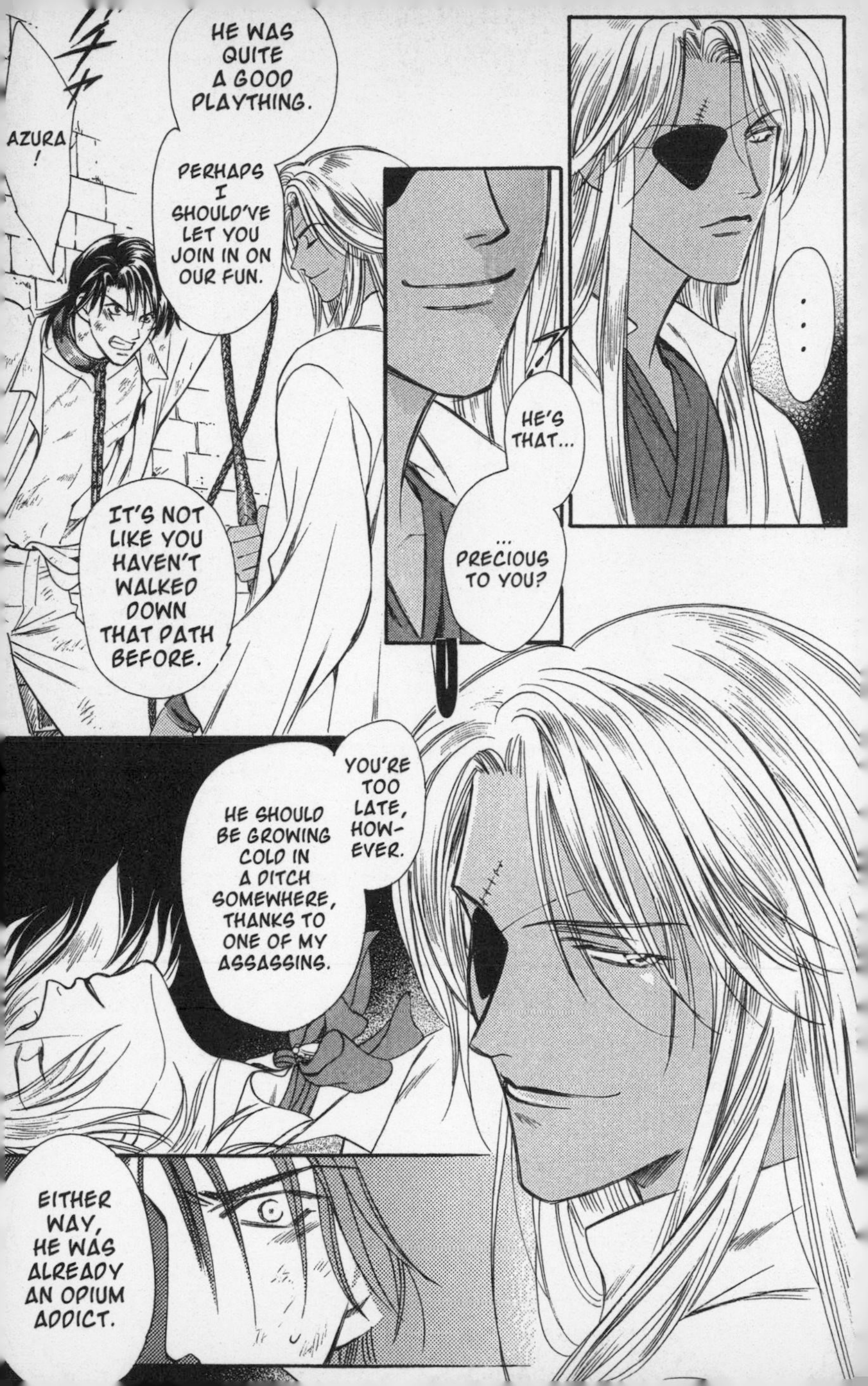
...
HE'S THAT...
... PRECIOUS TO YOU?
HE WAS QUITE A GOOD PLAYTHING.
AZURA!
PERHAPS I SHOULD'VE LET YOU JOIN IN ON OUR FUN.
IT'S NOT LIKE YOU HAVEN'T WALKED DOWN THAT PATH BEFORE.
YOU'RE TOO LATE, HOW-EVER.
HE SHOULD BE GROWING COLD IN A DITCH SOMEWHERE, THANKS TO ONE OF MY ASSASSINS.
EITHER WAY, HE WAS ALREADY AN OPIUM ADDICT.

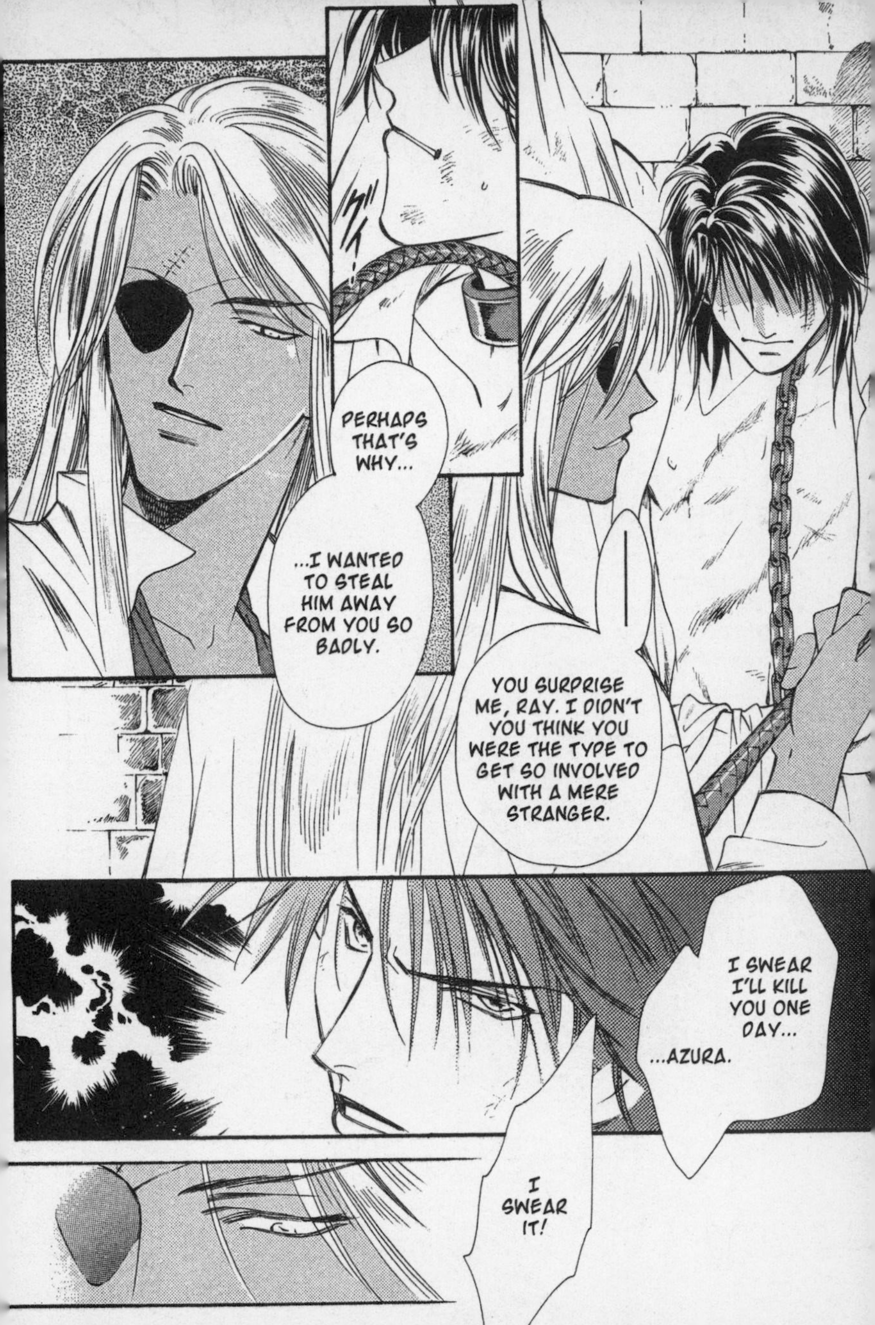
PERHAPS THAT'S WHY...
...I WANTED TO STEAL HIM AWAY FROM YOU SO BADLY.
YOU SURPRISE ME, RAY. I DIDN'T YOU THINK YOU WERE THE TYPE TO GET SO INVOLVED WITH A MERE STRANGER.
I SWEAR I'LL KILL YOU ONE DAY...
...AZURA.
I SWEAR IT!

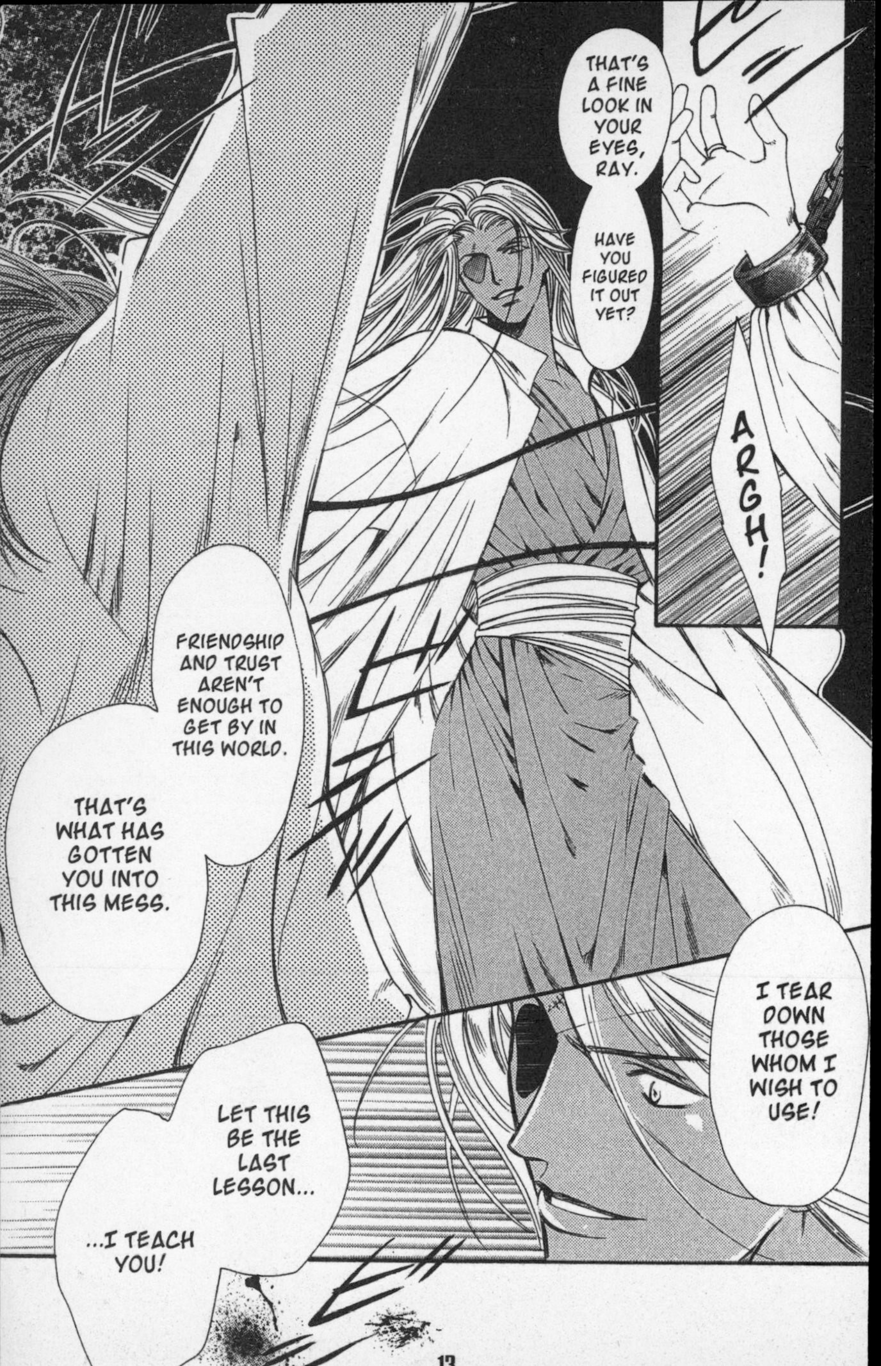
ARGH!
THAT'S A FINE LOOK IN YOUR EYES, RAY.
HAVE YOU FIGURED IT OUT YET?
FRIENDSHIP AND TRUST AREN'T ENOUGH TO GET BY IN THIS WORLD.
THAT'S WHAT HAS GOTTEN YOU INTO THIS MESS.
I TEAR DOWN THOSE WHOM I WISH TO USE!
LET THIS BE THE LAST LESSON...
...I TEACH YOU!

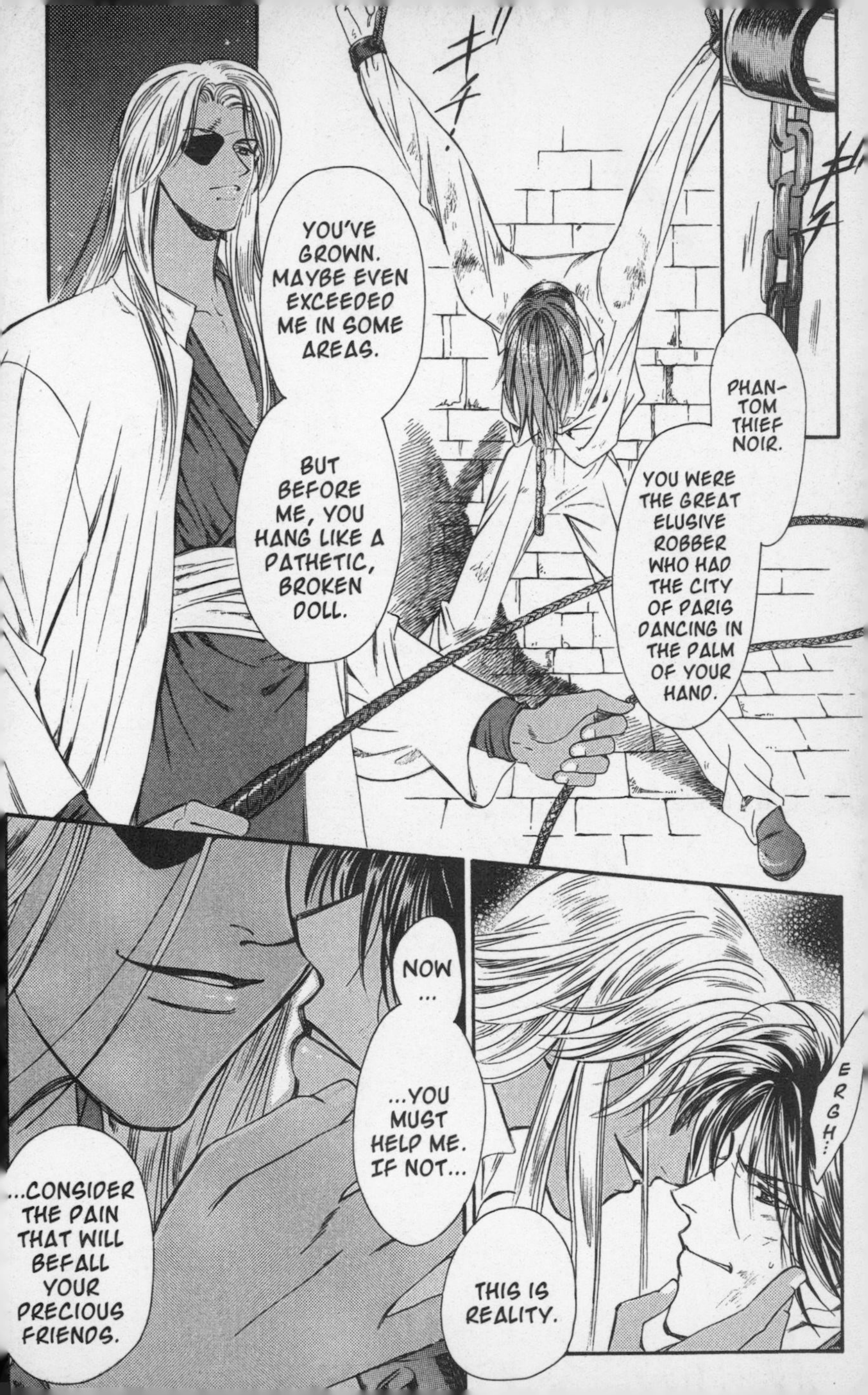
PHAN-TOM THIEF NOIR.
YOU WERE THE GREAT ELUSIVE ROBBER WHO HAD THE CITY OF PARIS DANCING IN THE PALM OF YOUR HAND.
YOU'VE GROWN. MAYBE EVEN EXCEEDED ME IN SOME AREAS.
BUT BEFORE ME, YOU HANG LIKE A PATHETIC, BROKEN DOLL.
ERGH...
THIS IS REALITY.
NOW...
...YOU MUST HELP ME. IF NOT...
...CONSIDER THE PAIN THAT WILL BEFALL YOUR PRECIOUS FRIENDS.

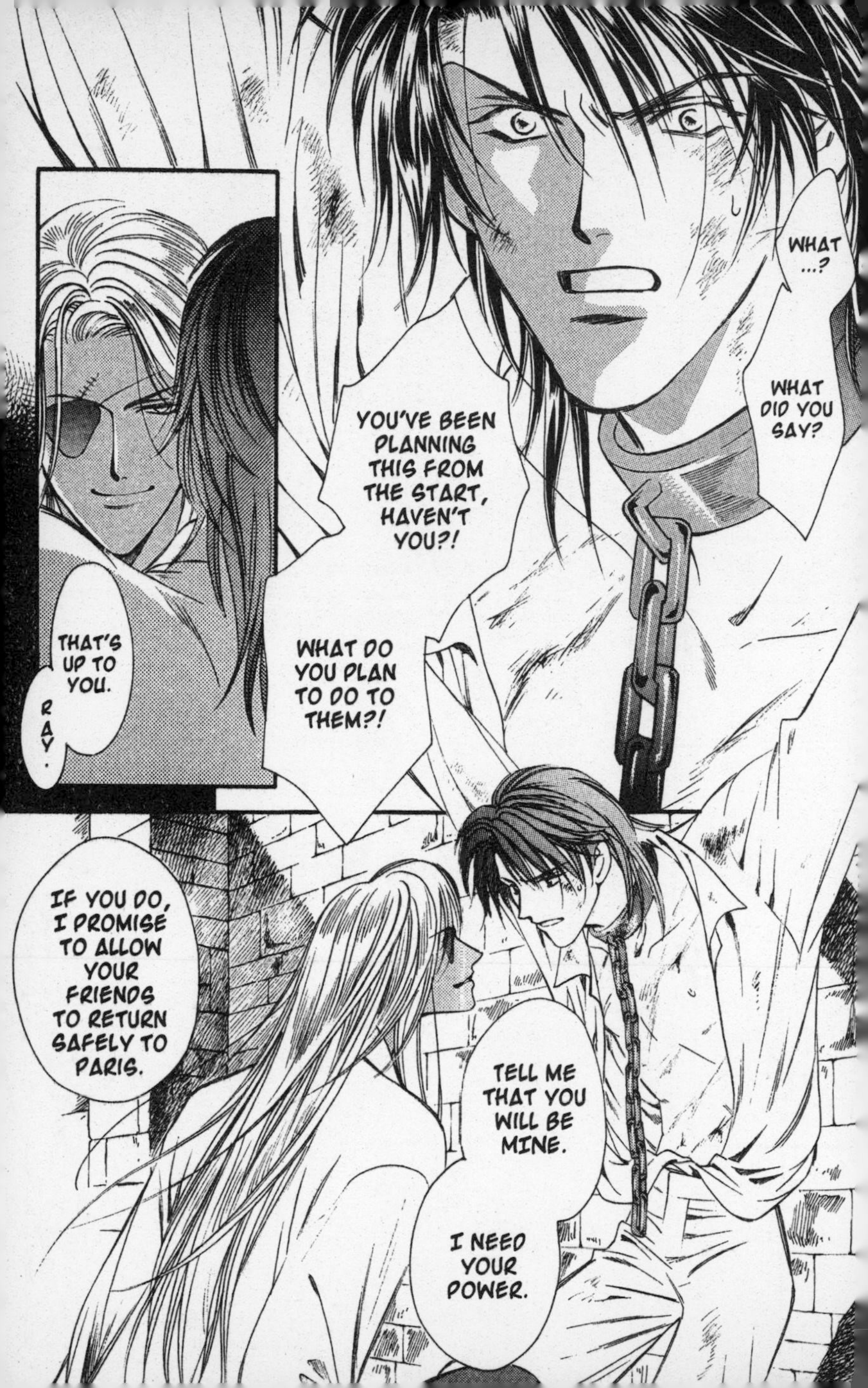
WHAT ...?
WHAT DID YOU SAY?
YOU'VE BEEN PLANNING THIS FROM THE START, HAVEN'T YOU?!
WHAT DO YOU PLAN TO DO TO THEM?!
THAT'S UP TO YOU.
RAY.
TELL ME THAT YOU WILL BE MINE.
IF YOU DO, I PROMISE TO ALLOW YOUR FRIENDS TO RETURN SAFELY TO PARIS.
I NEED YOUR POWER.

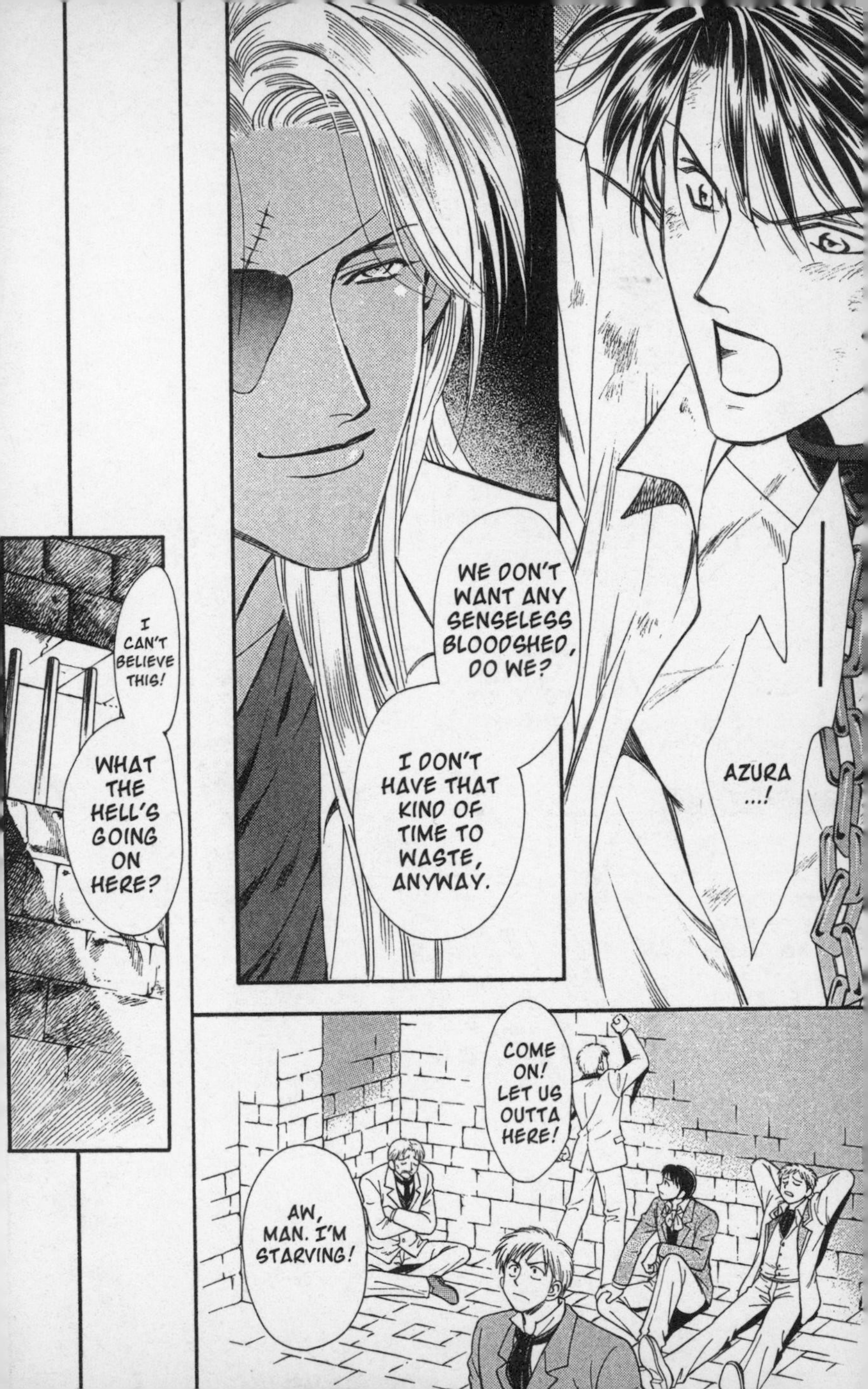
AZURA ...!
WE DON'T WANT ANY SENSELESS BLOODSHED, DO WE?
I DON'T HAVE THAT KIND OF TIME TO WASTE, ANYWAY.
I CAN'T BELIEVE THIS!
WHAT THE HELL'S GOING ON HERE?
COME ON! LET US OUTTA HERE!
AW, MAN. I'M STARVING!

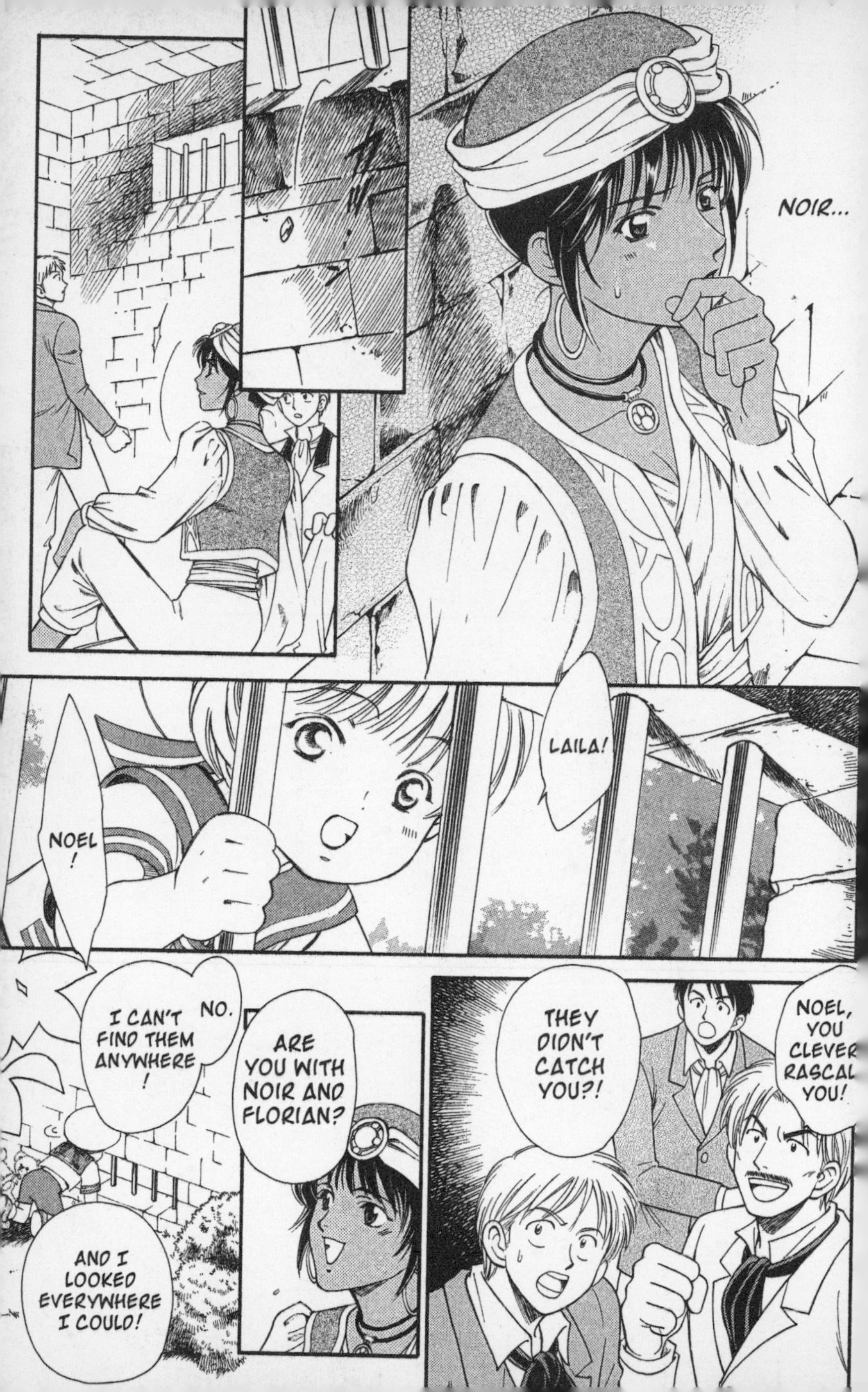
NOIR...
LAILA!
NOEL!
NOEL, YOU CLEVER RASCAL YOU!
THEY DIDN'T CATCH YOU?!
ARE YOU WITH NOIR AND FLORIAN?
NO.
I CAN'T FIND THEM ANYWHERE!
AND I LOOKED EVERYWHERE I COULD!

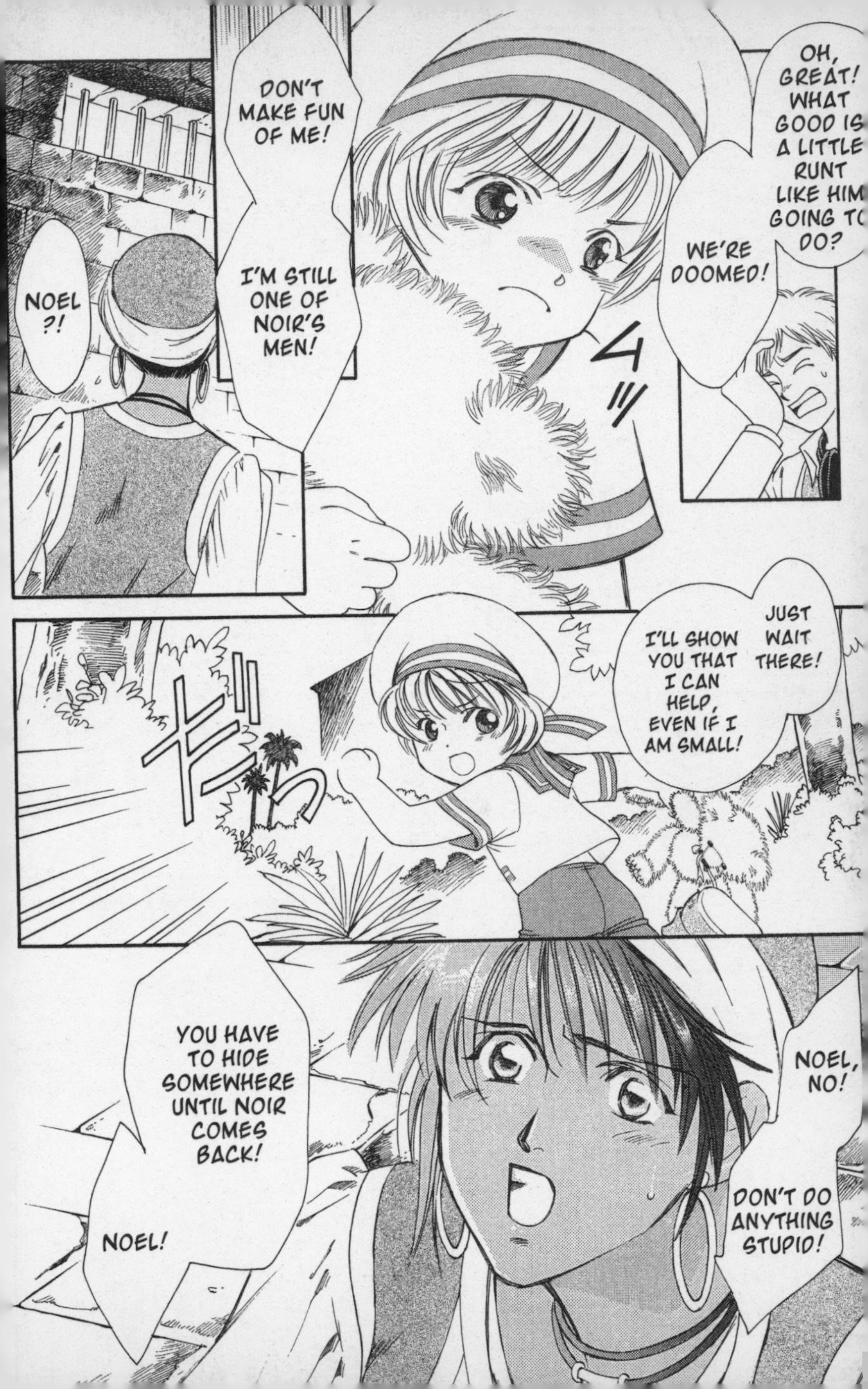
OH, GREAT! WHAT GOOD IS A LITTLE RUNT LIKE HIM GOING TO DO?
WE'RE DOOMED!
DON'T MAKE FUN OF ME!
I'M STILL ONE OF NOIR'S MEN!
ムッ
NOEL ?!
JUST WAIT THERE!
I'LL SHOW YOU THAT I CAN HELP, EVEN IF I AM SMALL!
NOEL, NO!
DON'T DO ANYTHING STUPID!
YOU HAVE TO HIDE SOMEWHERE UNTIL NOIR COMES BACK!
NOEL!

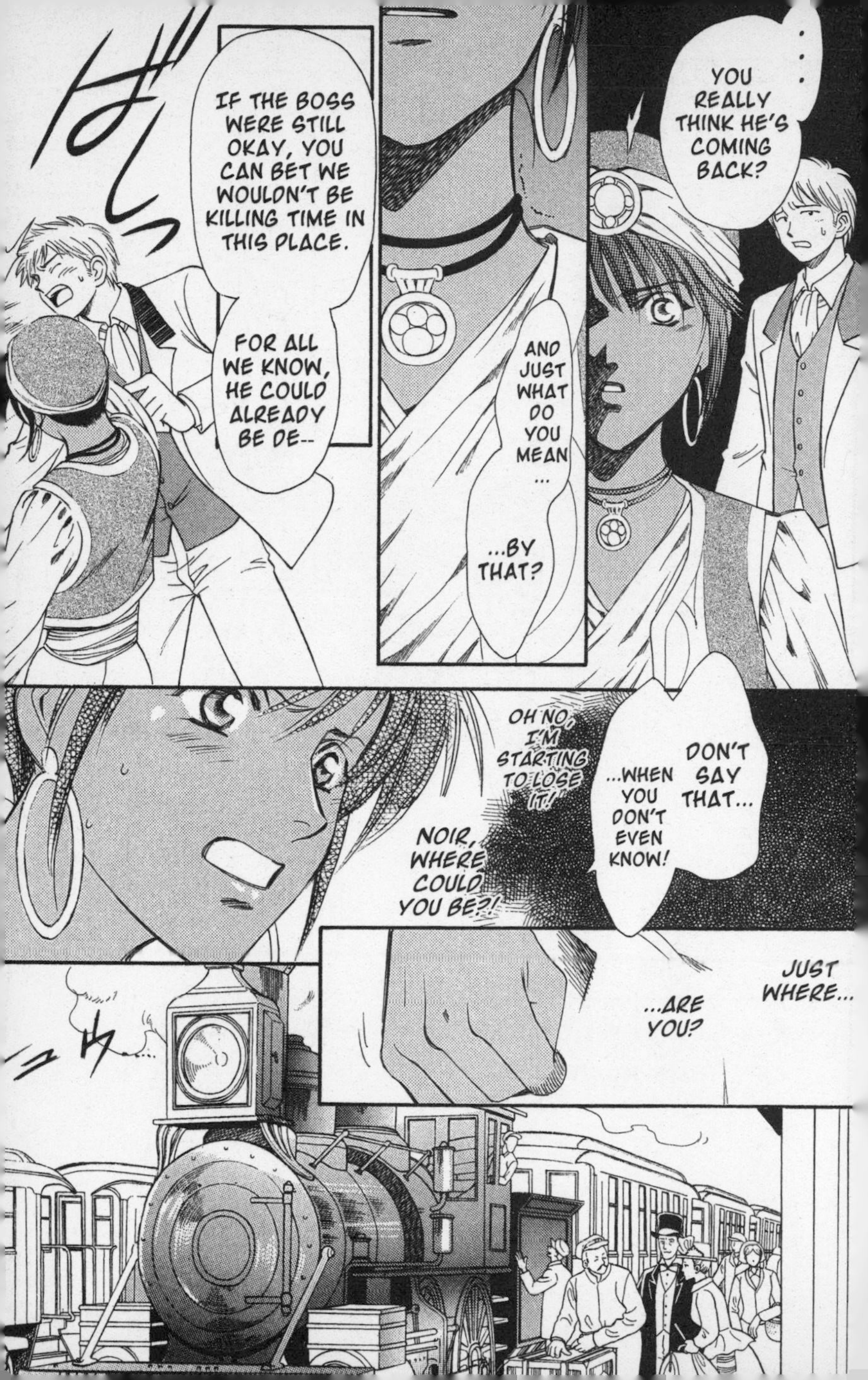
...
YOU REALLY THINK HE'S COMING BACK?
AND JUST WHAT DO YOU MEAN...
...BY THAT?
IF THE BOSS WERE STILL OKAY, YOU CAN BET WE WOULDN'T BE KILLING TIME IN THIS PLACE.
FOR ALL WE KNOW, HE COULD ALREADY BE DE--
DON'T SAY THAT...
...WHEN YOU DON'T EVEN KNOW!
OH NO, I'M STARTING TO LOSE IT!
NOIR, WHERE COULD YOU BE?!
JUST WHERE...
...ARE YOU?

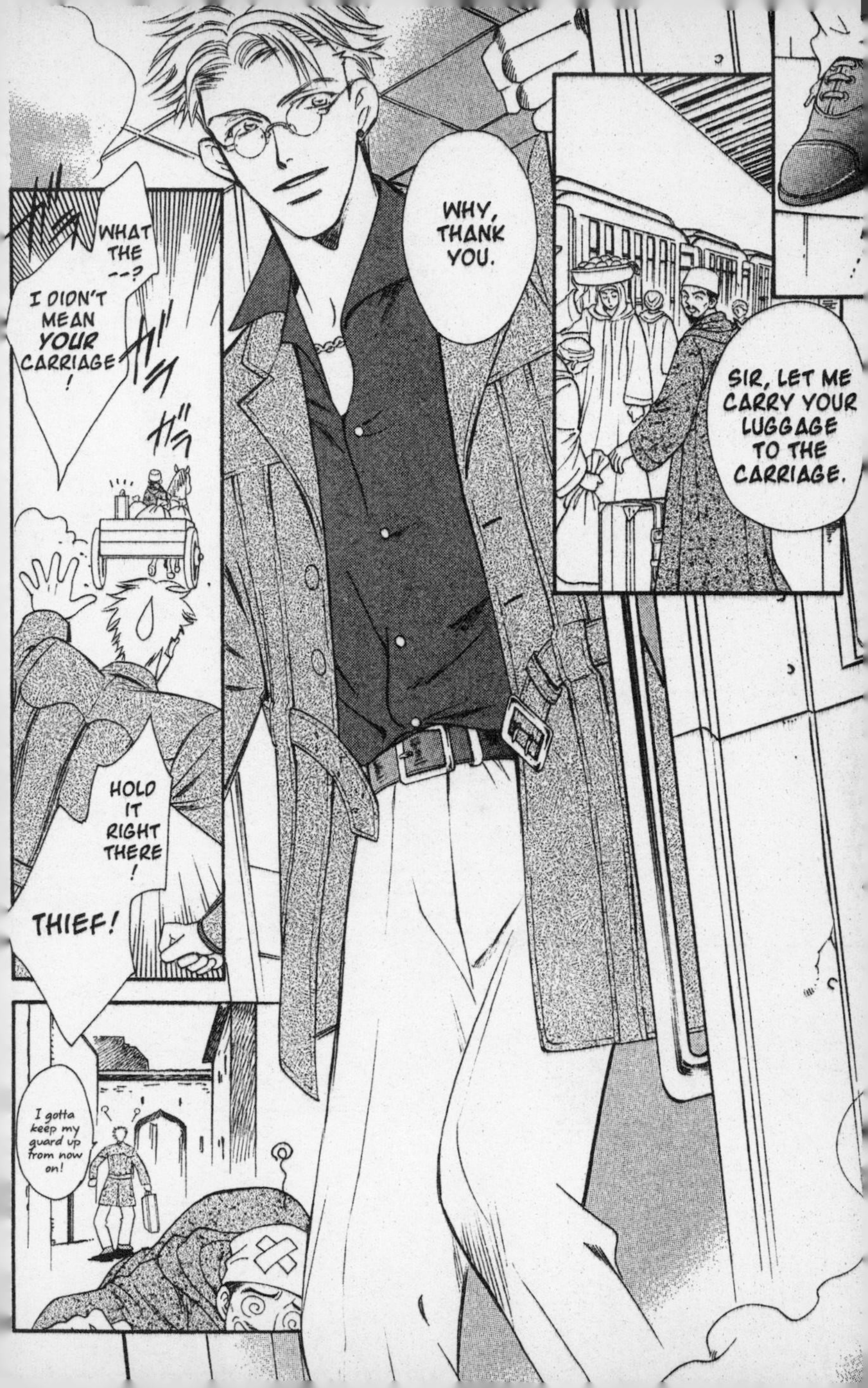
SIR, LET ME CARRY YOUR LUGGAGE TO THE CARRIAGE.
WHY, THANK YOU.
WHAT THE --?
I DIDN'T MEAN YOUR CARRIAGE!
HOLD IT RIGHT THERE!
THIEF!
I gotta keep my guard up from now on!

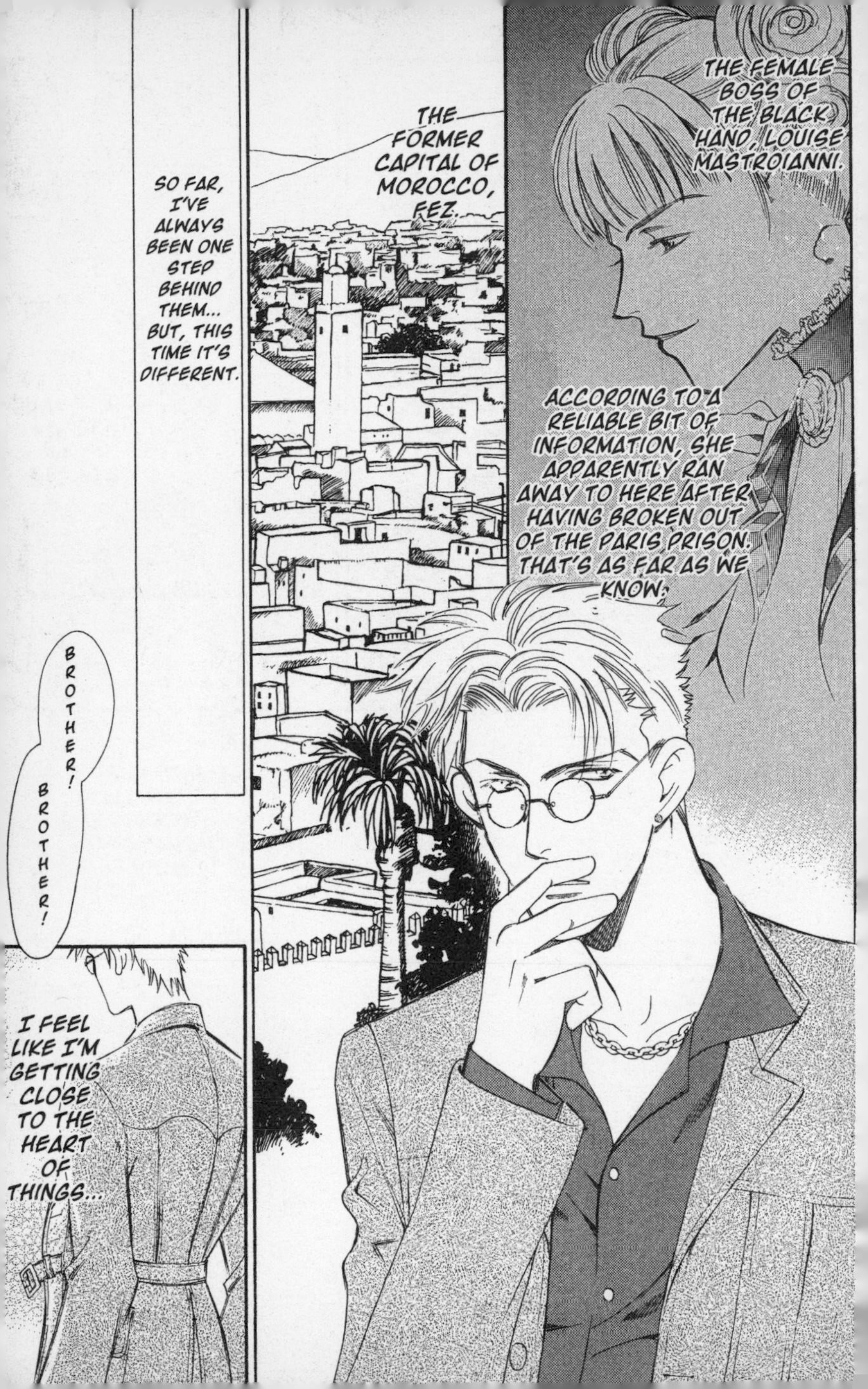
THE FEMALE BOSS OF THE BLACK HAND, LOUISE MASTROIANNI.
ACCORDING TO A RELIABLE BIT OF INFORMATION, SHE APPARENTLY RAN AWAY TO HERE AFTER HAVING BROKEN OUT OF THE PARIS PRISON. THAT'S AS FAR AS WE KNOW.
THE FORMER CAPITAL OF MOROCCO, FEZ.
SO FAR, I'VE ALWAYS BEEN ONE STEP BEHIND THEM... BUT, THIS TIME IT'S DIFFERENT.
BROTHER! BROTHER!
I FEEL LIKE I'M GETTING CLOSE TO THE HEART OF THINGS...

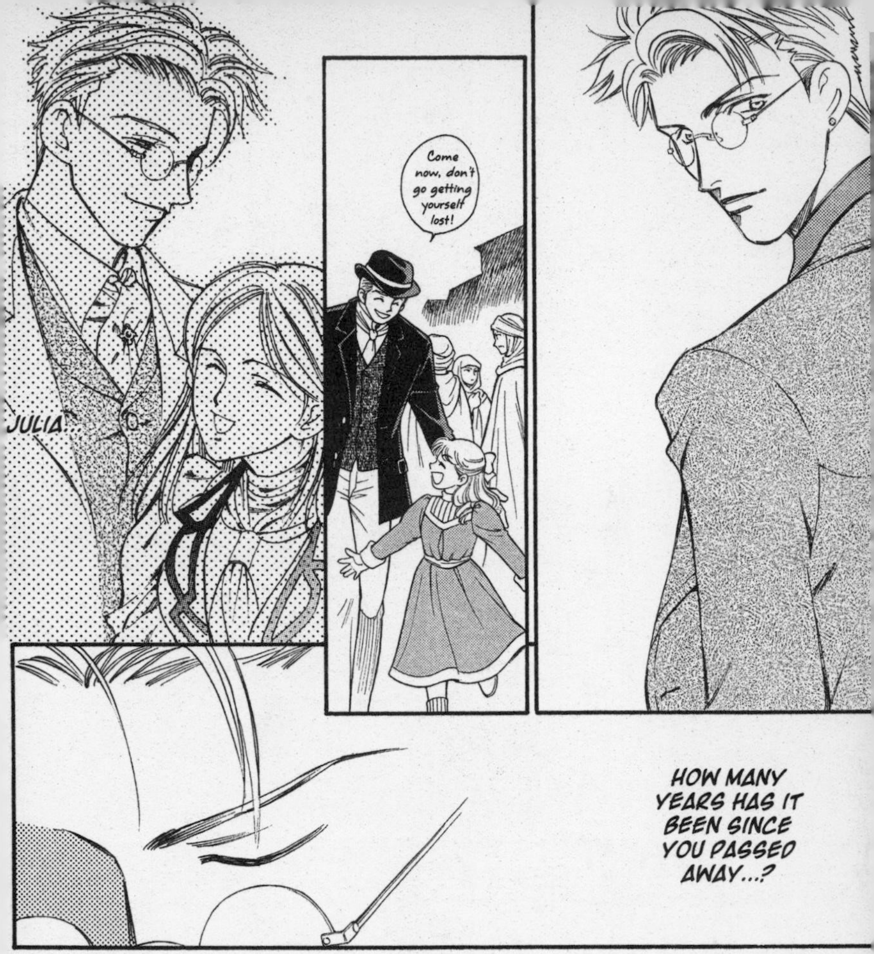
Come now, don't go getting yourself lost!
JULIA...
HOW MANY YEARS HAS IT BEEN SINCE YOU PASSED AWAY...?

BUT, JUST YOU WAIT. BEFORE LONG, I'LL FINALLY EXPOSE THE CRIME SYNDICATE THAT KILLED YOU.

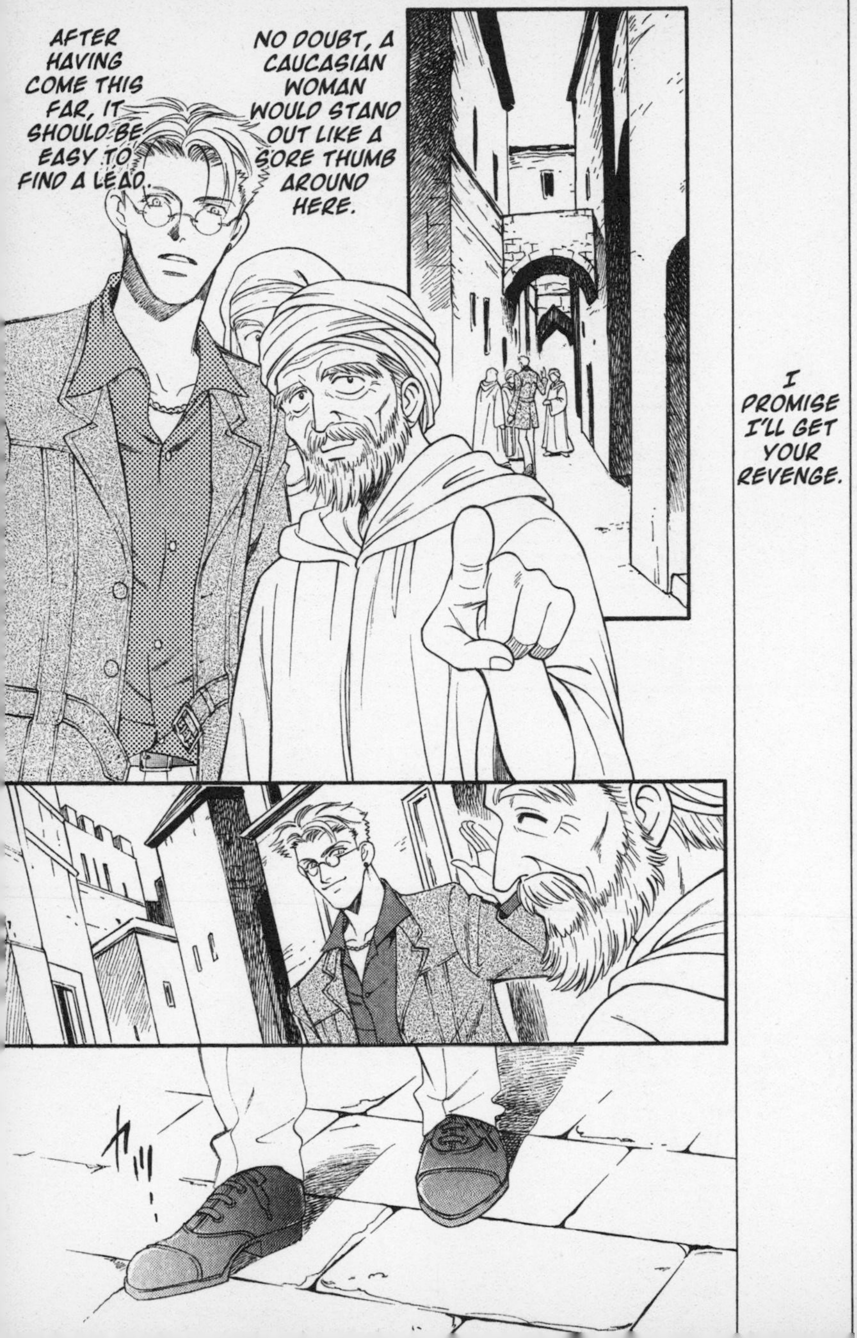
I PROMISE I'LL GET YOUR REVENGE.
NO DOUBT, A CAUCASIAN WOMAN WOULD STAND OUT LIKE A SORE THUMB AROUND HERE.
AFTER HAVING COME THIS FAR, IT SHOULD BE EASY TO FIND A LEAD.

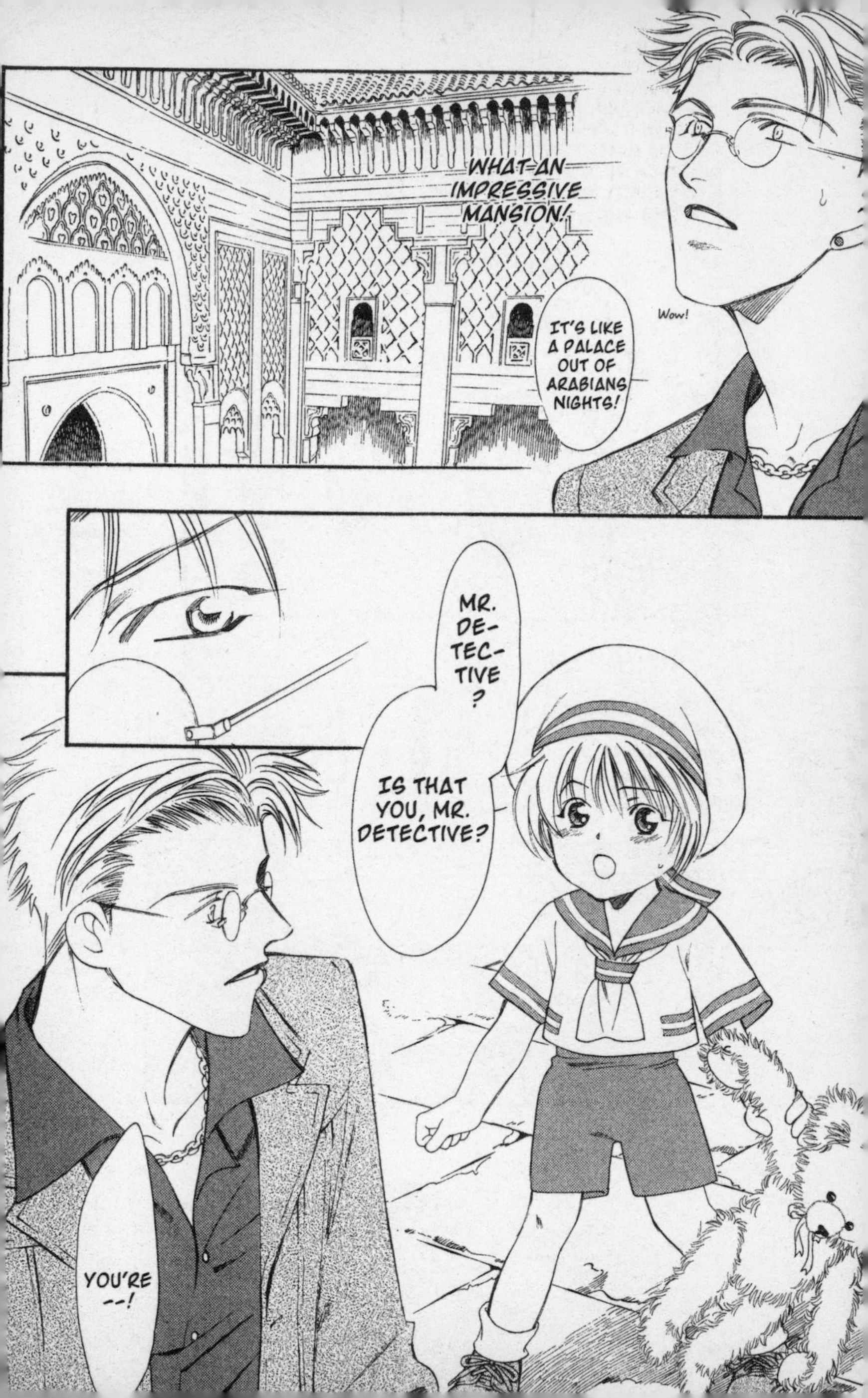
Wow!
WHAT AN IMPRESSIVE MANSION!
IT'S LIKE A PALACE OUT OF ARABIANS NIGHTS!
MR. DE-TEC-TIVE?
IS THAT YOU, MR. DETECTIVE?
YOU'RE --!

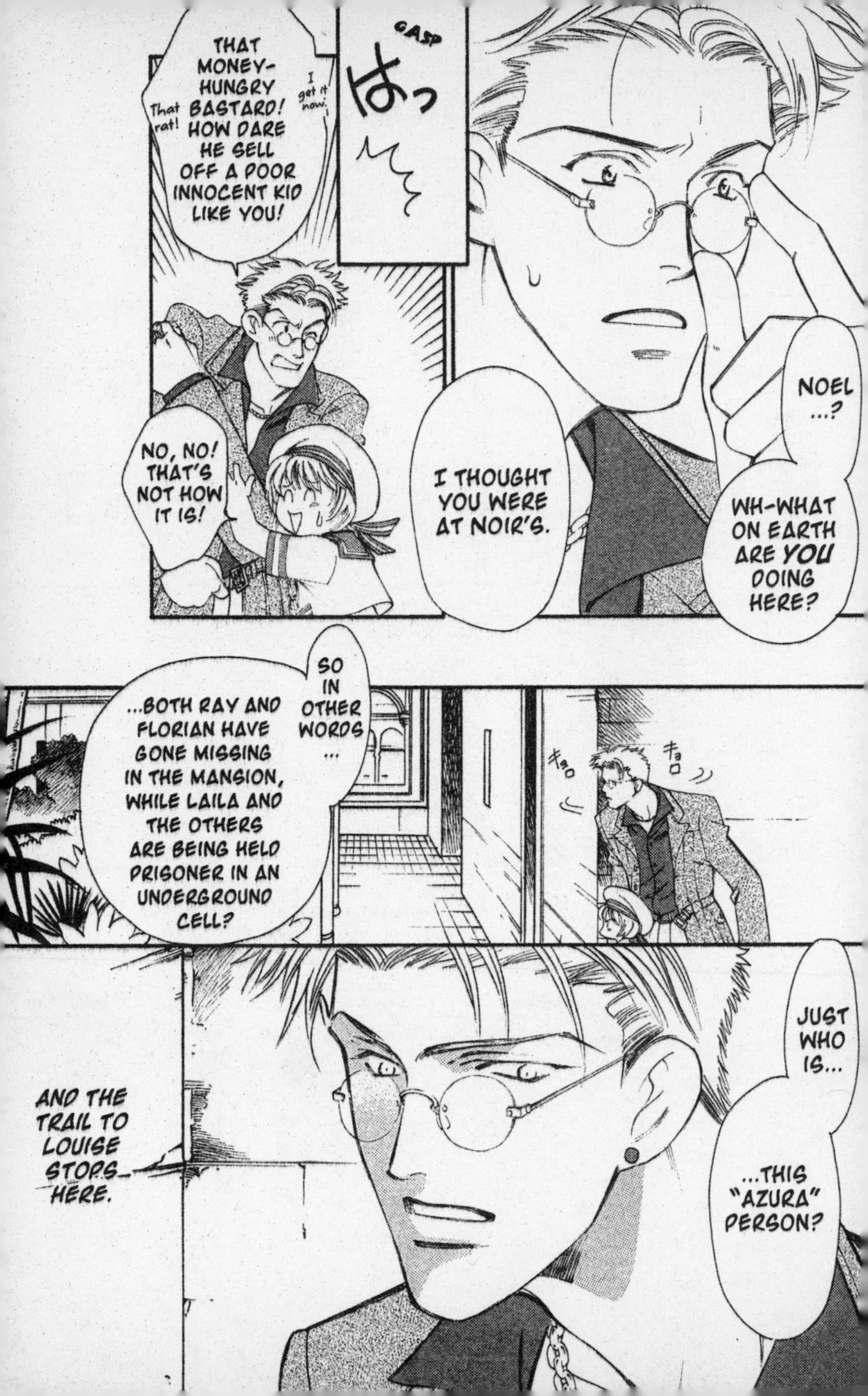
NOEL ...?
WH-WHAT ON EARTH ARE *YOU* DOING HERE?
I THOUGHT YOU WERE AT NOIR'S.
GASP
はっ
I get it now.
THAT MONEY-HUNGRY BASTARD! HOW DARE HE SELL OFF A POOR INNOCENT KID LIKE YOU!
That rat!
NO, NO! THAT'S NOT HOW IT IS!
キョロ
キョロ
SO IN OTHER WORDS...
...BOTH RAY AND FLORIAN HAVE GONE MISSING IN THE MANSION, WHILE LAILA AND THE OTHERS ARE BEING HELD PRISONER IN AN UNDERGROUND CELL?
JUST WHO IS...
...THIS "AZURA" PERSON?
AND THE TRAIL TO LOUISE STOPS HERE.

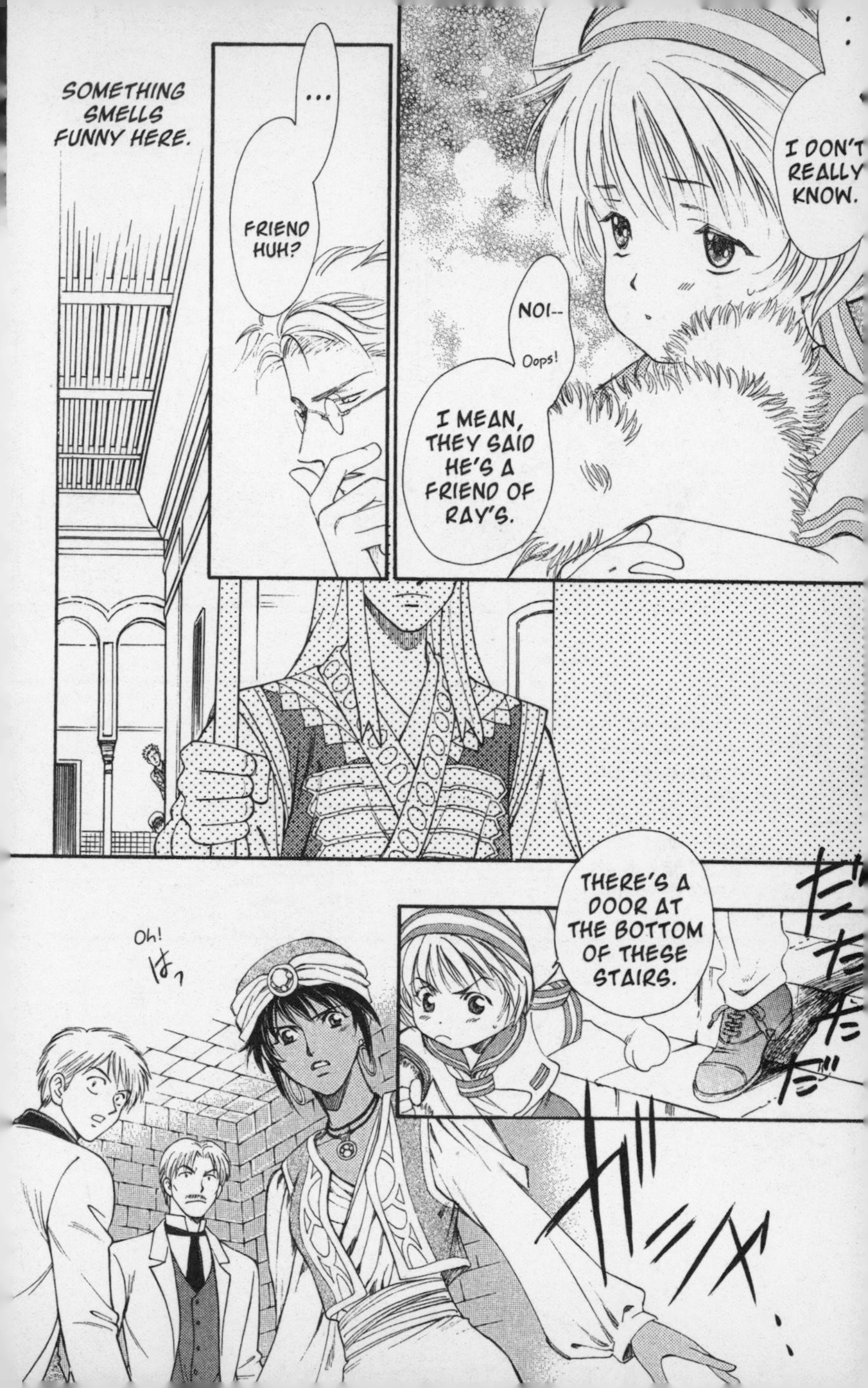
I DON'T REALLY KNOW.
NOI--
Oops!
I MEAN, THEY SAID HE'S A FRIEND OF RAY'S.
...
FRIEND HUH?
SOMETHING SMELLS FUNNY HERE.
THERE'S A DOOR AT THE BOTTOM OF THESE STAIRS.
Oh!

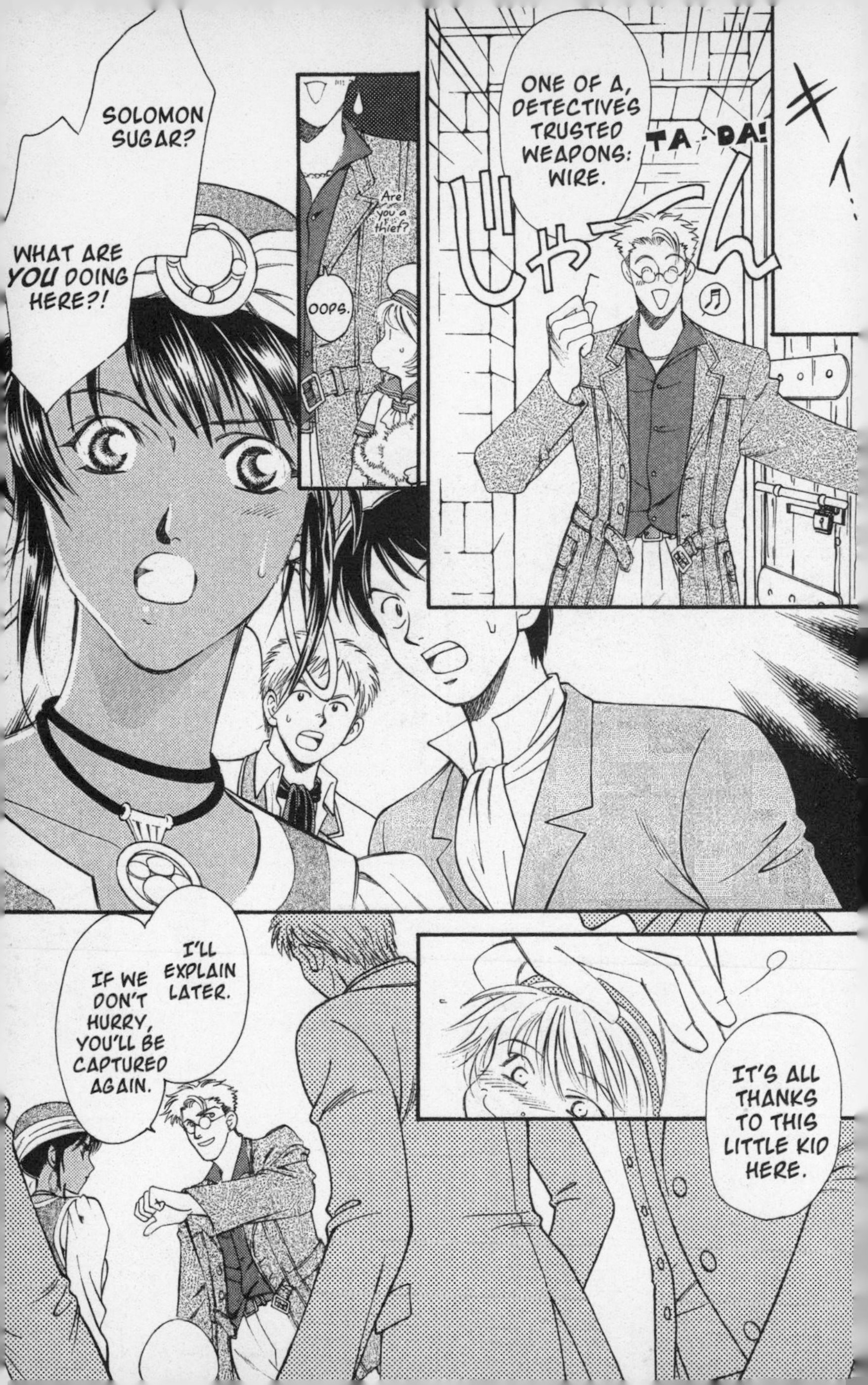

ONE OF A, DETECTIVES TRUSTED WEAPONS: WIRE.
TA-DA!
じゃーん
Are you a thief?
OOPS.
SOLOMON SUGAR?
WHAT ARE *YOU* DOING HERE?!
IT'S ALL THANKS TO THIS LITTLE KID HERE.
I'LL EXPLAIN LATER.
IF WE DON'T HURRY, YOU'LL BE CAPTURED AGAIN.

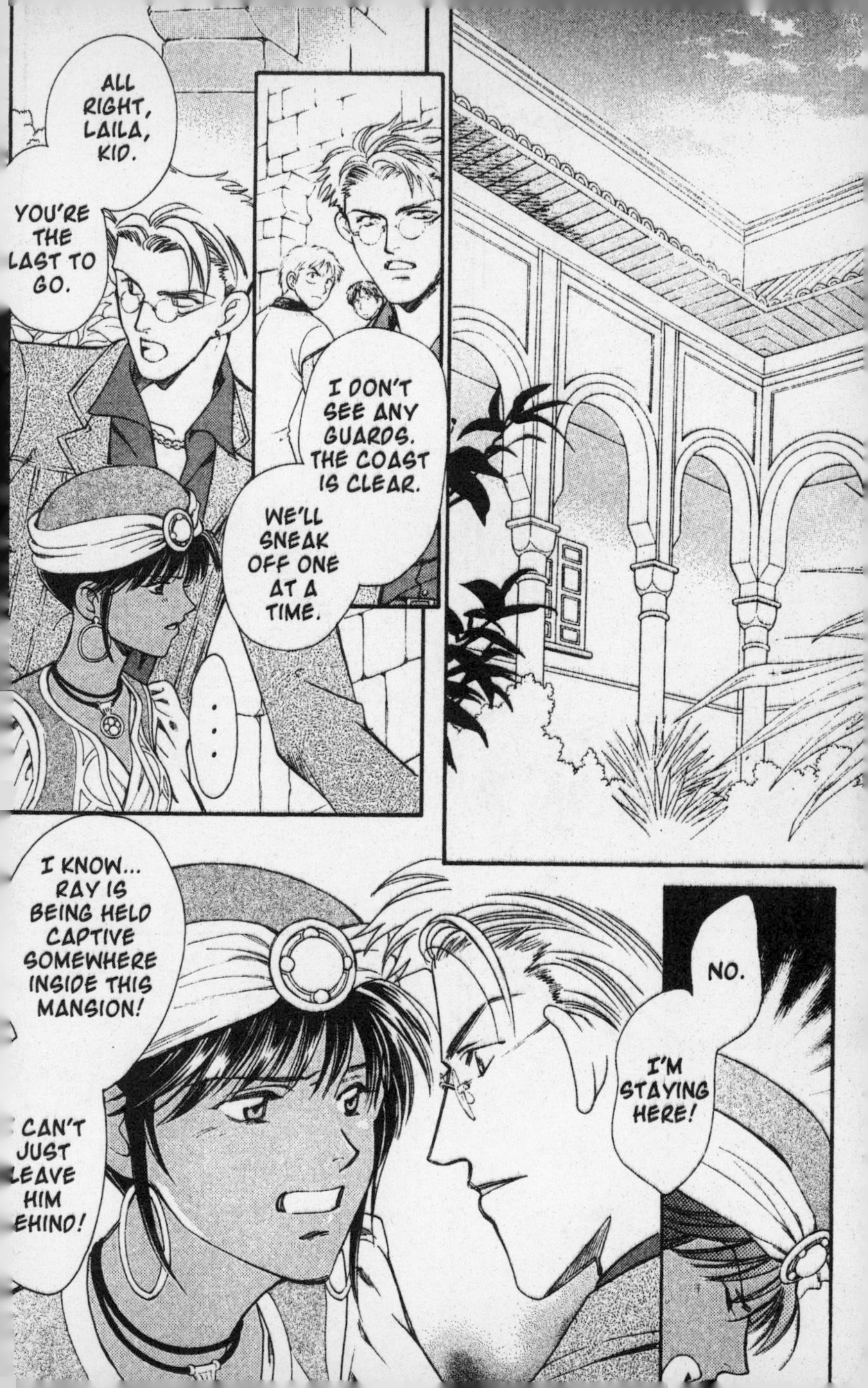

I DON'T SEE ANY GUARDS. THE COAST IS CLEAR.
WE'LL SNEAK OFF ONE AT A TIME.
ALL RIGHT, LAILA, KID.
YOU'RE THE LAST TO GO.
...
NO.
I'M STAYING HERE!
I KNOW... RAY IS BEING HELD CAPTIVE SOMEWHERE INSIDE THIS MANSION!
CAN'T JUST EAVE HIM EHIND!

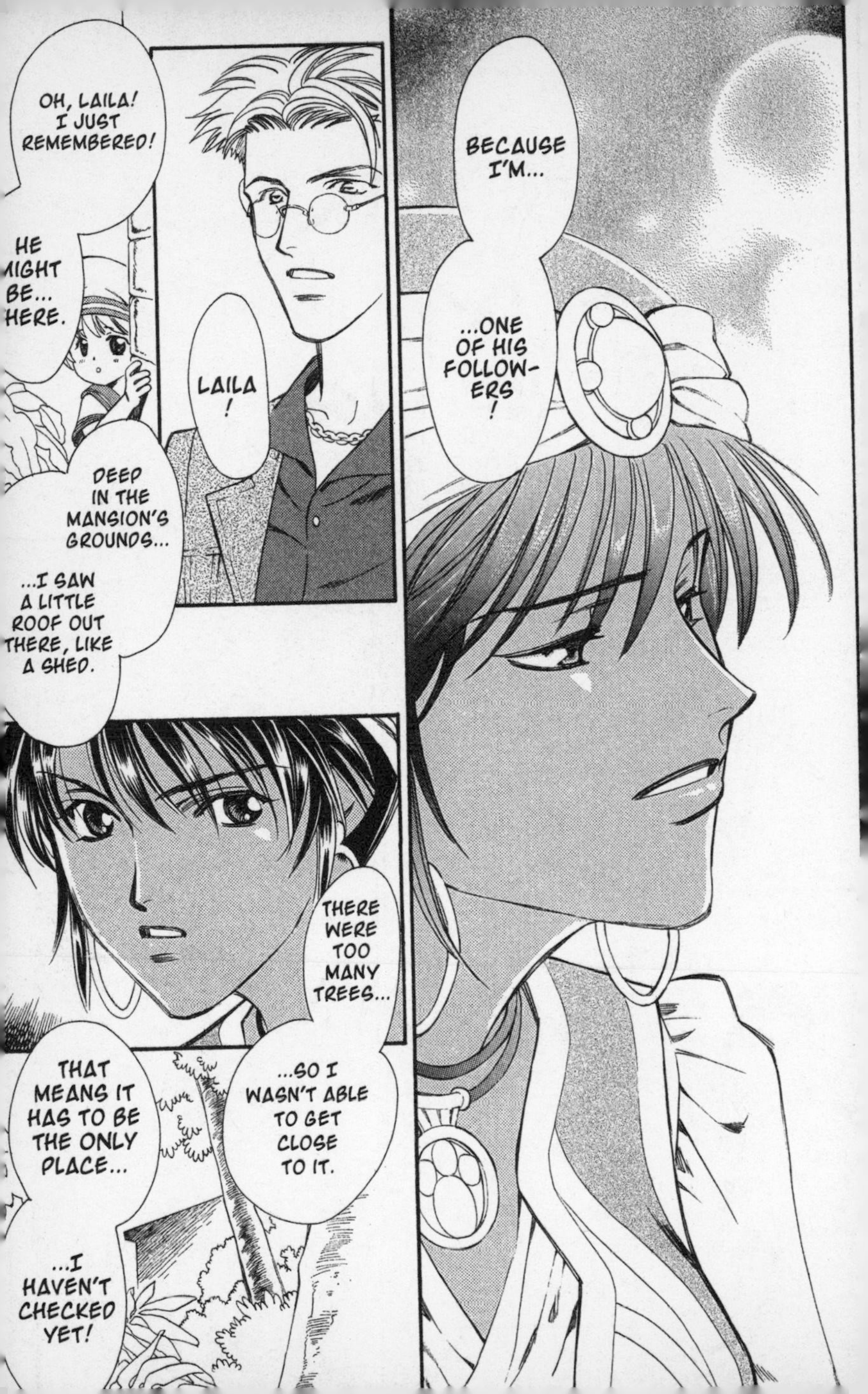
BECAUSE I'M...
...ONE OF HIS FOLLOW-ERS!
OH, LAILA! I JUST REMEMBERED!
LAILA!
HE IGHT BE... HERE.
DEEP IN THE MANSION'S GROUNDS...
...I SAW A LITTLE ROOF OUT THERE, LIKE A SHED.
THERE WERE TOO MANY TREES...
...SO I WASN'T ABLE TO GET CLOSE TO IT.
THAT MEANS IT HAS TO BE THE ONLY PLACE...
...I HAVEN'T CHECKED YET!

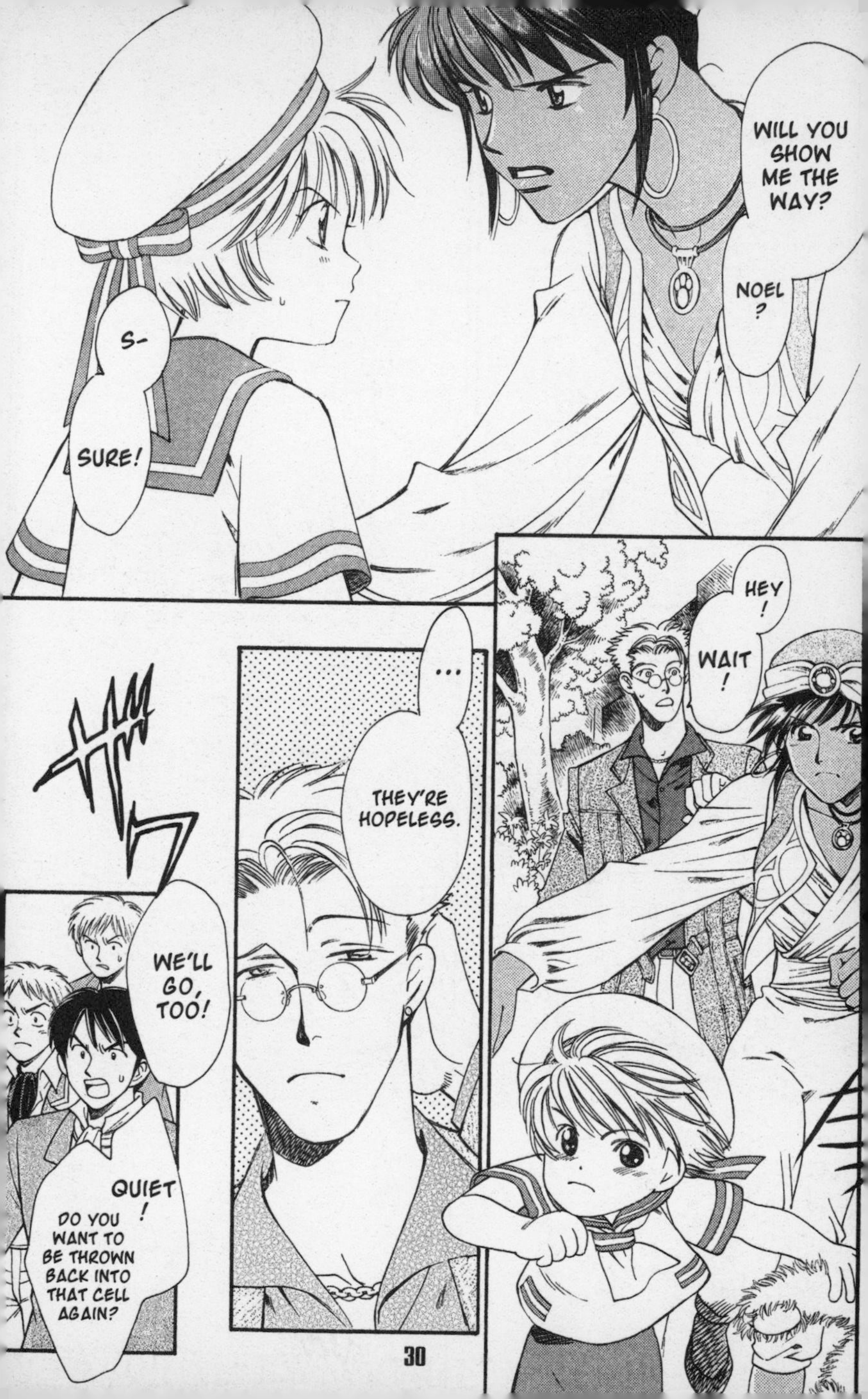
WILL YOU SHOW ME THE WAY?
NOEL?
S-
SURE!
HEY! WAIT!
...
THEY'RE HOPELESS.
WE'LL GO, TOO!
QUIET!
DO YOU WANT TO BE THROWN BACK INTO THAT CELL AGAIN?

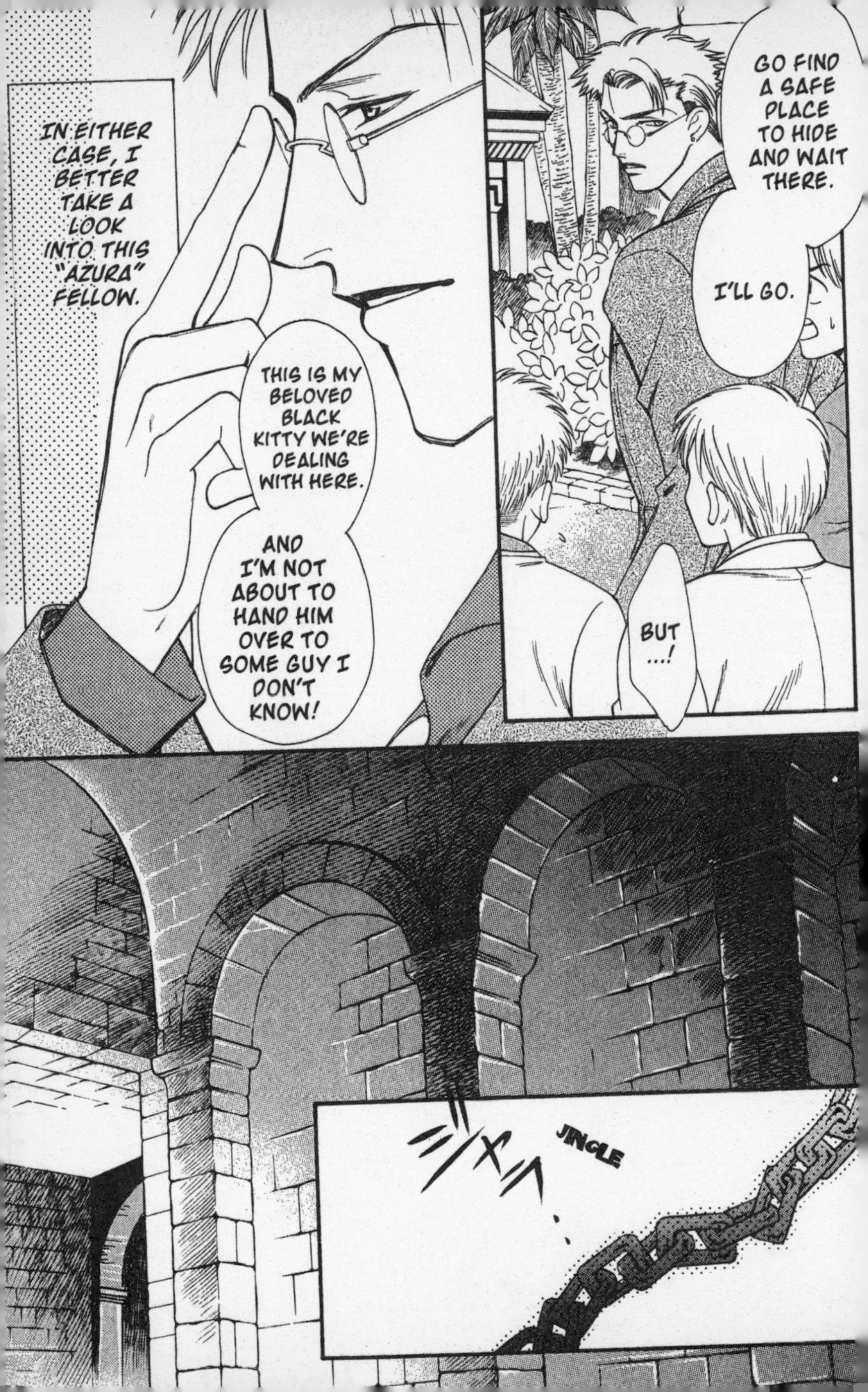
GO FIND A SAFE PLACE TO HIDE AND WAIT THERE.
I'LL GO.
BUT ...!
THIS IS MY BELOVED BLACK KITTY WE'RE DEALING WITH HERE.
AND I'M NOT ABOUT TO HAND HIM OVER TO SOME GUY I DON'T KNOW!
IN EITHER CASE, I BETTER TAKE A LOOK INTO THIS "AZURA" FELLOW.
JINGLE

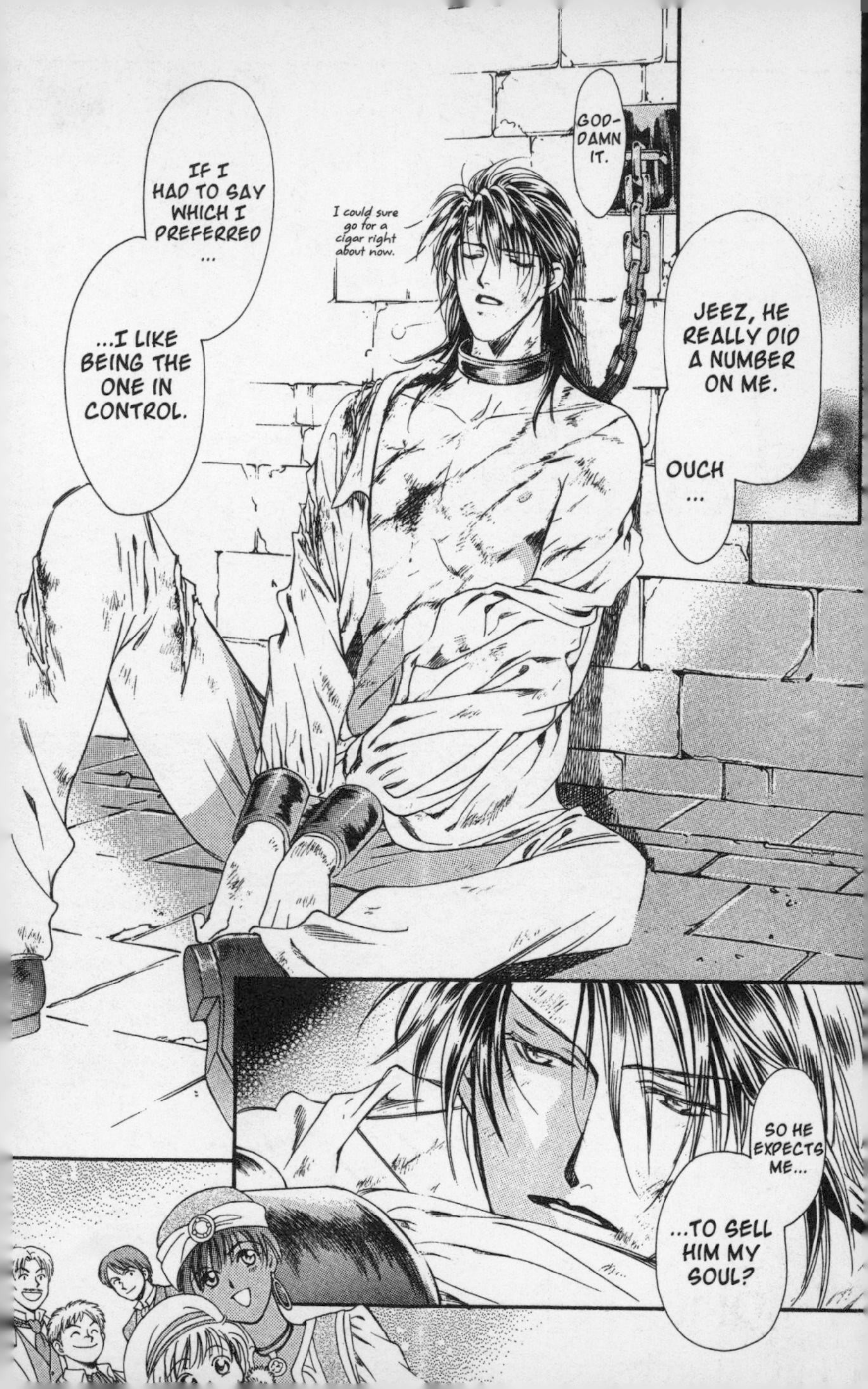
GOD-DAMN IT.
JEEZ, HE REALLY DID A NUMBER ON ME.
OUCH ...
I could sure go for a cigar right about now.
IF I HAD TO SAY WHICH I PREFERRED ...
...I LIKE BEING THE ONE IN CONTROL.
SO HE EXPECTS ME...
...TO SELL HIM MY SOUL?

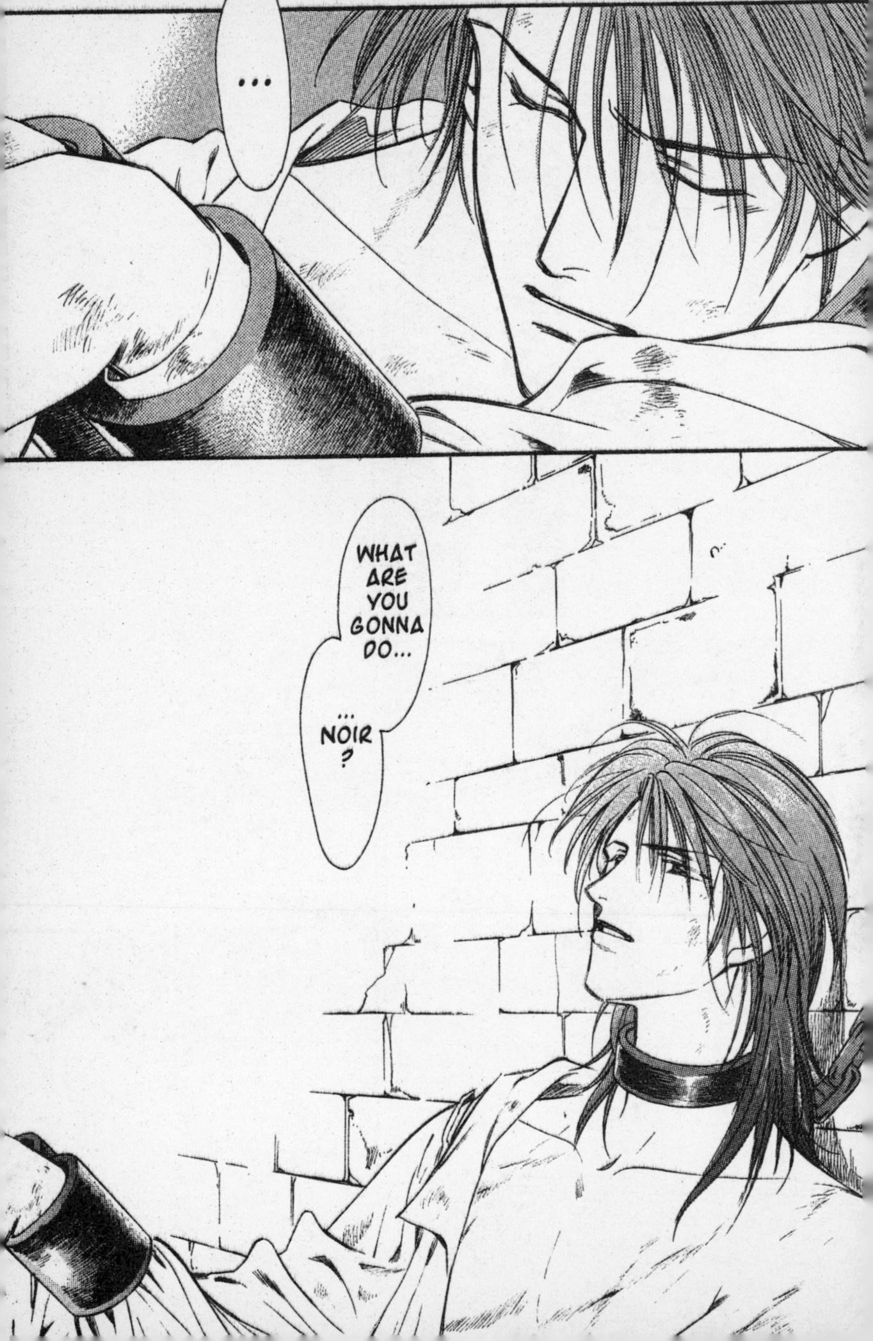
...
WHAT ARE YOU GONNA DO...
... NOIR ?

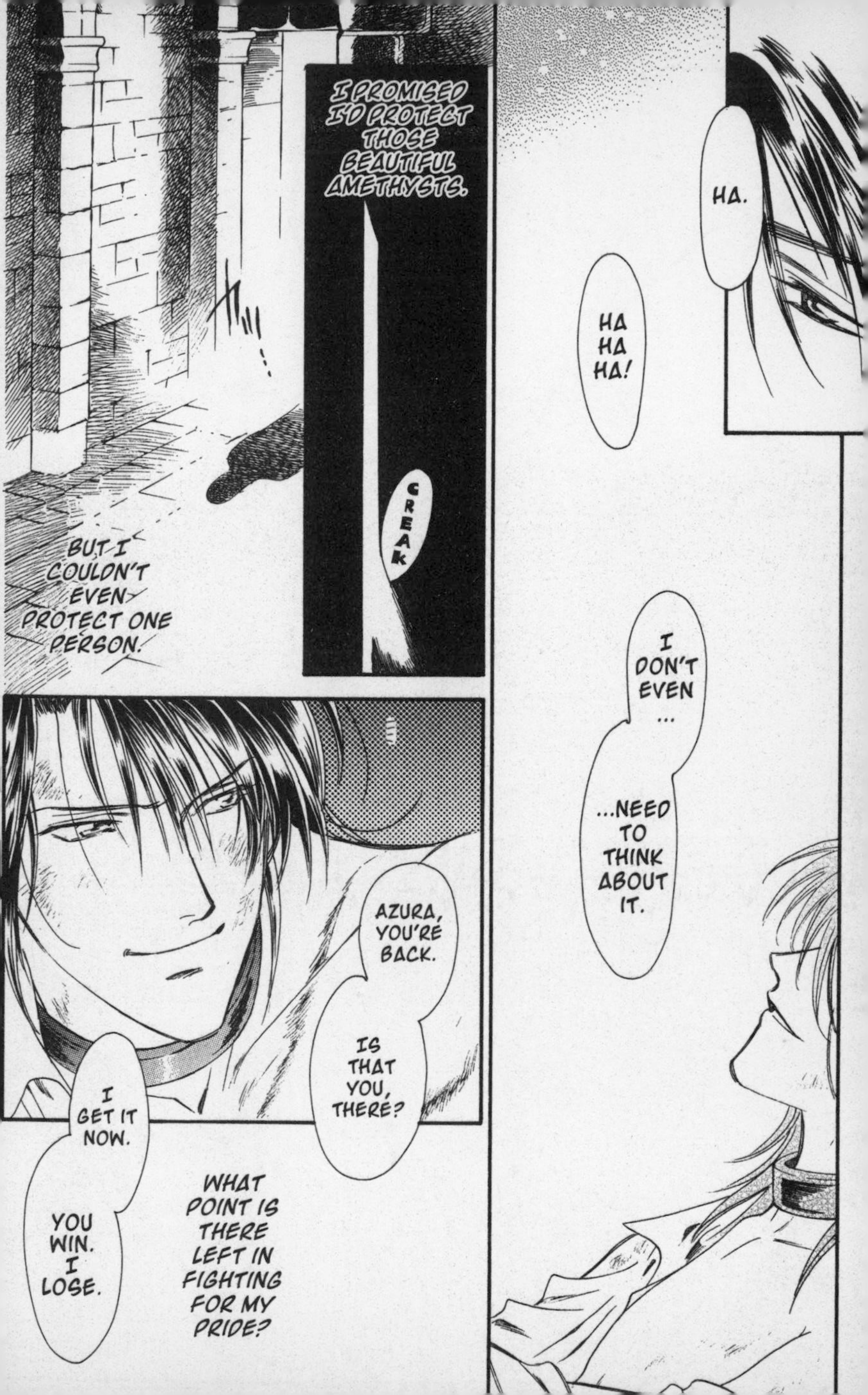

HA.
HA HA HA!
I DON'T EVEN...
...NEED TO THINK ABOUT IT.
I PROMISED I'D PROTECT THOSE BEAUTIFUL AMETHYSTS.
CREAK
BUT I COULDN'T EVEN PROTECT ONE PERSON.
AZURA, YOU'RE BACK.
IS THAT YOU, THERE?
I GET IT NOW.
WHAT POINT IS THERE LEFT IN FIGHTING FOR MY PRIDE?
YOU WIN. I LOSE.

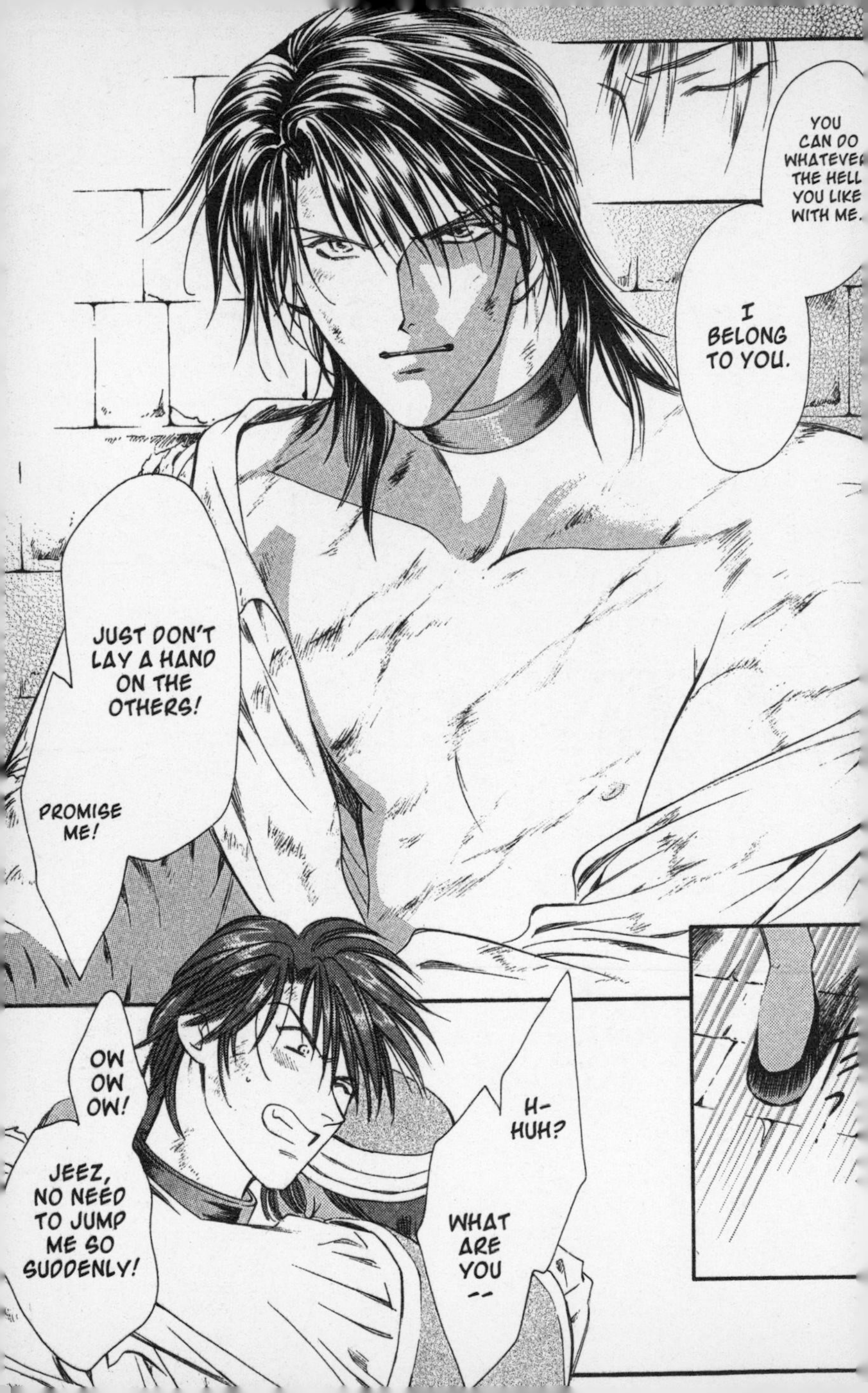
YOU CAN DO WHATEVER THE HELL YOU LIKE WITH ME.
I BELONG TO YOU.
JUST DON'T LAY A HAND ON THE OTHERS!
PROMISE ME!
H-HUH?
WHAT ARE YOU --
OW OW OW!
JEEZ, NO NEED TO JUMP ME SO SUDDENLY!

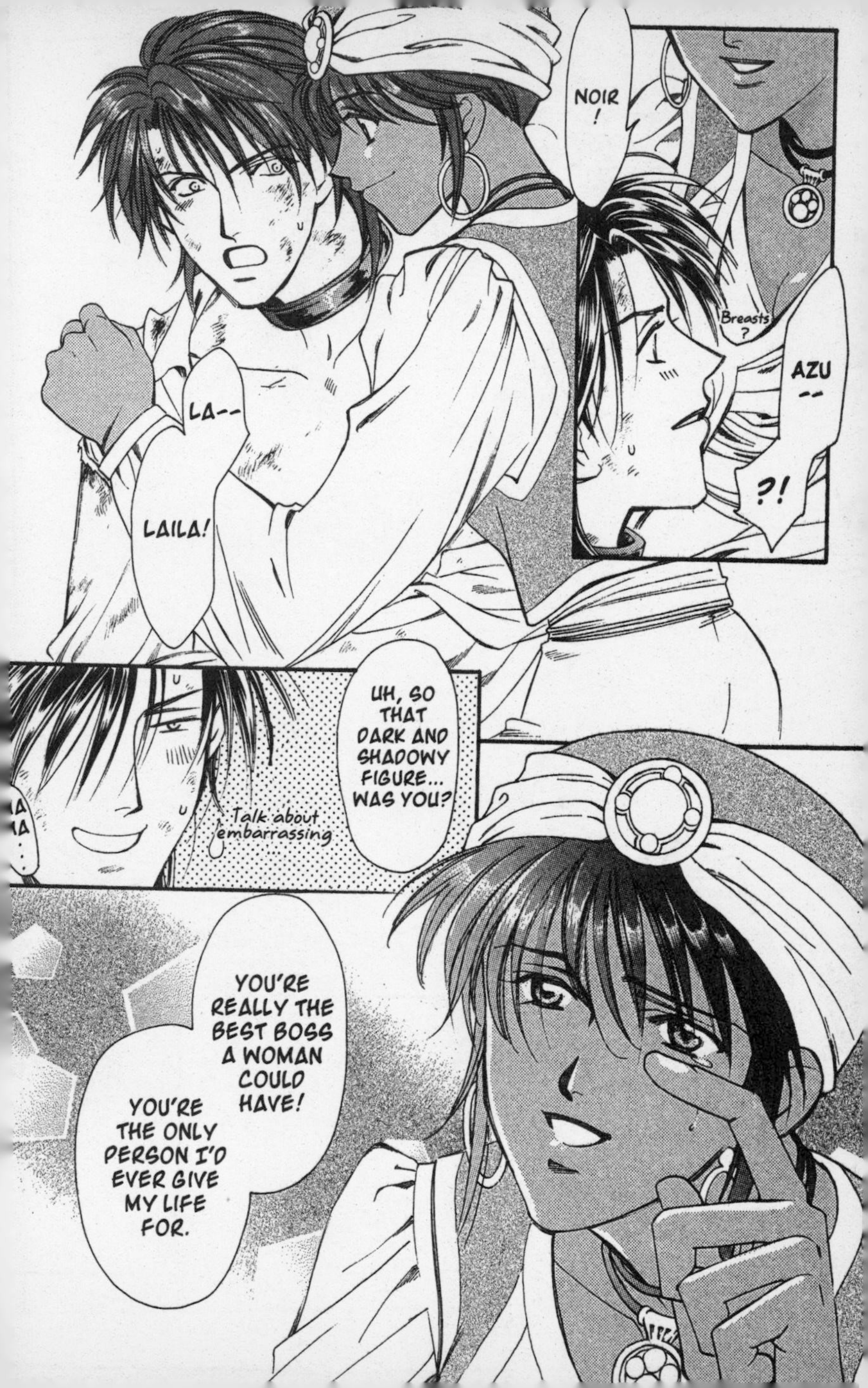
NOIR!
Breasts?
AZU--
?!
LA--
LAILA!
UH, SO THAT DARK AND SHADOWY FIGURE... WAS YOU?
Talk about embarrassing
YOU'RE REALLY THE BEST BOSS A WOMAN COULD HAVE!
YOU'RE THE ONLY PERSON I'D EVER GIVE MY LIFE FOR.

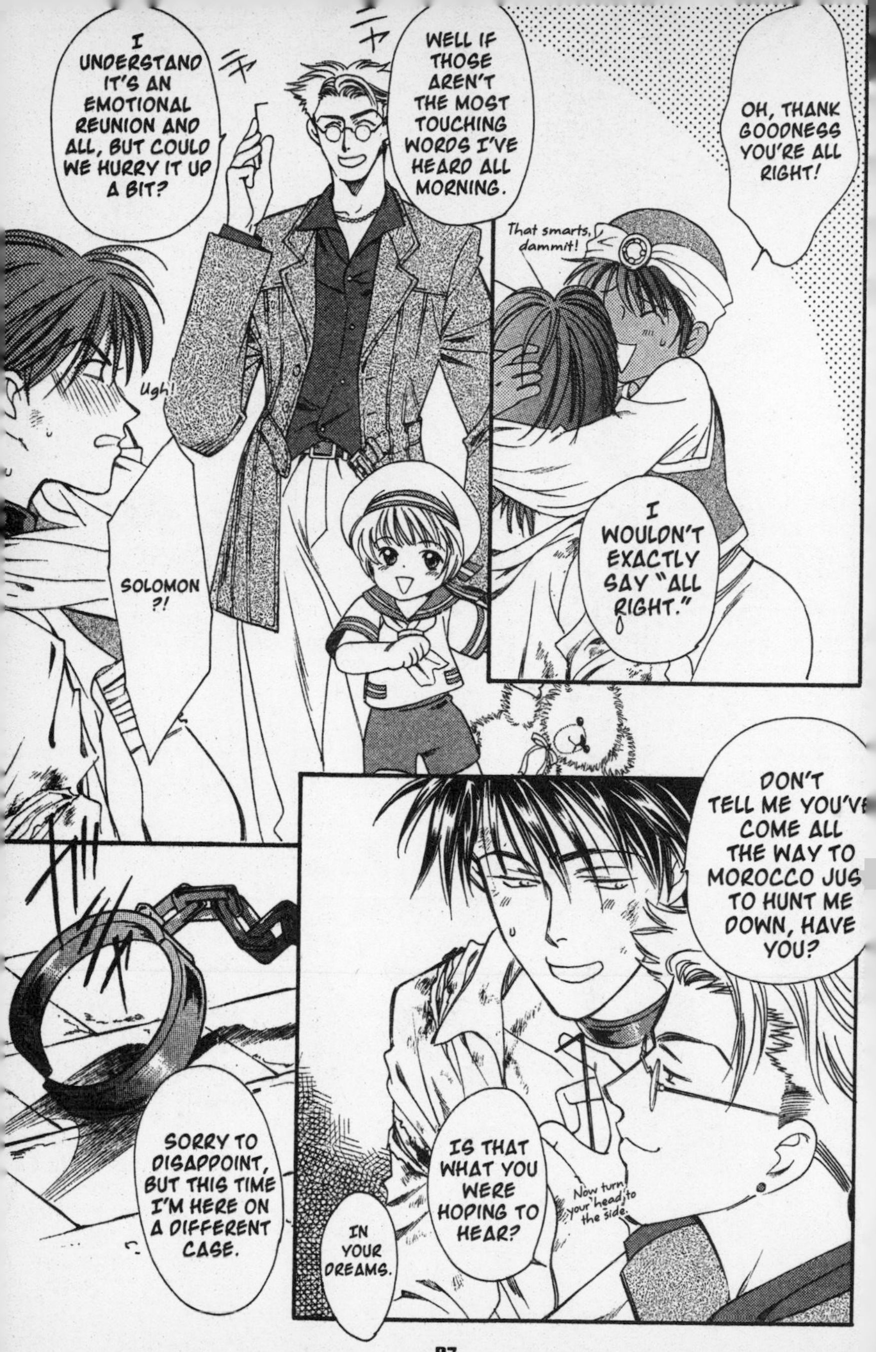
OH, THANK GOODNESS YOU'RE ALL RIGHT!
That smarts, dammit!
I WOULDN'T EXACTLY SAY "ALL RIGHT."
ニヤ
WELL IF THOSE AREN'T THE MOST TOUCHING WORDS I'VE HEARD ALL MORNING.
I UNDERSTAND IT'S AN EMOTIONAL REUNION AND ALL, BUT COULD WE HURRY IT UP A BIT?
Ugh!
SOLOMON ?!
DON'T TELL ME YOU'V COME ALL THE WAY TO MOROCCO JUS TO HUNT ME DOWN, HAVE YOU?
IS THAT WHAT YOU WERE HOPING TO HEAR?
Now turn your head to the side.
IN YOUR DREAMS.
SORRY TO DISAPPOINT, BUT THIS TIME I'M HERE ON A DIFFERENT CASE.

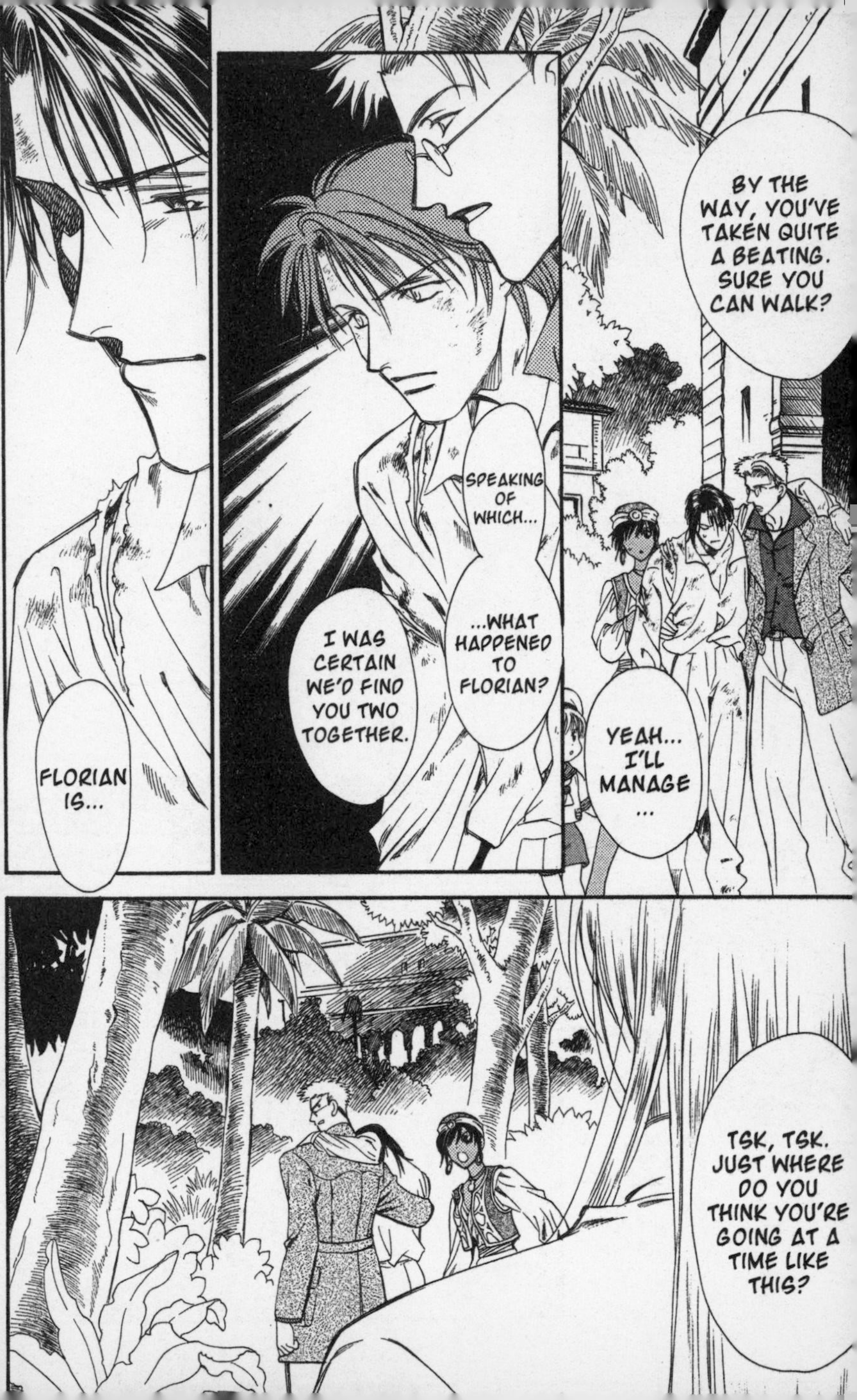
BY THE WAY, YOU'VE TAKEN QUITE A BEATING. SURE YOU CAN WALK?
YEAH... I'LL MANAGE ...
SPEAKING OF WHICH...
...WHAT HAPPENED TO FLORIAN?
I WAS CERTAIN WE'D FIND YOU TWO TOGETHER.
FLORIAN IS...
TSK, TSK. JUST WHERE DO YOU THINK YOU'RE GOING AT A TIME LIKE THIS?

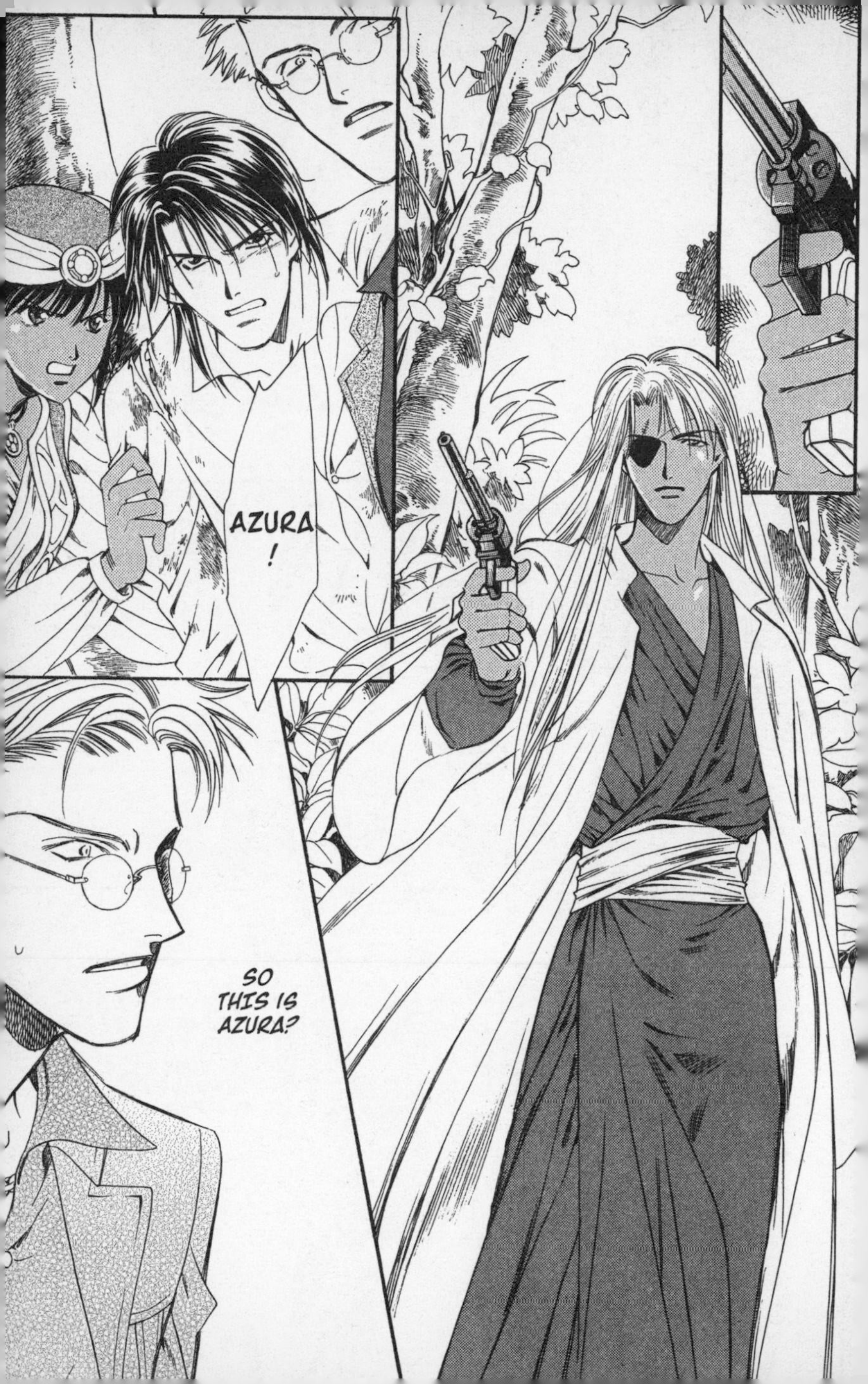
AZURA!
SO THIS IS AZURA?

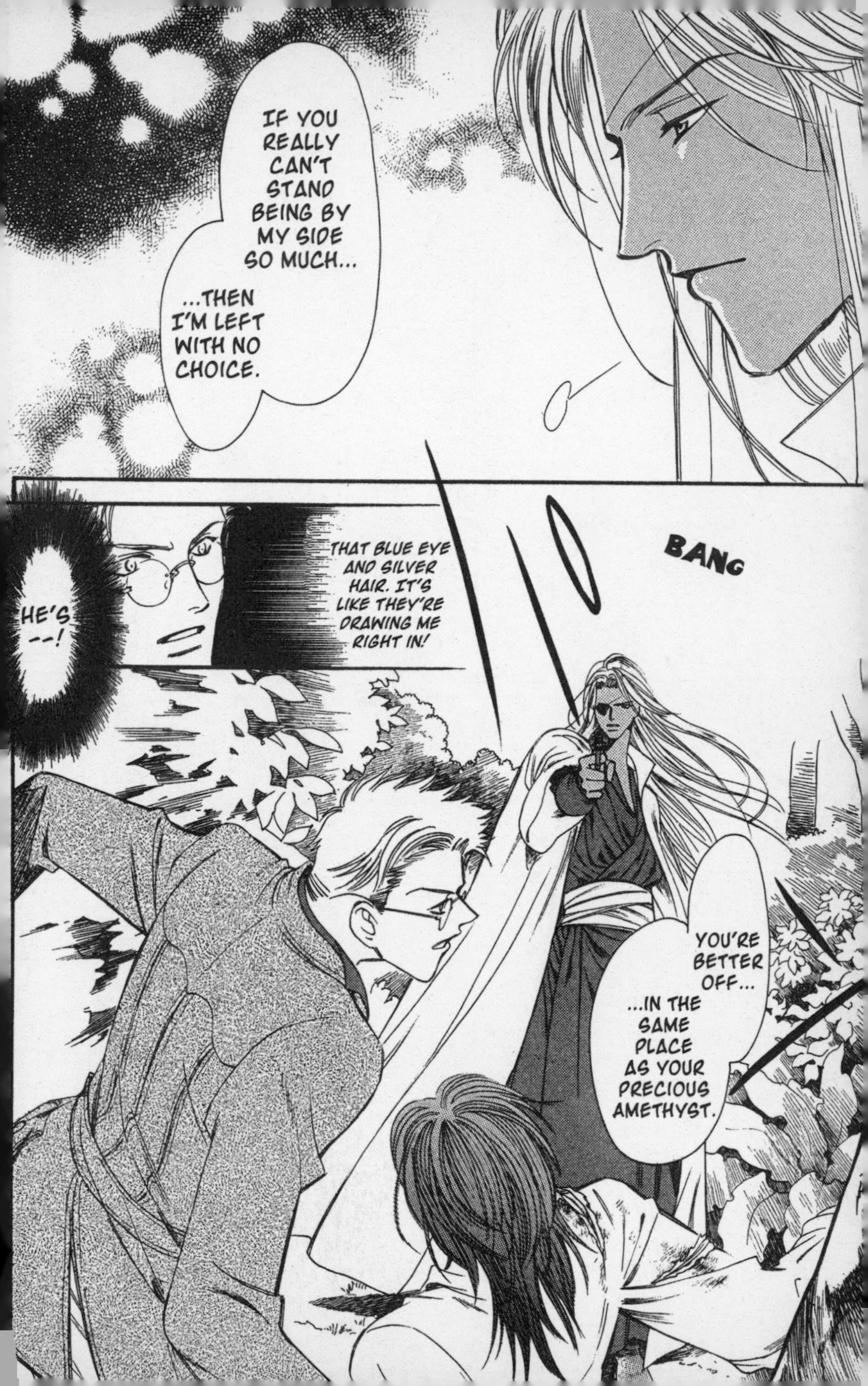
IF YOU REALLY CAN'T STAND BEING BY MY SIDE SO MUCH...
...THEN I'M LEFT WITH NO CHOICE.
BANG
THAT BLUE EYE AND SILVER HAIR. IT'S LIKE THEY'RE DRAWING ME RIGHT IN!
HE'S --!
YOU'RE BETTER OFF...
...IN THE SAME PLACE AS YOUR PRECIOUS AMETHYST.

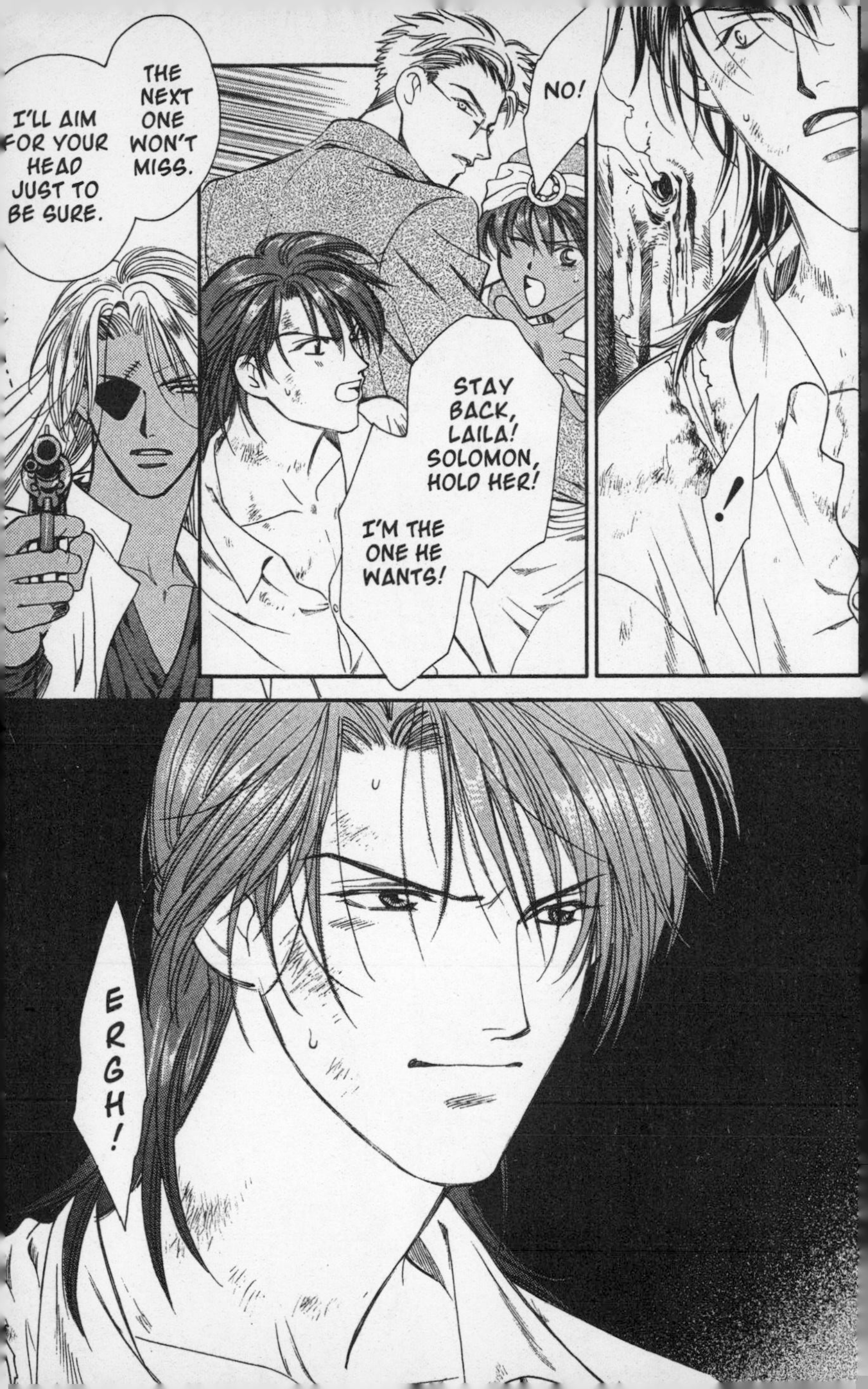
!
NO!
STAY BACK, LAILA! SOLOMON, HOLD HER!
I'M THE ONE HE WANTS!
THE NEXT ONE WON'T MISS.
I'LL AIM FOR YOUR HEAD JUST TO BE SURE.
ERGH!

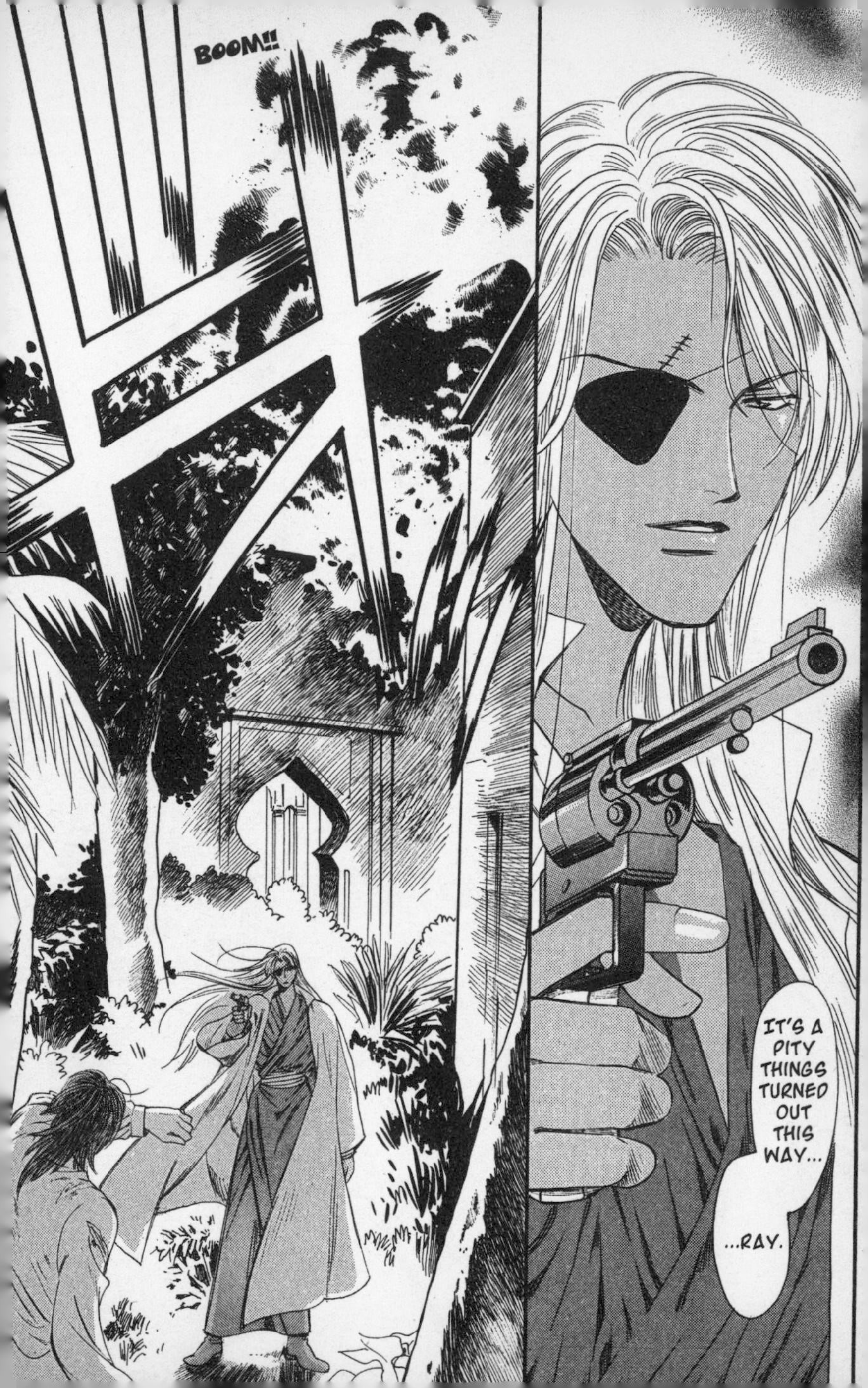
IT'S A PITY THINGS TURNED OUT THIS WAY...
...RAY.
BOOM!!

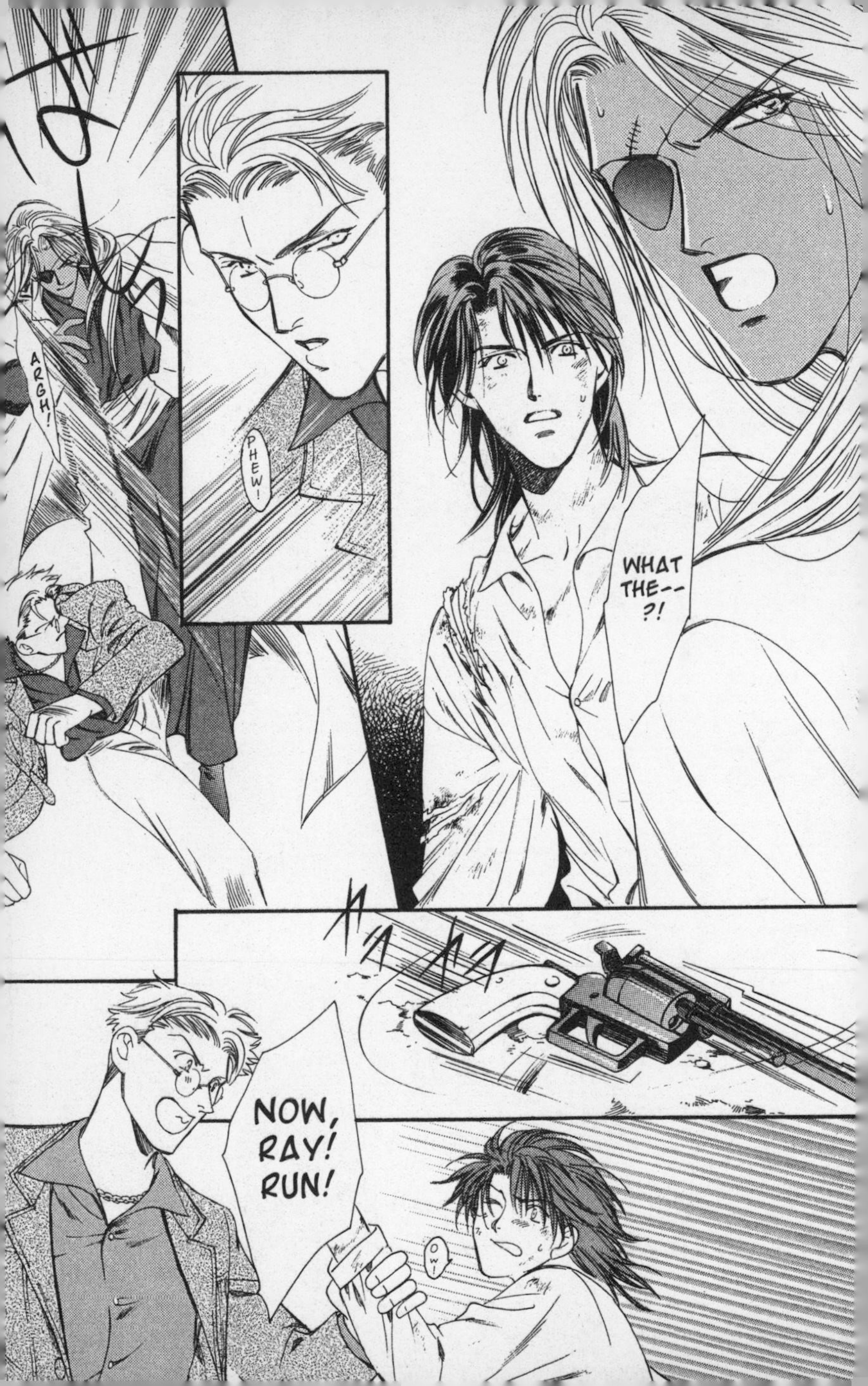
WHAT THE--?!
PHEW!
ARGH!
NOW, RAY! RUN!
OW!

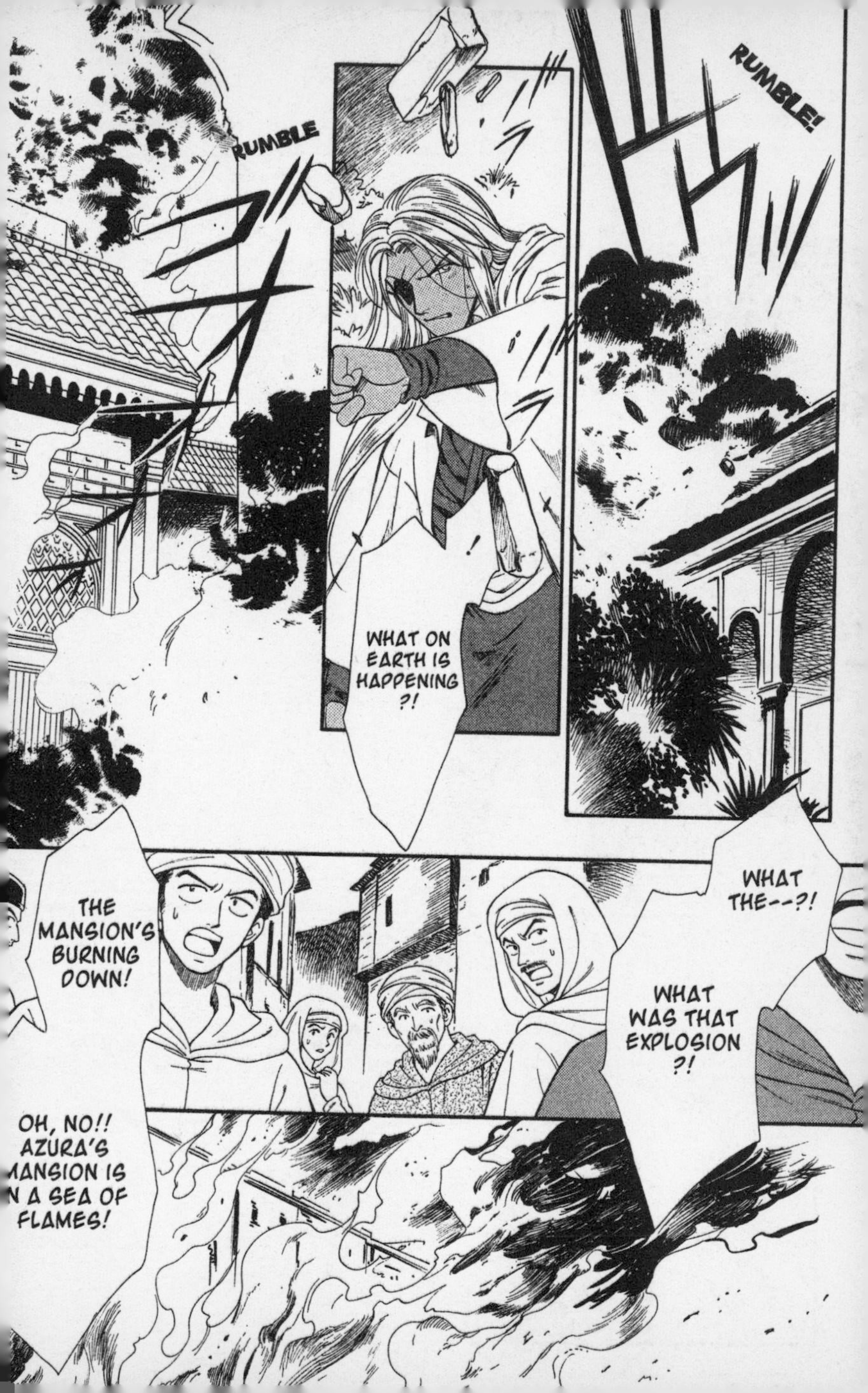
RUMBLE!
WHAT ON EARTH IS HAPPENING?!
RUMBLE
WHAT THE--?!
WHAT WAS THAT EXPLOSION?!
THE MANSION'S BURNING DOWN!
OH, NO!! AZURA'S MANSION IS N A SEA OF FLAMES!

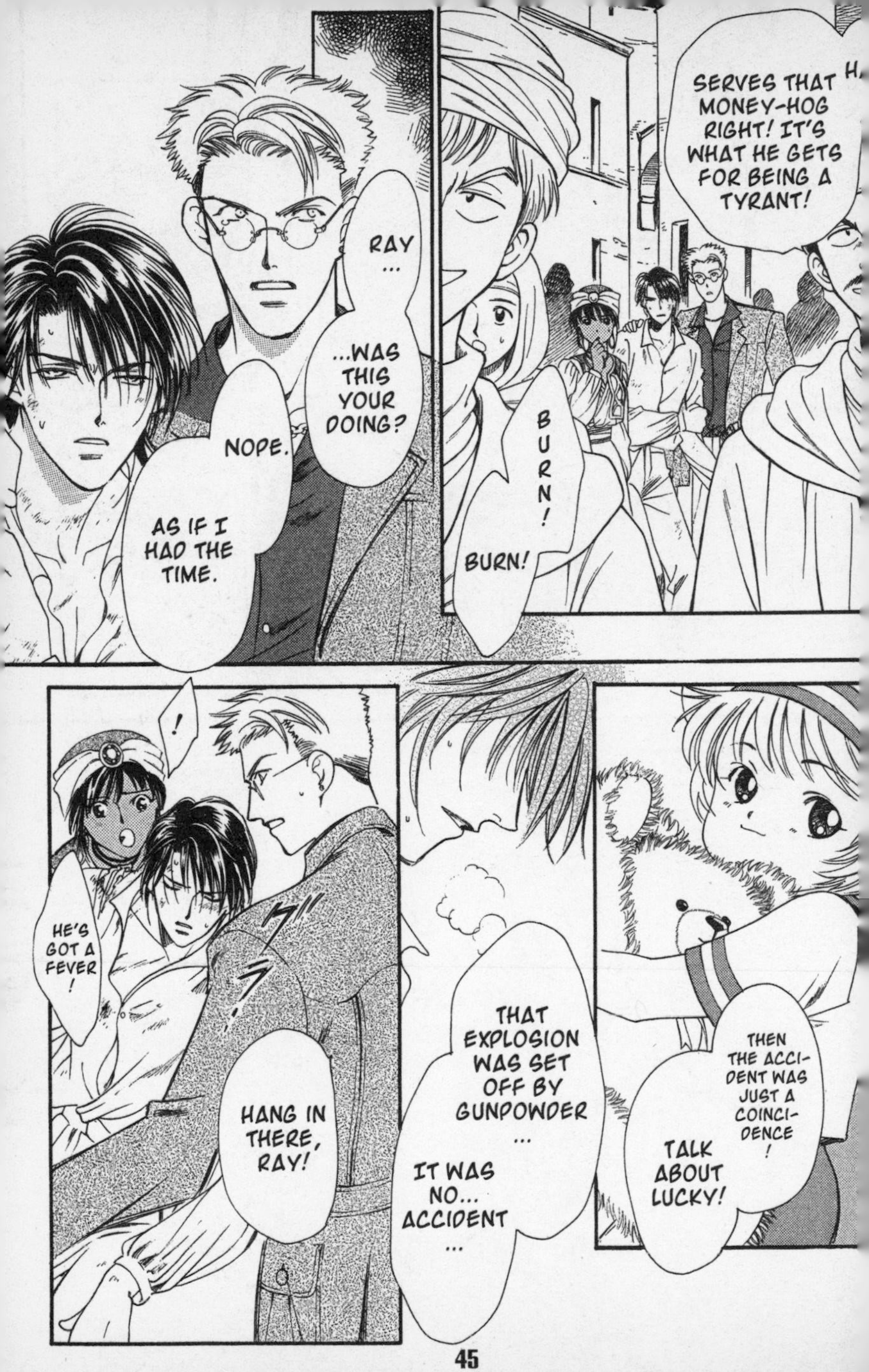
SERVES THAT MONEY-HOG RIGHT! IT'S WHAT HE GETS FOR BEING A TYRANT!
BURN!
BURN!
RAY ...
...WAS THIS YOUR DOING?
NOPE.
AS IF I HAD THE TIME.
THEN THE ACCI-DENT WAS JUST A COINCI-DENCE!
TALK ABOUT LUCKY!
THAT EXPLOSION WAS SET OFF BY GUNPOWDER ...
IT WAS NO... ACCIDENT ...
!
HE'S GOT A FEVER!
HANG IN THERE, RAY!

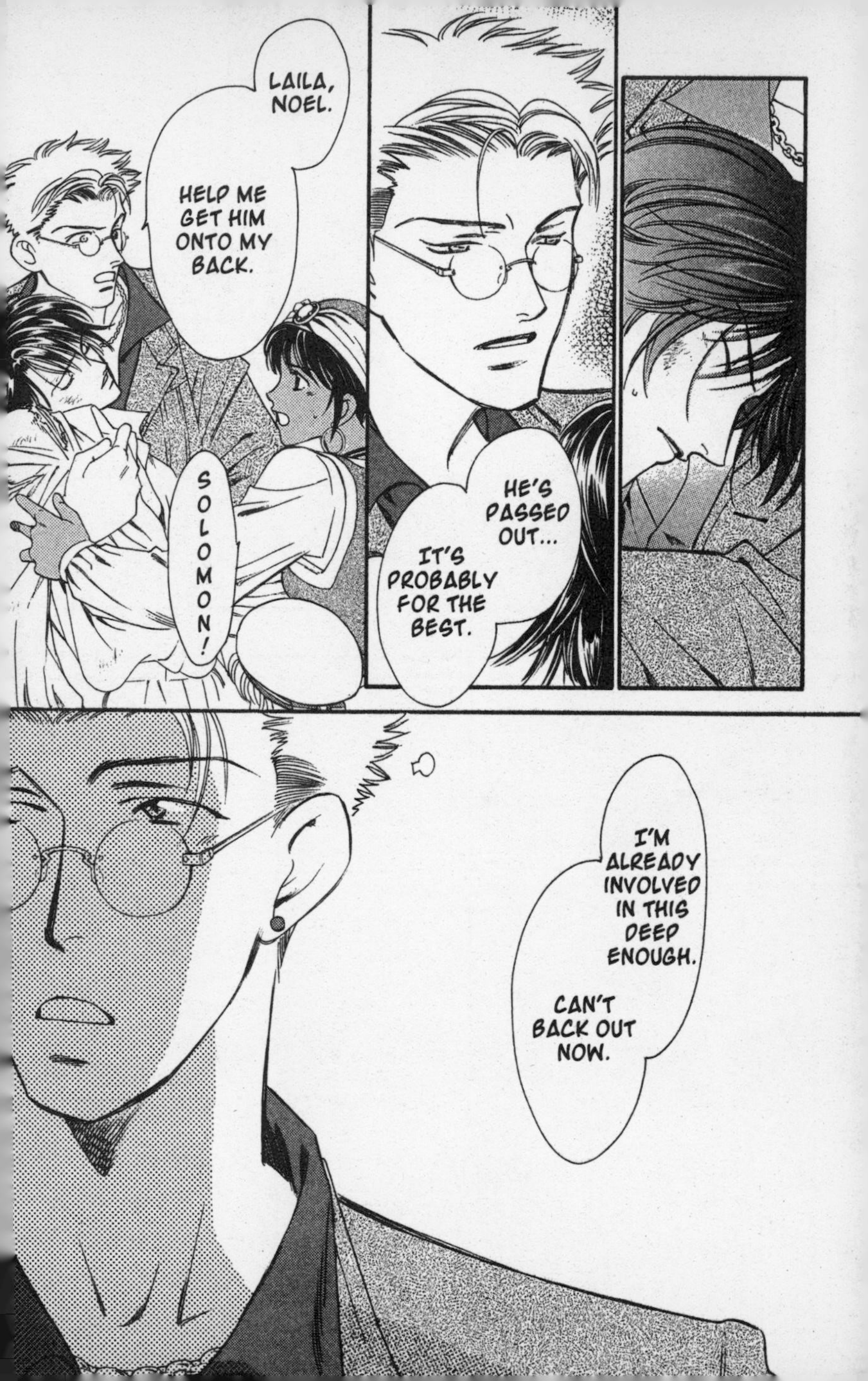
HE'S PASSED OUT...
IT'S PROBABLY FOR THE BEST.
LAILA, NOEL.
HELP ME GET HIM ONTO MY BACK.
SOLOMON!
I'M ALREADY INVOLVED IN THIS DEEP ENOUGH.
CAN'T BACK OUT NOW.

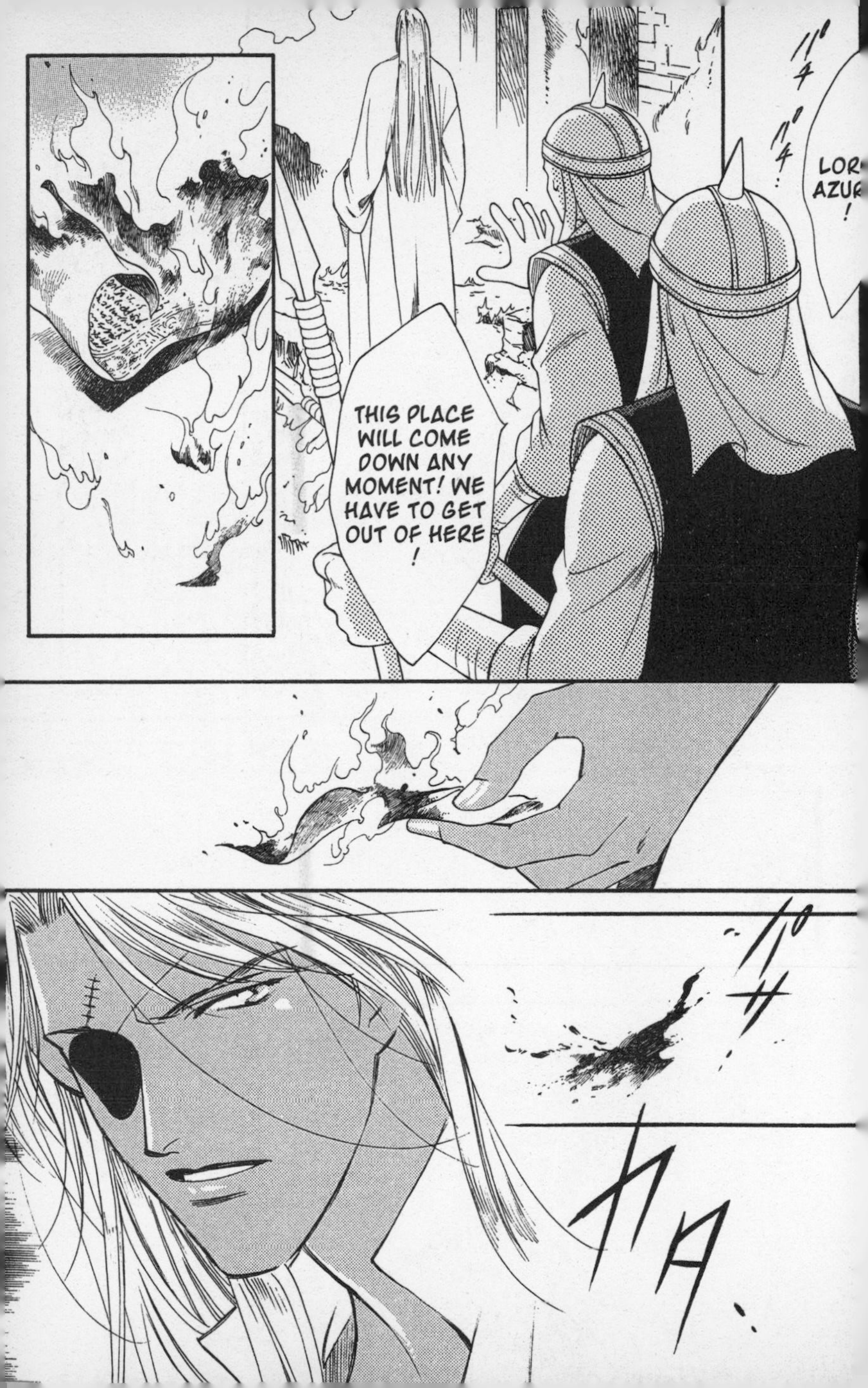
パチパチ…
LOR AZUR !
THIS PLACE WILL COME DOWN ANY MOMENT! WE HAVE TO GET OUT OF HERE !
パサ!

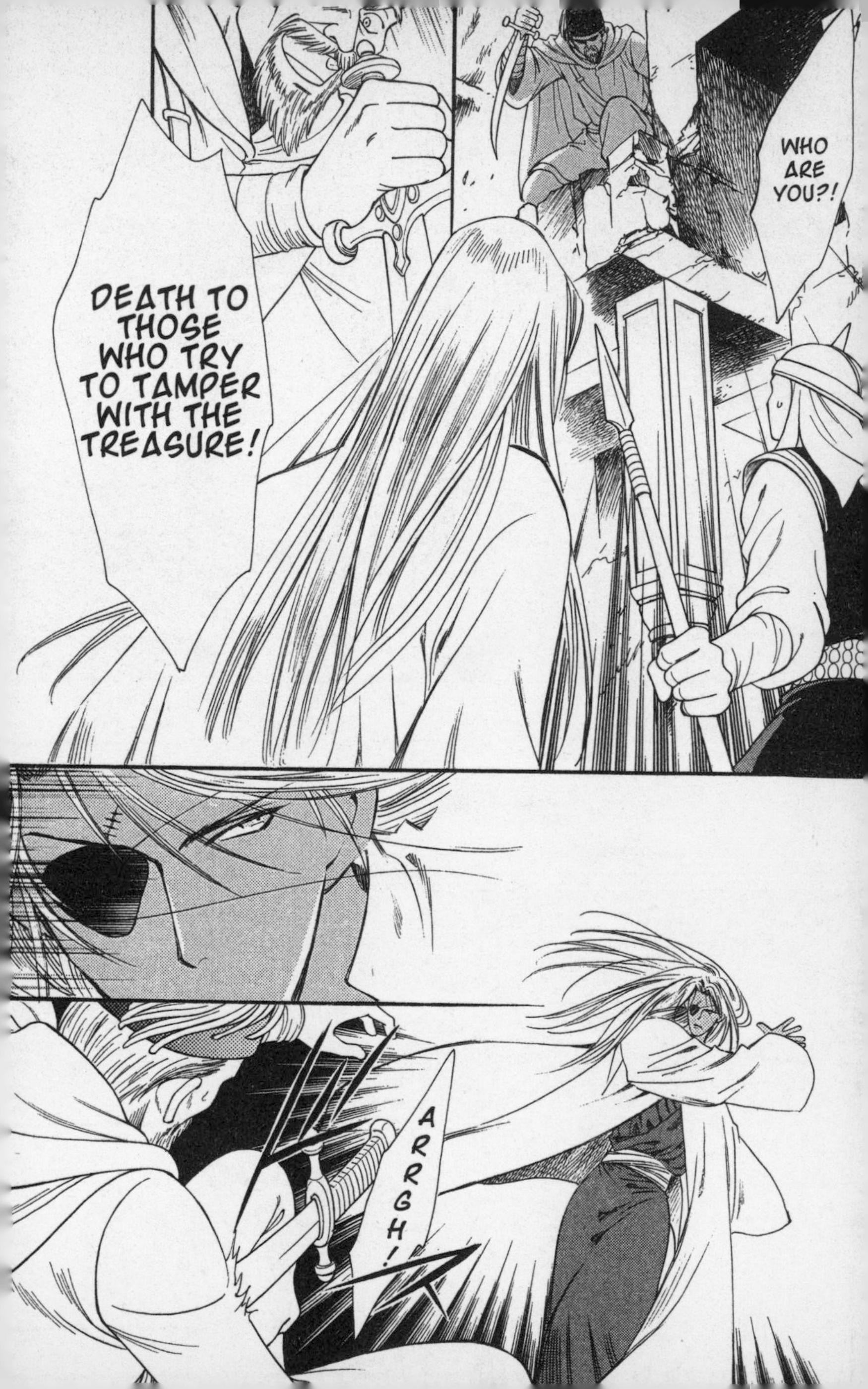
WHO ARE YOU?!
DEATH TO THOSE WHO TRY TO TAMPER WITH THE TREASURE!
ARRGH!

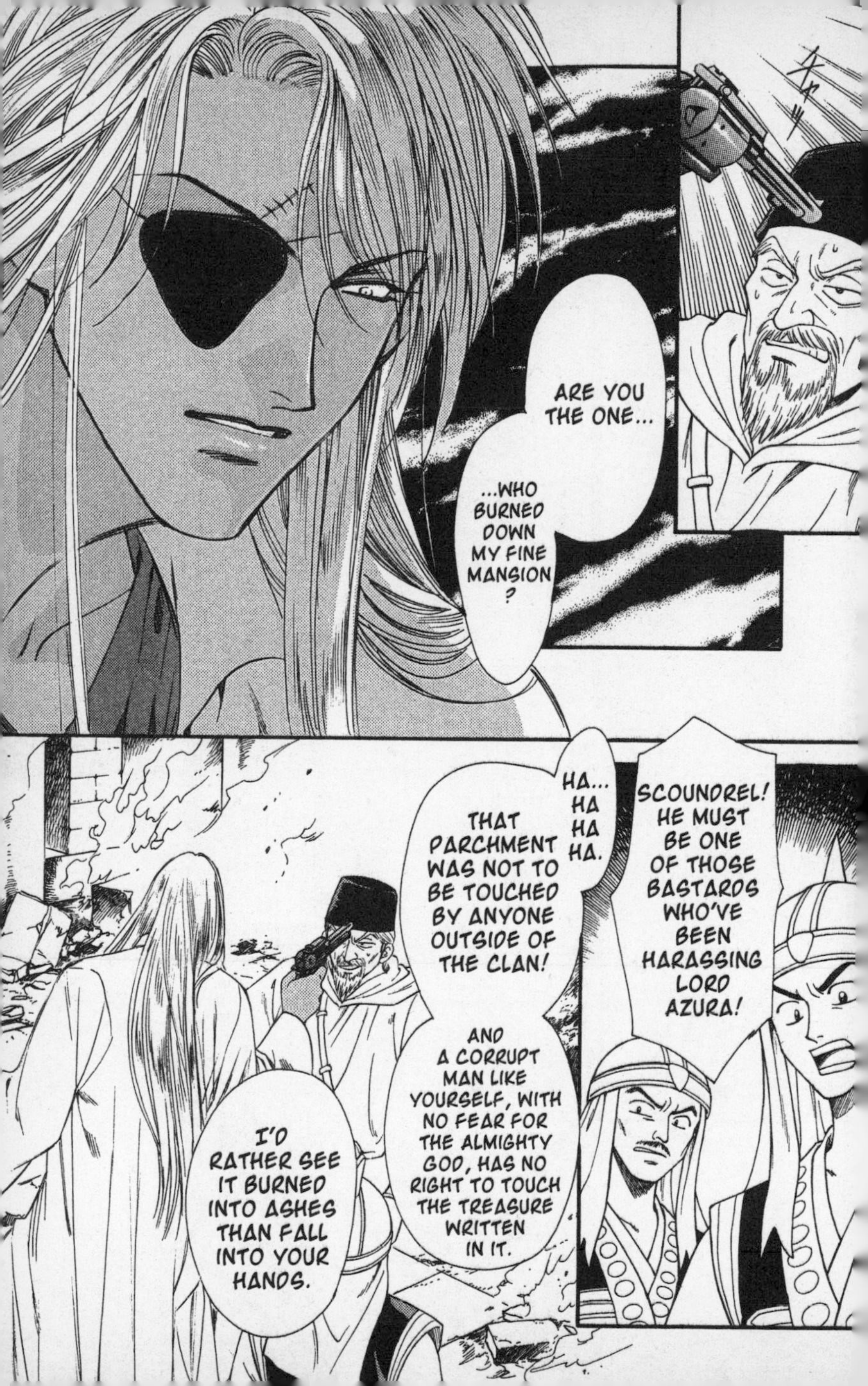
ARE YOU THE ONE...
...WHO BURNED DOWN MY FINE MANSION?
SCOUNDREL! HE MUST BE ONE OF THOSE BASTARDS WHO'VE BEEN HARASSING LORD AZURA!
HA... HA HA HA.
THAT PARCHMENT WAS NOT TO BE TOUCHED BY ANYONE OUTSIDE OF THE CLAN!
AND A CORRUPT MAN LIKE YOURSELF, WITH NO FEAR FOR THE ALMIGHTY GOD, HAS NO RIGHT TO TOUCH THE TREASURE WRITTEN IN IT.
I'D RATHER SEE IT BURNED INTO ASHES THAN FALL INTO YOUR HANDS.

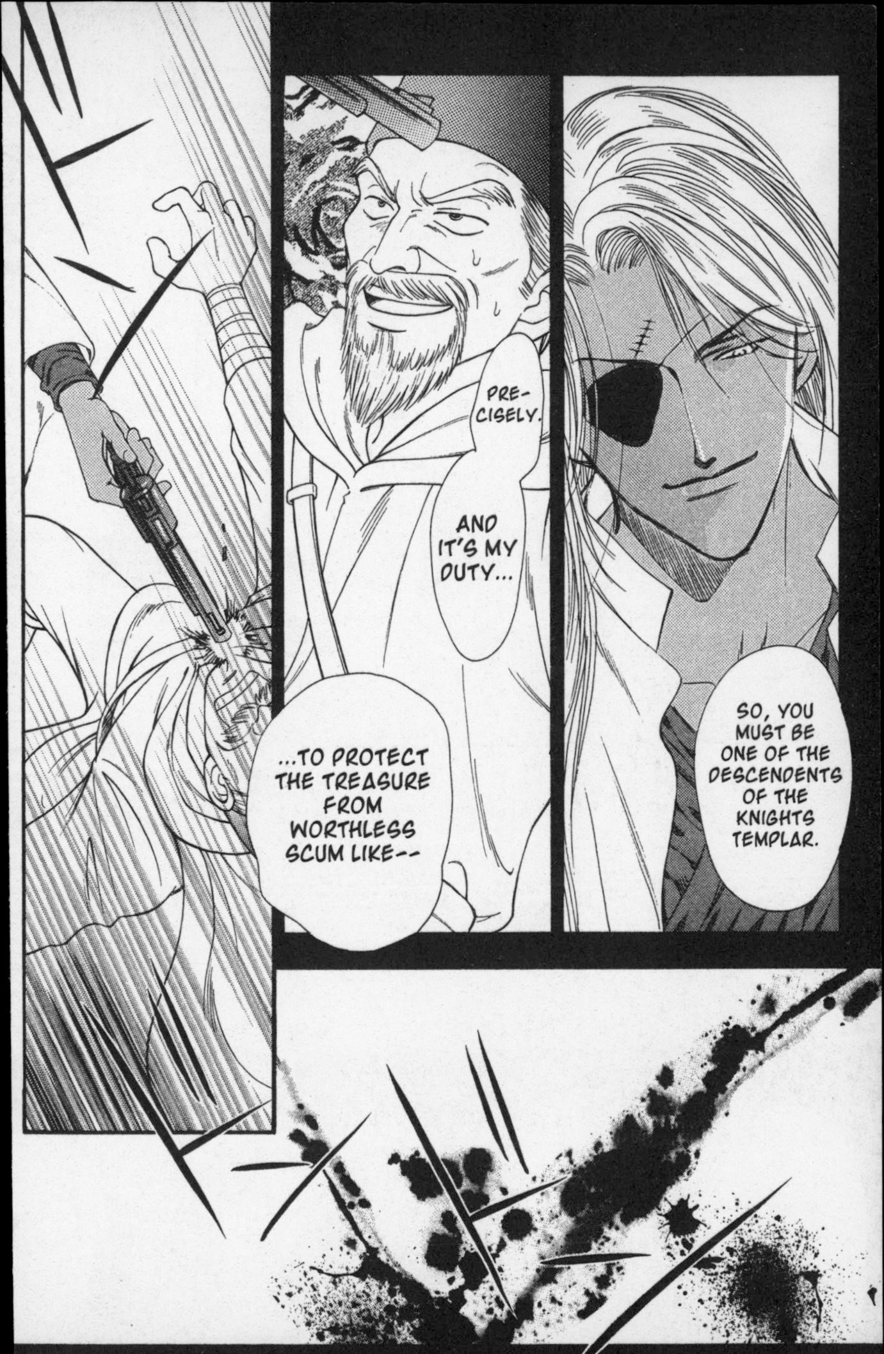
SO, YOU MUST BE ONE OF THE DESCENDENTS OF THE KNIGHTS TEMPLAR.
PRE-CISELY.
AND IT'S MY DUTY...
...TO PROTECT THE TREASURE FROM WORTHLESS SCUM LIKE--

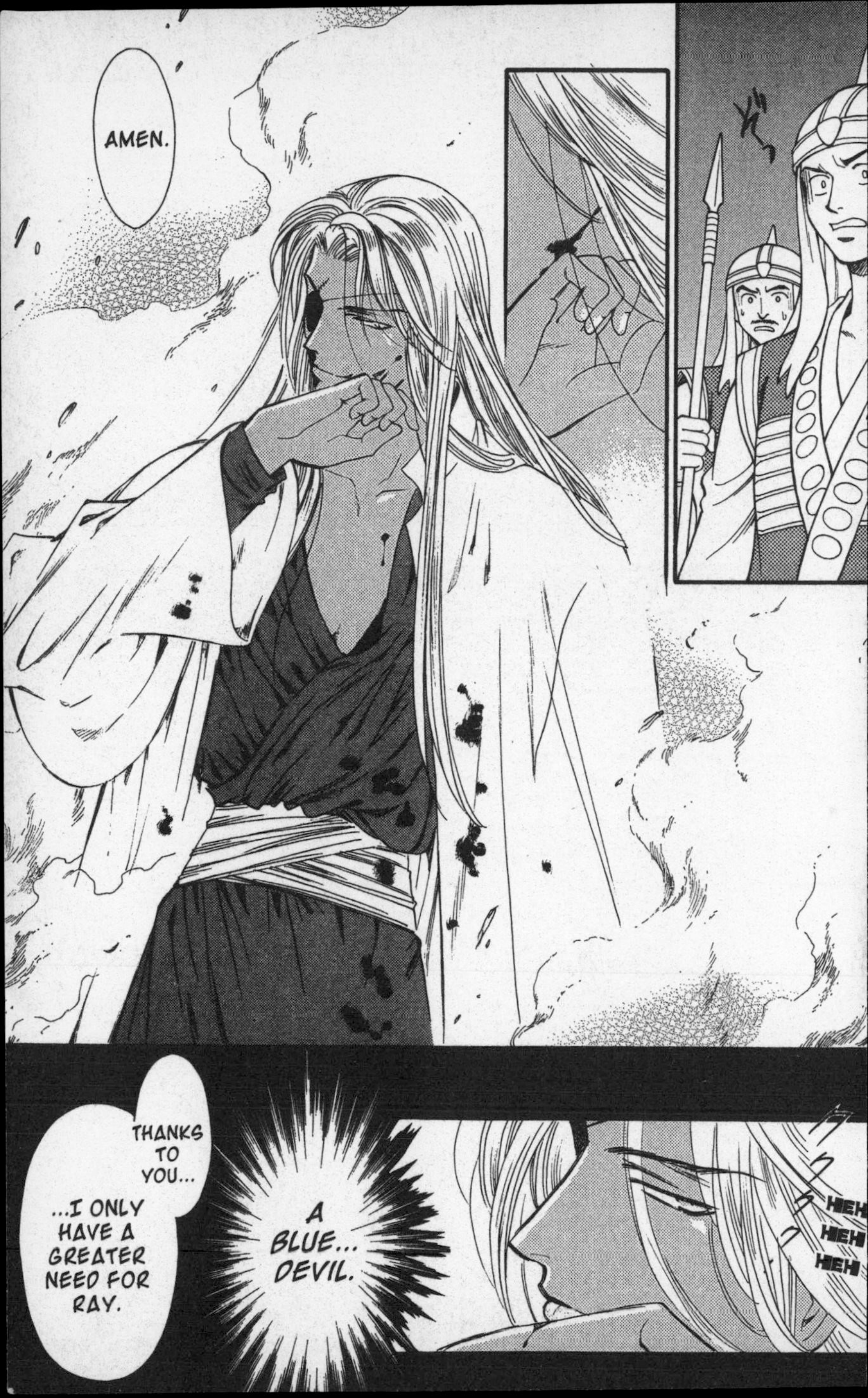
AMEN.
THANKS TO YOU...
...I ONLY HAVE A GREATER NEED FOR RAY.
A BLUE... DEVIL.
HEH HEH HEH

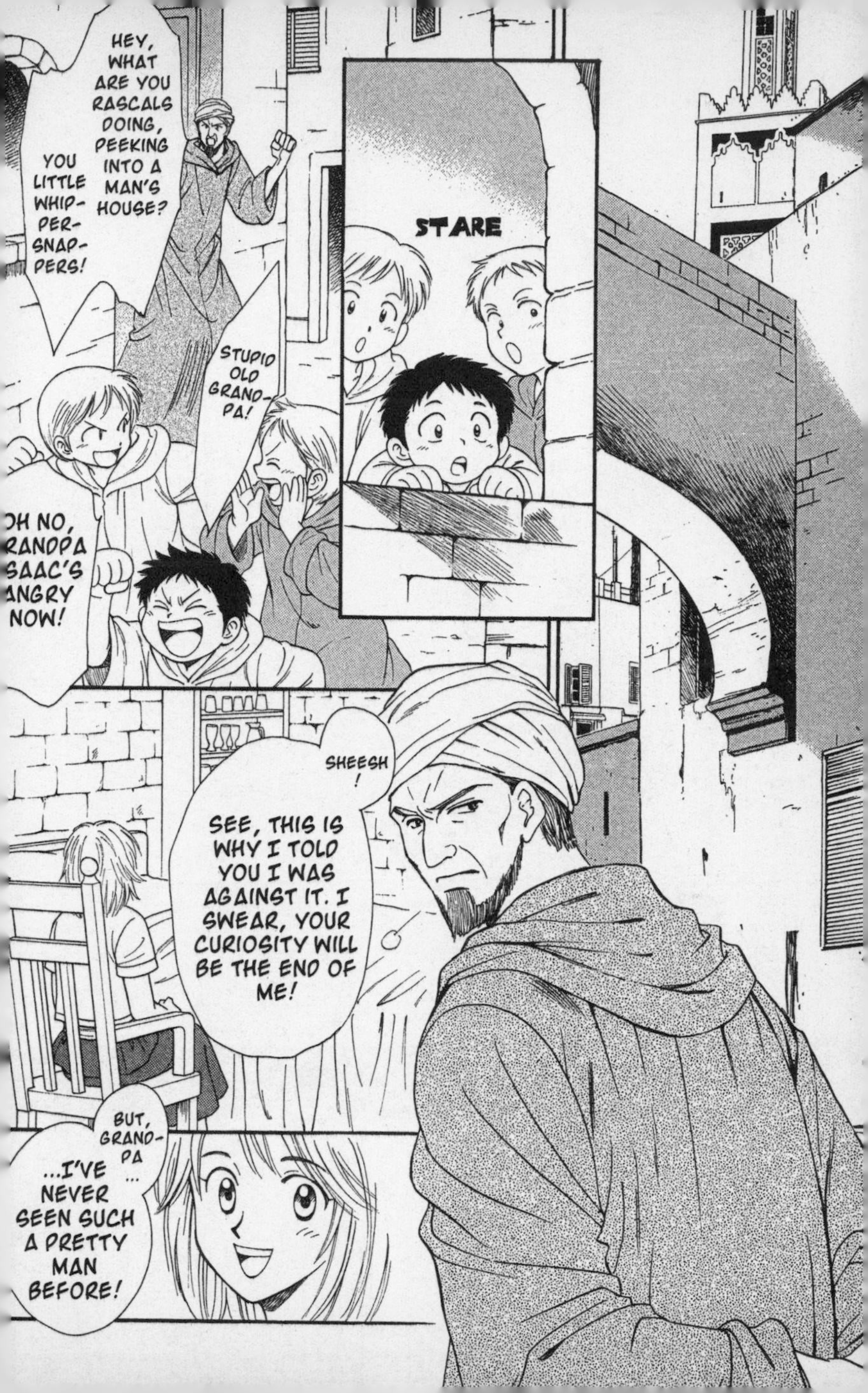
STARE
HEY, WHAT ARE YOU RASCALS DOING, PEEKING INTO A MAN'S HOUSE?
YOU LITTLE WHIP-PER-SNAP-PERS!
STUPID OLD GRAND-PA!
OH NO, RANDPA SAAC'S ANGRY NOW!
SHEESH!
SEE, THIS IS WHY I TOLD YOU I WAS AGAINST IT. I SWEAR, YOUR CURIOSITY WILL BE THE END OF ME!
BUT, GRAND-PA...
...I'VE NEVER SEEN SUCH A PRETTY MAN BEFORE!

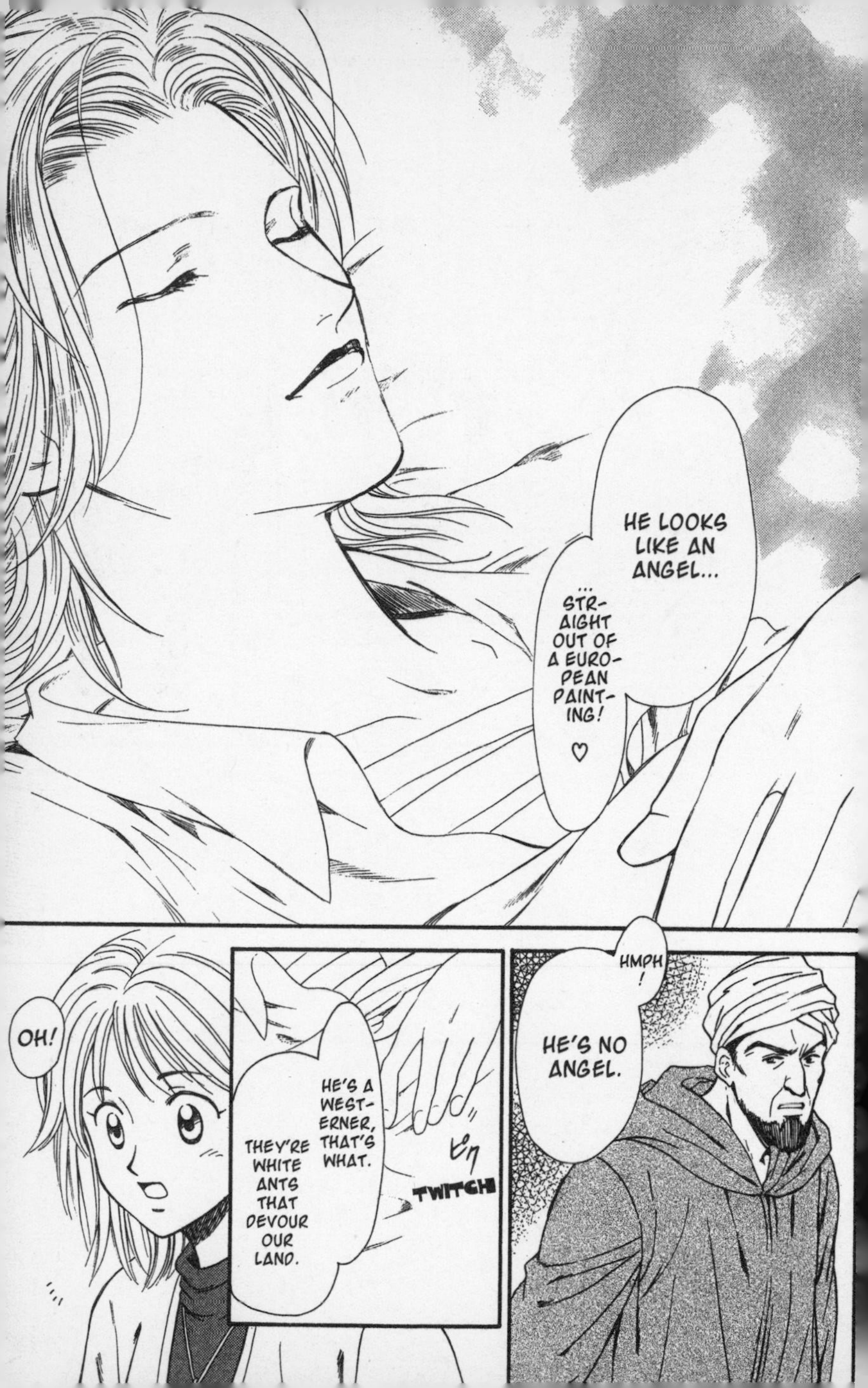
HE LOOKS LIKE AN ANGEL...
...STR-AIGHT OUT OF A EURO-PEAN PAINT-ING! ♡
HMPH!
HE'S NO ANGEL.
HE'S A WEST-ERNER, THAT'S WHAT.
THEY'RE WHITE ANTS THAT DEVOUR OUR LAND.
ピク
TWITCH
OH!

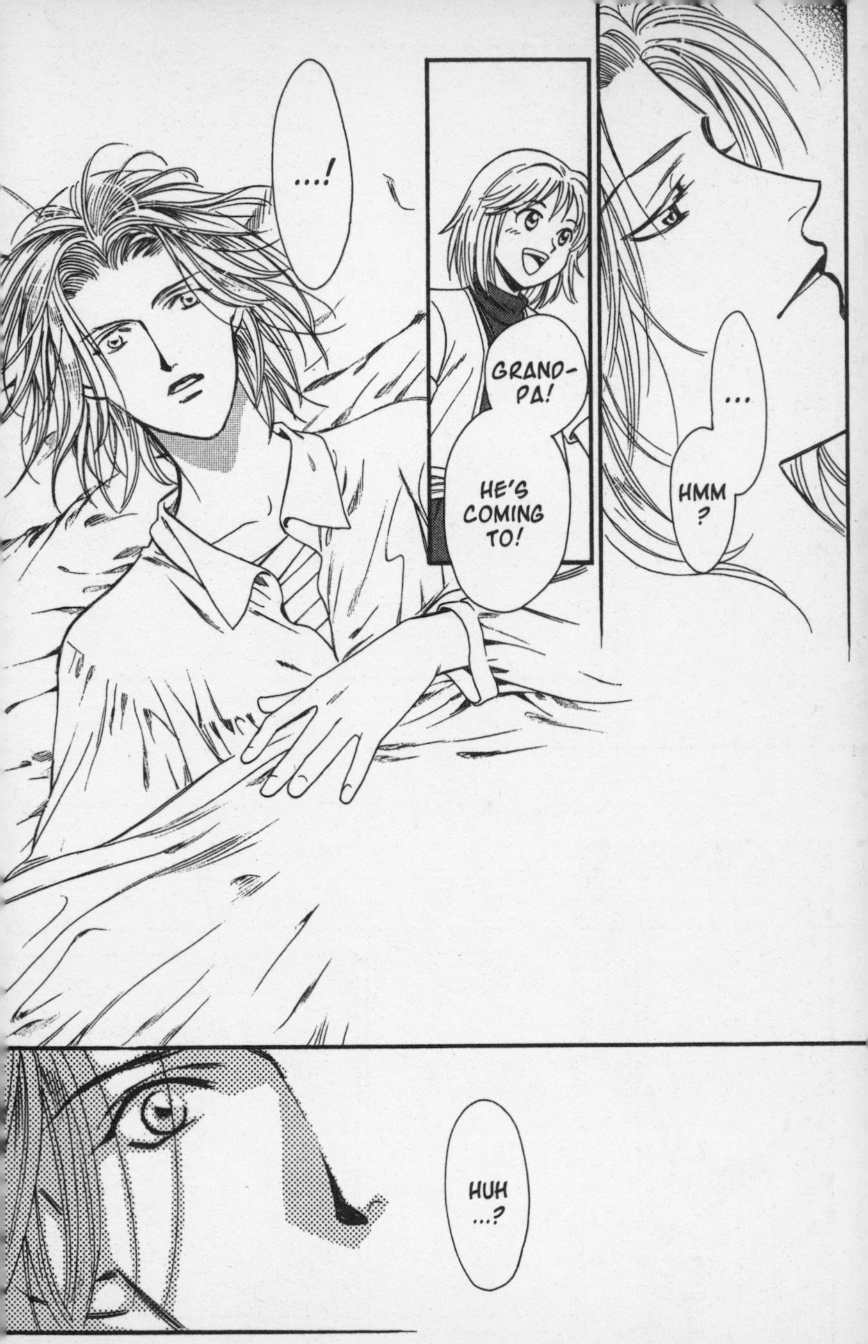
...
HMM ?
GRAND-PA!
HE'S COMING TO!
...!
HUH ...?

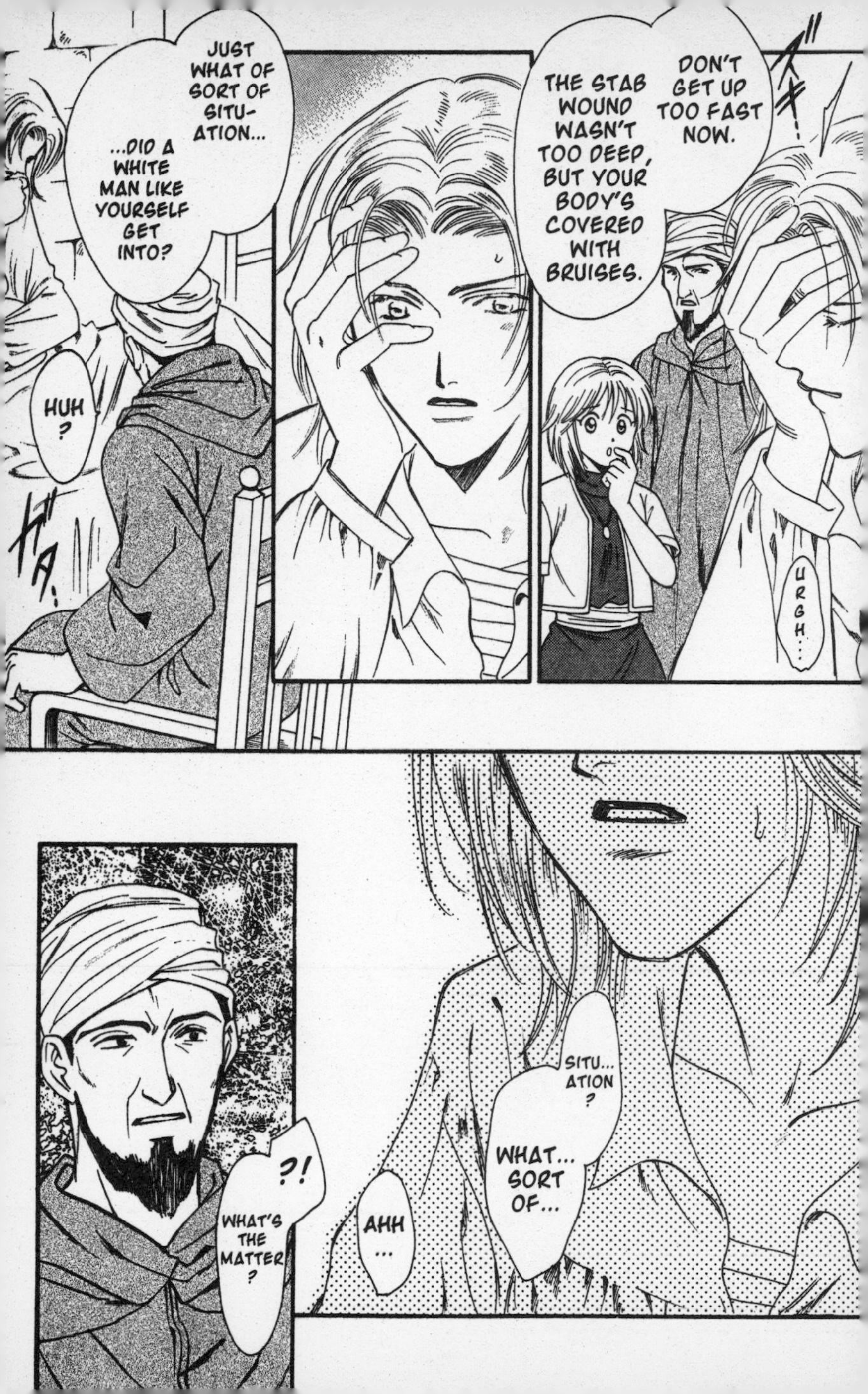
DON'T GET UP TOO FAST NOW.
THE STAB WOUND WASN'T TOO DEEP, BUT YOUR BODY'S COVERED WITH BRUISES.
URGH...
JUST WHAT OF SORT OF SITU- ATION...
...DID A WHITE MAN LIKE YOURSELF GET INTO?
HUH?
SITU... ATION?
WHAT... SORT OF...
AHH...
?!
WHAT'S THE MATTER?

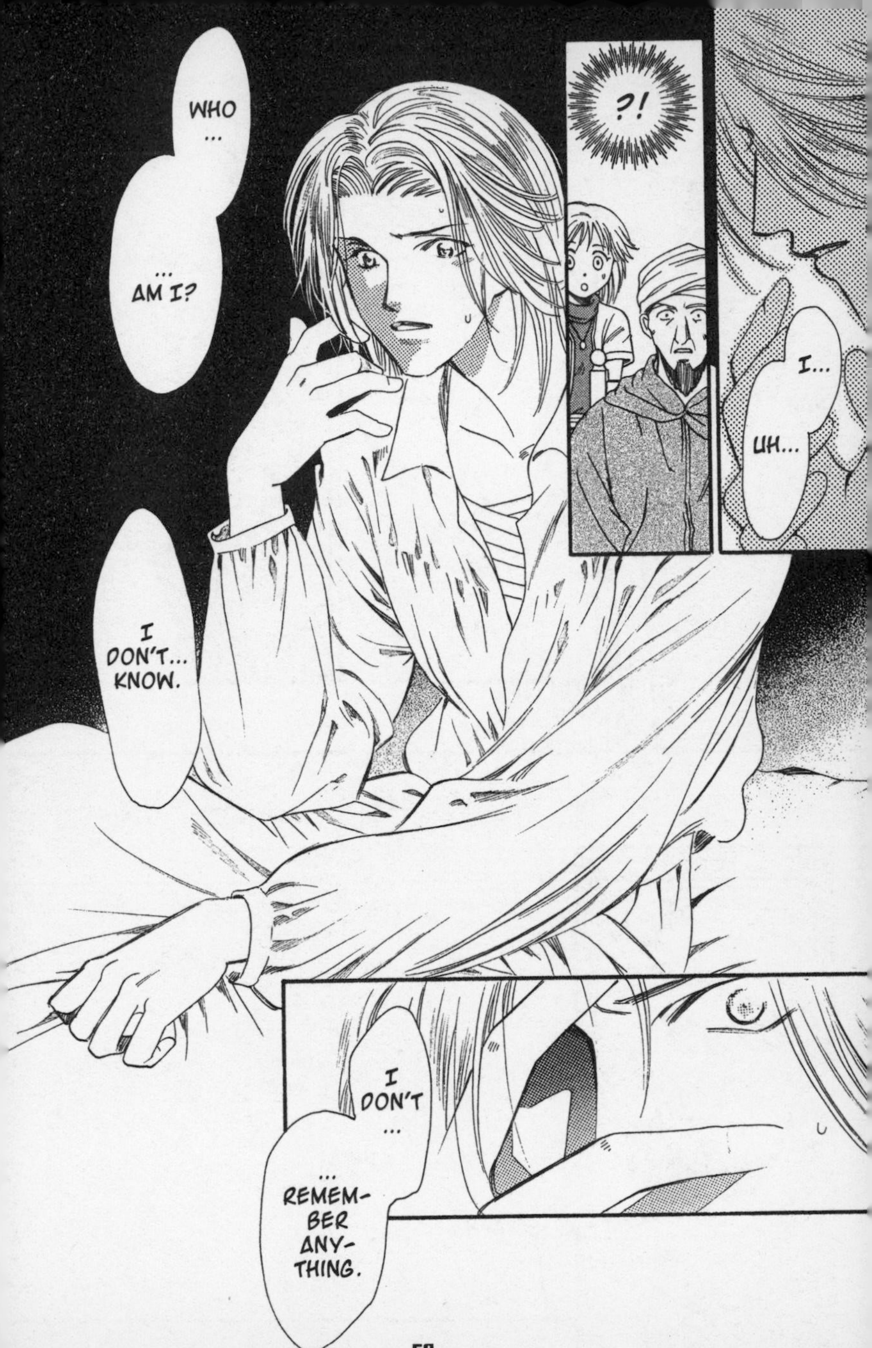
I... UH...
?!
WHO ... ... AM I?
I DON'T... KNOW.
I DON'T ... ... REMEMBER ANYTHING.

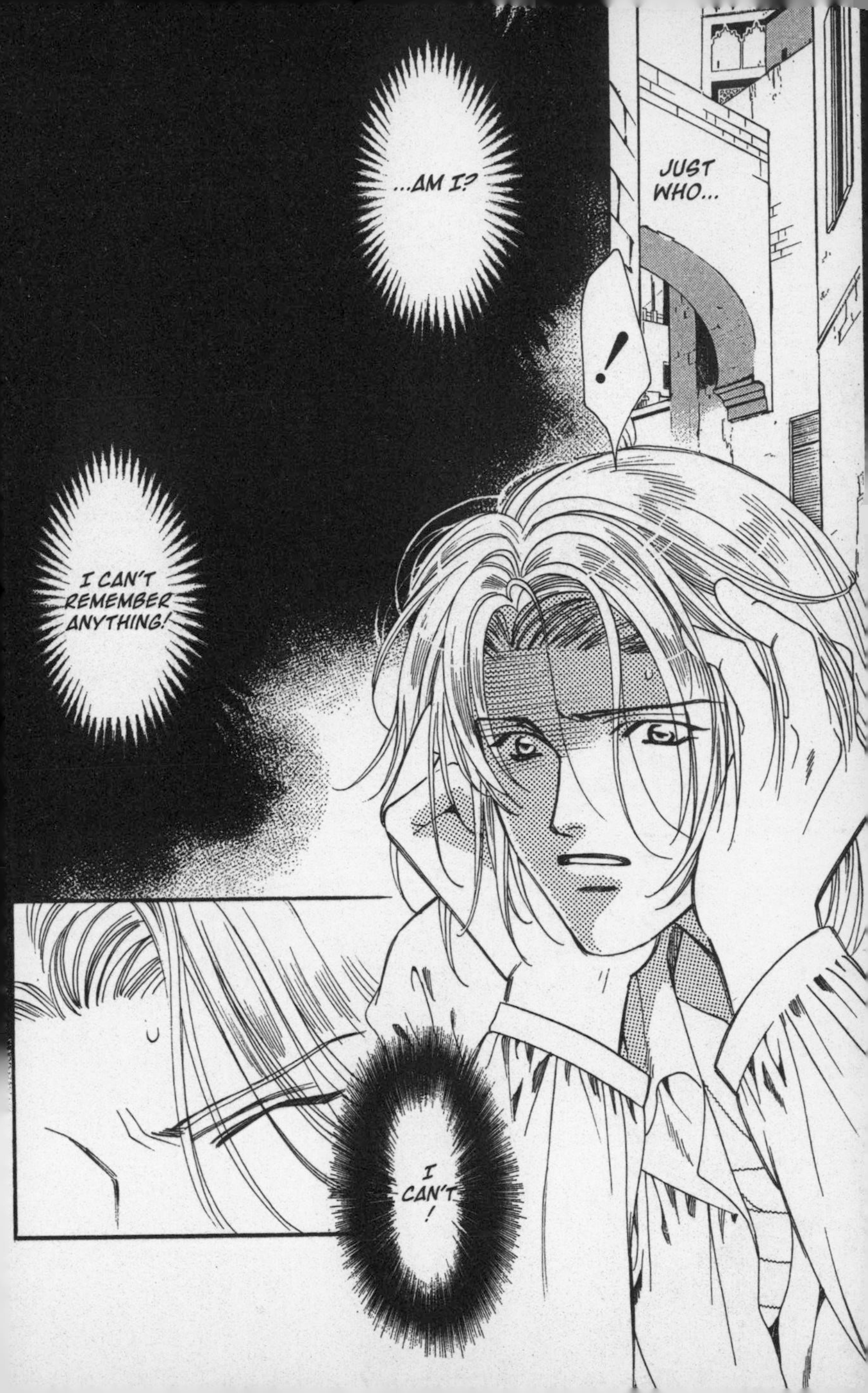
JUST WHO...
!
...AM I?
I CAN'T REMEMBER ANYTHING!
I CAN'T!

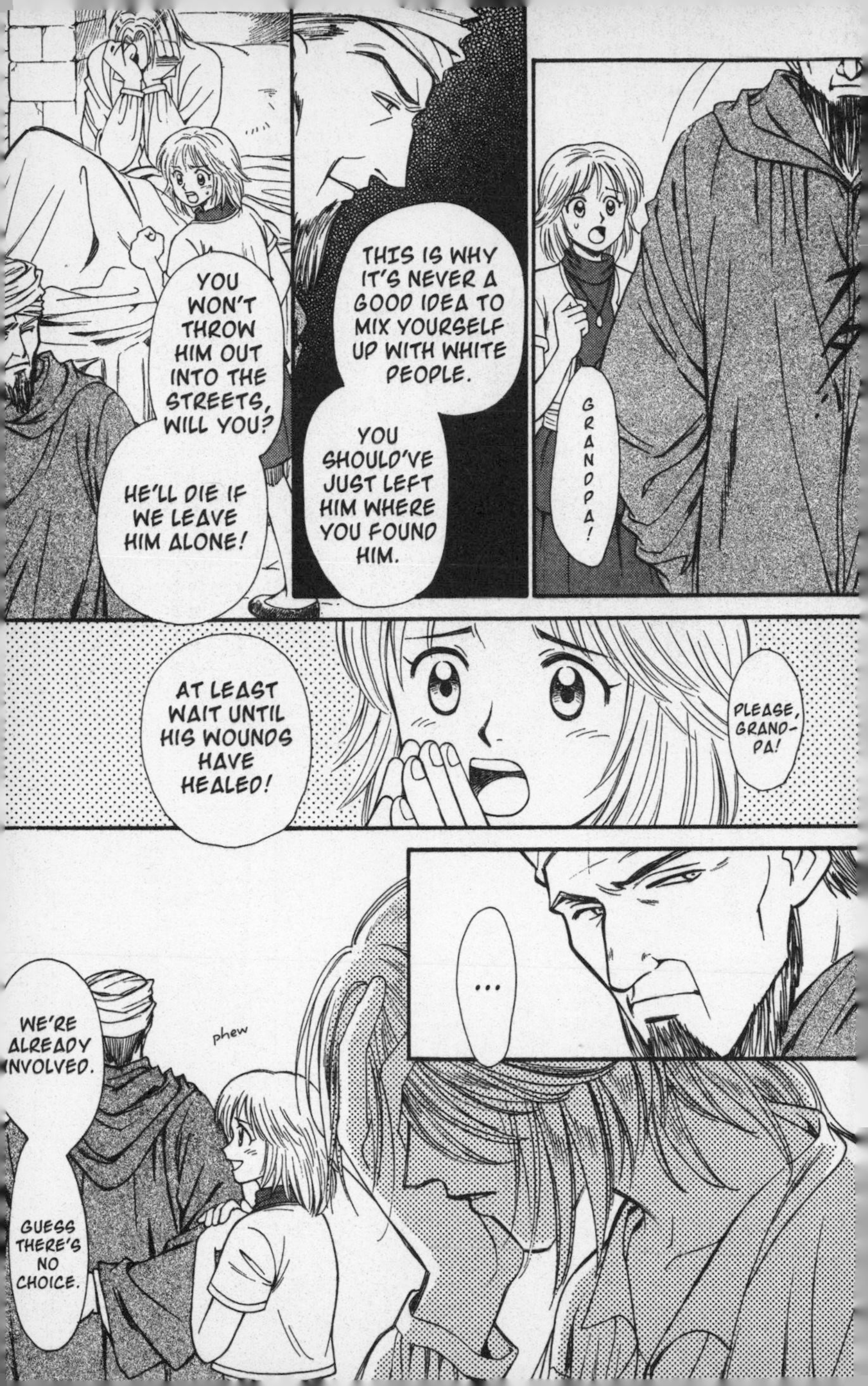
GRANDPA!
THIS IS WHY IT'S NEVER A GOOD IDEA TO MIX YOURSELF UP WITH WHITE PEOPLE.
YOU SHOULD'VE JUST LEFT HIM WHERE YOU FOUND HIM.
YOU WON'T THROW HIM OUT INTO THE STREETS, WILL YOU?
HE'LL DIE IF WE LEAVE HIM ALONE!
PLEASE, GRANDPA!
AT LEAST WAIT UNTIL HIS WOUNDS HAVE HEALED!
...
phew
WE'RE ALREADY INVOLVED.
GUESS THERE'S NO CHOICE.

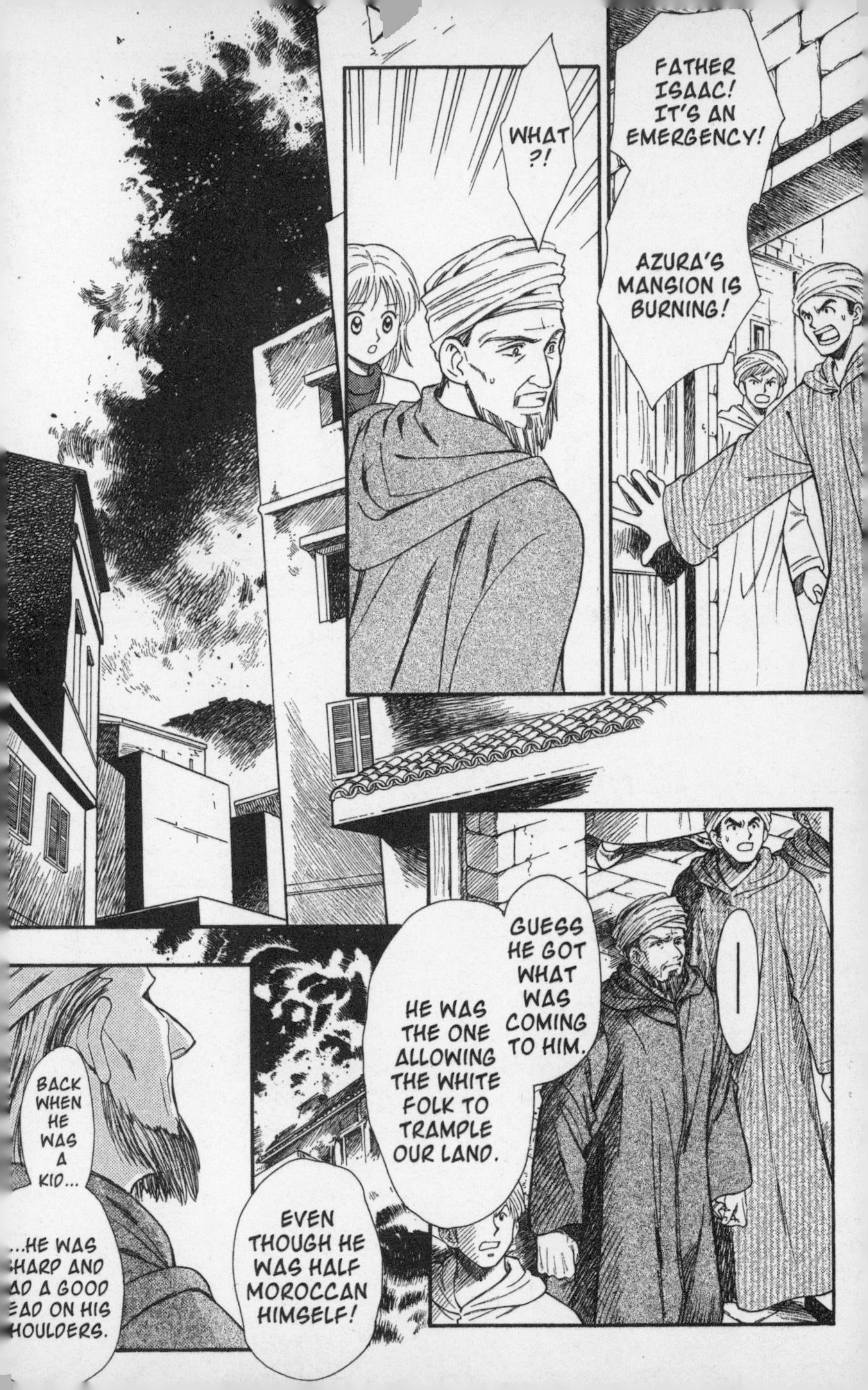
FATHER ISAAC! IT'S AN EMERGENCY!
AZURA'S MANSION IS BURNING!
WHAT?!
GUESS HE GOT WHAT WAS COMING TO HIM.
HE WAS THE ONE ALLOWING THE WHITE FOLK TO TRAMPLE OUR LAND.
EVEN THOUGH HE WAS HALF MOROCCAN HIMSELF!
BACK WHEN HE WAS A KID...
...HE WAS SHARP AND AD A GOOD EAD ON HIS HOULDERS.

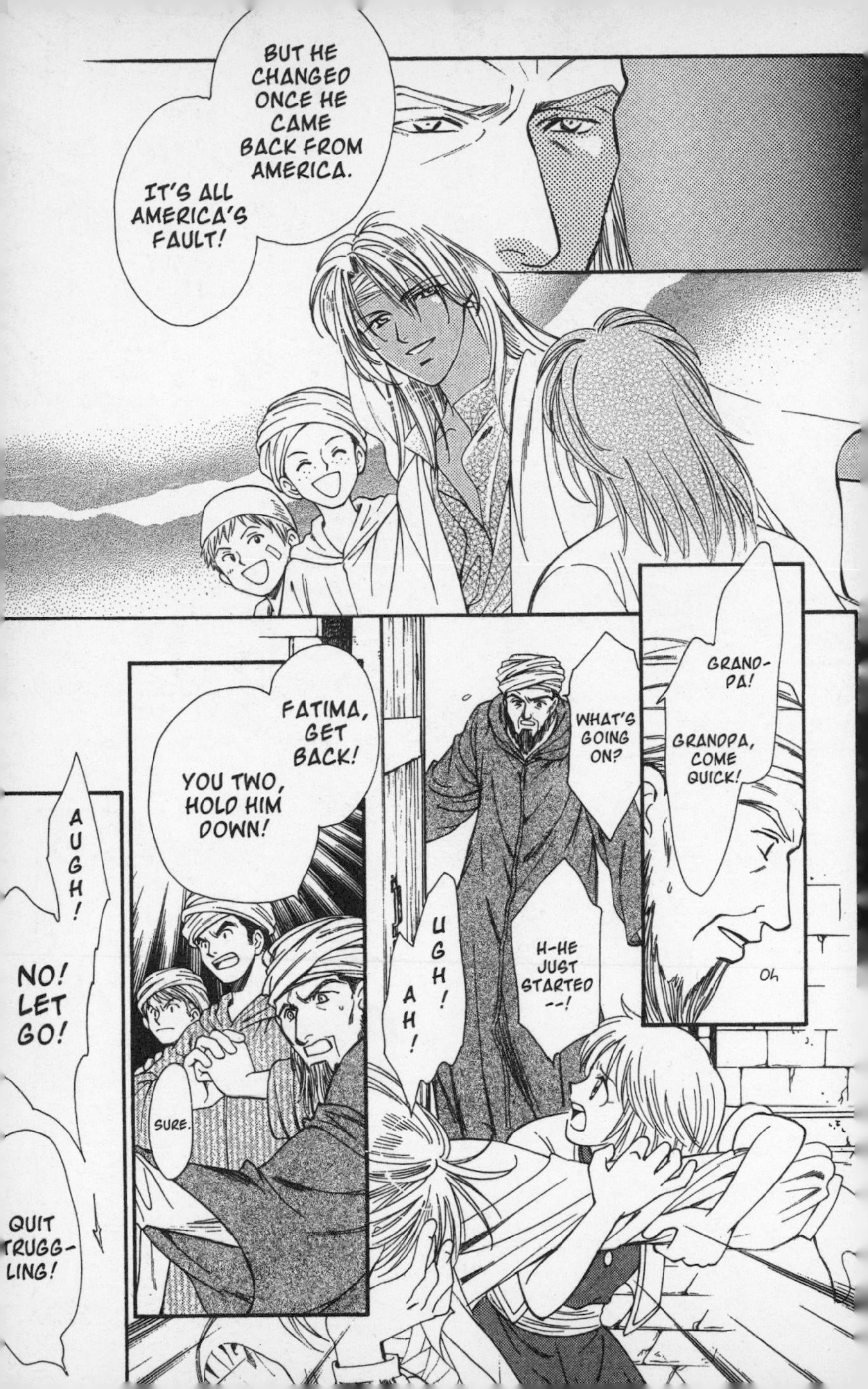
BUT HE CHANGED ONCE HE CAME BACK FROM AMERICA.
IT'S ALL AMERICA'S FAULT!
GRAND-PA!
GRANDPA, COME QUICK!
Oh
WHAT'S GOING ON?
H-HE JUST STARTED--!
UGH!
AH!
FATIMA, GET BACK!
YOU TWO, HOLD HIM DOWN!
SURE.
AUGH!
NO! LET GO!
QUIT TRUGG-LING!

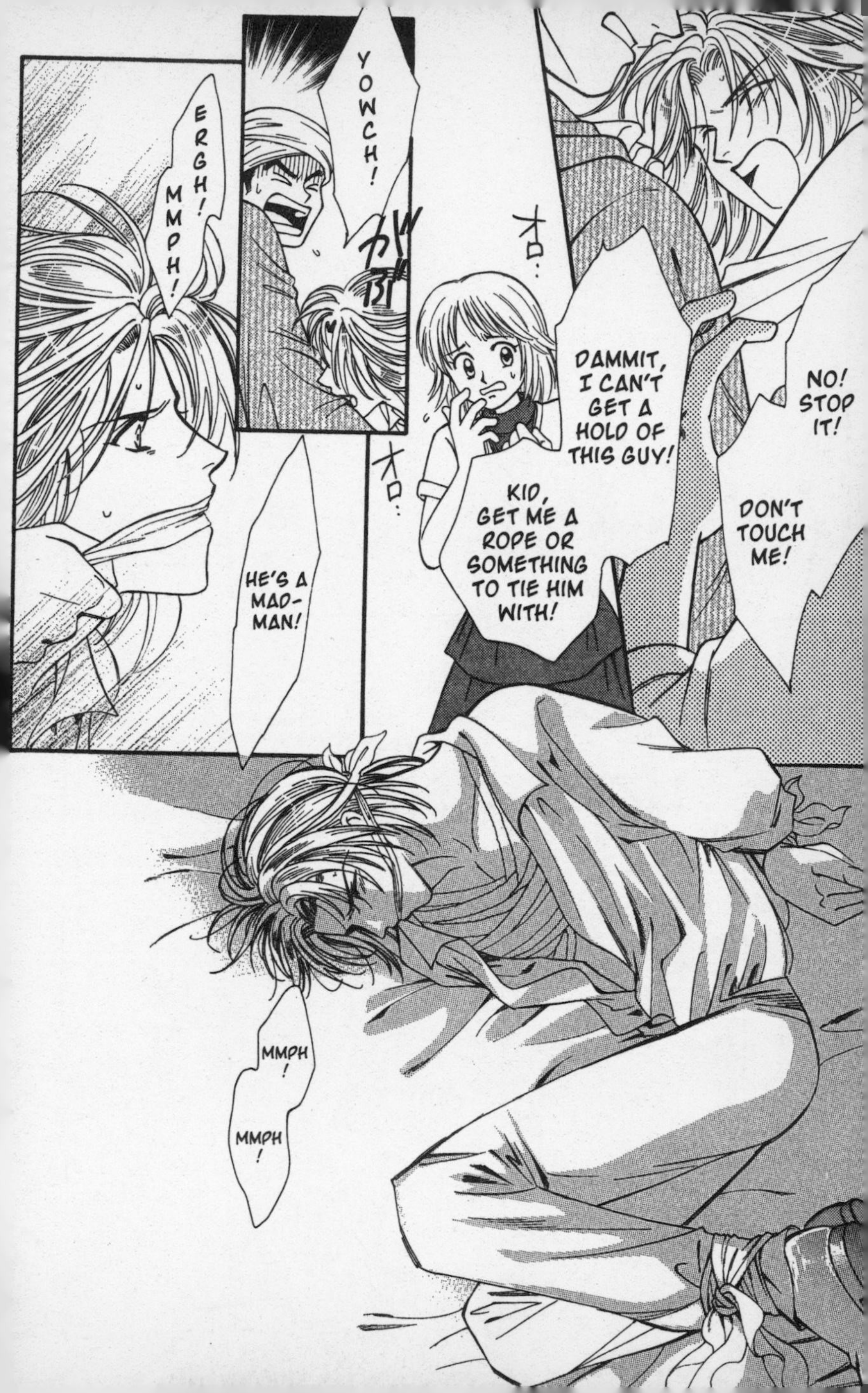
NO! STOP IT!
DON'T TOUCH ME!
DAMMIT, I CAN'T GET A HOLD OF THIS GUY!
KID, GET ME A ROPE OR SOMETHING TO TIE HIM WITH!
オロ…
YOWCH!
ガバ
ERGH! MMPH!
オロ…
HE'S A MAD-MAN!
MMPH! MMPH!

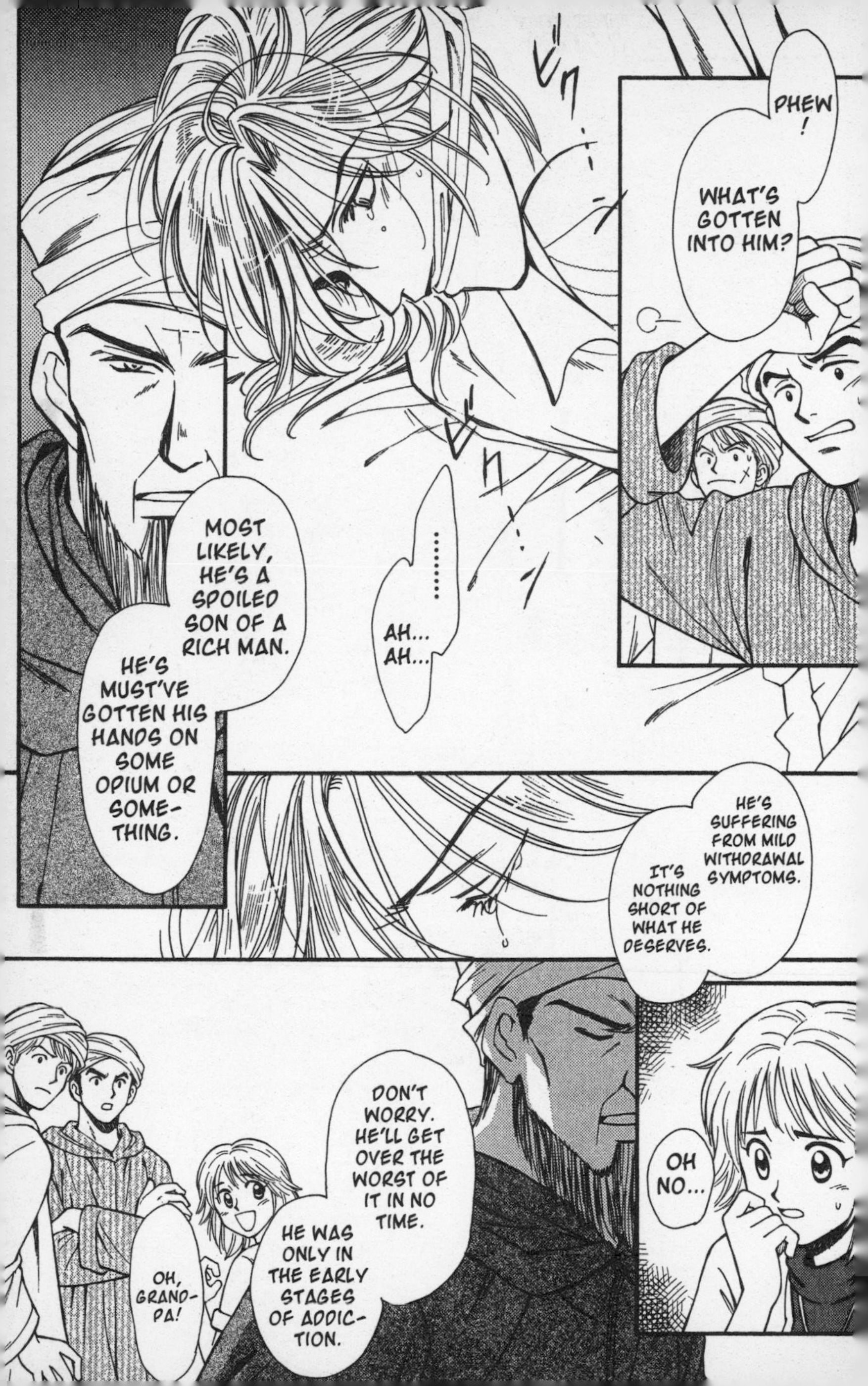
PHEW!
WHAT'S GOTTEN INTO HIM?
......
AH... AH...
MOST LIKELY, HE'S A SPOILED SON OF A RICH MAN.
HE'S MUST'VE GOTTEN HIS HANDS ON SOME OPIUM OR SOME-THING.
HE'S SUFFERING FROM MILD WITHDRAWAL SYMPTOMS.
IT'S NOTHING SHORT OF WHAT HE DESERVES.
OH NO...
DON'T WORRY. HE'LL GET OVER THE WORST OF IT IN NO TIME.
HE WAS ONLY IN THE EARLY STAGES OF ADDIC-TION.
OH, GRAND-PA!

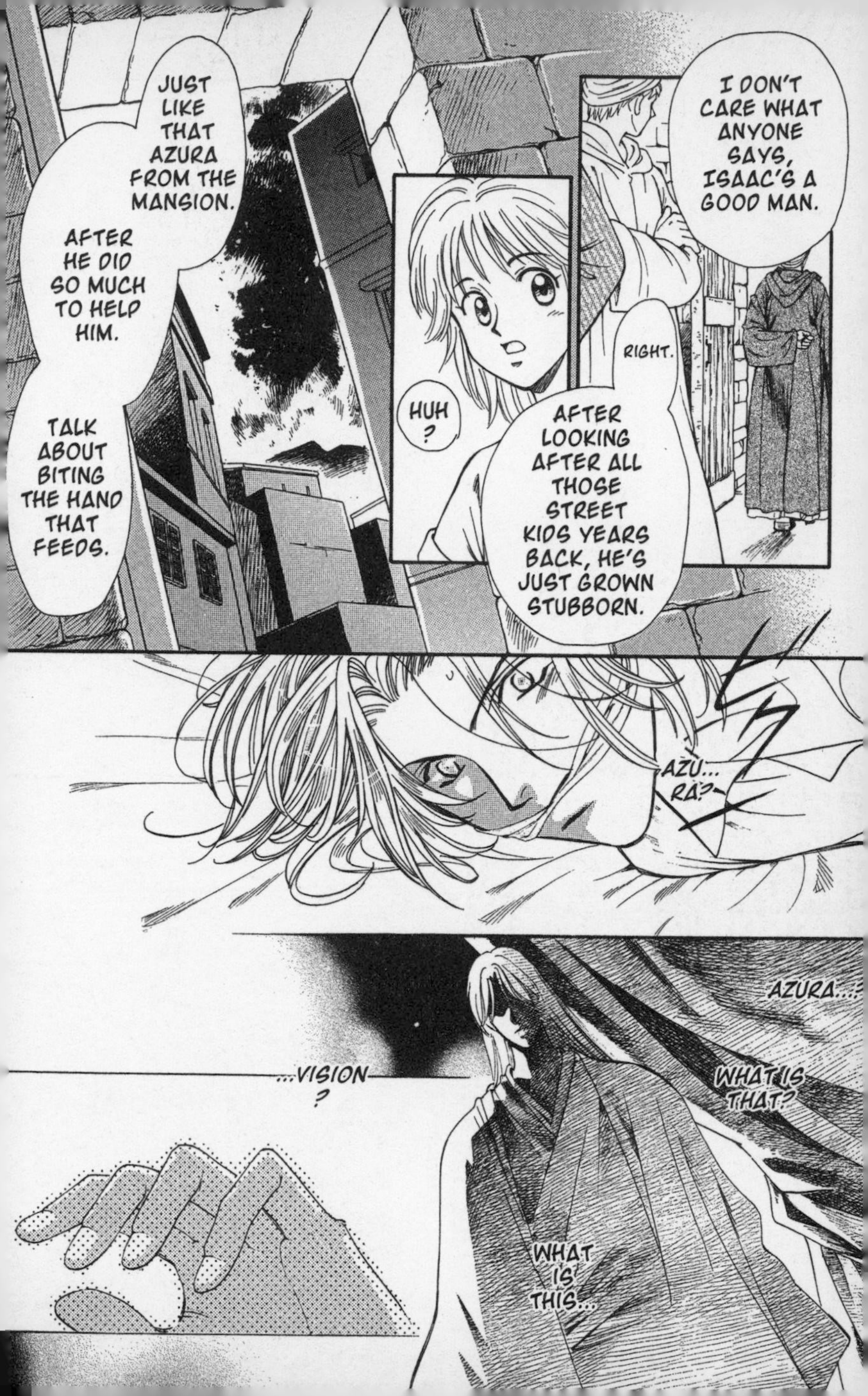
I DON'T CARE WHAT ANYONE SAYS, ISAAC'S A GOOD MAN.
RIGHT.
AFTER LOOKING AFTER ALL THOSE STREET KIDS YEARS BACK, HE'S JUST GROWN STUBBORN.
HUH?
JUST LIKE THAT AZURA FROM THE MANSION.
AFTER HE DID SO MUCH TO HELP HIM.
TALK ABOUT BITING THE HAND THAT FEEDS.
AZU... RA?
AZURA...?
WHAT IS THAT?
...VISION?
WHAT IS THIS...

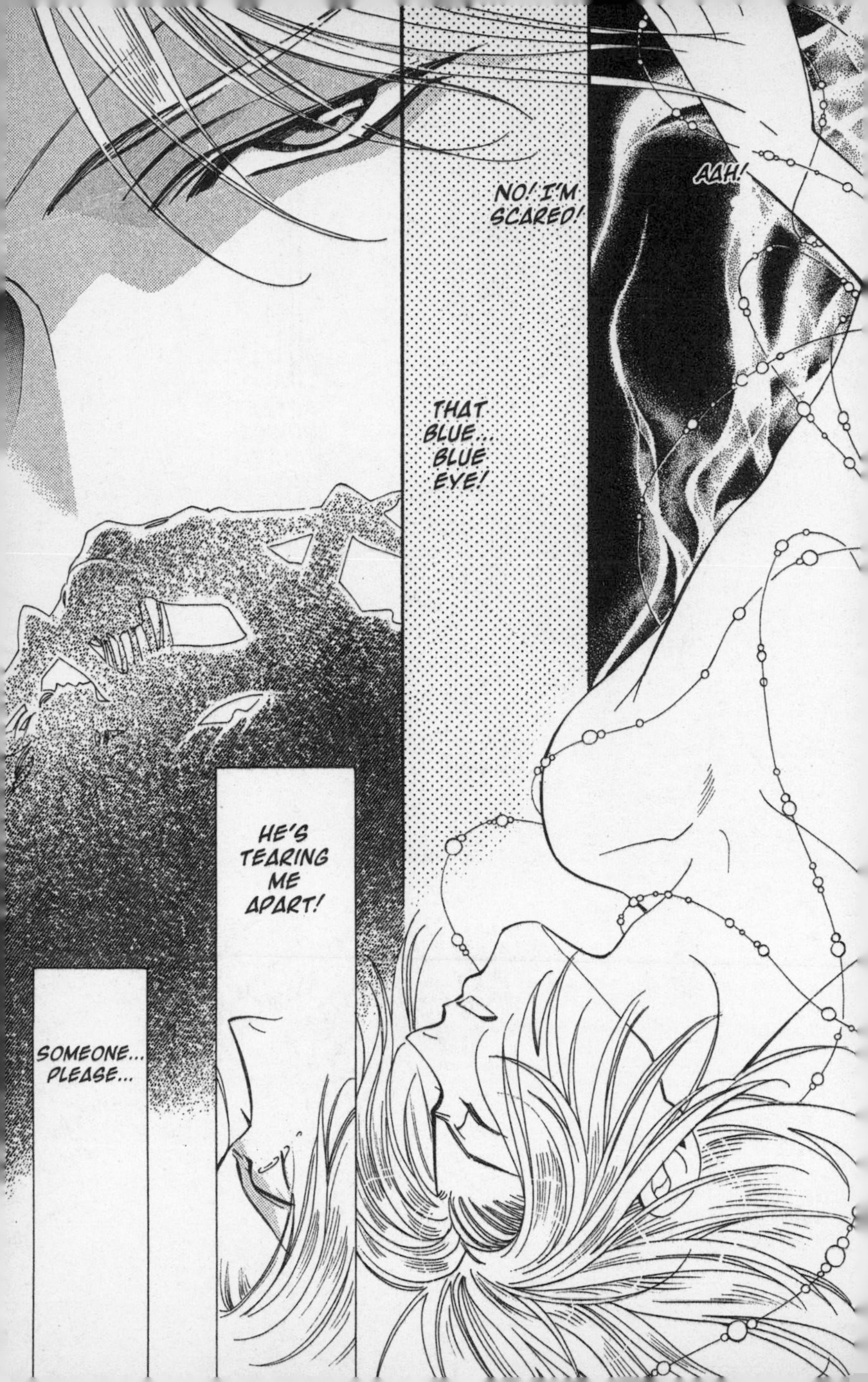
AAH!
NO! I'M SCARED!
THAT BLUE... BLUE EYE!
HE'S TEARING ME APART!
SOMEONE... PLEASE...

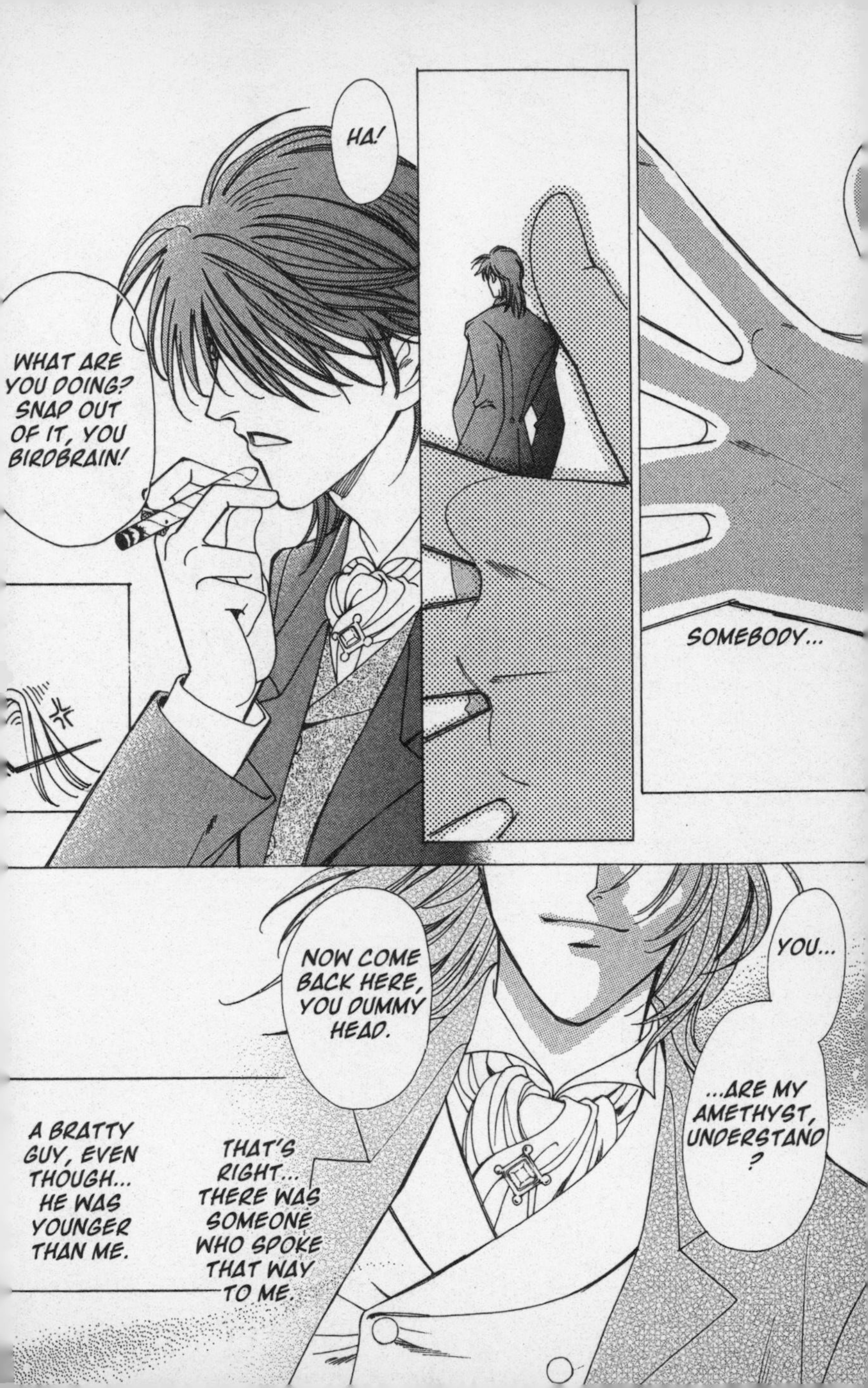
SOMEBODY...
HA!
WHAT ARE YOU DOING? SNAP OUT OF IT, YOU BIRDBRAIN!
YOU...
...ARE MY AMETHYST, UNDERSTAND?
NOW COME BACK HERE, YOU DUMMY HEAD.
THAT'S RIGHT... THERE WAS SOMEONE WHO SPOKE THAT WAY TO ME.
A BRATTY GUY, EVEN THOUGH... HE WAS YOUNGER THAN ME.

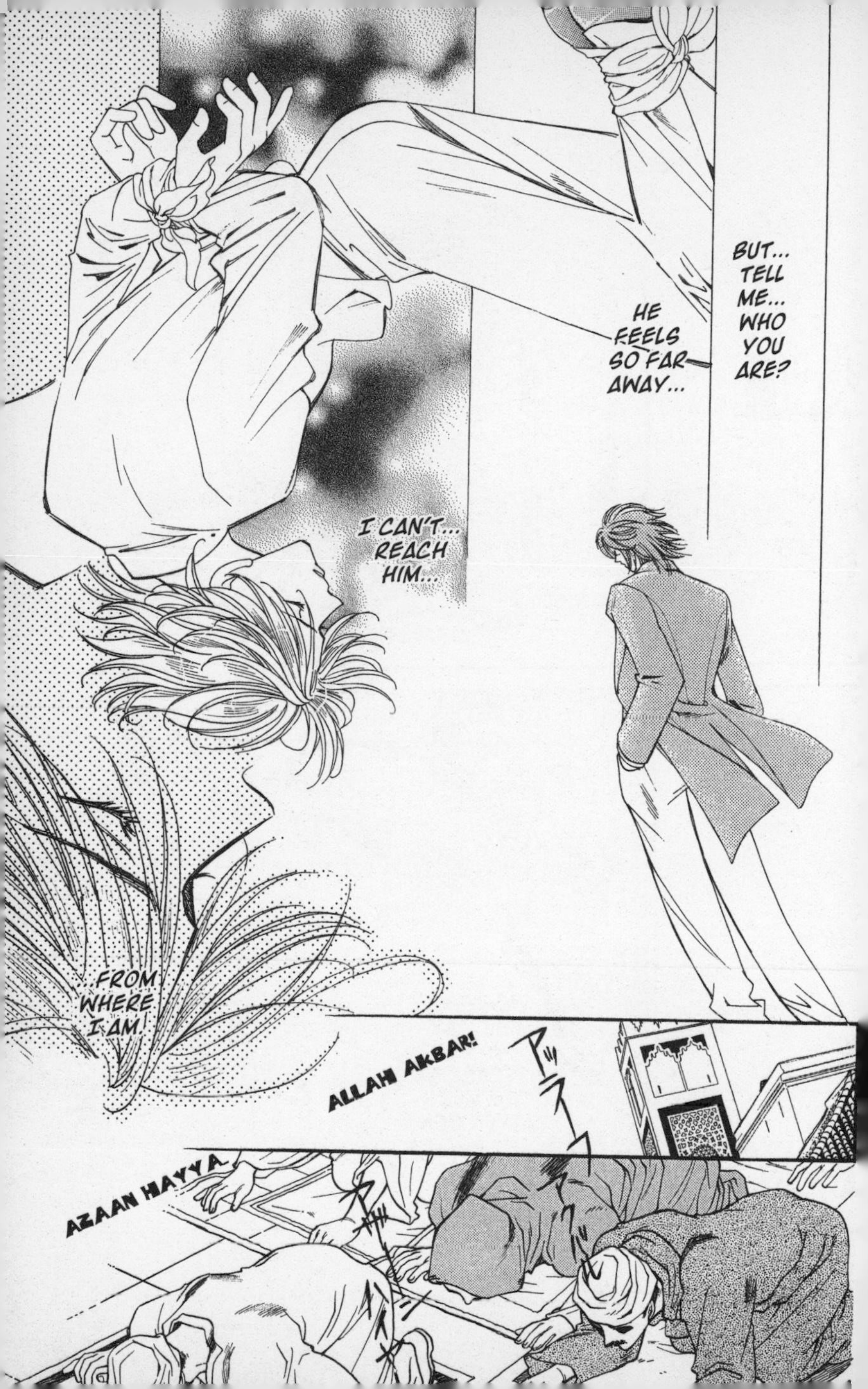
BUT... TELL ME... WHO YOU ARE?
HE FEELS SO FAR AWAY...
I CAN'T... REACH HIM...
...FROM WHERE I AM.
ALLAH AKBAR!
AZAAN HAYYA

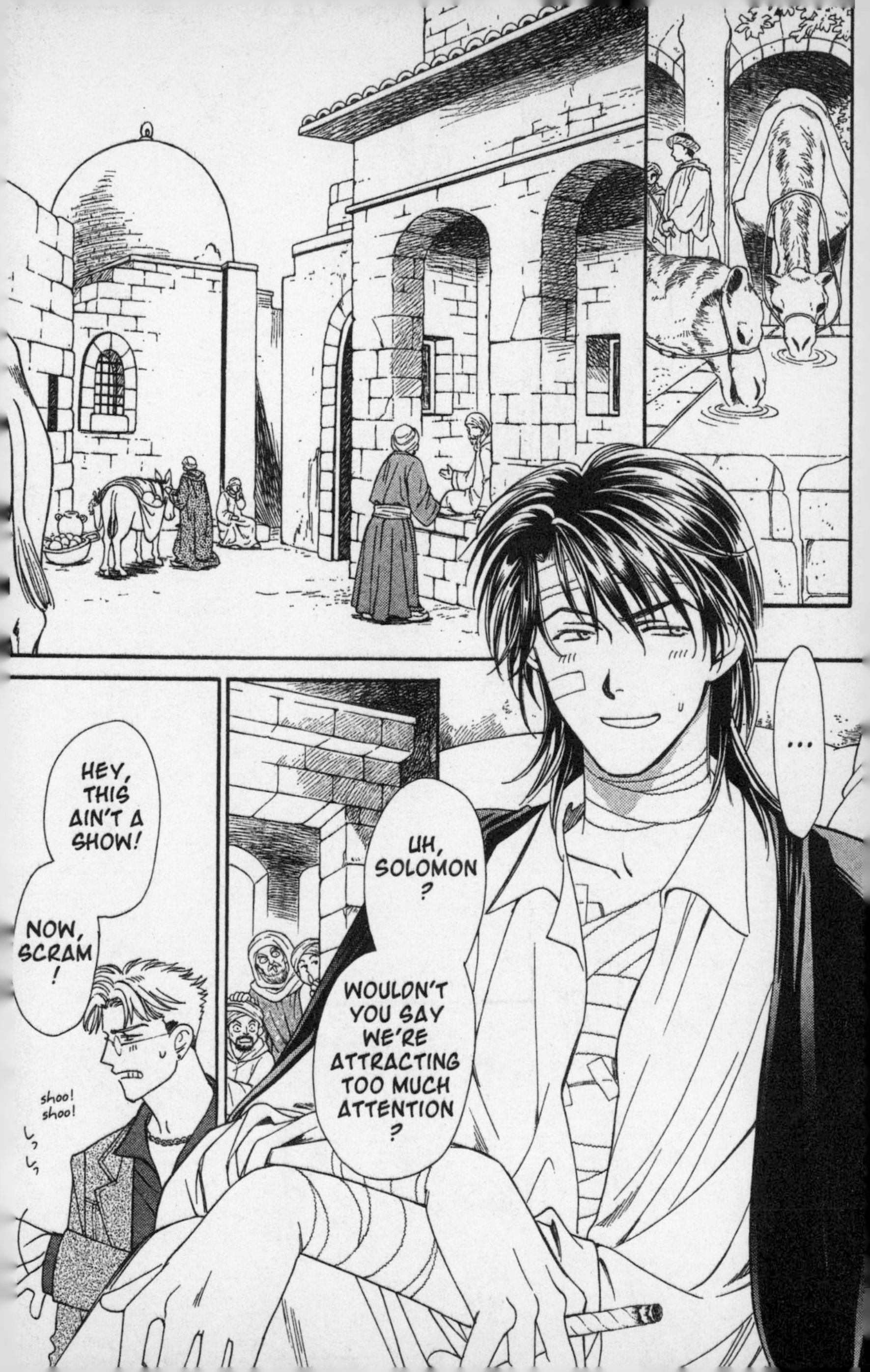
...
UH, SOLOMON?
WOULDN'T YOU SAY WE'RE ATTRACTING TOO MUCH ATTENTION?
HEY, THIS AIN'T A SHOW!
NOW, SCRAM!
shoo! shoo!
しっしっ

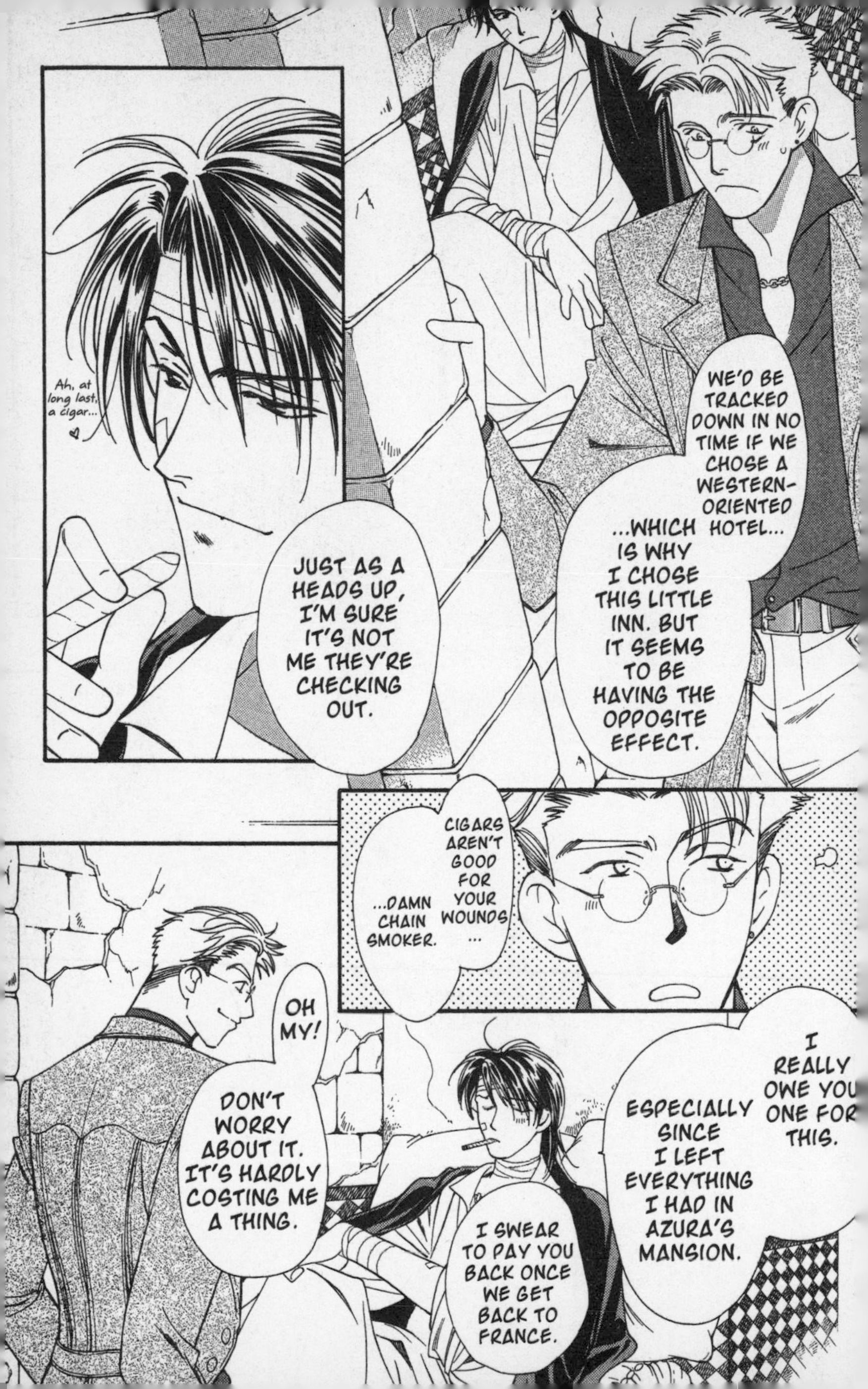
WE'D BE TRACKED DOWN IN NO TIME IF WE CHOSE A WESTERN-ORIENTED HOTEL...
...WHICH IS WHY I CHOSE THIS LITTLE INN. BUT IT SEEMS TO BE HAVING THE OPPOSITE EFFECT.
Ah, at long last, a cigar... ♥
JUST AS A HEADS UP, I'M SURE IT'S NOT ME THEY'RE CHECKING OUT.
CIGARS AREN'T GOOD FOR YOUR WOUNDS...
...DAMN CHAIN SMOKER.
I REALLY OWE YOU ONE FOR THIS.
ESPECIALLY SINCE I LEFT EVERYTHING I HAD IN AZURA'S MANSION.
I SWEAR TO PAY YOU BACK ONCE WE GET BACK TO FRANCE.
OH MY!
DON'T WORRY ABOUT IT. IT'S HARDLY COSTING ME A THING.

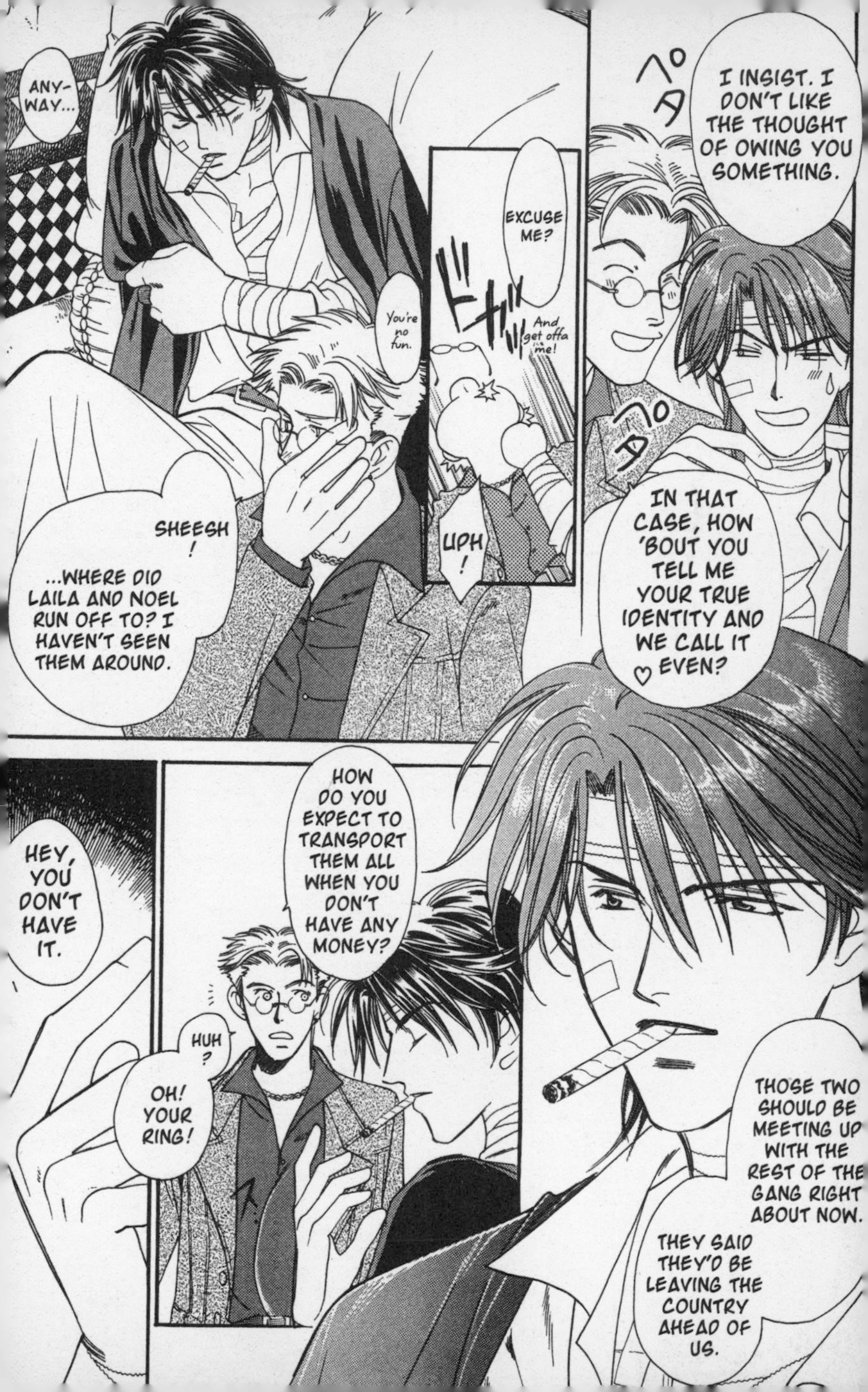
ペタ
I INSIST. I DON'T LIKE THE THOUGHT OF OWING YOU SOMETHING.
ペタ
IN THAT CASE, HOW 'BOUT YOU TELL ME YOUR TRUE IDENTITY AND WE CALL IT ♡ EVEN?
EXCUSE ME?
And get offa me!
UPH!
You're no fun.
SHEESH!
...WHERE DID LAILA AND NOEL RUN OFF TO? I HAVEN'T SEEN THEM AROUND.
ANY-WAY...
THOSE TWO SHOULD BE MEETING UP WITH THE REST OF THE GANG RIGHT ABOUT NOW.
THEY SAID THEY'D BE LEAVING THE COUNTRY AHEAD OF US.
HOW DO YOU EXPECT TO TRANSPORT THEM ALL WHEN YOU DON'T HAVE ANY MONEY?
HUH?
OH! YOUR RING!
HEY, YOU DON'T HAVE IT.

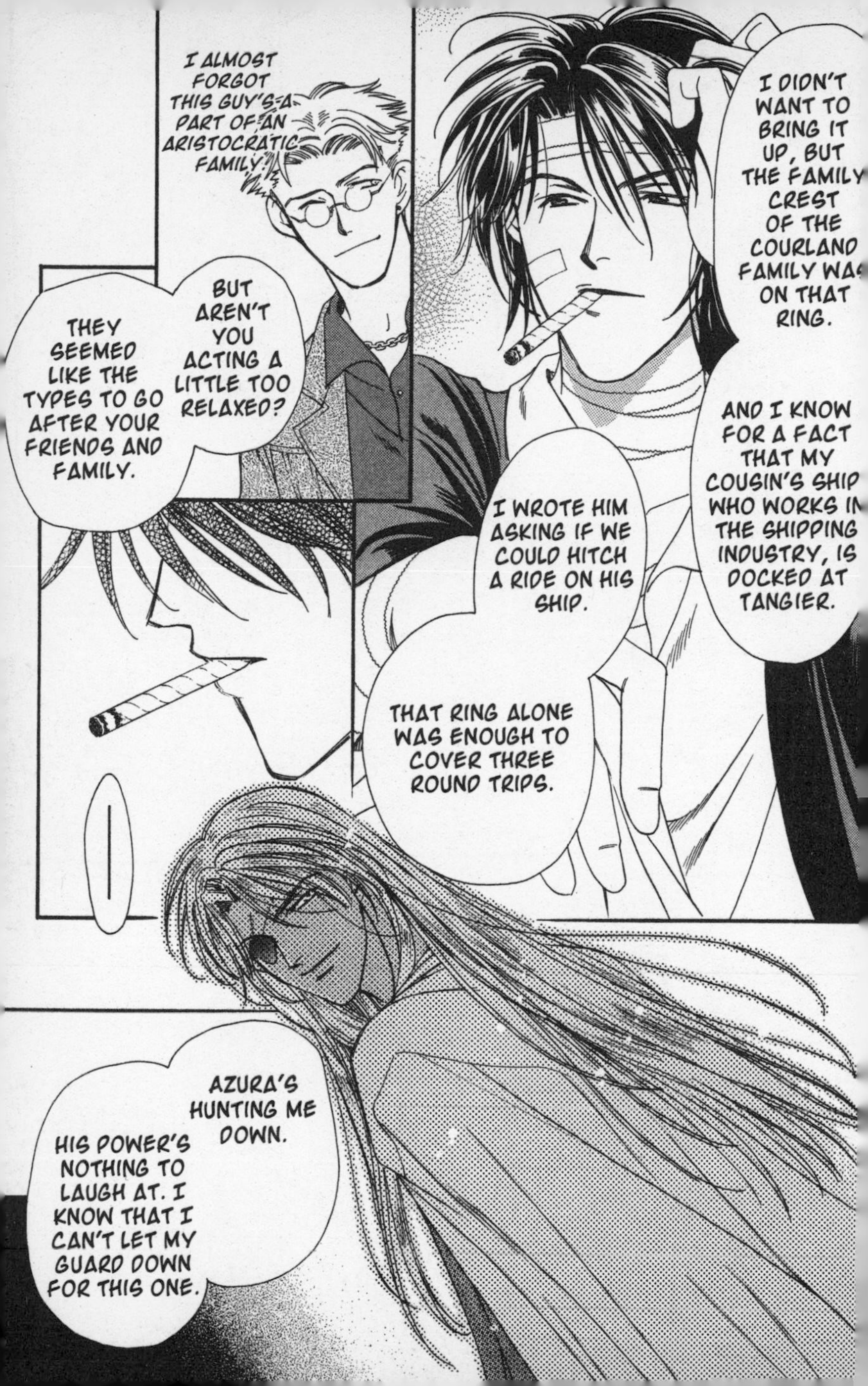
I DIDN'T WANT TO BRING IT UP, BUT THE FAMILY CREST OF THE COURLAND FAMILY WAS ON THAT RING.
AND I KNOW FOR A FACT THAT MY COUSIN'S SHIP WHO WORKS IN THE SHIPPING INDUSTRY, IS DOCKED AT TANGIER.
I ALMOST FORGOT THIS GUY'S A PART OF AN ARISTOCRATIC FAMILY.
I WROTE HIM ASKING IF WE COULD HITCH A RIDE ON HIS SHIP.
THAT RING ALONE WAS ENOUGH TO COVER THREE ROUND TRIPS.
BUT AREN'T YOU ACTING A LITTLE TOO RELAXED?
THEY SEEMED LIKE THE TYPES TO GO AFTER YOUR FRIENDS AND FAMILY.
AZURA'S HUNTING ME DOWN.
HIS POWER'S NOTHING TO LAUGH AT. I KNOW THAT I CAN'T LET MY GUARD DOWN FOR THIS ONE.

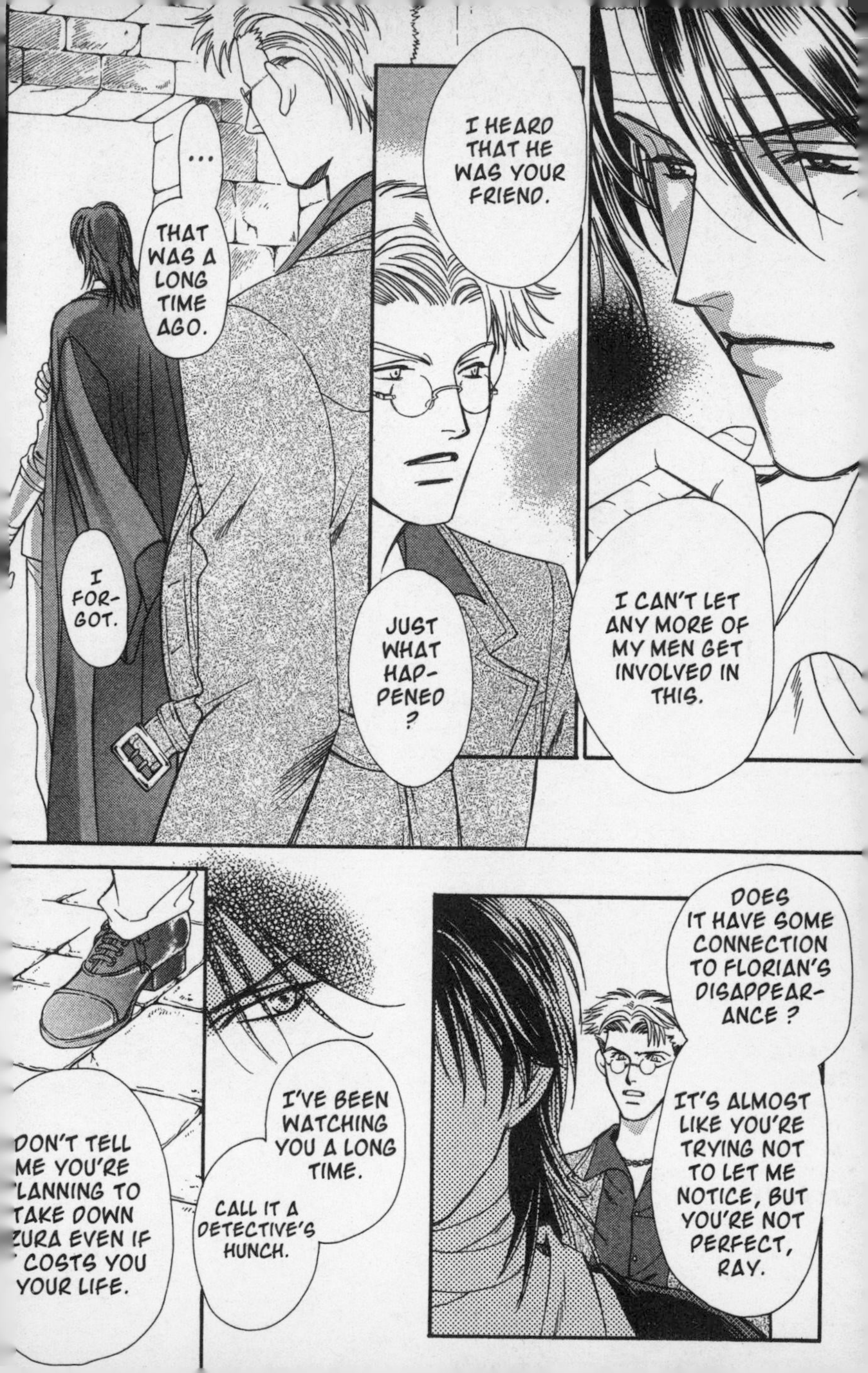
I CAN'T LET ANY MORE OF MY MEN GET INVOLVED IN THIS.
I HEARD THAT HE WAS YOUR FRIEND.
JUST WHAT HAP-PENED ?
...
THAT WAS A LONG TIME AGO.
I FOR-GOT.
DOES IT HAVE SOME CONNECTION TO FLORIAN'S DISAPPEAR-ANCE ?
IT'S ALMOST LIKE YOU'RE TRYING NOT TO LET ME NOTICE, BUT YOU'RE NOT PERFECT, RAY.
I'VE BEEN WATCHING YOU A LONG TIME.
CALL IT A DETECTIVE'S HUNCH.
DON'T TELL ME YOU'RE LANNING TO TAKE DOWN ZURA EVEN IF COSTS YOU YOUR LIFE.

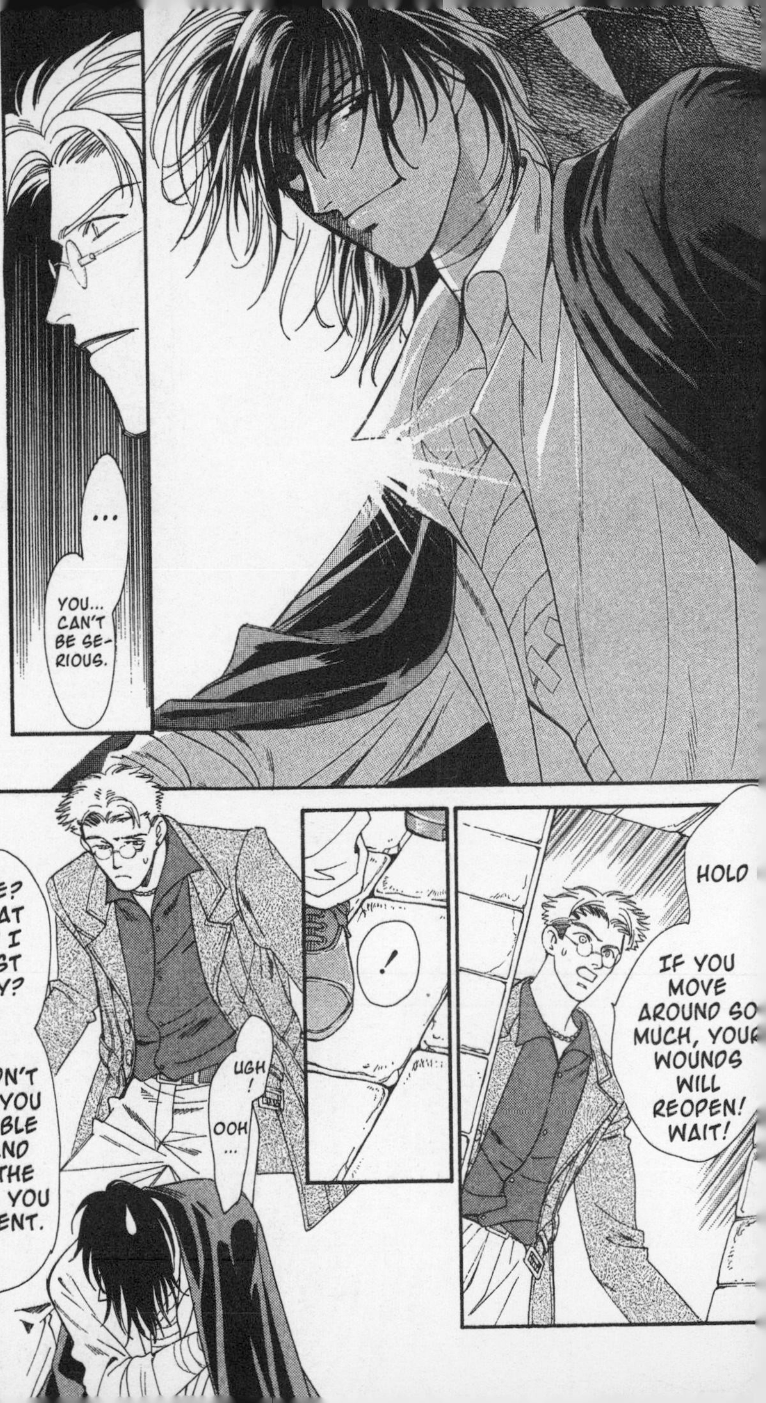
...
YOU... CAN'T BE SE-RIOUS.
HOLD
IF YOU MOVE AROUND SO MUCH, YOUR WOUNDS WILL REOPEN! WAIT!
!
UGH!
OOH...
SEE? WHAT DID I JUST SAY?
I WOULDN'T EXPECT YOU TO BE ABLE TO STAND AFTER THE TORTURE YOU UNDERWENT.

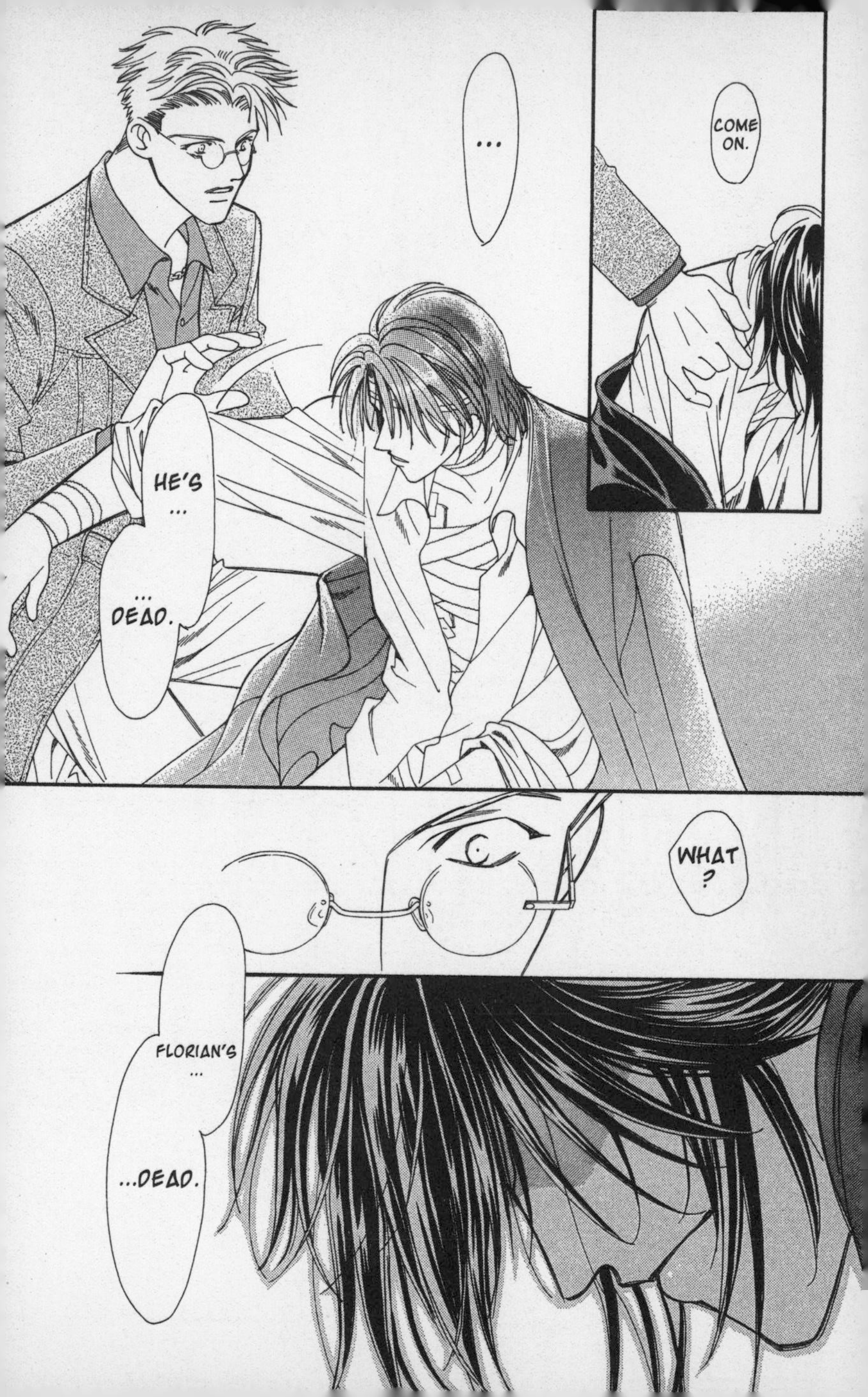
COME ON.
...
HE'S ...
... DEAD.
WHAT?
FLORIAN'S ...
...DEAD.

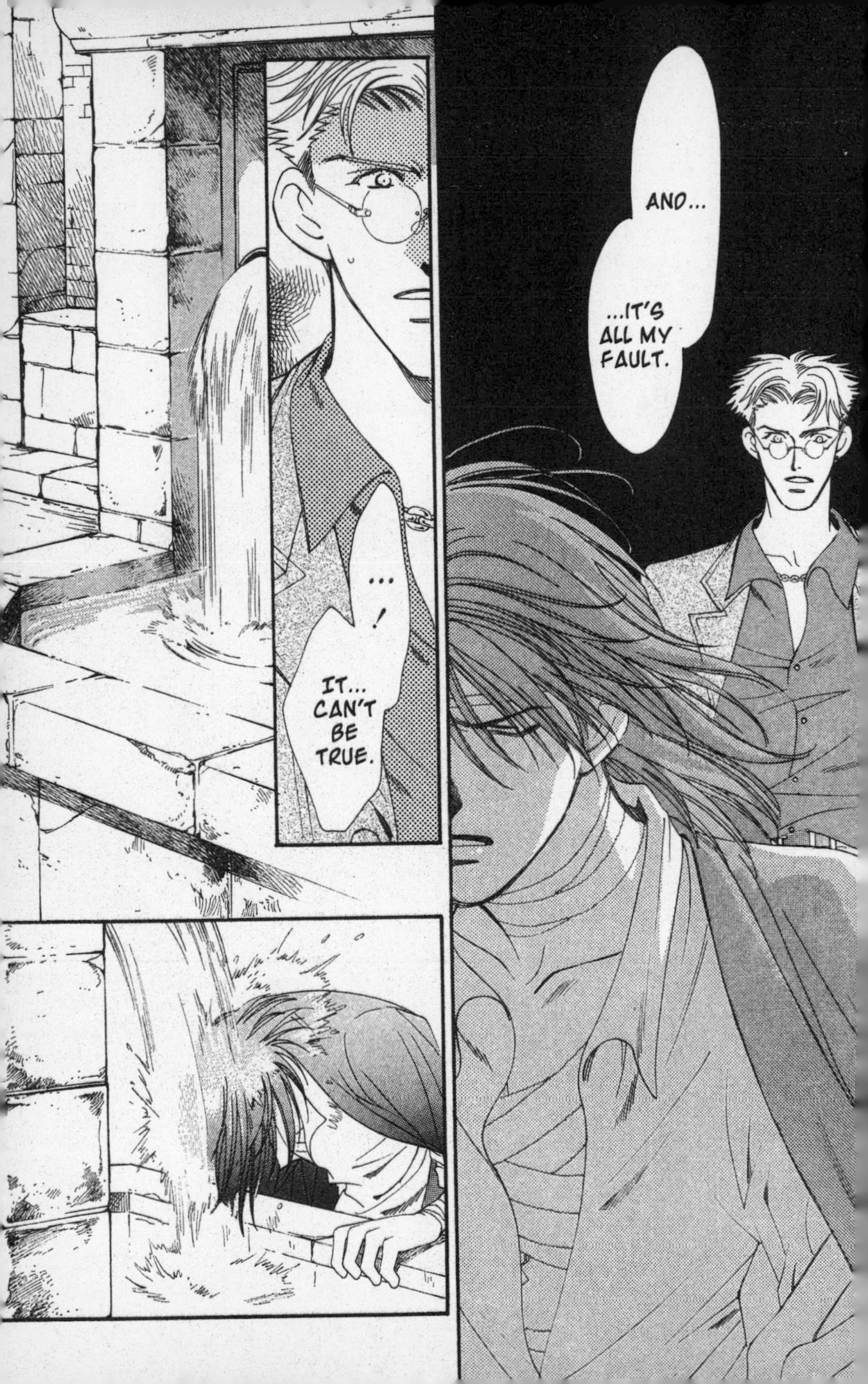
AND...
...IT'S ALL MY FAULT.
... !
IT... CAN'T BE TRUE.

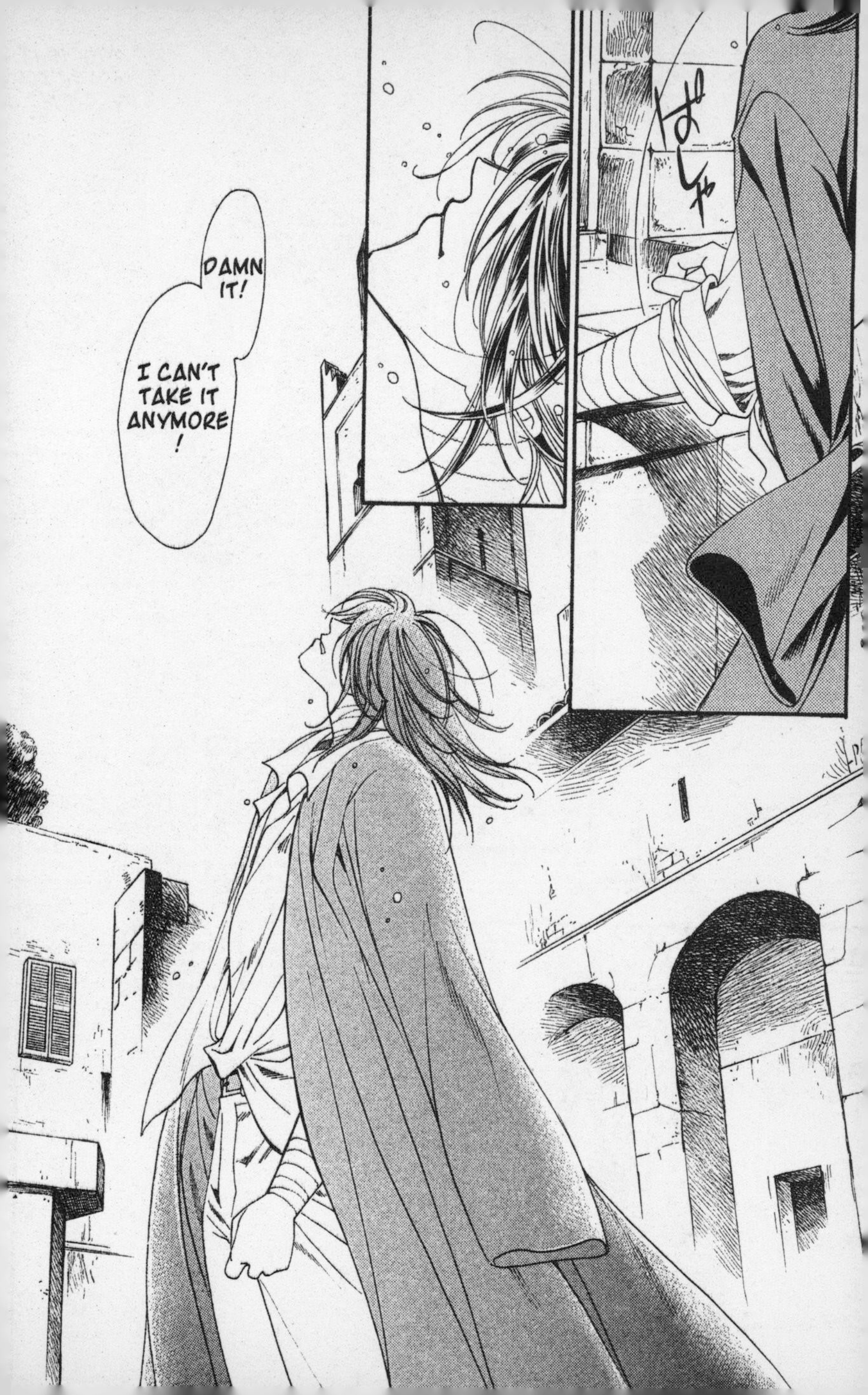
ぱしゃ
DAMN IT! I CAN'T TAKE IT ANYMORE!

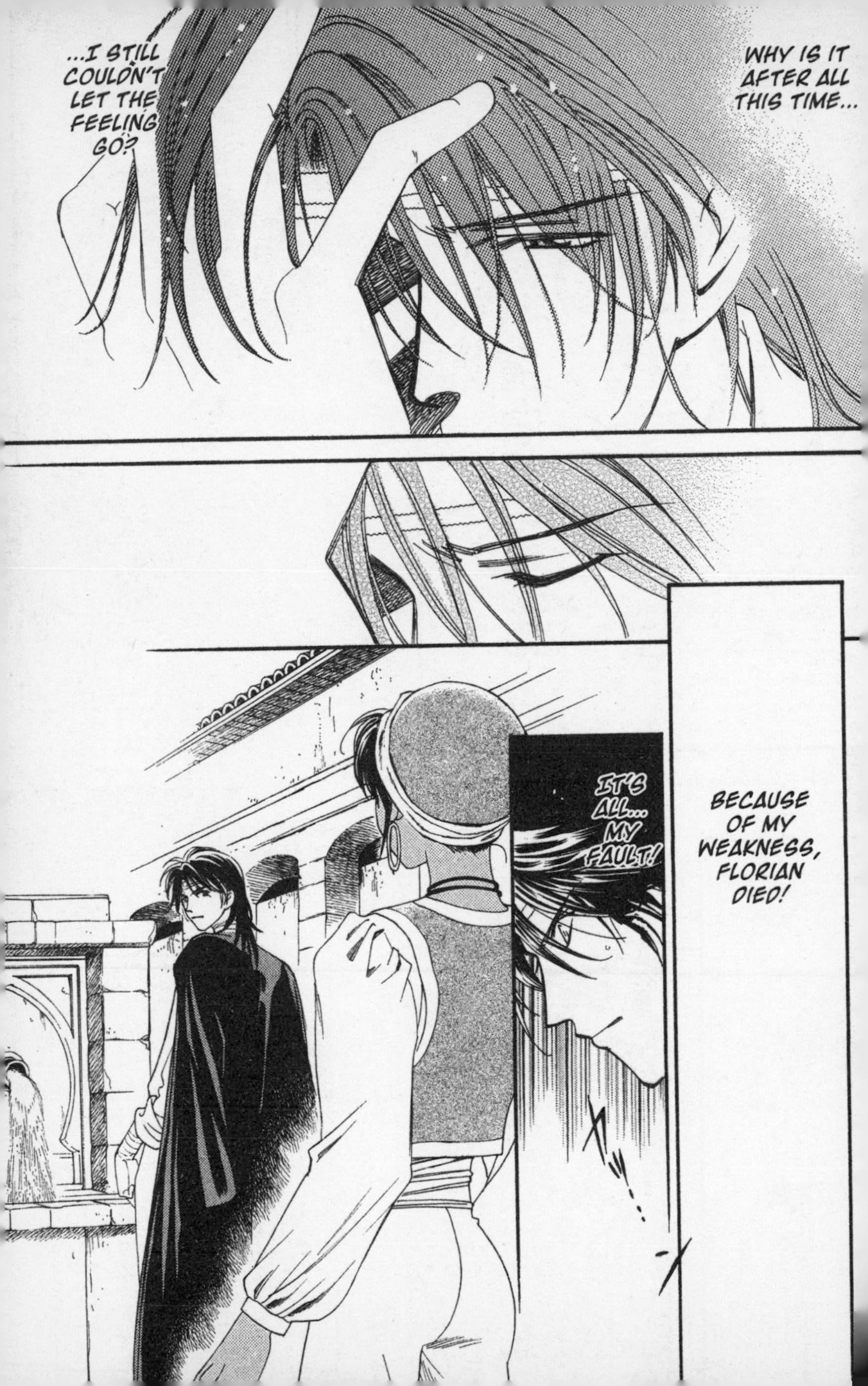
WHY IS IT AFTER ALL THIS TIME...
...I STILL COULDN'T LET THE FEELING GO?
BECAUSE OF MY WEAKNESS, FLORIAN DIED!
IT'S ALL... MY FAULT!

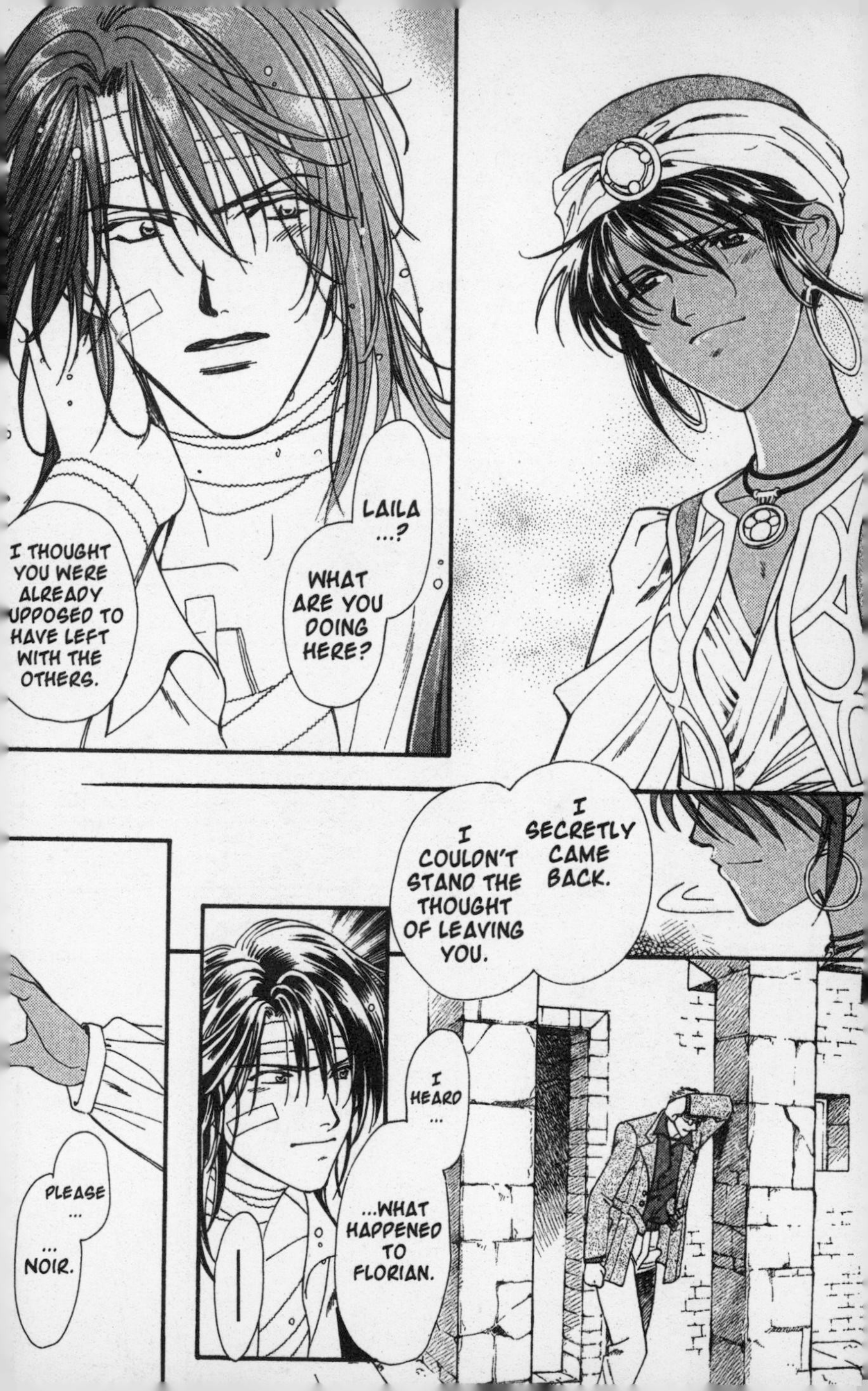
LAILA ...?
WHAT ARE YOU DOING HERE?
I THOUGHT YOU WERE ALREADY UPPOSED TO HAVE LEFT WITH THE OTHERS.
I SECRETLY CAME BACK.
I COULDN'T STAND THE THOUGHT OF LEAVING YOU.
I HEARD ...
...WHAT HAPPENED TO FLORIAN.
PLEASE ...
... NOIR.

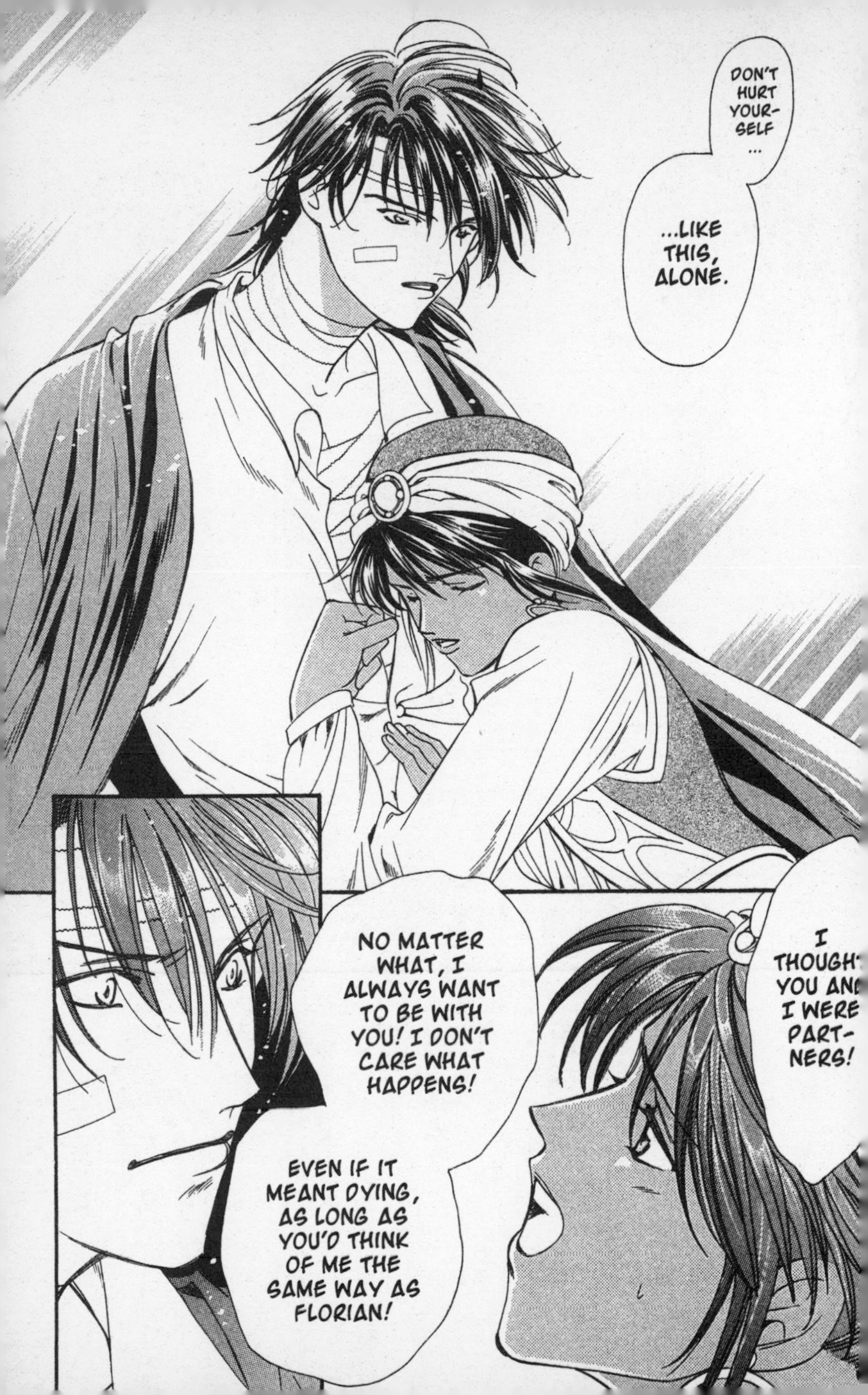
DON'T HURT YOUR-SELF ...
...LIKE THIS, ALONE.
I THOUGHT YOU AND I WERE PART-NERS!
NO MATTER WHAT, I ALWAYS WANT TO BE WITH YOU! I DON'T CARE WHAT HAPPENS!
EVEN IF IT MEANT DYING, AS LONG AS YOU'D THINK OF ME THE SAME WAY AS FLORIAN!

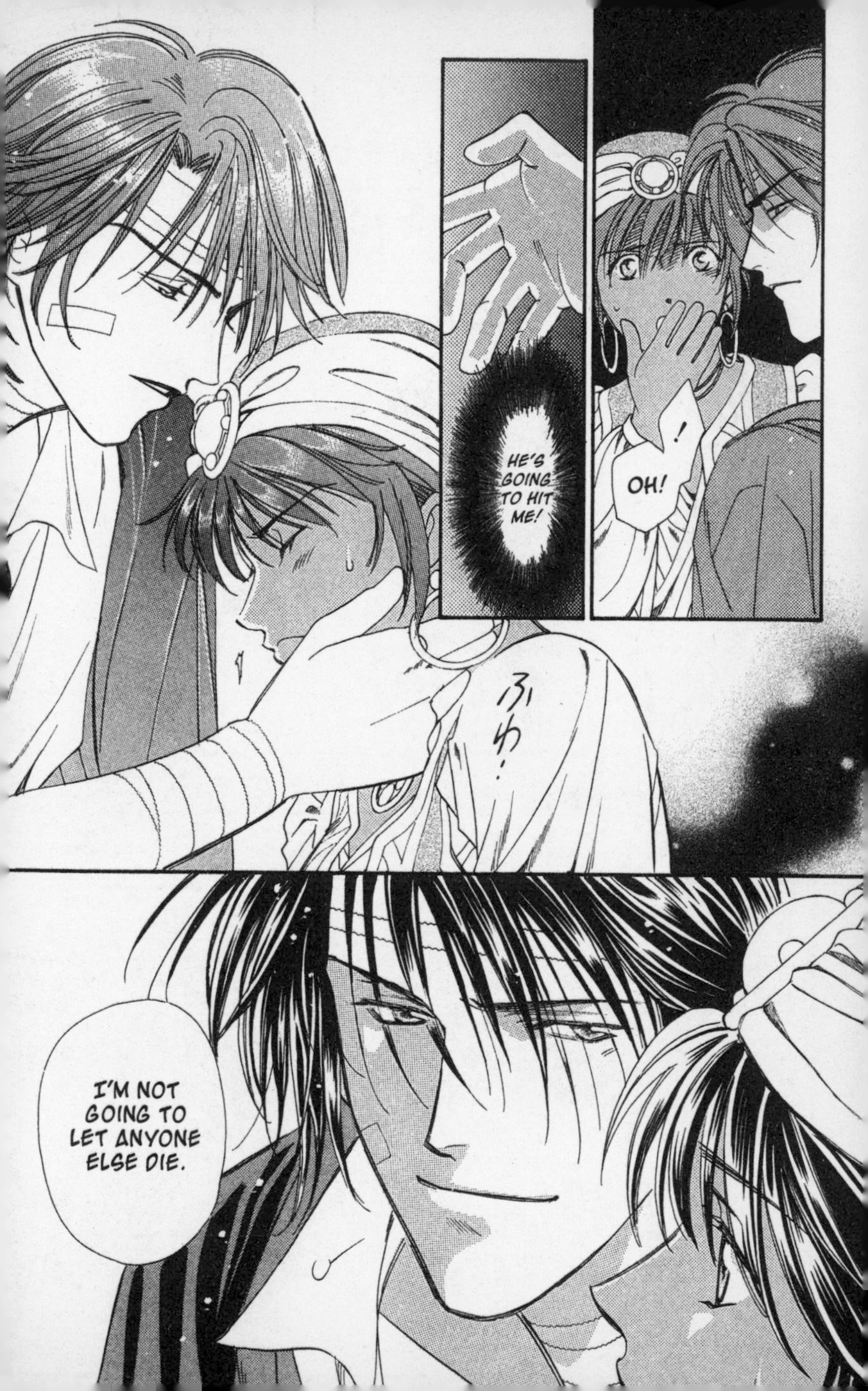
!
OH!
HE'S GOING TO HIT ME!
ふわ…
I'M NOT GOING TO LET ANYONE ELSE DIE.

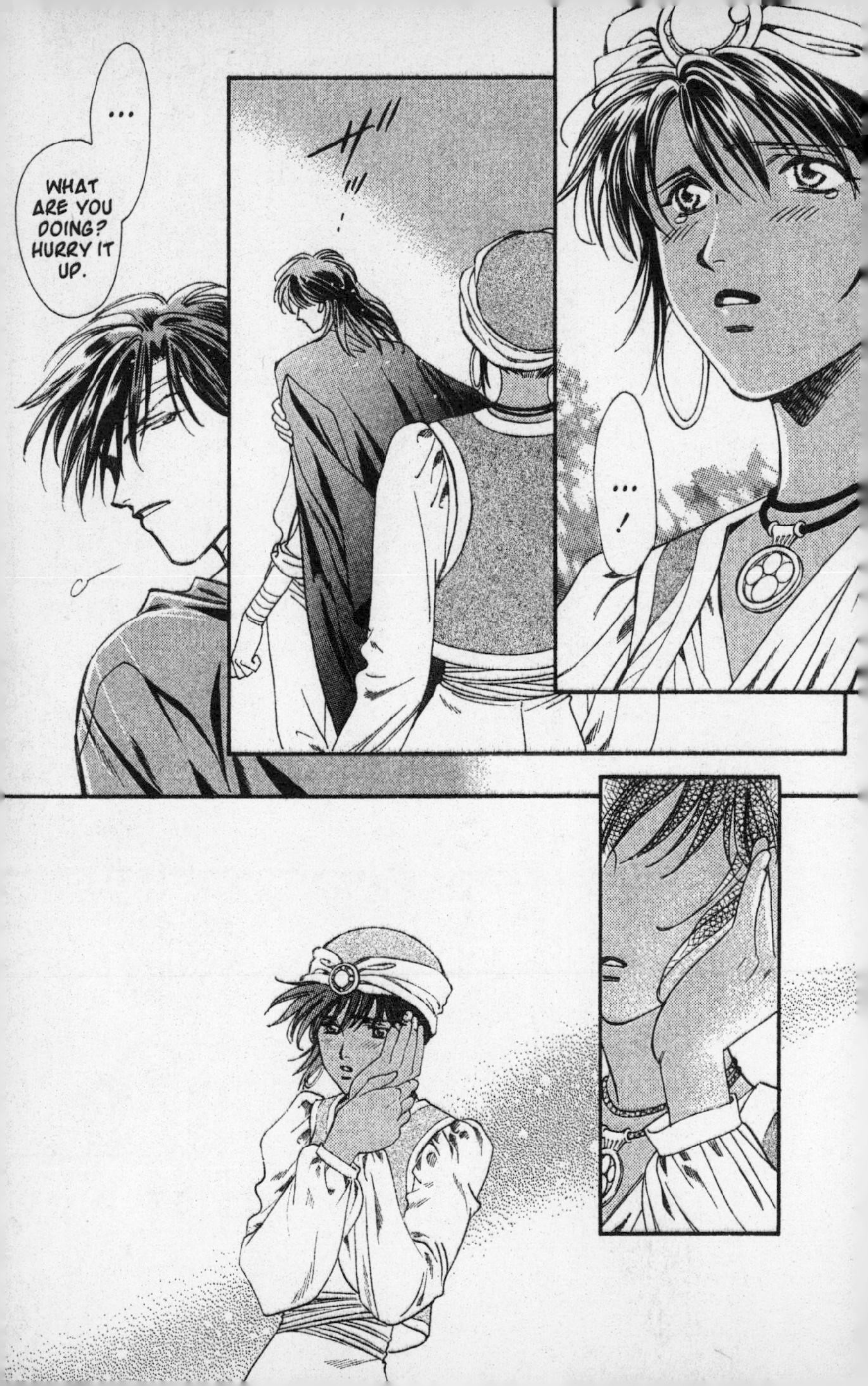
...!
...
WHAT ARE YOU DOING? HURRY IT UP.

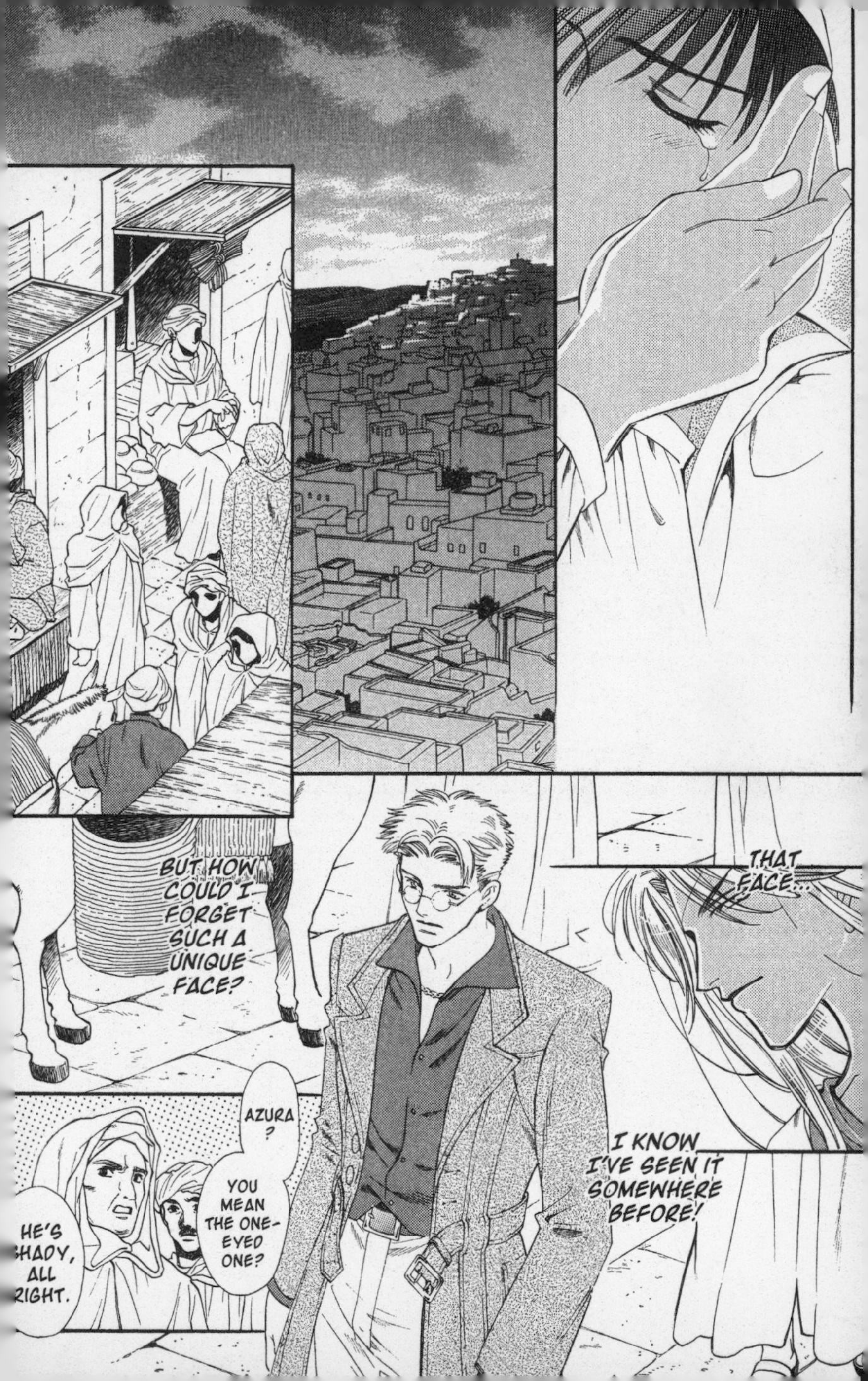

THAT FACE...
I KNOW I'VE SEEN IT SOMEWHERE BEFORE!
BUT HOW COULD I FORGET SUCH A UNIQUE FACE?
AZURA?
YOU MEAN THE ONE-EYED ONE?
HE'S SHADY, ALL RIGHT.

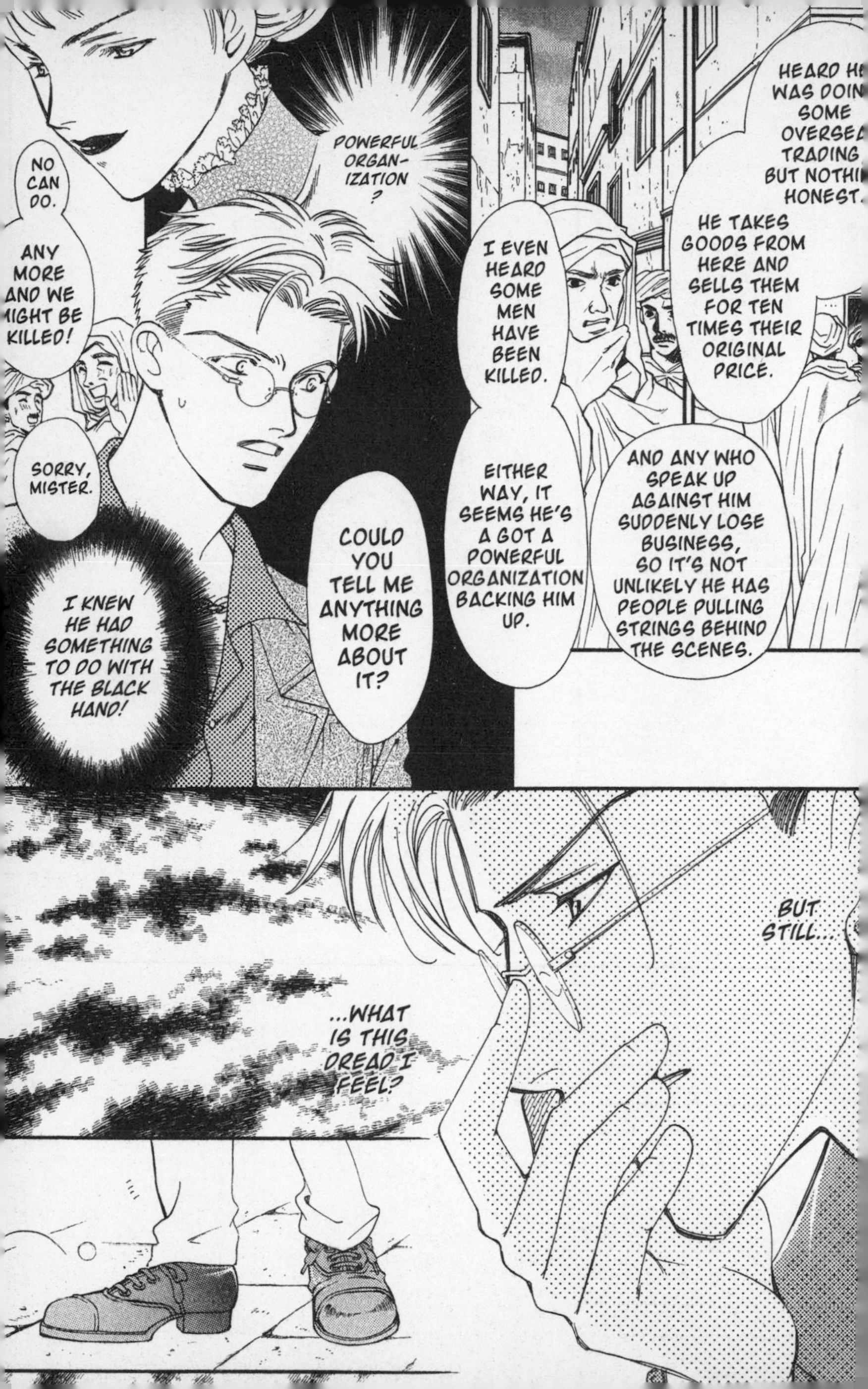
HEARD HE WAS DOIN SOME OVERSEA TRADING BUT NOTHI HONEST.
HE TAKES GOODS FROM HERE AND SELLS THEM FOR TEN TIMES THEIR ORIGINAL PRICE.
I EVEN HEARD SOME MEN HAVE BEEN KILLED.
AND ANY WHO SPEAK UP AGAINST HIM SUDDENLY LOSE BUSINESS, SO IT'S NOT UNLIKELY HE HAS PEOPLE PULLING STRINGS BEHIND THE SCENES.
EITHER WAY, IT SEEMS HE'S A GOT A POWERFUL ORGANIZATION BACKING HIM UP.
POWERFUL ORGAN-IZATION ?
COULD YOU TELL ME ANYTHING MORE ABOUT IT?
NO CAN DO.
ANY MORE AND WE MIGHT BE KILLED!
SORRY, MISTER.
I KNEW HE HAD SOMETHING TO DO WITH THE BLACK HAND!
BUT STILL...
...WHAT IS THIS DREAD I FEEL?

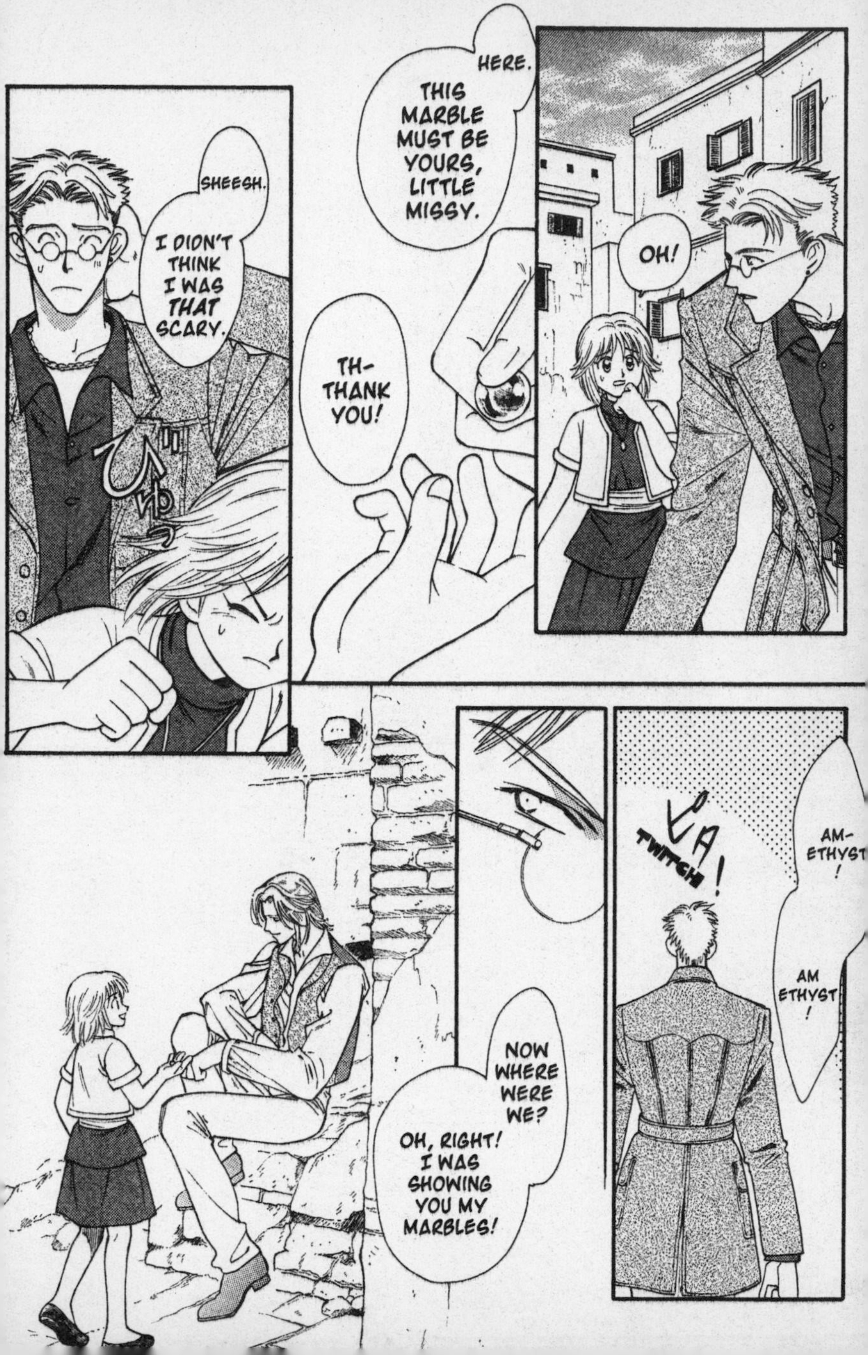
OH!
HERE.
THIS MARBLE MUST BE YOURS, LITTLE MISSY.
TH-THANK YOU!
SHEESH.
I DIDN'T THINK I WAS THAT SCARY.
TWITCH!
AM-ETHYST!
AM ETHYST!
NOW WHERE WERE WE?
OH, RIGHT! I WAS SHOWING YOU MY MARBLES!

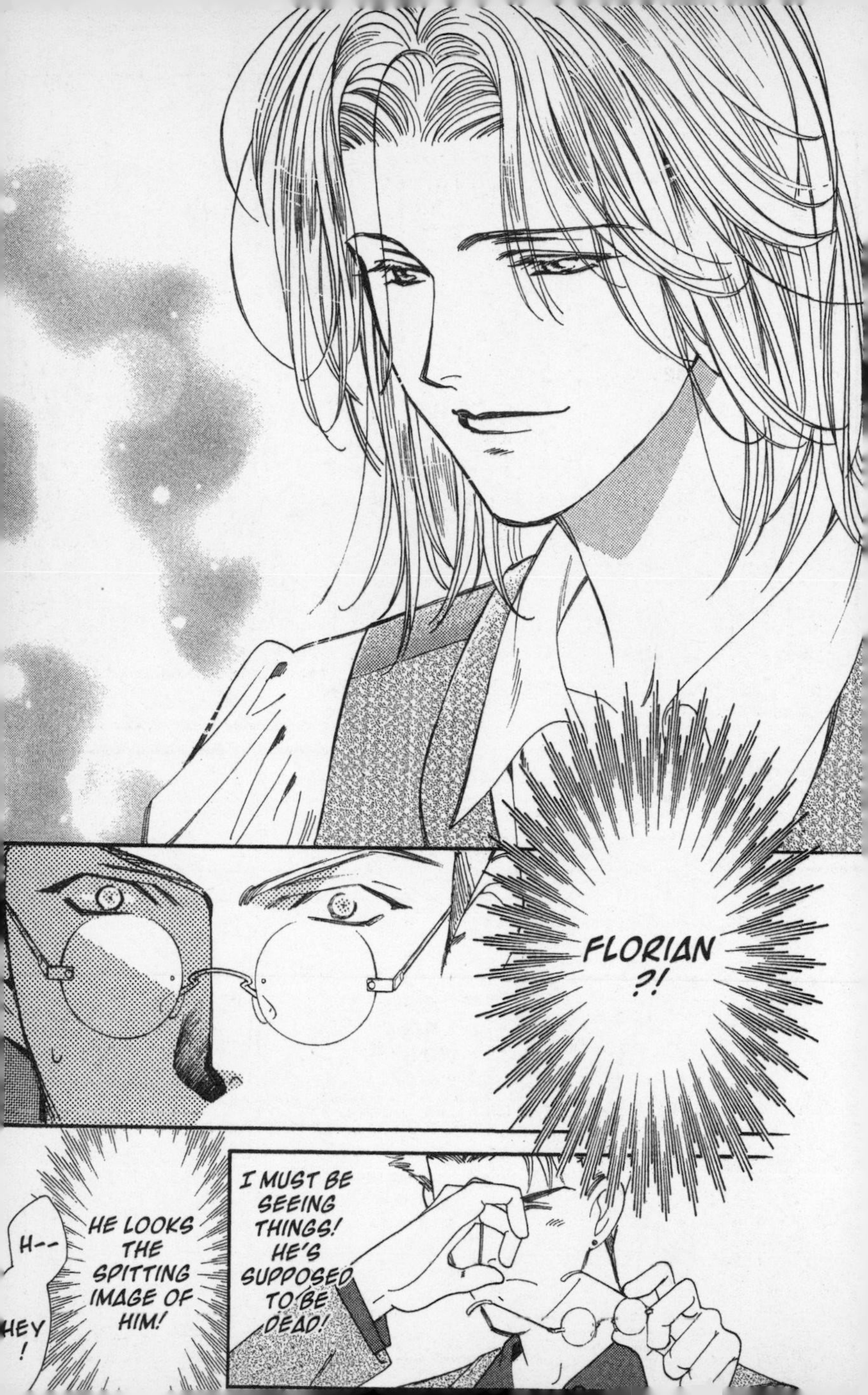
FLORIAN ?!
I MUST BE SEEING THINGS! HE'S SUPPOSED TO BE DEAD!
HE LOOKS THE SPITTING IMAGE OF HIM!
H-- HEY!

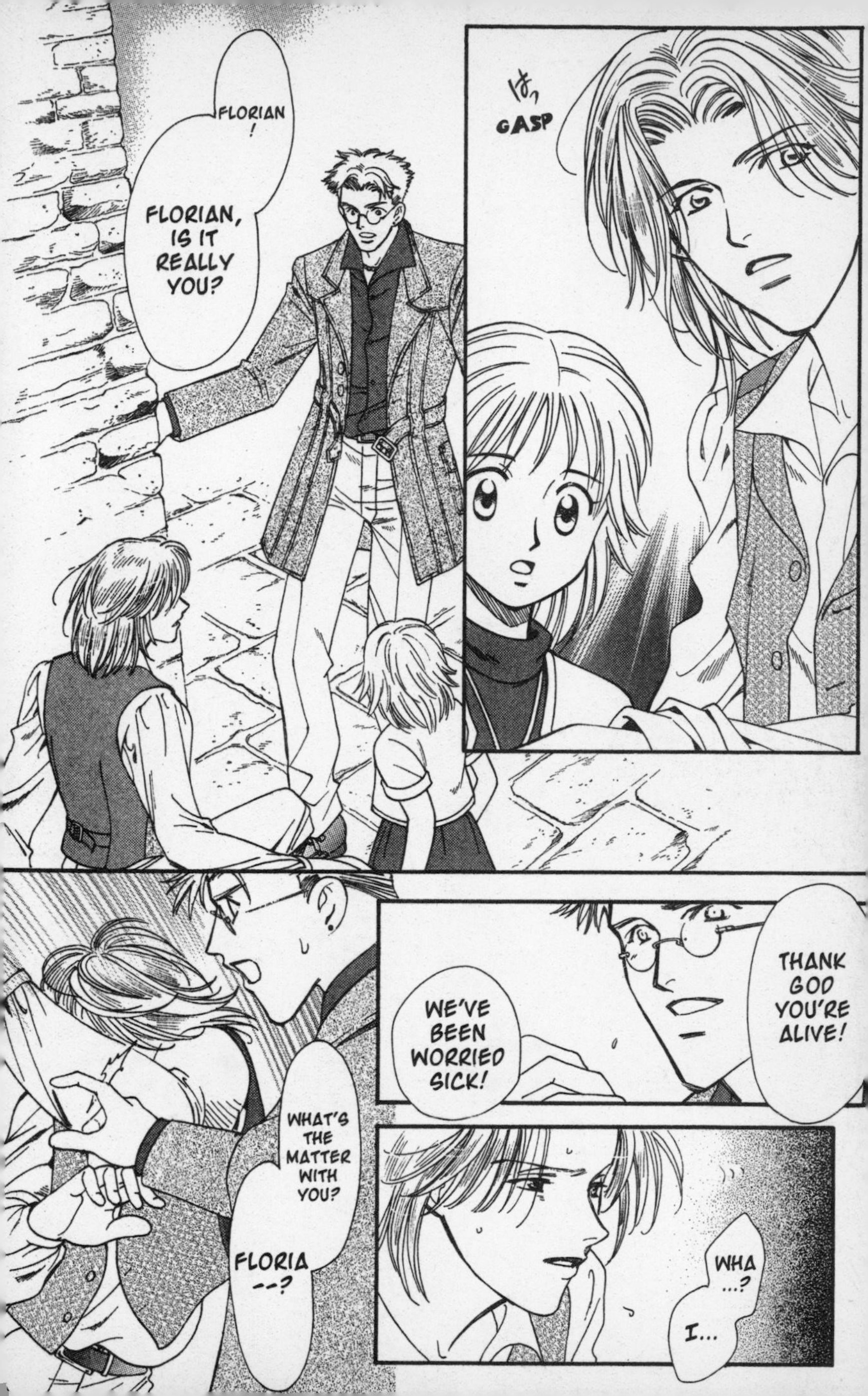
はっ
GASP
FLORIAN!
FLORIAN, IS IT REALLY YOU?
THANK GOD YOU'RE ALIVE!
WE'VE BEEN WORRIED SICK!
WHA...?
I...
WHAT'S THE MATTER WITH YOU?
FLORIA--?

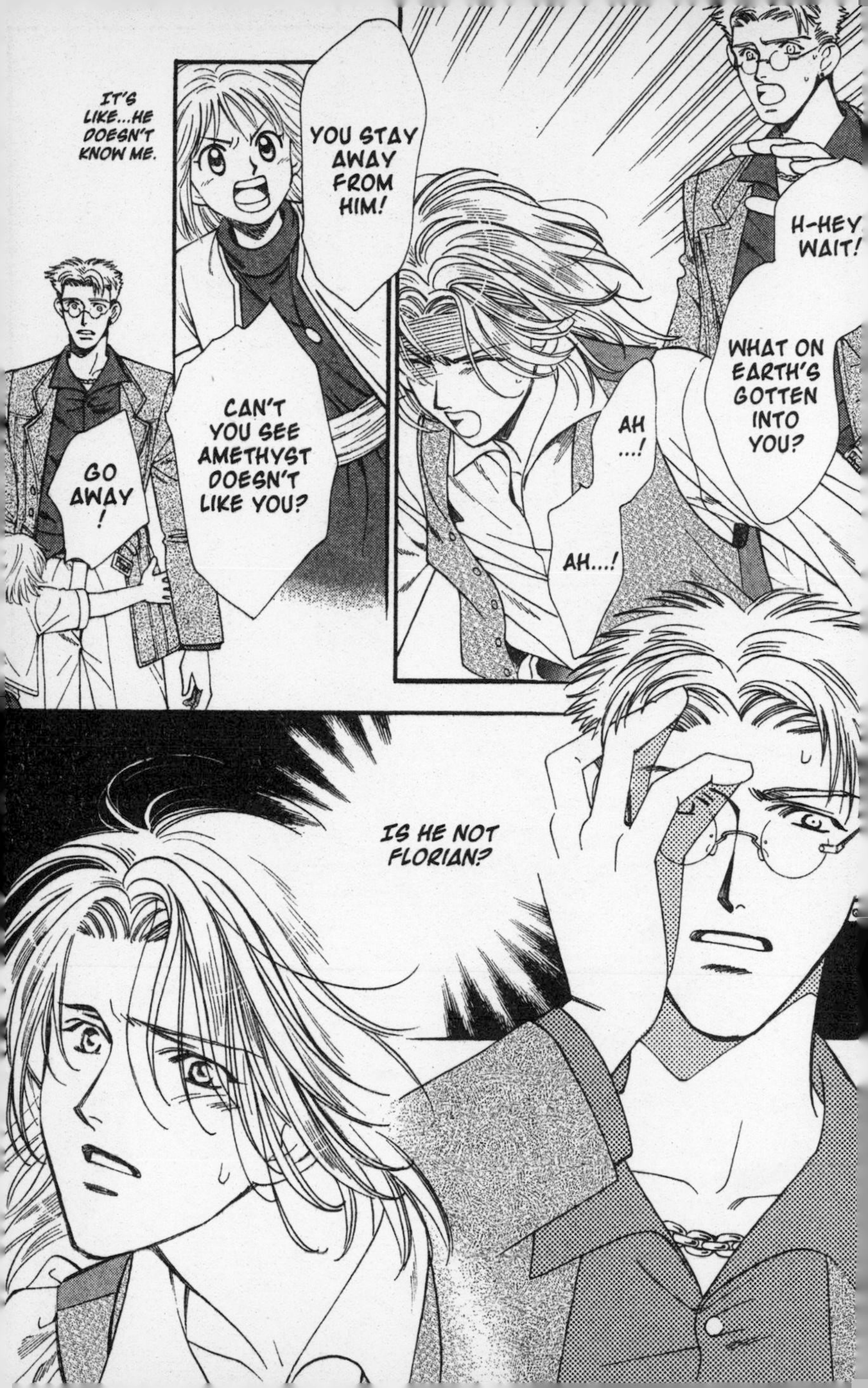
H-HEY WAIT!
WHAT ON EARTH'S GOTTEN INTO YOU?
AH ...!
AH...!
YOU STAY AWAY FROM HIM!
CAN'T YOU SEE AMETHYST DOESN'T LIKE YOU?
IT'S LIKE...HE DOESN'T KNOW ME.
GO AWAY!
IS HE NOT FLORIAN?

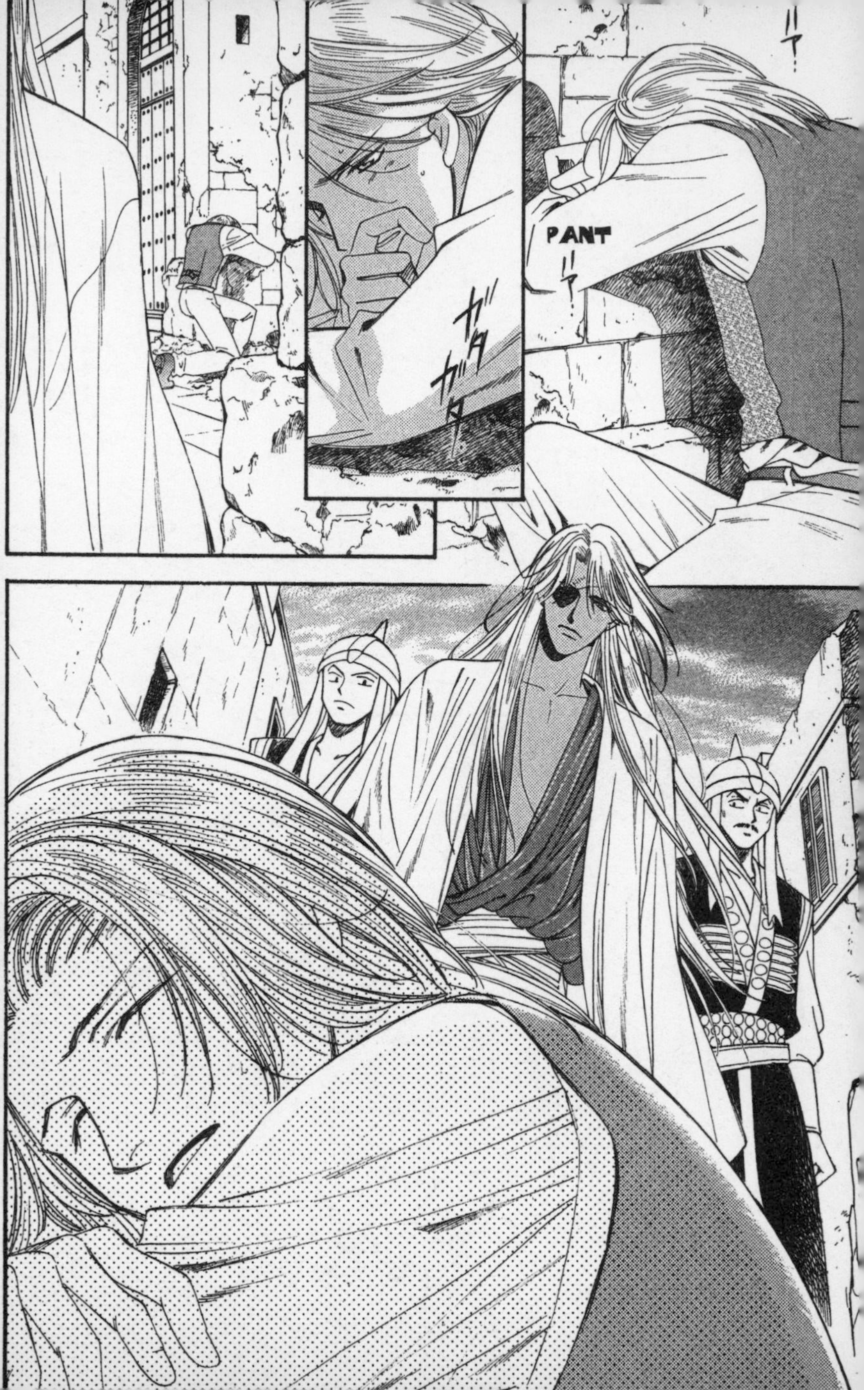
ハァ
PANT
ハァ
ガタ
ガタ

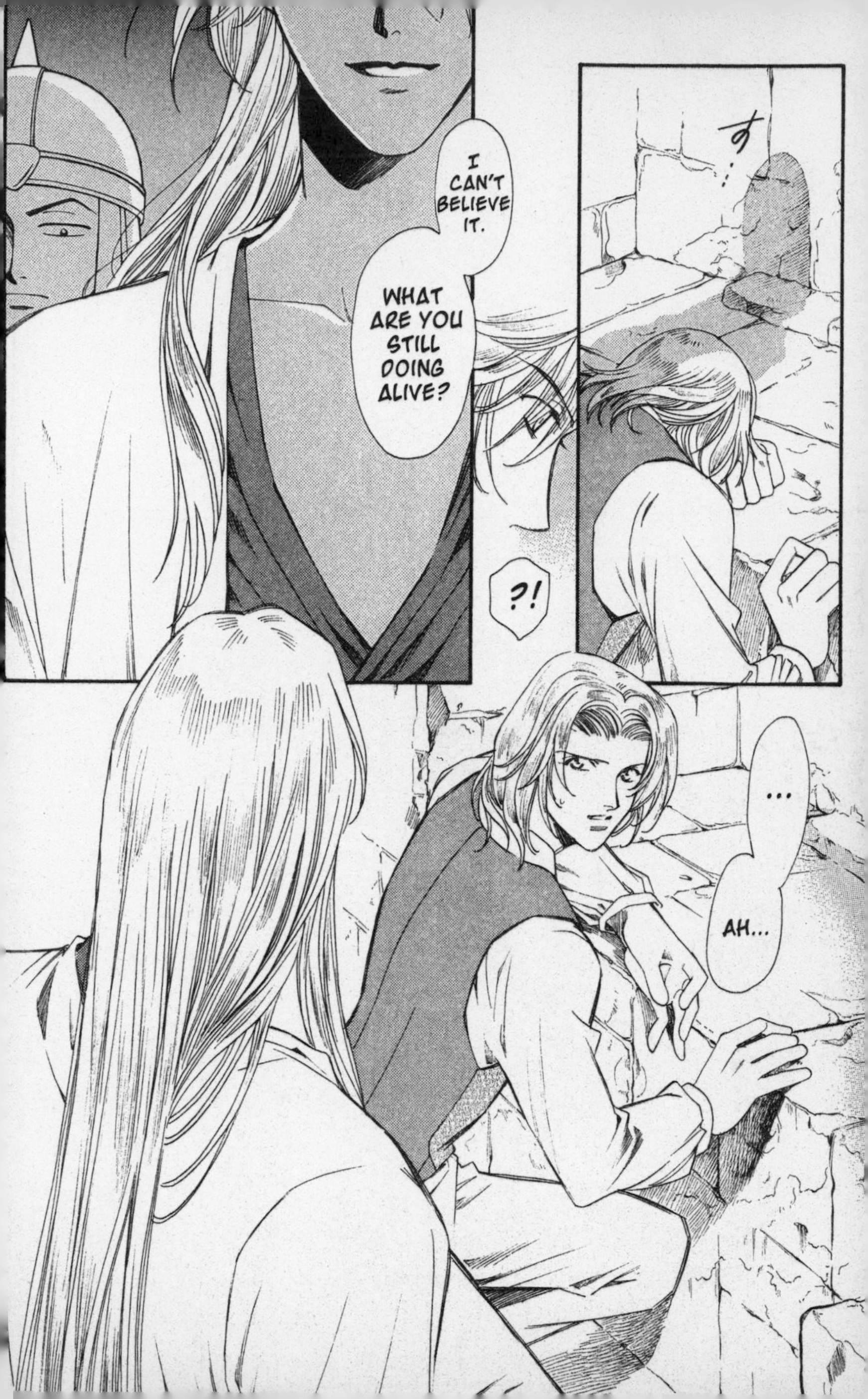
す・・
I CAN'T BELIEVE IT.
WHAT ARE YOU STILL DOING ALIVE?
?!
...
AH...

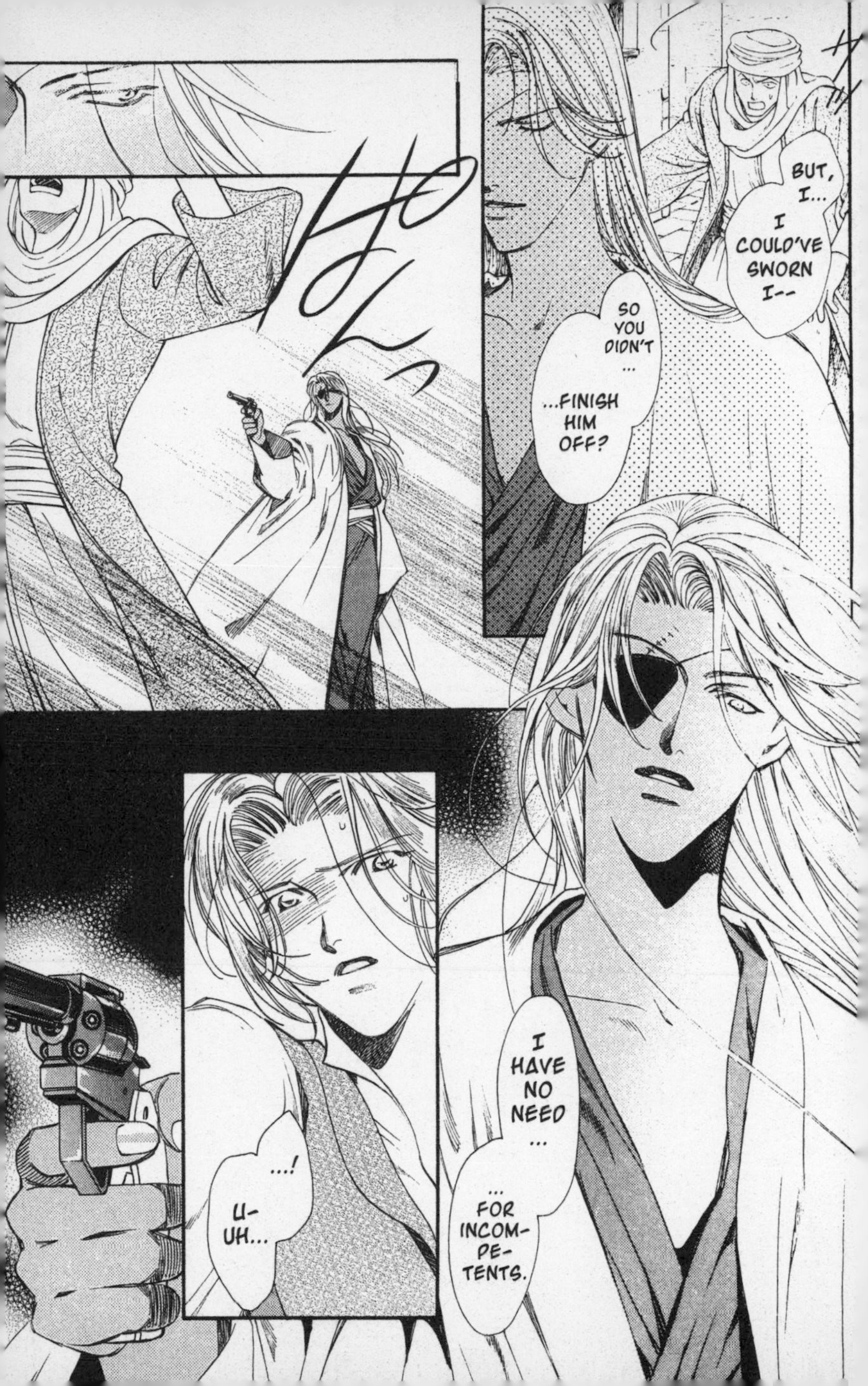
BUT, I... I COULD'VE SWORN I--
SO YOU DIDN'T ... ...FINISH HIM OFF?
I HAVE NO NEED ...
... FOR INCOM-PE-TENTS.
...!
U-UH...

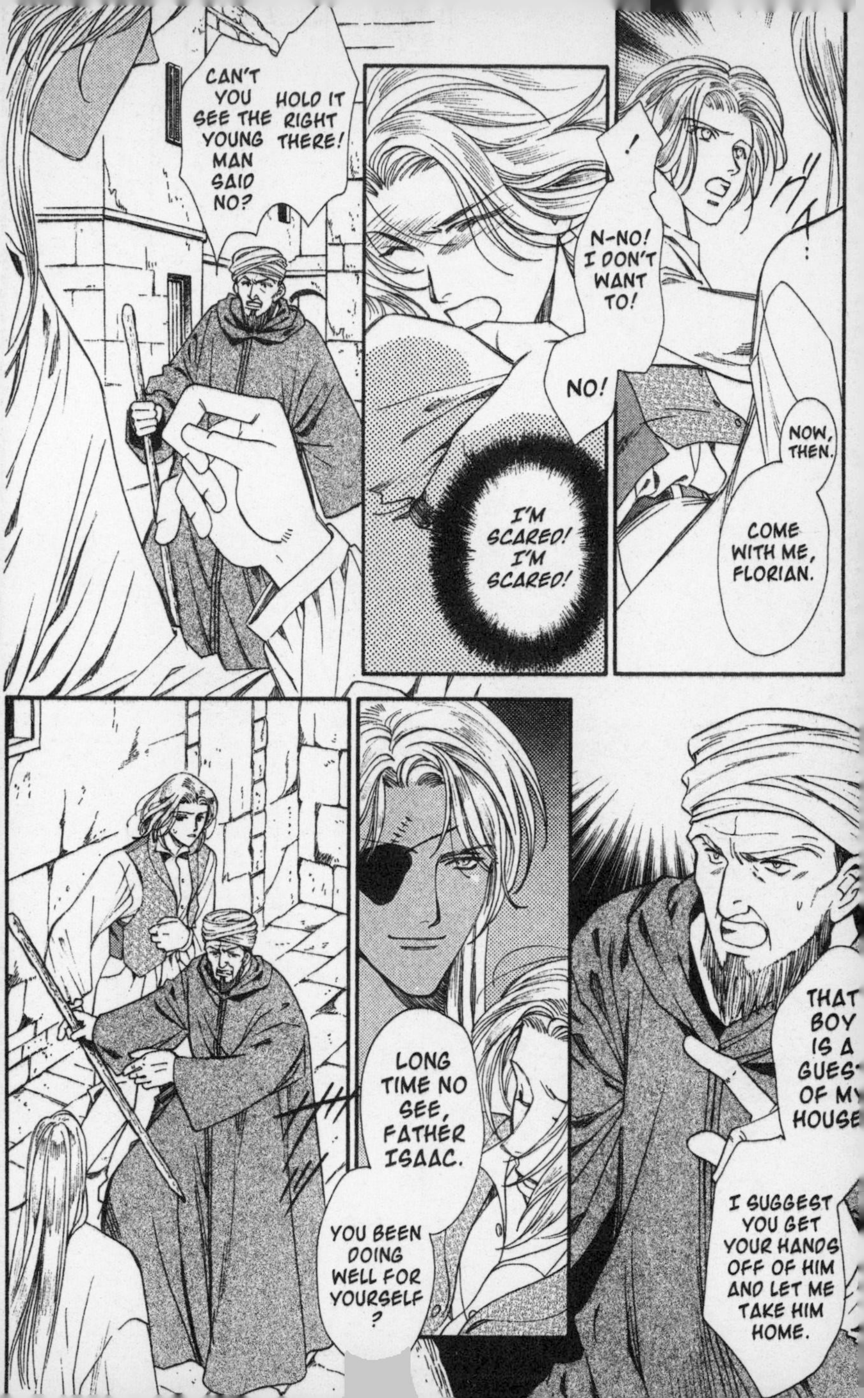
NOW, THEN.
COME WITH ME, FLORIAN.
!
N-NO! I DON'T WANT TO!
NO!
I'M SCARED! I'M SCARED!
HOLD IT RIGHT THERE!
CAN'T YOU SEE THE YOUNG MAN SAID NO?
THAT BOY IS A GUES OF MY HOUSE
I SUGGEST YOU GET YOUR HANDS OFF OF HIM AND LET ME TAKE HIM HOME.
LONG TIME NO SEE, FATHER ISAAC.
YOU BEEN DOING WELL FOR YOURSELF?

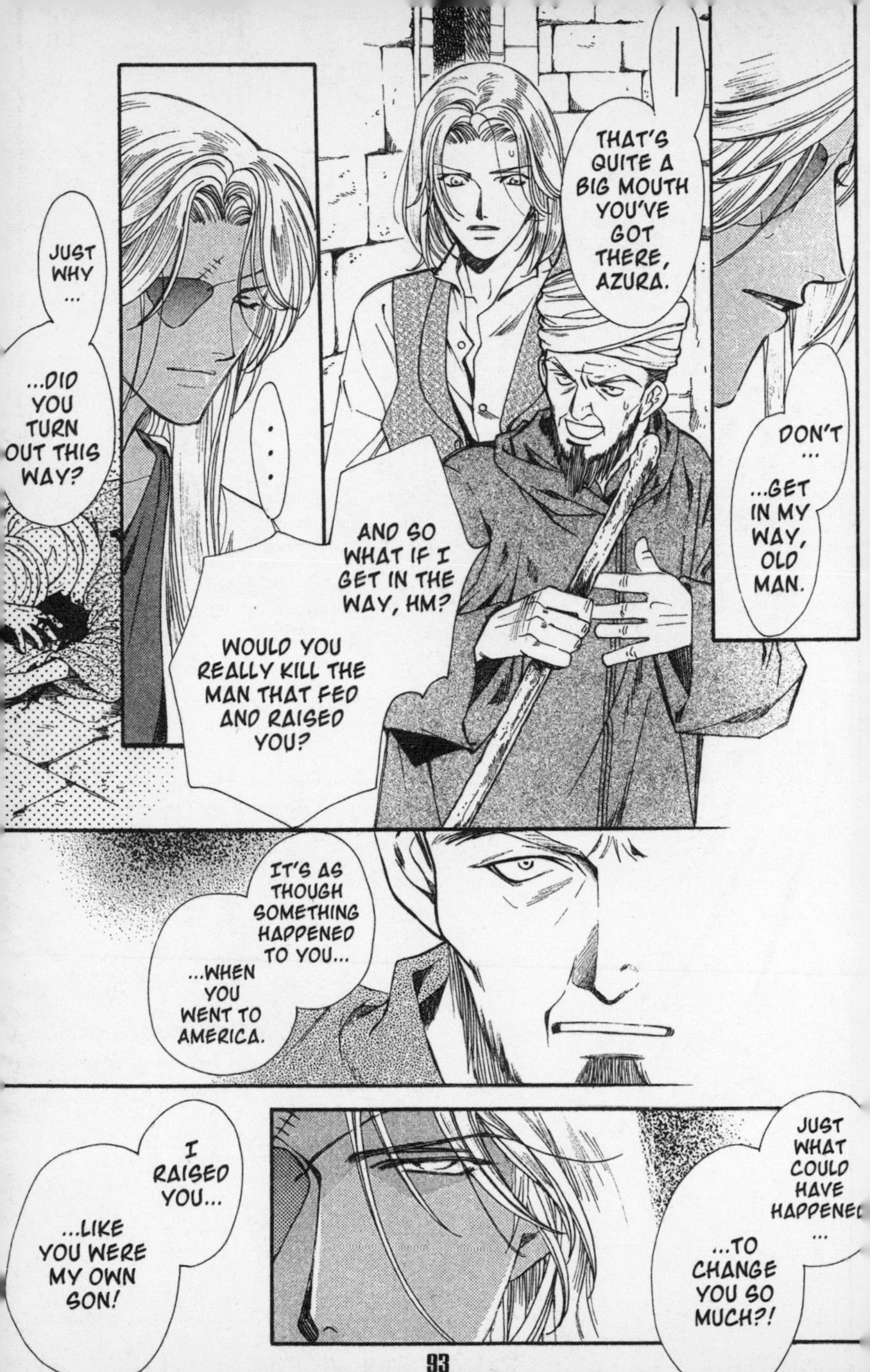
DON'T ...
...GET IN MY WAY, OLD MAN.
!
THAT'S QUITE A BIG MOUTH YOU'VE GOT THERE, AZURA.
AND SO WHAT IF I GET IN THE WAY, HM?
WOULD YOU REALLY KILL THE MAN THAT FED AND RAISED YOU?
...
JUST WHY ...
...DID YOU TURN OUT THIS WAY?
IT'S AS THOUGH SOMETHING HAPPENED TO YOU...
...WHEN YOU WENT TO AMERICA.
JUST WHAT COULD HAVE HAPPENED ...
...TO CHANGE YOU SO MUCH?!
I RAISED YOU...
...LIKE YOU WERE MY OWN SON!

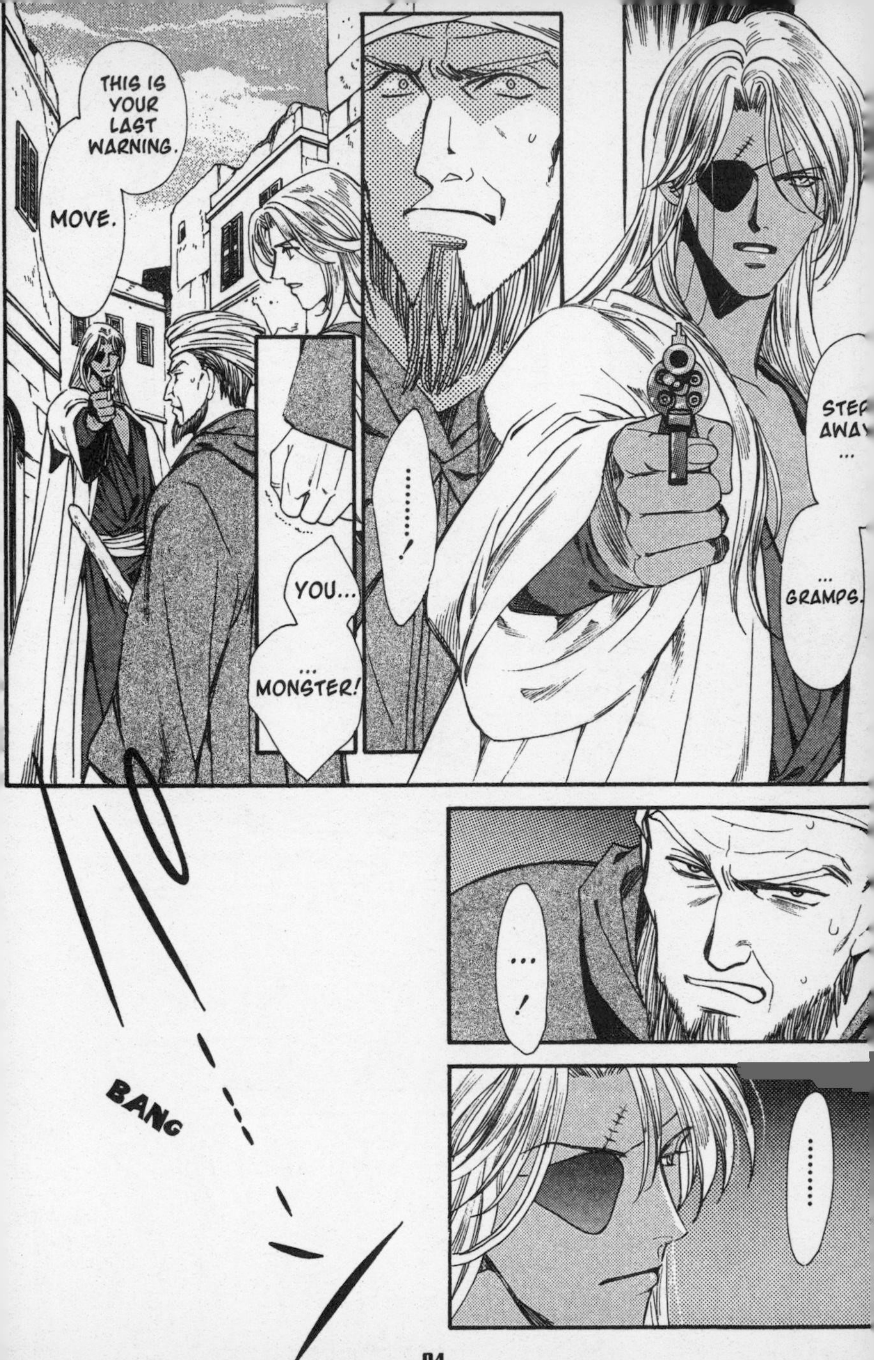
STEP AWAY ...
... GRAMPS.
......!
YOU...
... MONSTER!
THIS IS YOUR LAST WARNING.
MOVE.
...!
....
BANG

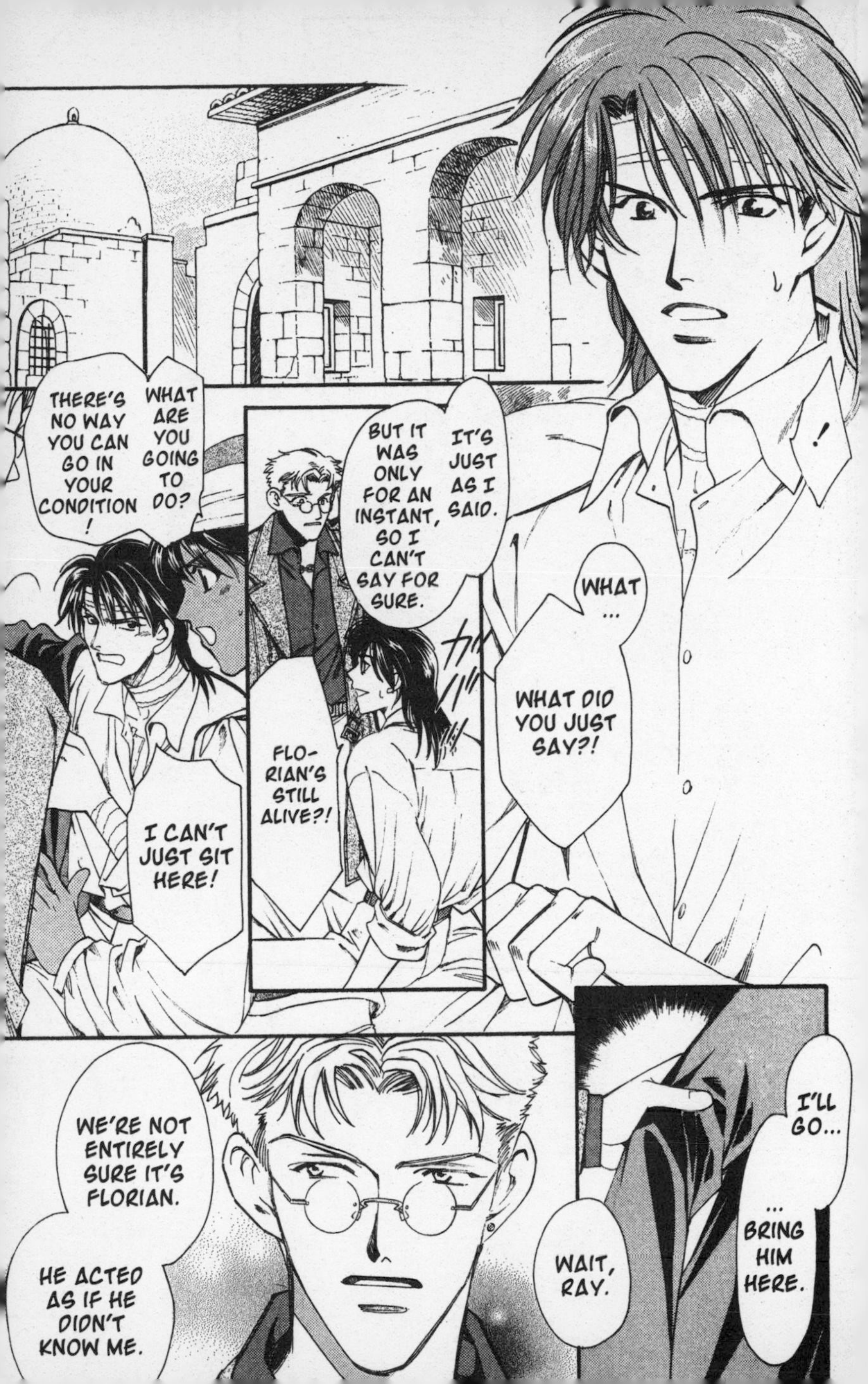
!
WHAT...
WHAT DID YOU JUST SAY?!
IT'S JUST AS I SAID.
BUT IT WAS ONLY FOR AN INSTANT, SO I CAN'T SAY FOR SURE.
FLO-RIAN'S STILL ALIVE?!
WHAT ARE YOU GOING TO DO?
THERE'S NO WAY YOU CAN GO IN YOUR CONDITION!
I CAN'T JUST SIT HERE!
I'LL GO...
...BRING HIM HERE.
WAIT, RAY.
WE'RE NOT ENTIRELY SURE IT'S FLORIAN.
HE ACTED AS IF HE DIDN'T KNOW ME.

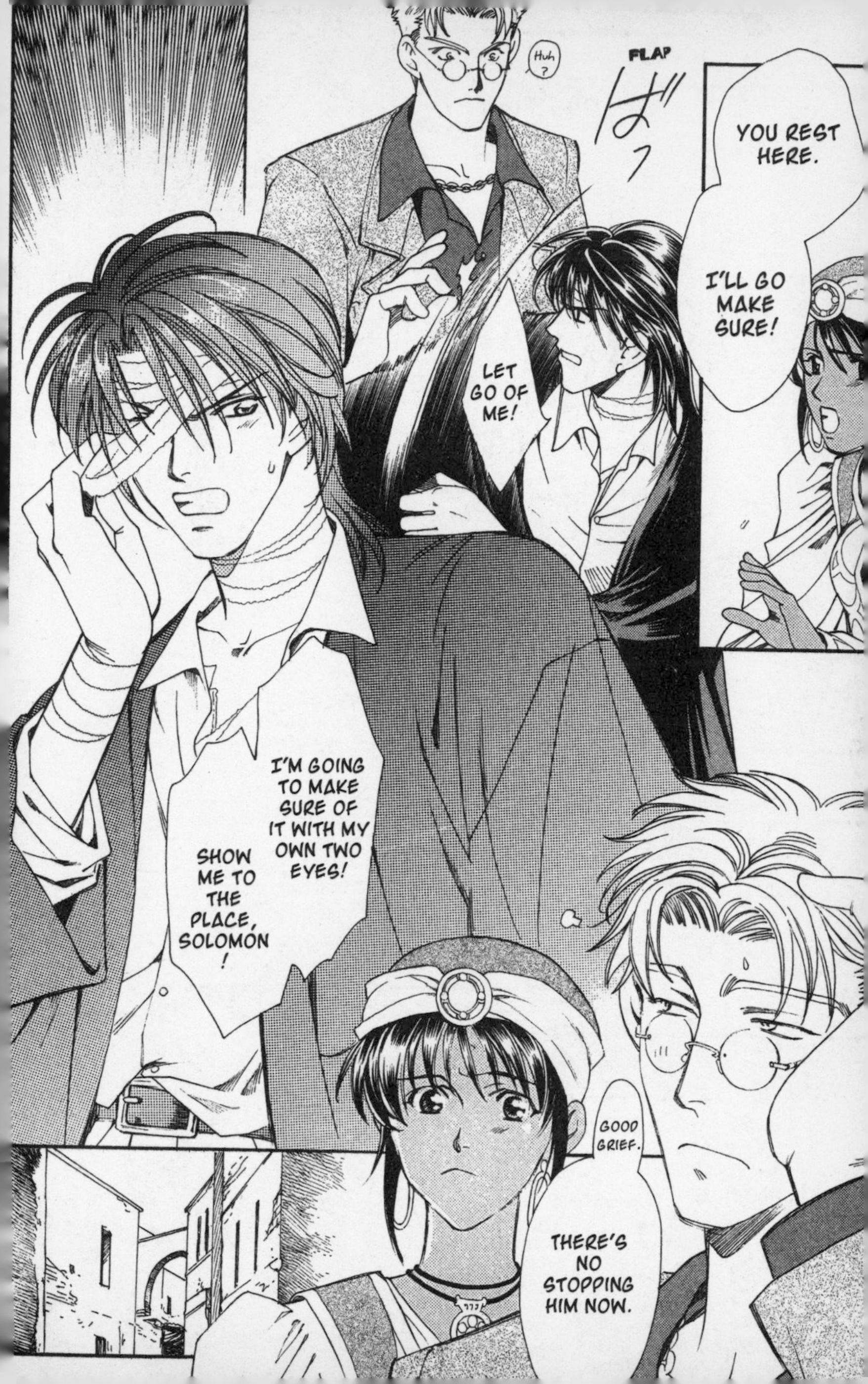
YOU REST HERE.
I'LL GO MAKE SURE!
FLAP
ばっ
Huh?
LET GO OF ME!
I'M GOING TO MAKE SURE OF IT WITH MY OWN TWO EYES!
SHOW ME TO THE PLACE, SOLOMON!
GOOD GRIEF.
THERE'S NO STOPPING HIM NOW.

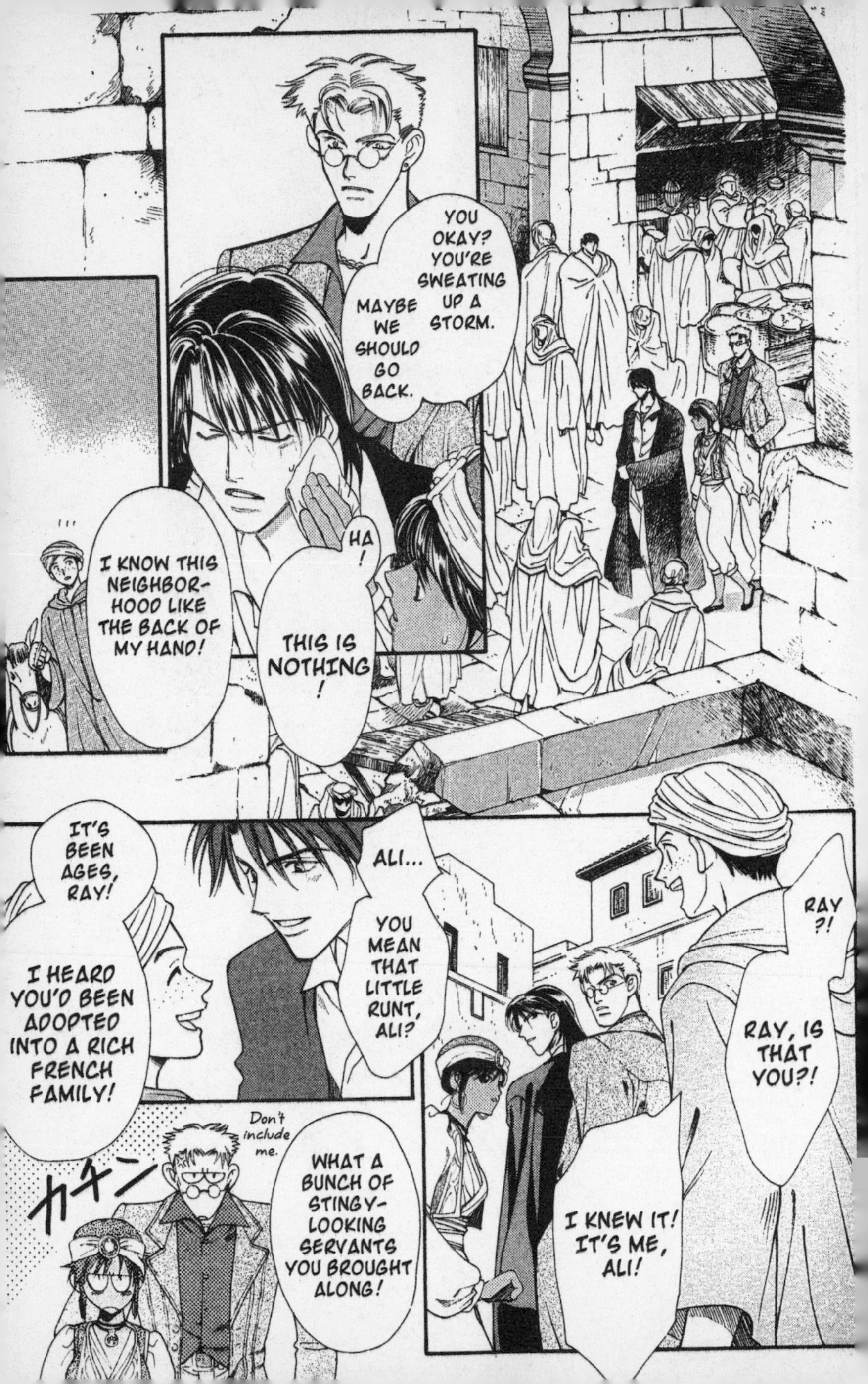
YOU OKAY? YOU'RE SWEATING UP A STORM.
MAYBE WE SHOULD GO BACK.
HA!
THIS IS NOTHING!
I KNOW THIS NEIGHBOR-HOOD LIKE THE BACK OF MY HAND!
!!!
RAY?!
RAY, IS THAT YOU?!
I KNEW IT! IT'S ME, ALI!
ALI...
YOU MEAN THAT LITTLE RUNT, ALI?
IT'S BEEN AGES, RAY!
I HEARD YOU'D BEEN ADOPTED INTO A RICH FRENCH FAMILY!
WHAT A BUNCH OF STINGY-LOOKING SERVANTS YOU BROUGHT ALONG!
Don't include me.
カチーン

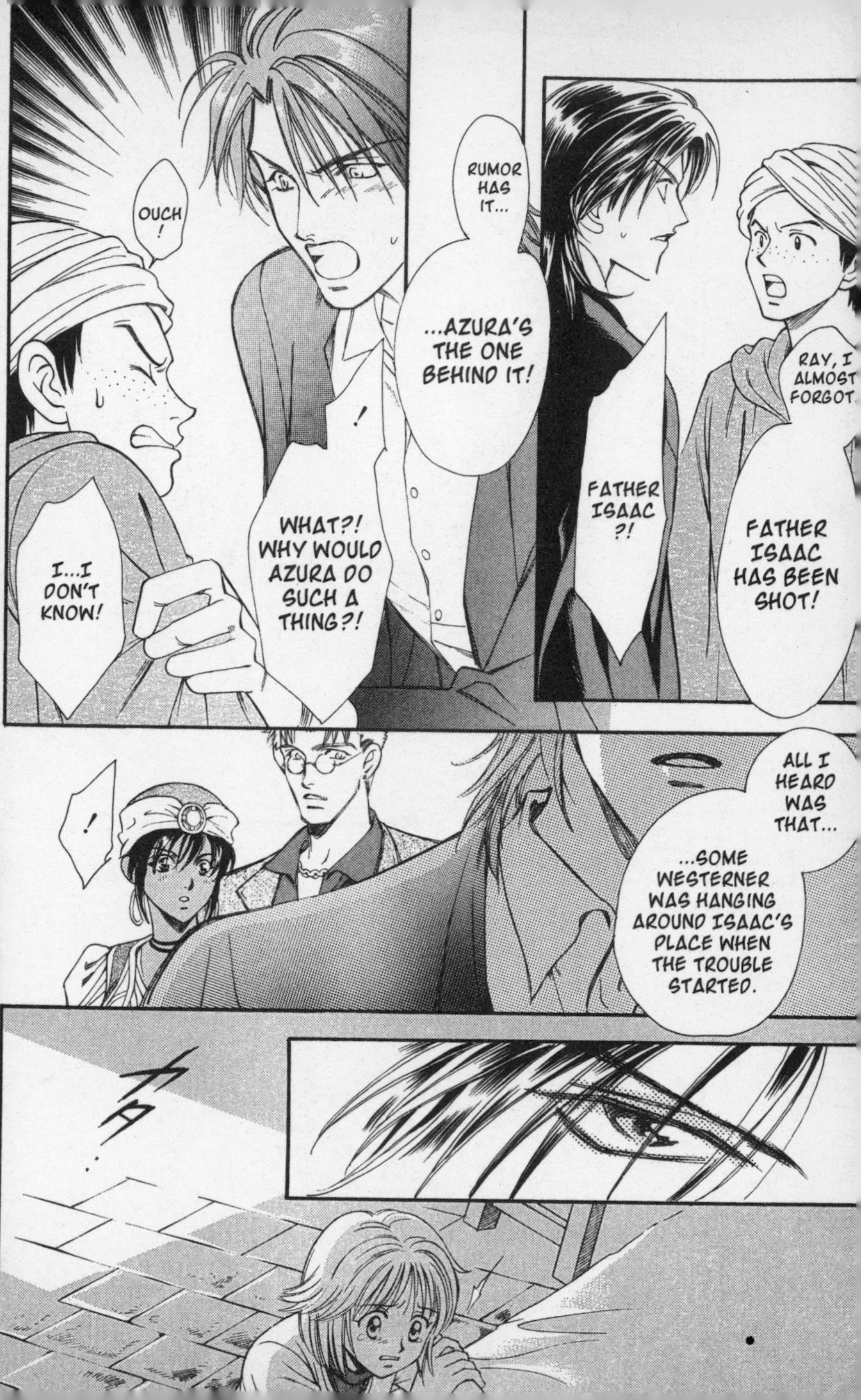
RAY, I ALMOST FORGOT.
FATHER ISAAC HAS BEEN SHOT!
FATHER ISAAC ?!
RUMOR HAS IT...
...AZURA'S THE ONE BEHIND IT!
!
WHAT?! WHY WOULD AZURA DO SUCH A THING?!
OUCH!
I...I DON'T KNOW!
ALL I HEARD WAS THAT...
...SOME WESTERNER WAS HANGING AROUND ISAAC'S PLACE WHEN THE TROUBLE STARTED.
!
カタ..

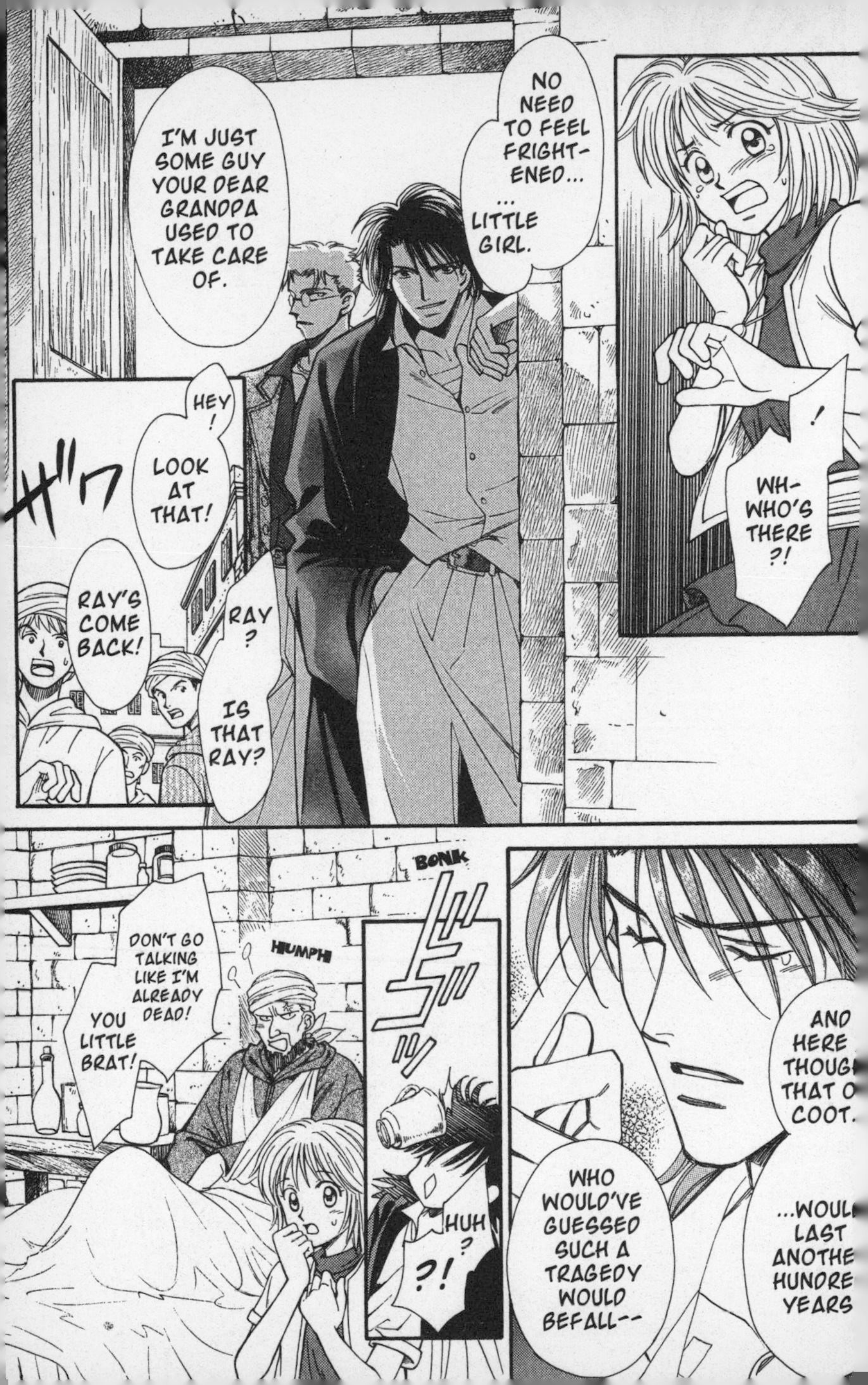
!
WH- WHO'S THERE ?!
NO NEED TO FEEL FRIGHT- ENED... ... LITTLE GIRL.
I'M JUST SOME GUY YOUR DEAR GRANDPA USED TO TAKE CARE OF.
HEY !
LOOK AT THAT!
RAY ?
IS THAT RAY?
ザワ
RAY'S COME BACK!
WHO WOULD'VE GUESSED SUCH A TRAGEDY WOULD BEFALL--
AND HERE THOUG THAT O COOT.
...WOUL LAST ANOTHE HUNDRE YEARS
BONK
HUH ?
?!
HUMPH!
DON'T GO TALKING LIKE I'M ALREADY DEAD!
YOU LITTLE BRAT!

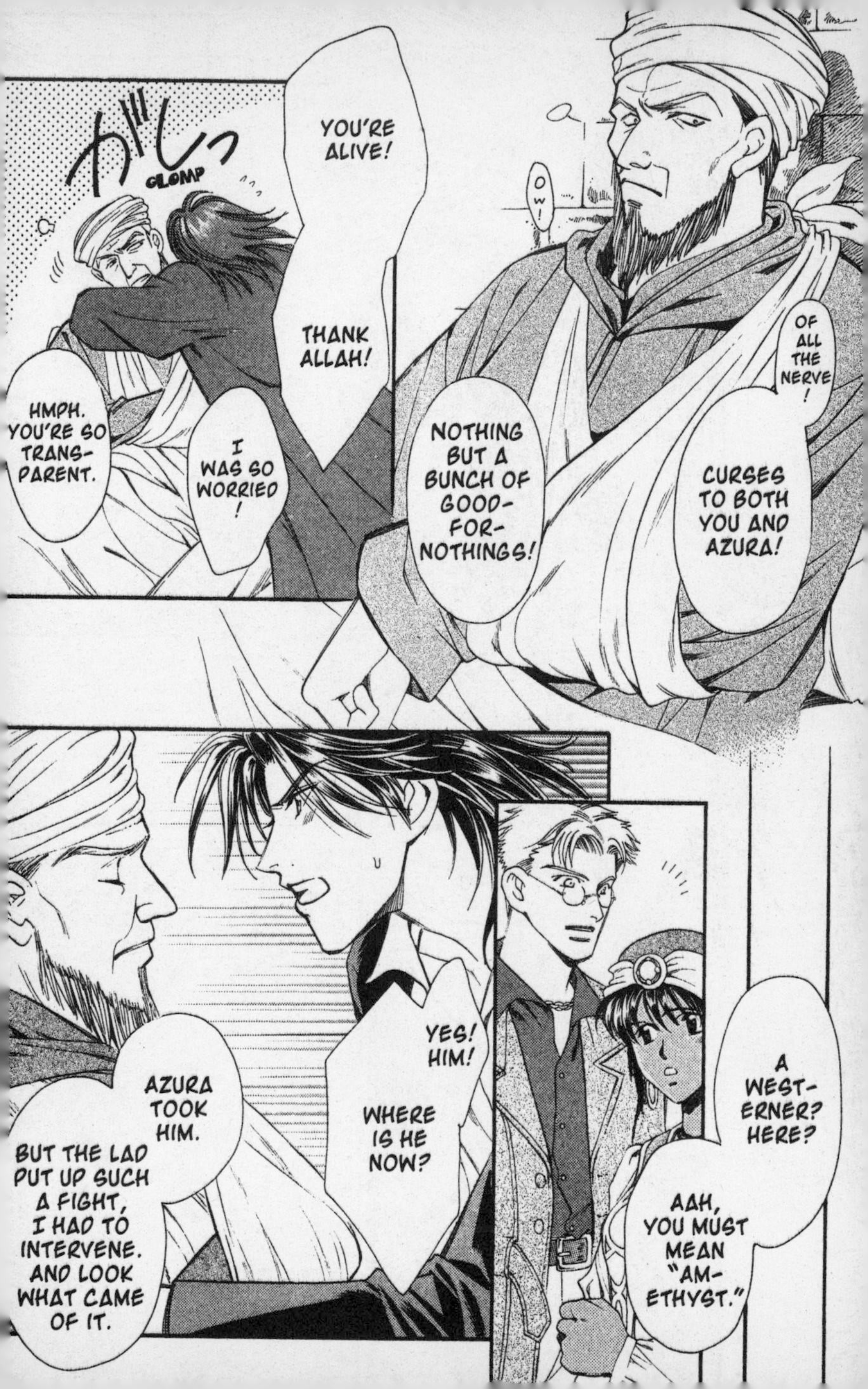
OW!
OF ALL THE NERVE!
CURSES TO BOTH YOU AND AZURA!
NOTHING BUT A BUNCH OF GOOD-FOR-NOTHINGS!
がしっ
GLOMP
YOU'RE ALIVE!
THANK ALLAH!
I WAS SO WORRIED!
HMPH. YOU'RE SO TRANS-PARENT.
A WEST-ERNER? HERE?
AAH, YOU MUST MEAN "AM-ETHYST."
YES! HIM!
WHERE IS HE NOW?
AZURA TOOK HIM.
BUT THE LAD PUT UP SUCH A FIGHT, I HAD TO INTERVENE. AND LOOK WHAT CAME OF IT.

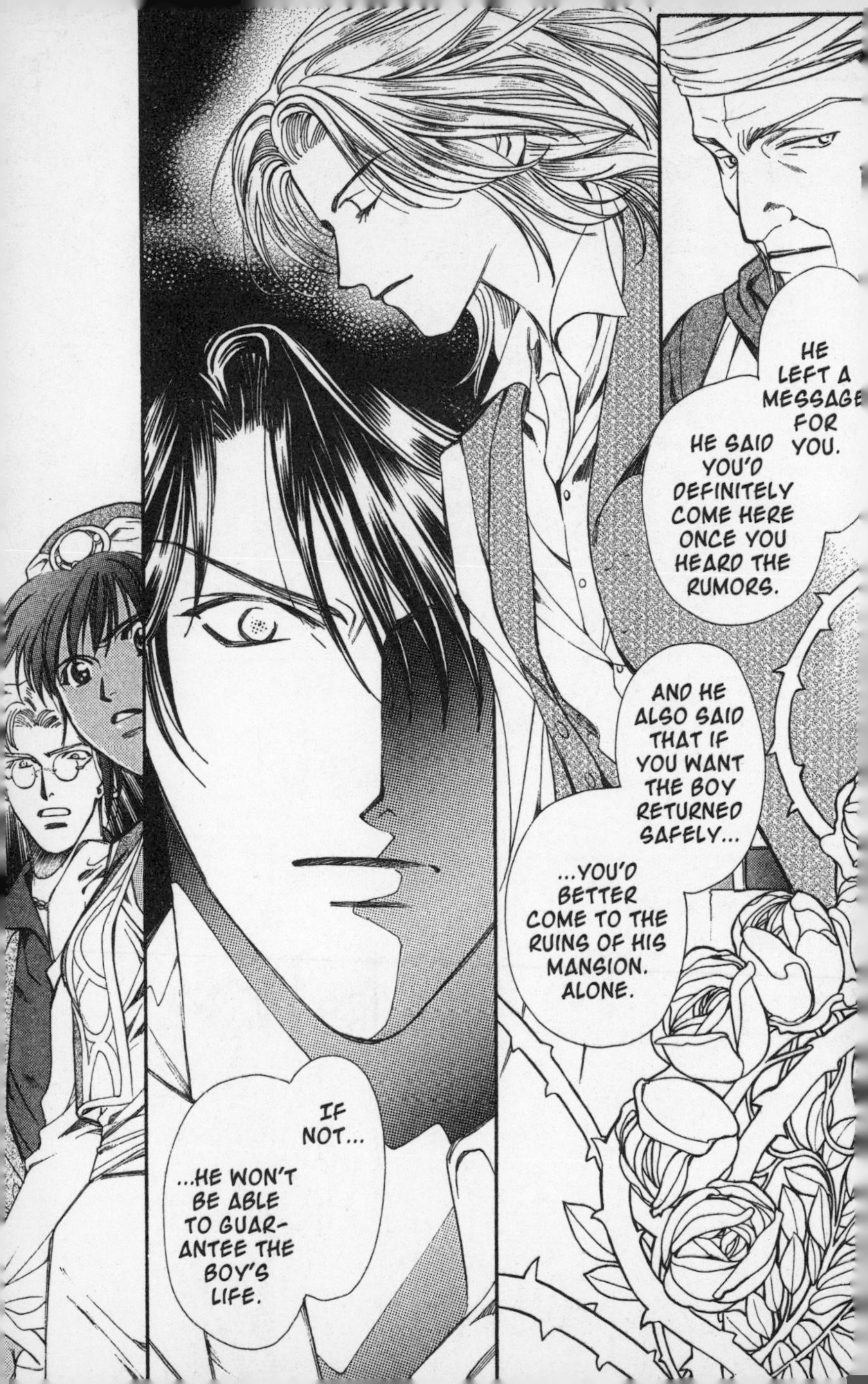
HE LEFT A MESSAGE FOR YOU.
HE SAID YOU'D DEFINITELY COME HERE ONCE YOU HEARD THE RUMORS.
AND HE ALSO SAID THAT IF YOU WANT THE BOY RETURNED SAFELY...
...YOU'D BETTER COME TO THE RUINS OF HIS MANSION. ALONE.
IF NOT...
...HE WON'T BE ABLE TO GUAR-ANTEE THE BOY'S LIFE.

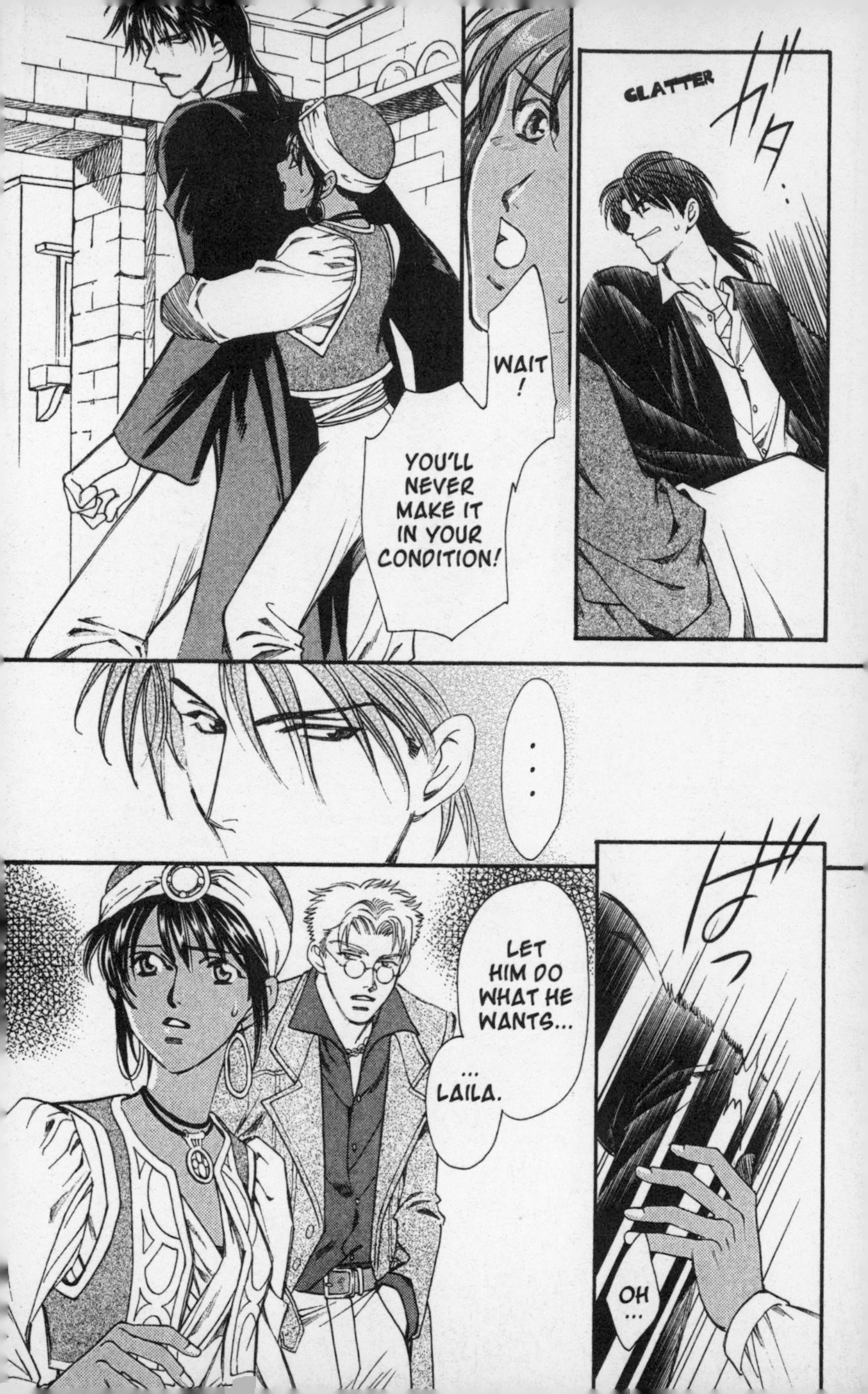
CLATTER
WAIT!
YOU'LL NEVER MAKE IT IN YOUR CONDITION!
...
OH ...
LET HIM DO WHAT HE WANTS...
... LAILA.

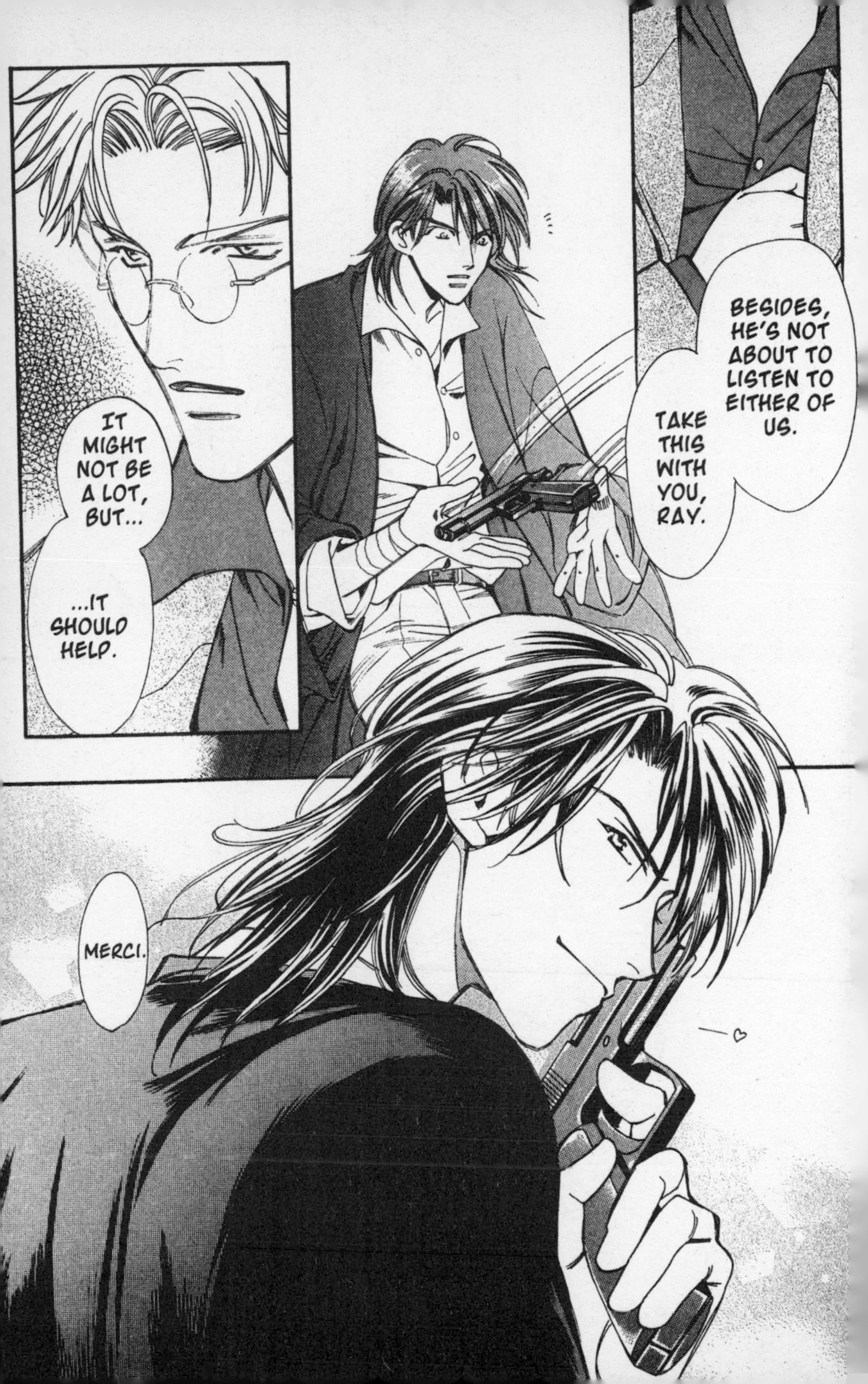
BESIDES, HE'S NOT ABOUT TO LISTEN TO EITHER OF US.
TAKE THIS WITH YOU, RAY.
IT MIGHT NOT BE A LOT, BUT...
...IT SHOULD HELP.
MERCI.
—♡

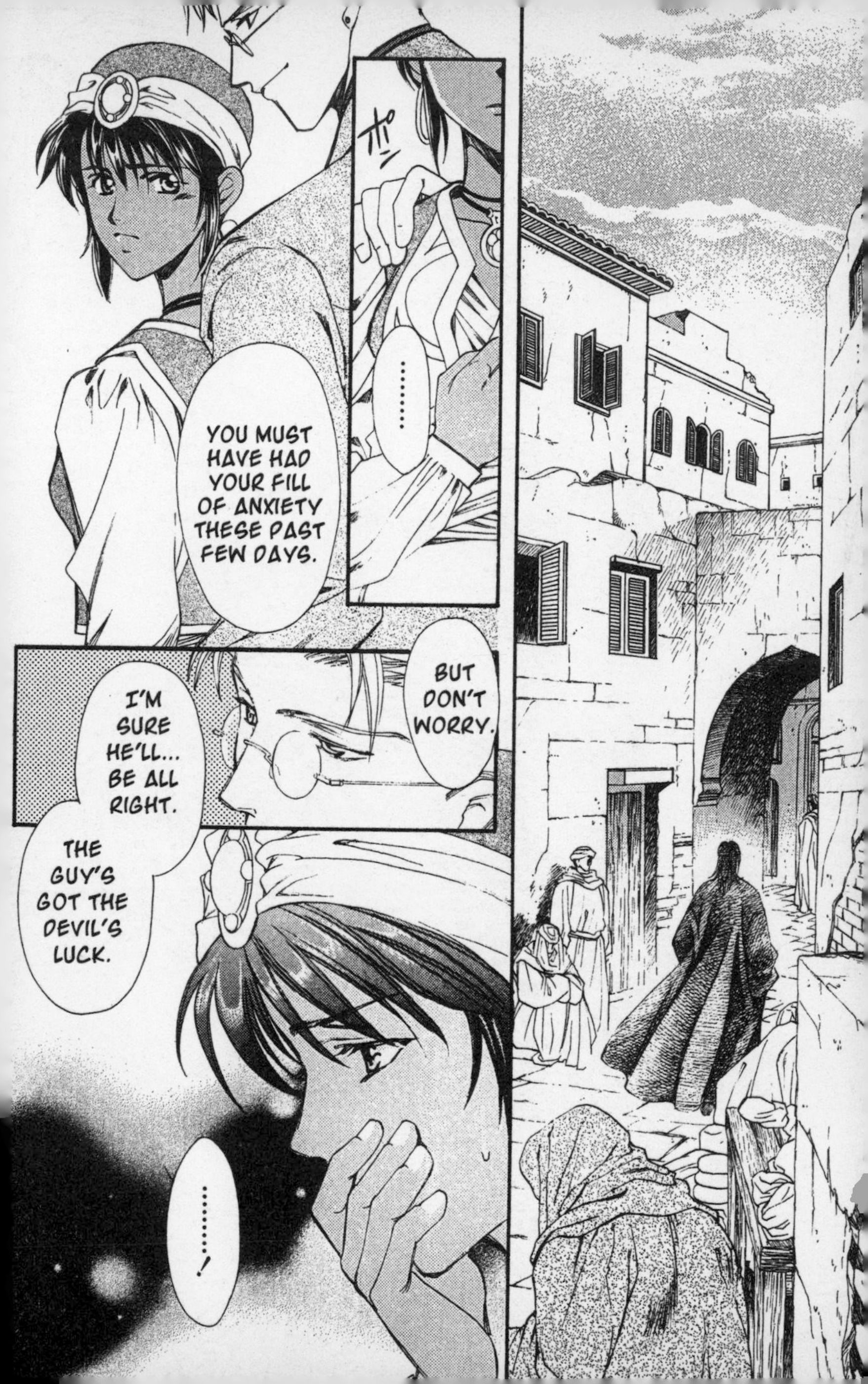
ポン
......
YOU MUST HAVE HAD YOUR FILL OF ANXIETY THESE PAST FEW DAYS.
BUT DON'T WORRY.
I'M SURE HE'LL... BE ALL RIGHT.
THE GUY'S GOT THE DEVIL'S LUCK.
......!

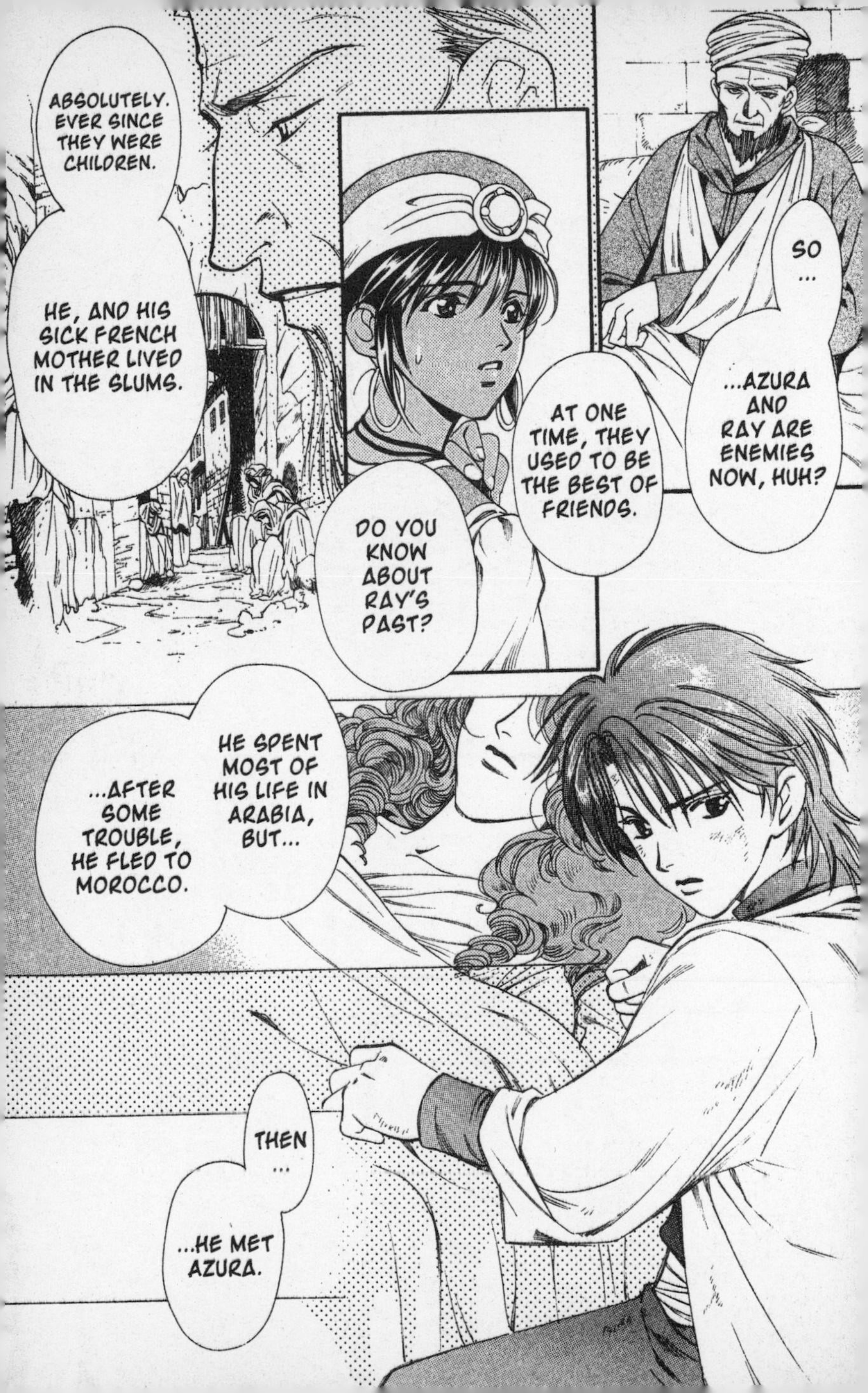
SO ...
...AZURA AND RAY ARE ENEMIES NOW, HUH?
AT ONE TIME, THEY USED TO BE THE BEST OF FRIENDS.
DO YOU KNOW ABOUT RAY'S PAST?
ABSOLUTELY. EVER SINCE THEY WERE CHILDREN.
HE, AND HIS SICK FRENCH MOTHER LIVED IN THE SLUMS.
HE SPENT MOST OF HIS LIFE IN ARABIA, BUT...
...AFTER SOME TROUBLE, HE FLED TO MOROCCO.
THEN ...
...HE MET AZURA.

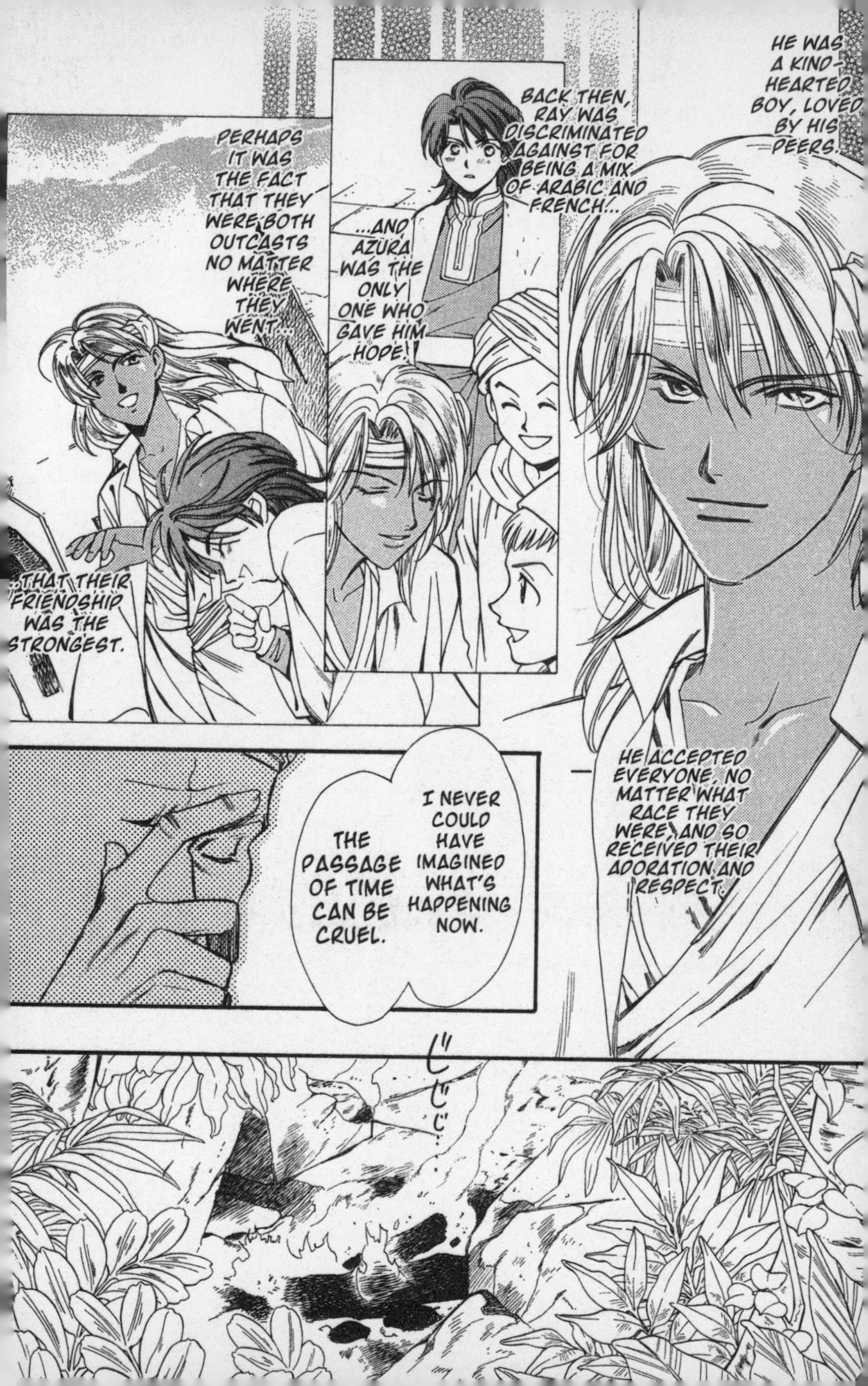
HE WAS A KIND-HEARTED BOY, LOVED BY HIS PEERS.
HE ACCEPTED EVERYONE, NO MATTER WHAT RACE THEY WERE, AND SO RECEIVED THEIR ADORATION AND RESPECT.
BACK THEN, RAY WAS DISCRIMINATED AGAINST FOR BEING A MIX OF ARABIC AND FRENCH...
...AND AZURA WAS THE ONLY ONE WHO GAVE HIM HOPE.
PERHAPS IT WAS THE FACT THAT THEY WERE BOTH OUTCASTS NO MATTER WHERE THEY WENT...
...THAT THEIR FRIENDSHIP WAS THE STRONGEST.
I NEVER COULD HAVE IMAGINED WHAT'S HAPPENING NOW.
THE PASSAGE OF TIME CAN BE CRUEL.
じじじ

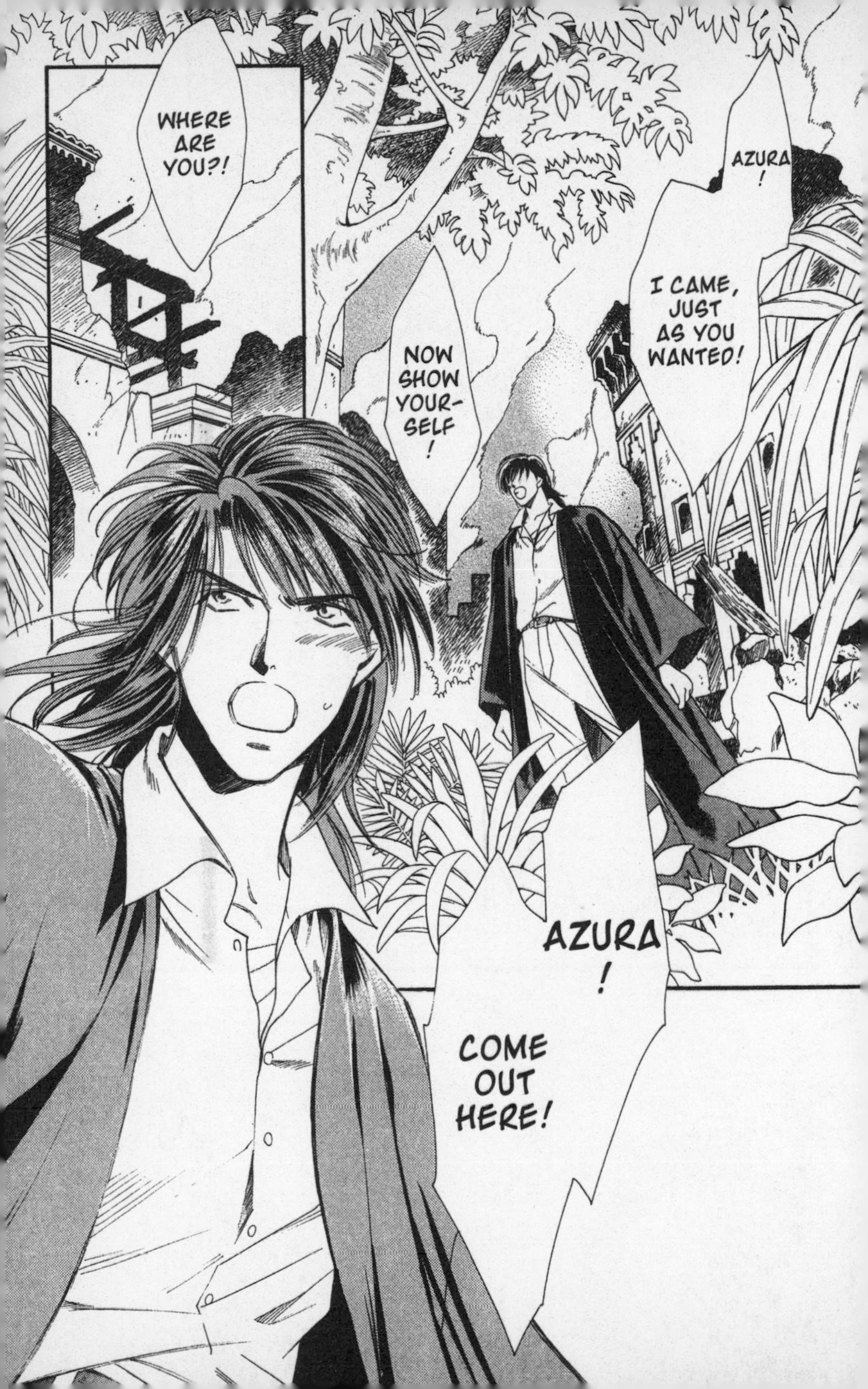
AZURA!
I CAME, JUST AS YOU WANTED!
NOW SHOW YOURSELF!
WHERE ARE YOU?!
AZURA!
COME OUT HERE!

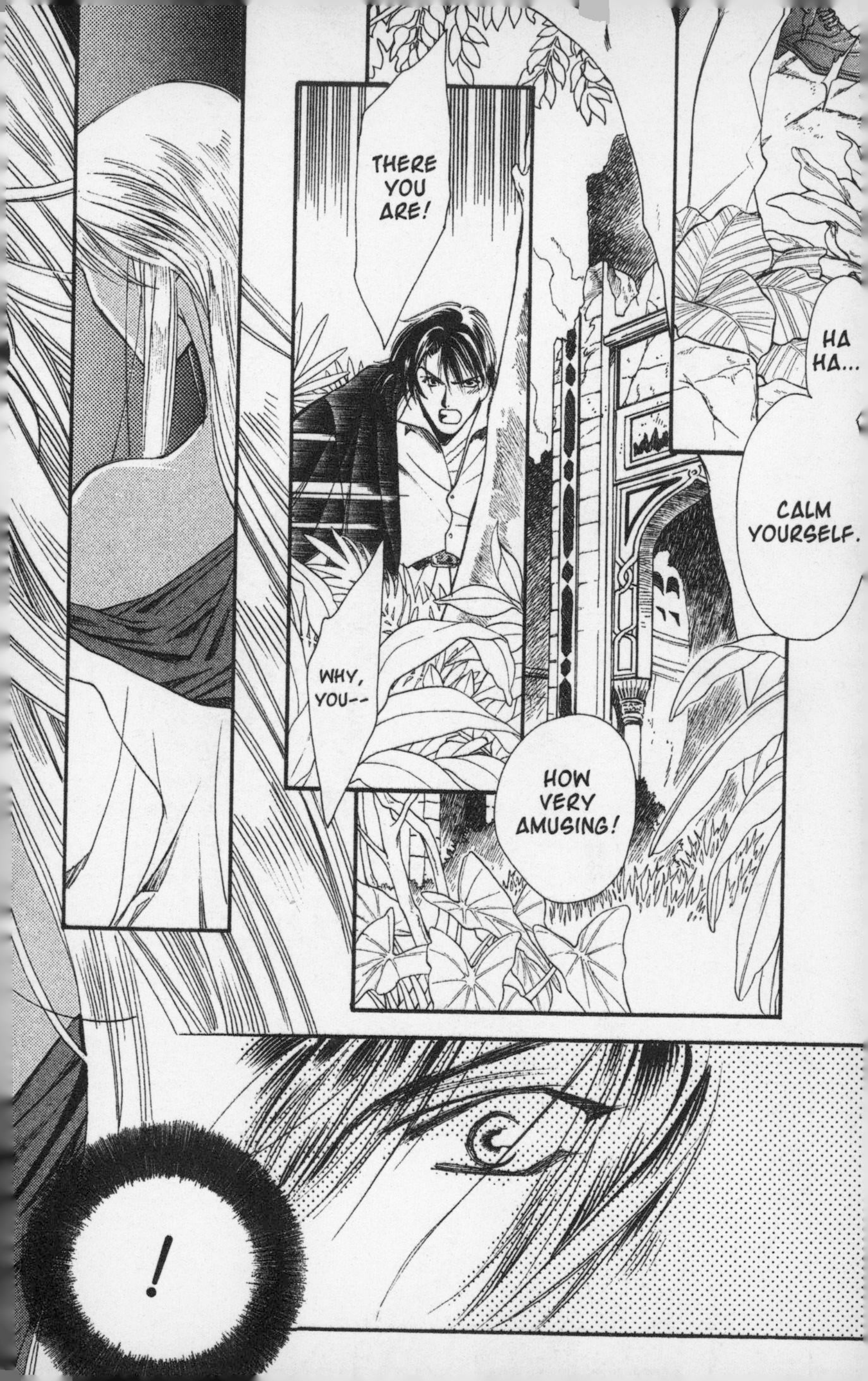
HA HA...
CALM YOURSELF.
HOW VERY AMUSING!
THERE YOU ARE!
WHY, YOU--
!

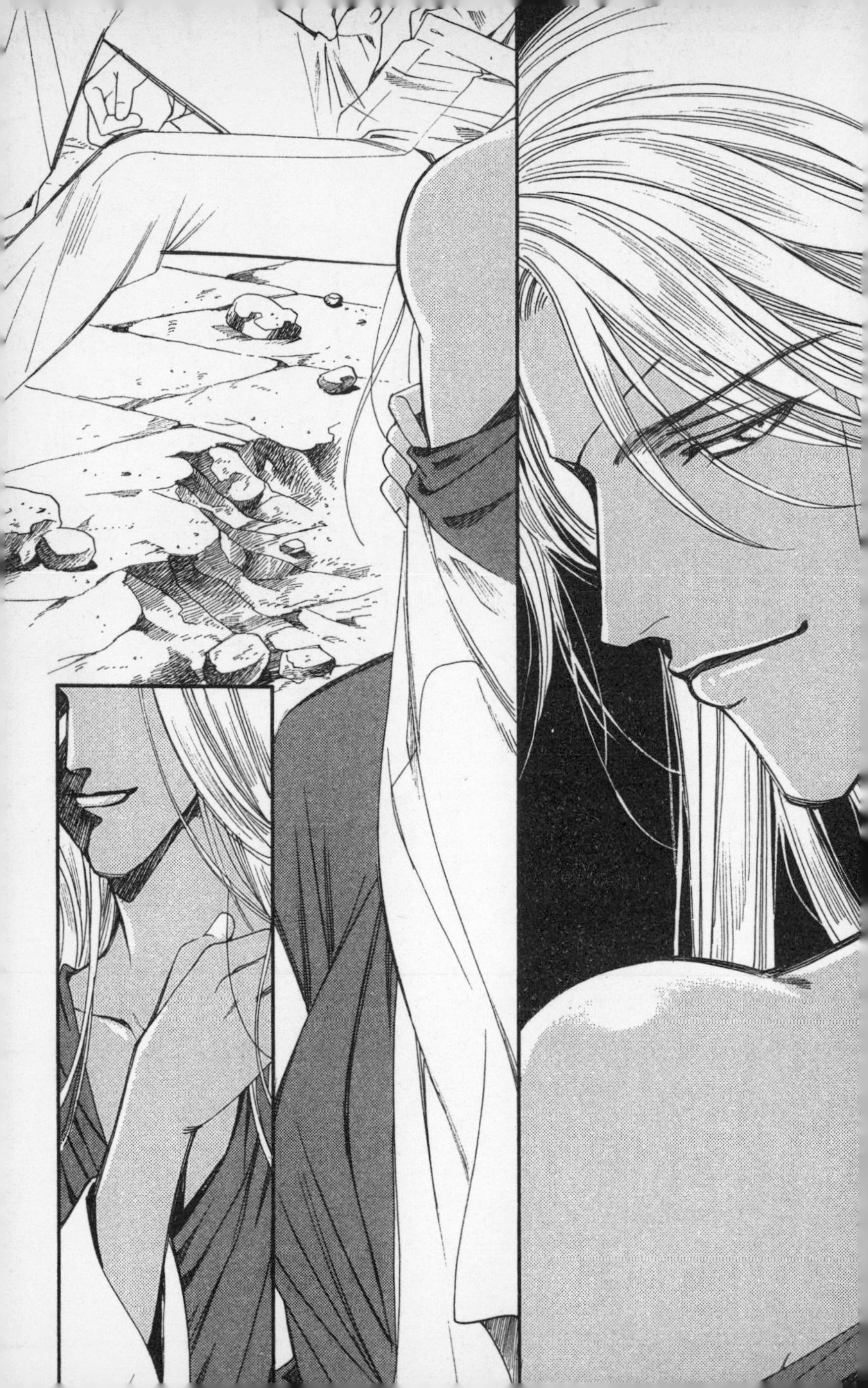

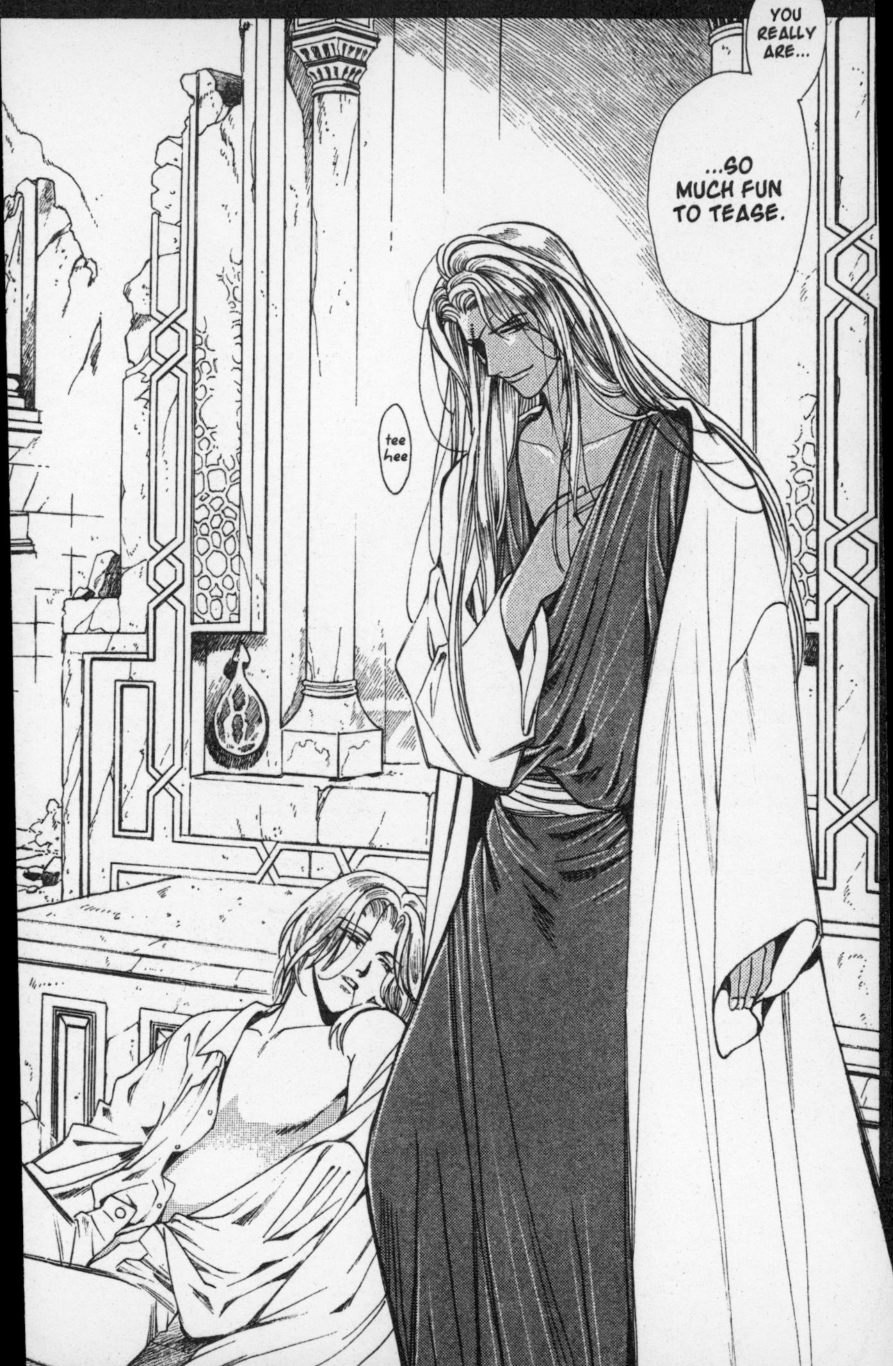
YOU REALLY ARE...
...SO MUCH FUN TO TEASE.
tee hee

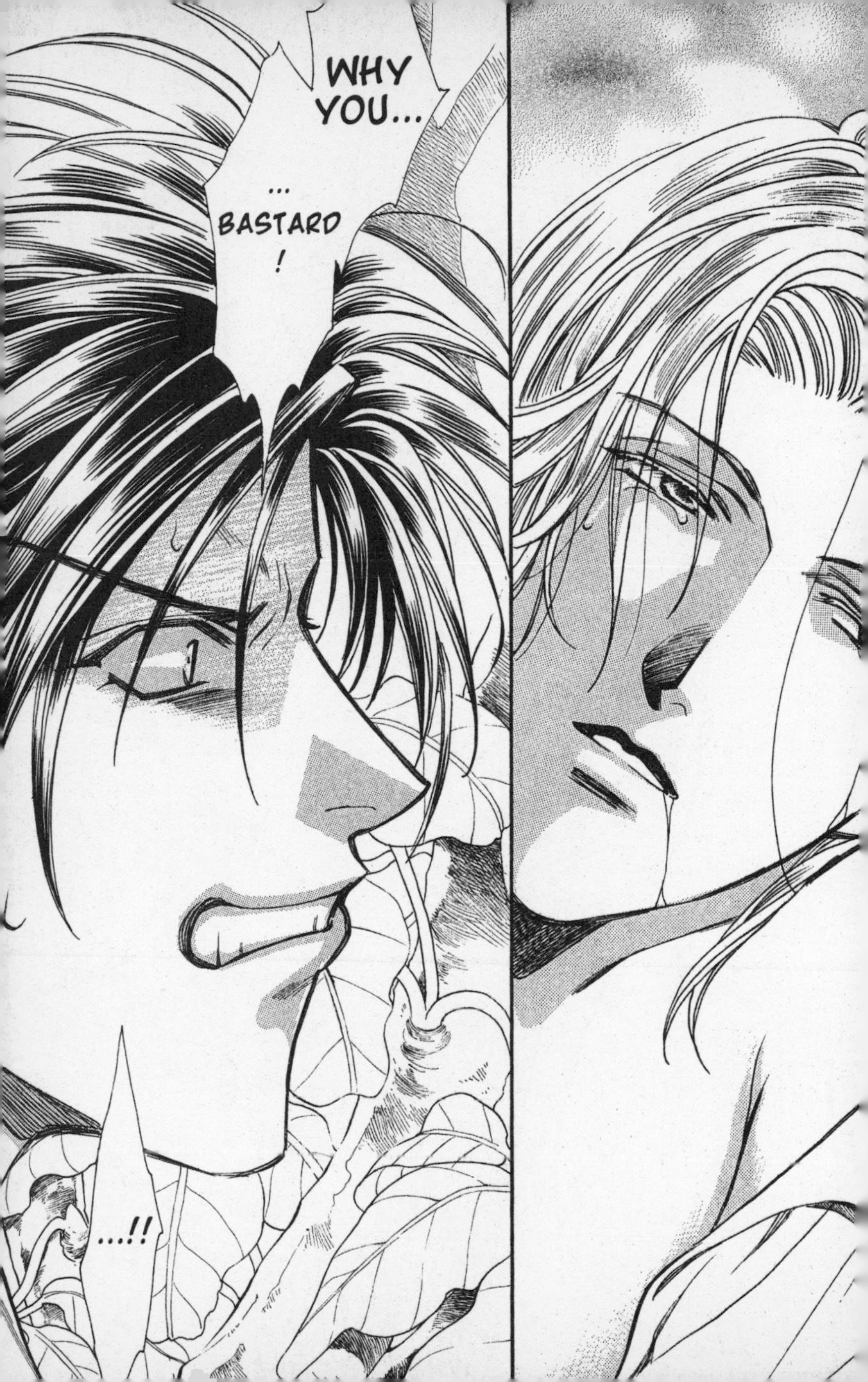
WHY YOU...
... BASTARD !
...!!

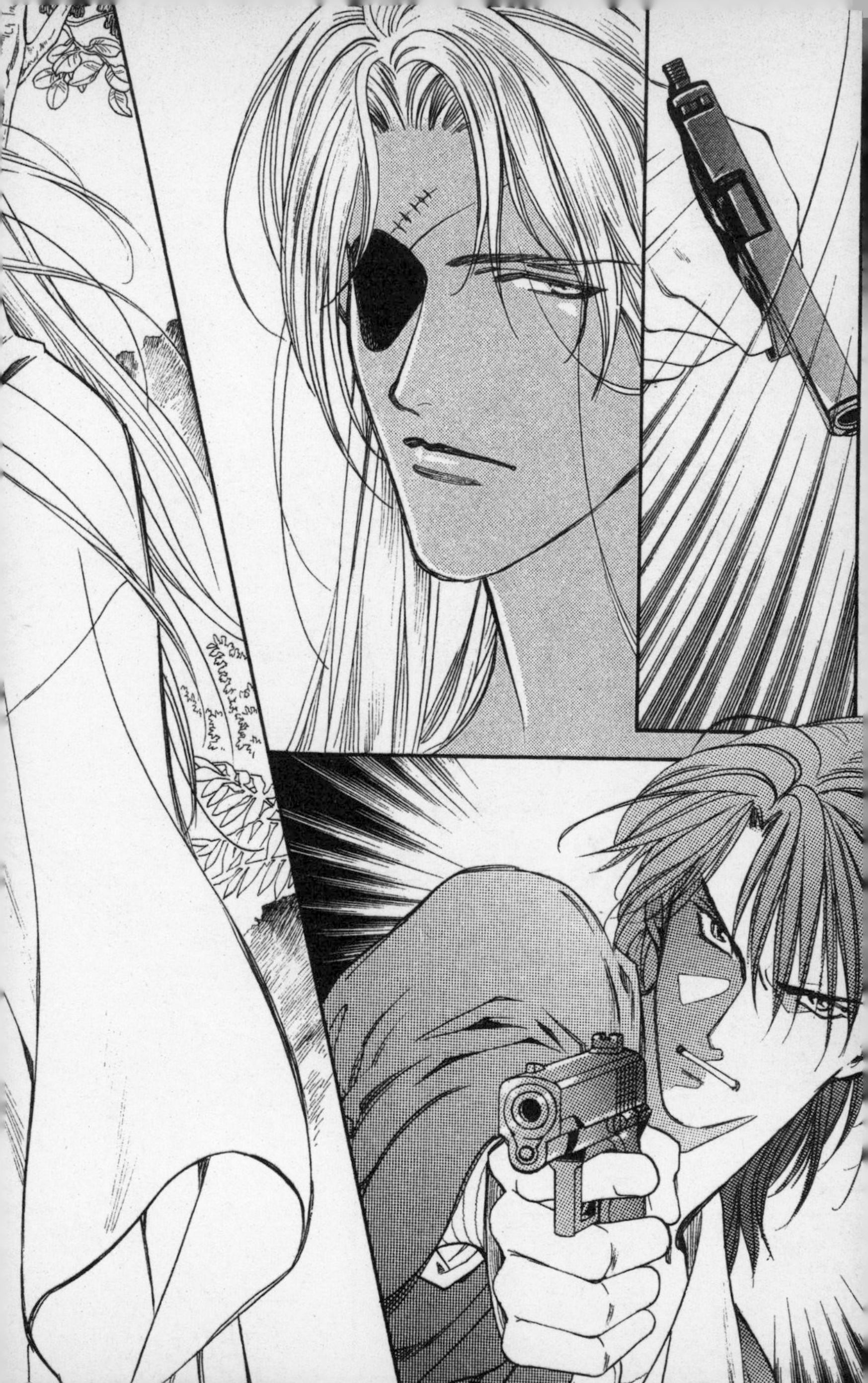

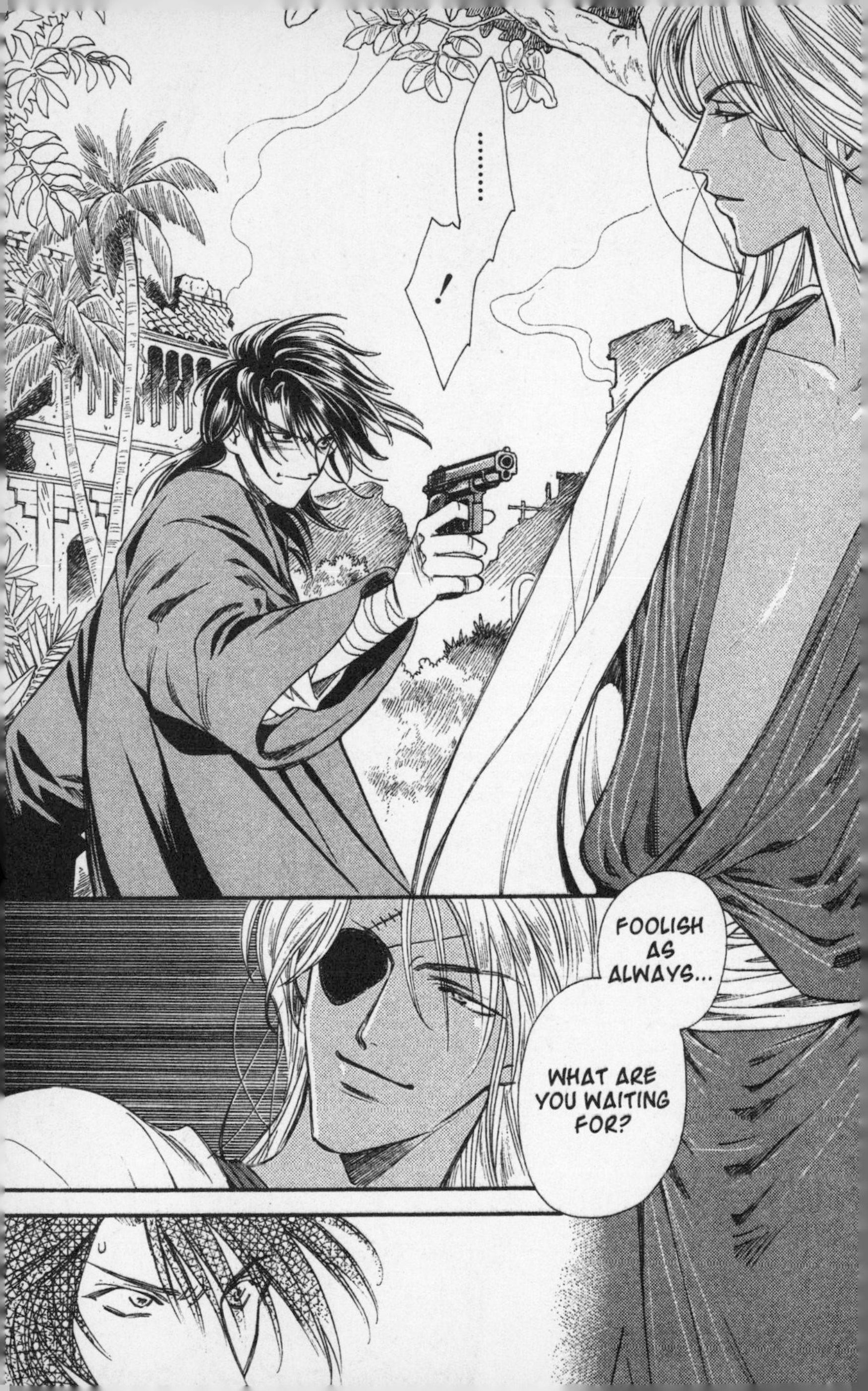
……!
FOOLISH AS ALWAYS...
WHAT ARE YOU WAITING FOR?

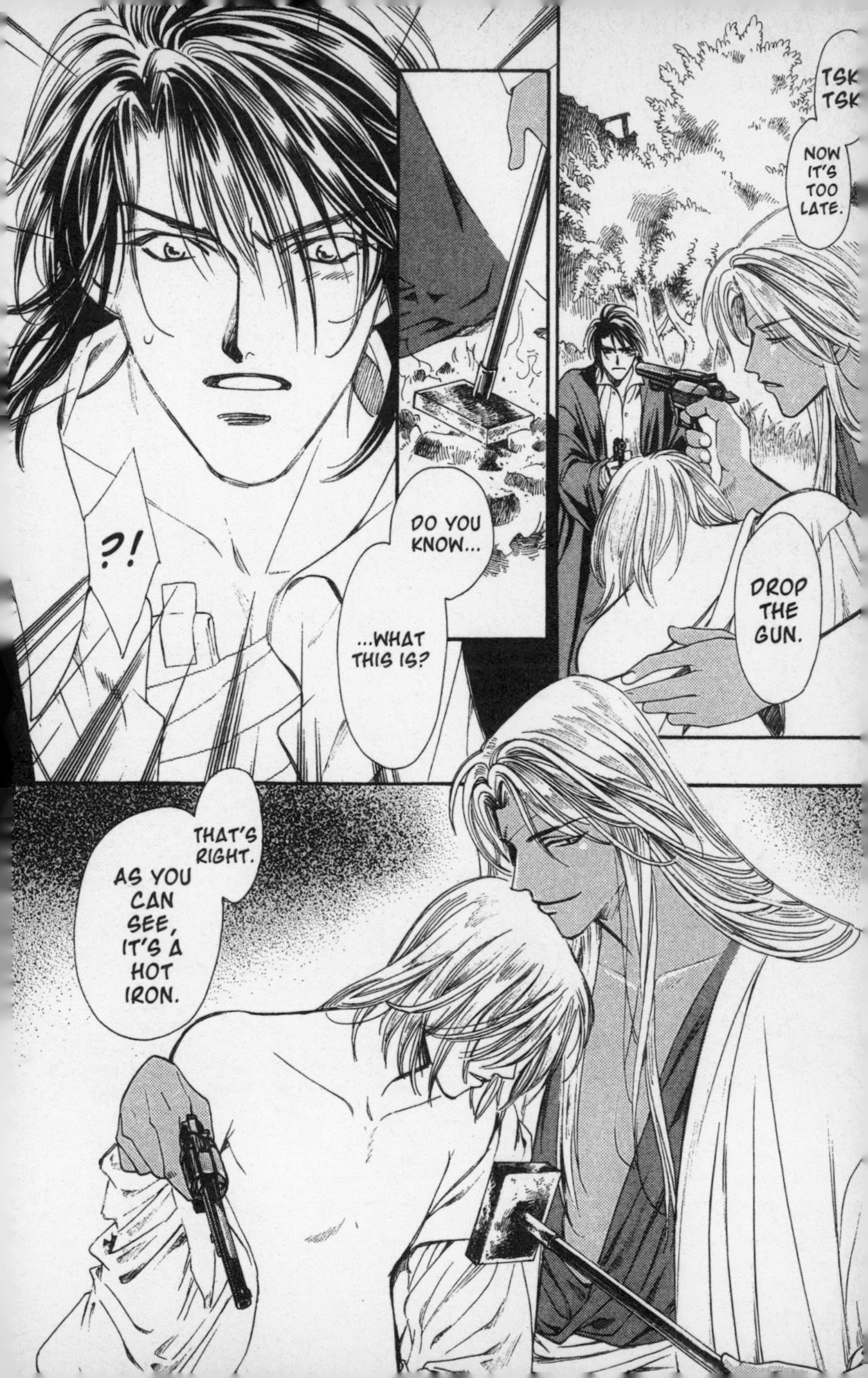
TSK TSK
NOW IT'S TOO LATE.
DROP THE GUN.
DO YOU KNOW...
...WHAT THIS IS?
?!
THAT'S RIGHT.
AS YOU CAN SEE, IT'S A HOT IRON.

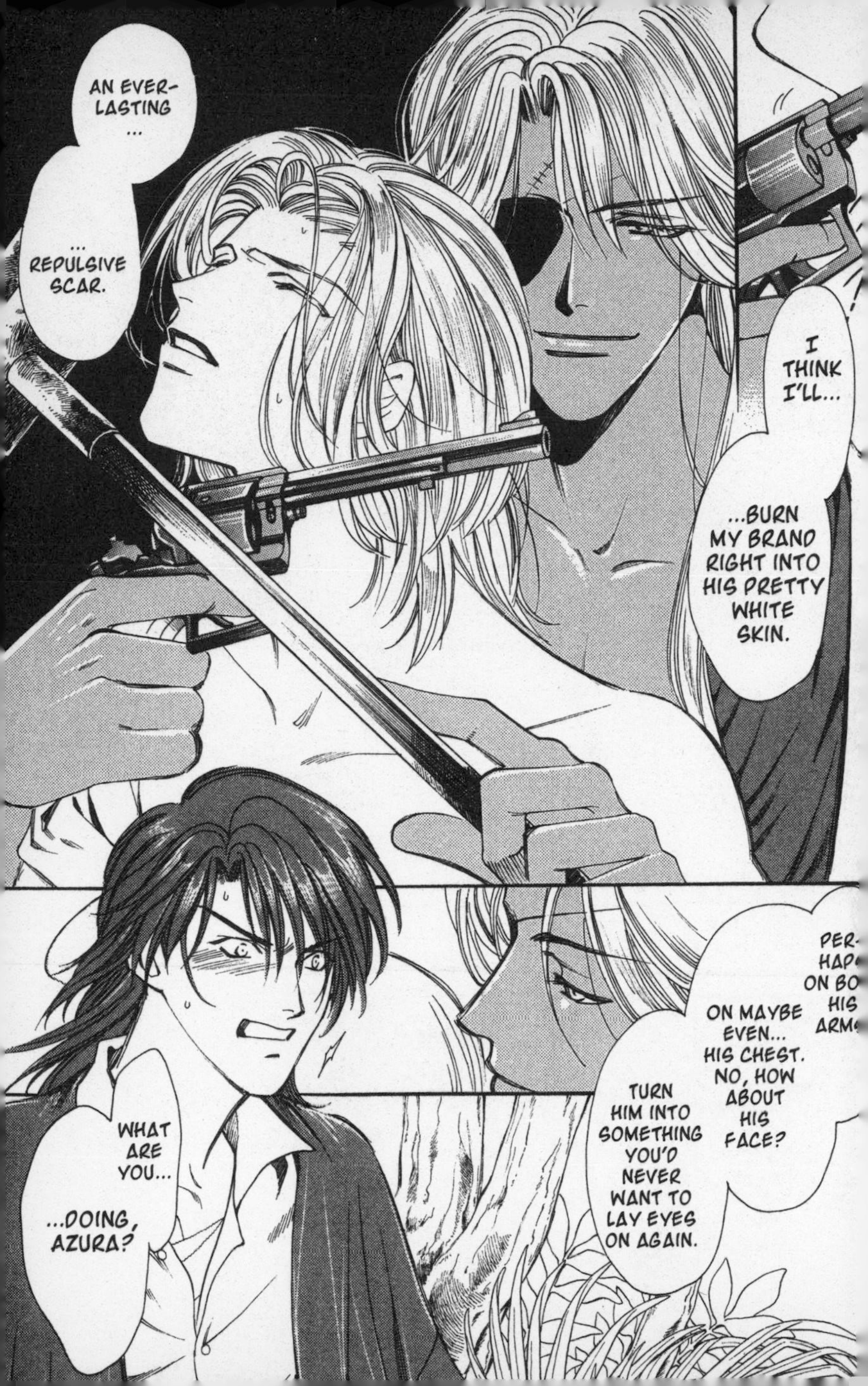
I THINK I'LL...
...BURN MY BRAND RIGHT INTO HIS PRETTY WHITE SKIN.
AN EVER-LASTING ...
... REPULSIVE SCAR.
PER-HAP ON BO HIS ARM
ON MAYBE EVEN... HIS CHEST. NO, HOW ABOUT HIS FACE?
TURN HIM INTO SOMETHING YOU'D NEVER WANT TO LAY EYES ON AGAIN.
WHAT ARE YOU...
...DOING, AZURA?

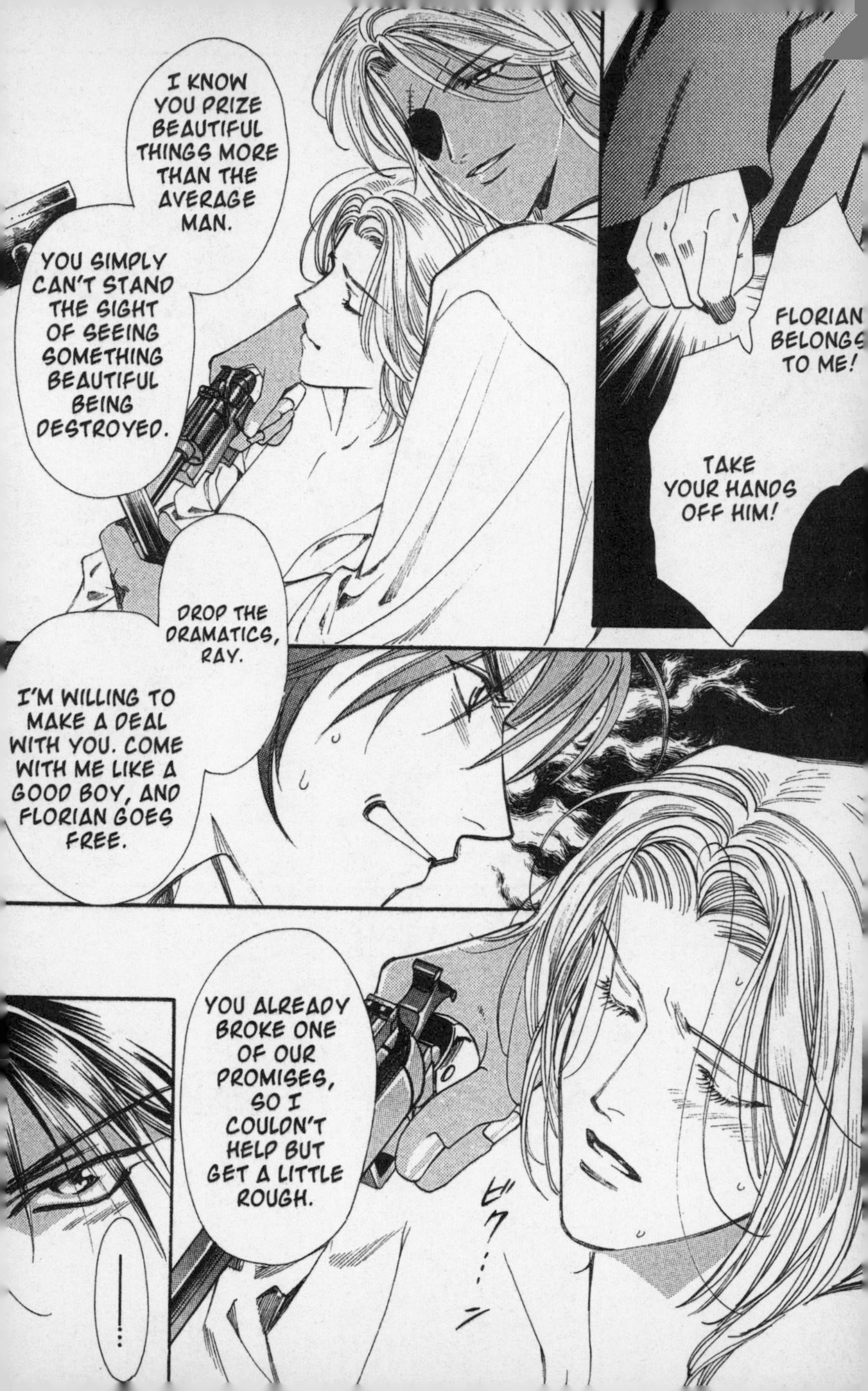
FLORIAN BELONGS TO ME!
TAKE YOUR HANDS OFF HIM!
I KNOW YOU PRIZE BEAUTIFUL THINGS MORE THAN THE AVERAGE MAN.
YOU SIMPLY CAN'T STAND THE SIGHT OF SEEING SOMETHING BEAUTIFUL BEING DESTROYED.
DROP THE DRAMATICS, RAY.
I'M WILLING TO MAKE A DEAL WITH YOU. COME WITH ME LIKE A GOOD BOY, AND FLORIAN GOES FREE.
YOU ALREADY BROKE ONE OF OUR PROMISES, SO I COULDN'T HELP BUT GET A LITTLE ROUGH.
ビク…
……

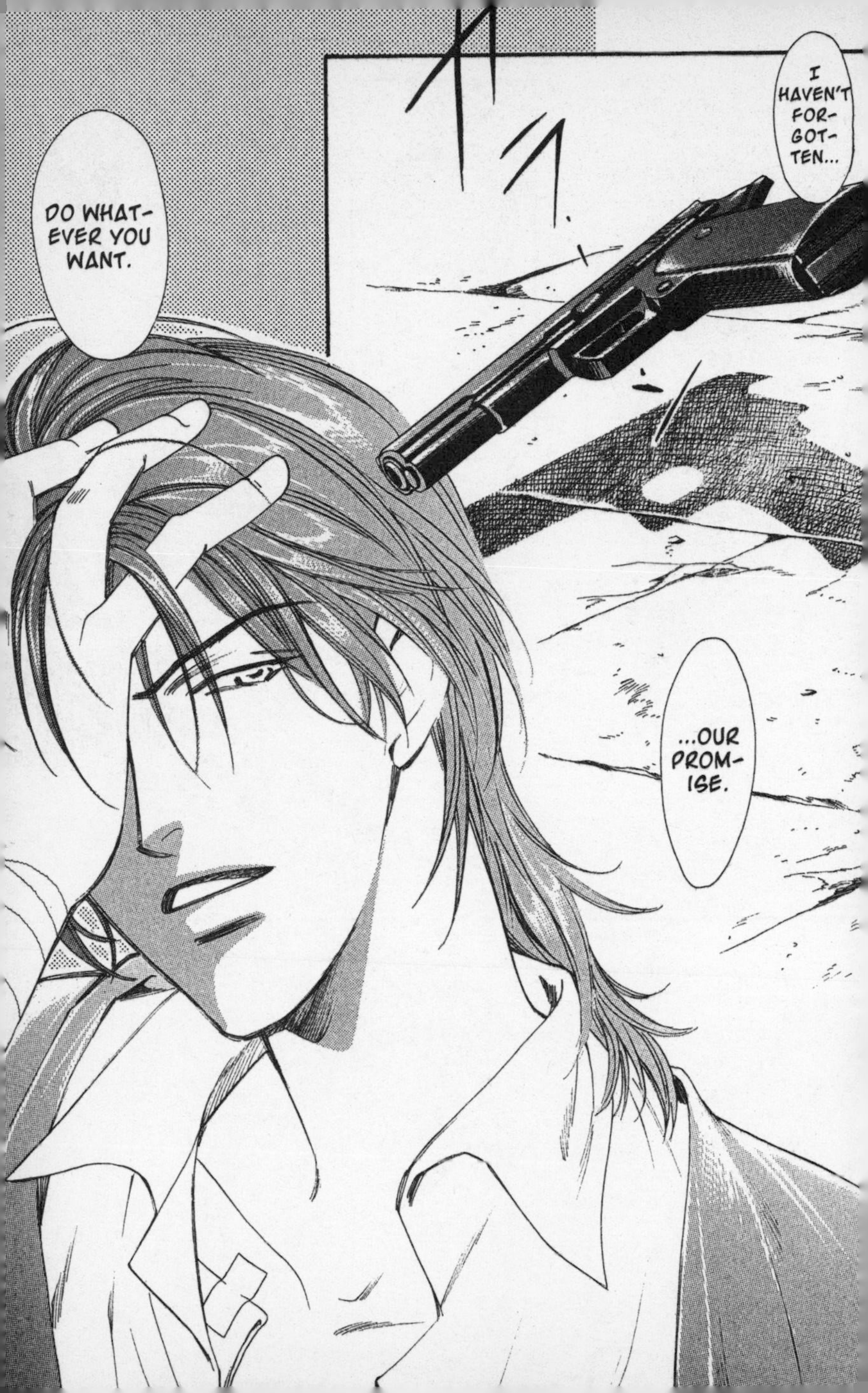
I HAVEN'T FOR-GOT-TEN...
...OUR PROM-ISE.
DO WHAT-EVER YOU WANT.

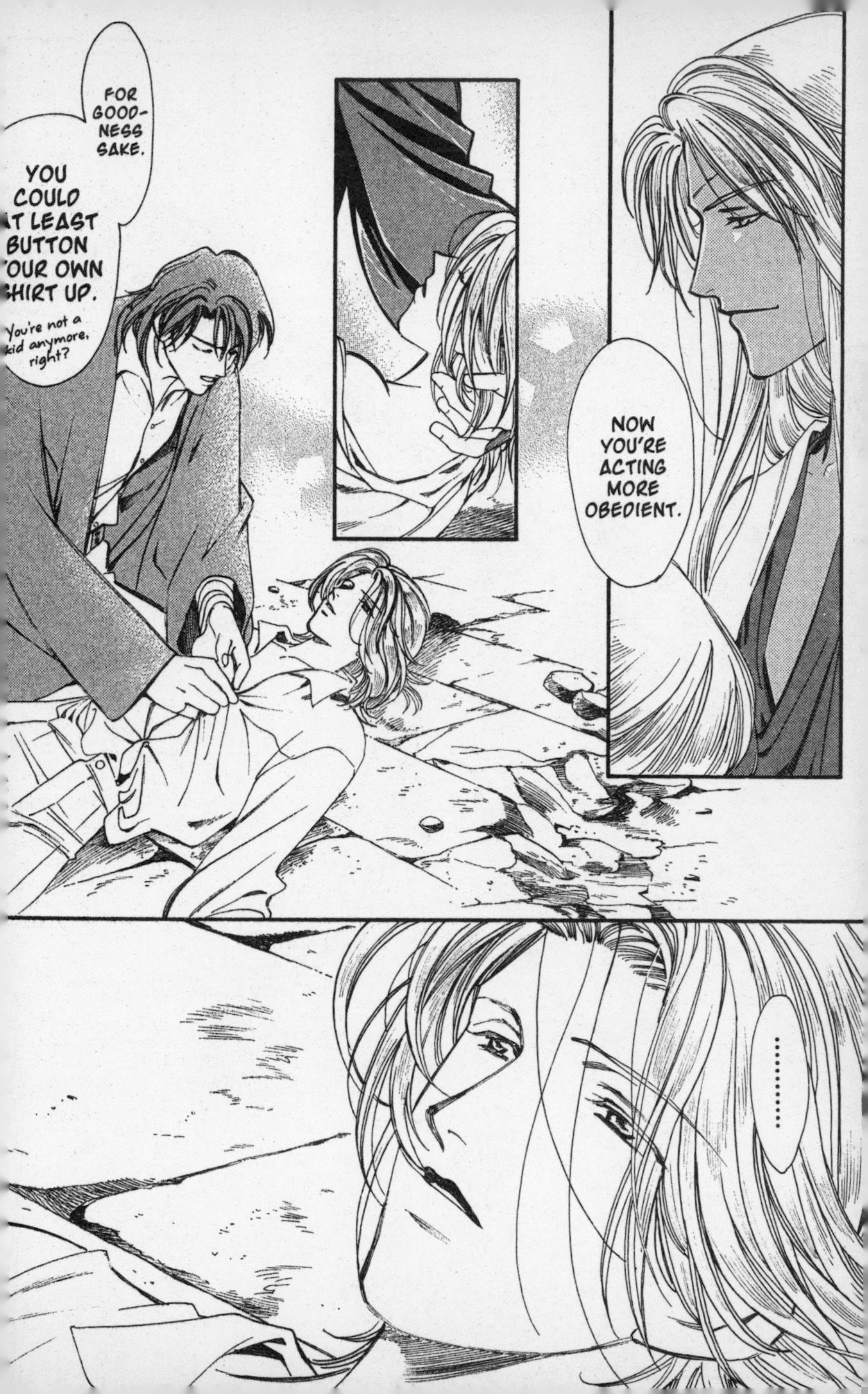
NOW YOU'RE ACTING MORE OBEDIENT.
FOR GOODNESS SAKE.
YOU COULD AT LEAST BUTTON YOUR OWN SHIRT UP.
You're not a kid anymore, right?
……

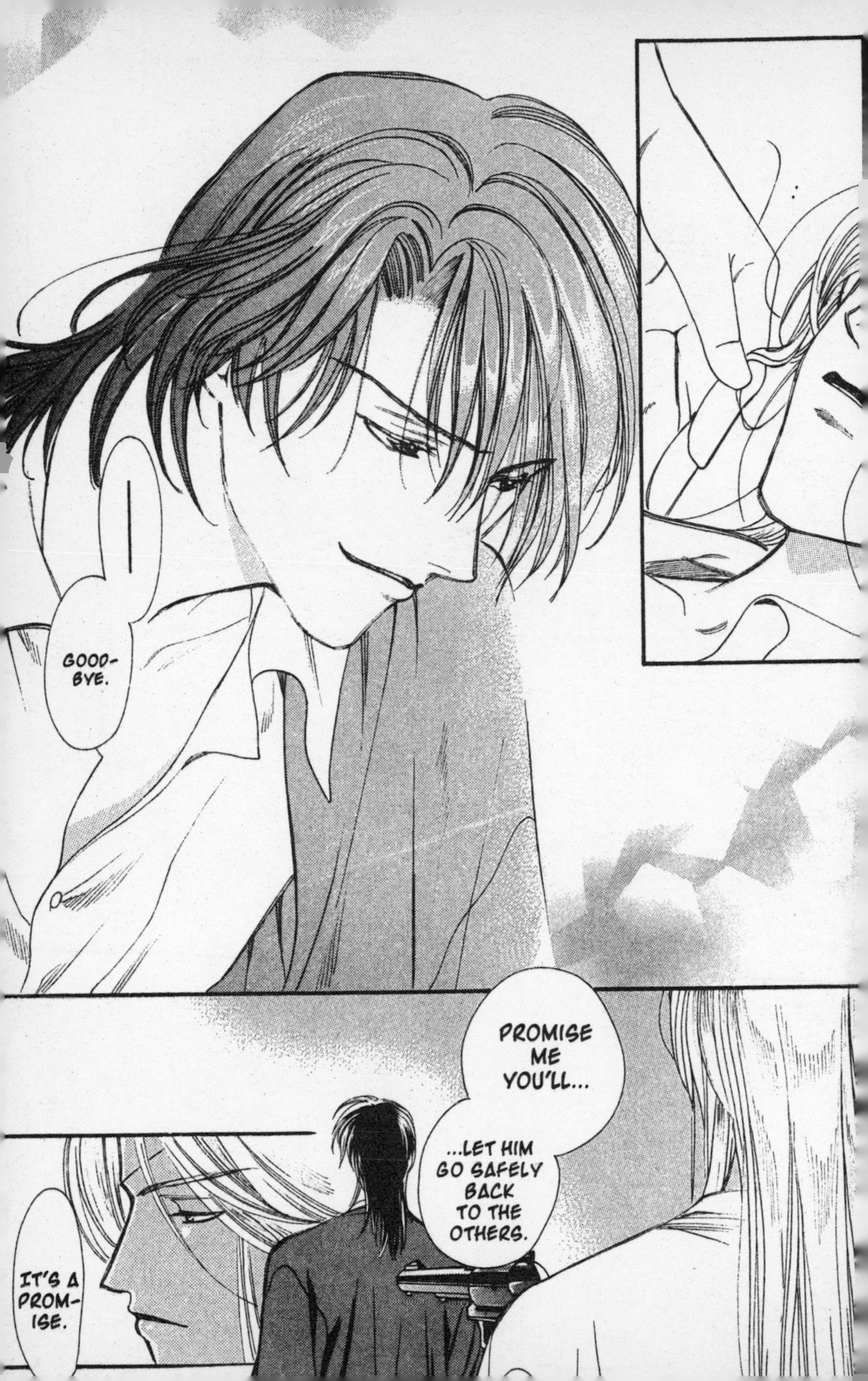
GOOD-BYE.
PROMISE ME YOU'LL...
...LET HIM GO SAFELY BACK TO THE OTHERS.
IT'S A PROM-ISE.

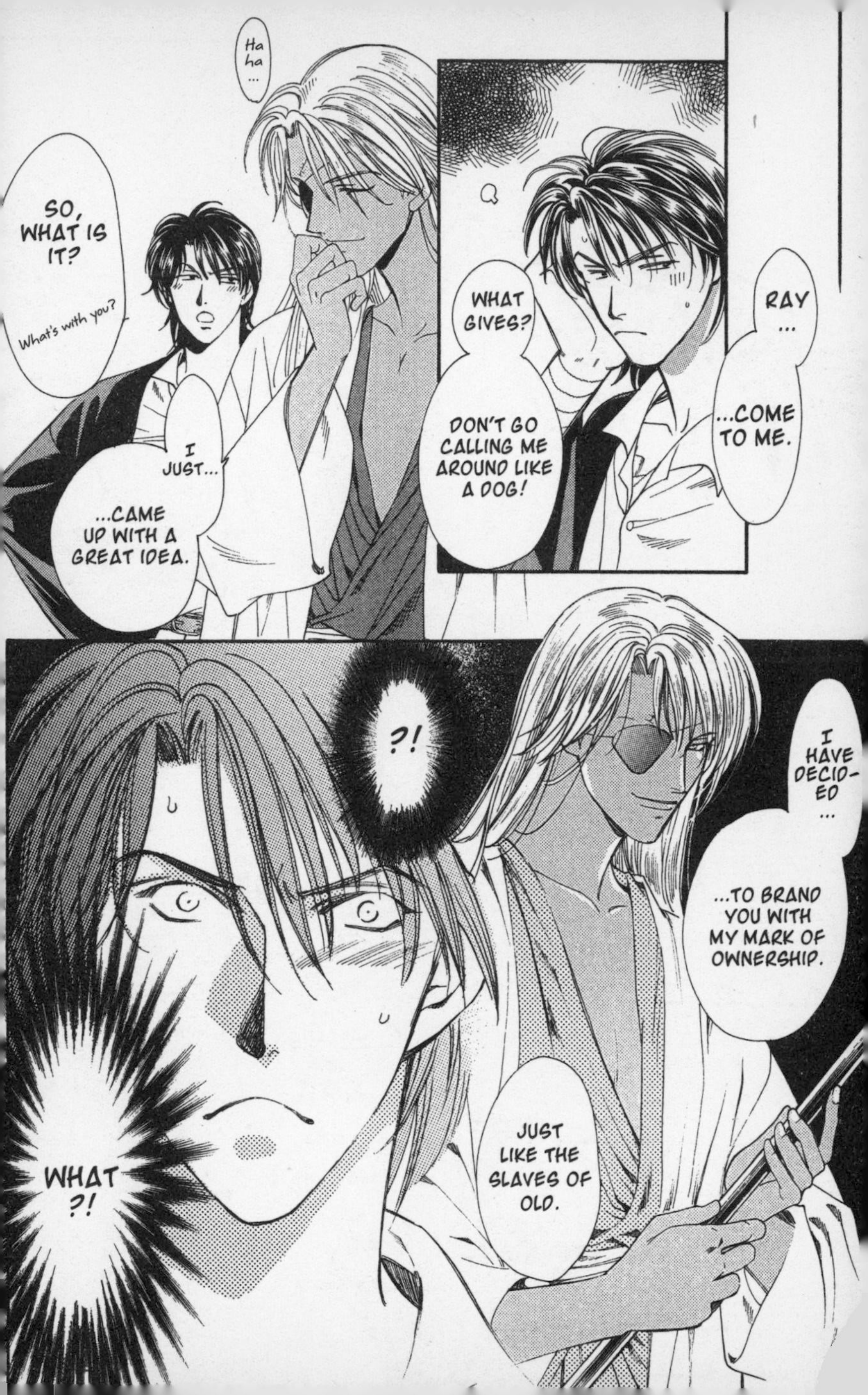

RAY ...
...COME TO ME.
WHAT GIVES?
DON'T GO CALLING ME AROUND LIKE A DOG!
Ha ha ...
SO, WHAT IS IT?
What's with you?
I JUST...
...CAME UP WITH A GREAT IDEA.
I HAVE DECID-ED ...
...TO BRAND YOU WITH MY MARK OF OWNERSHIP.
?!
JUST LIKE THE SLAVES OF OLD.
WHAT ?!

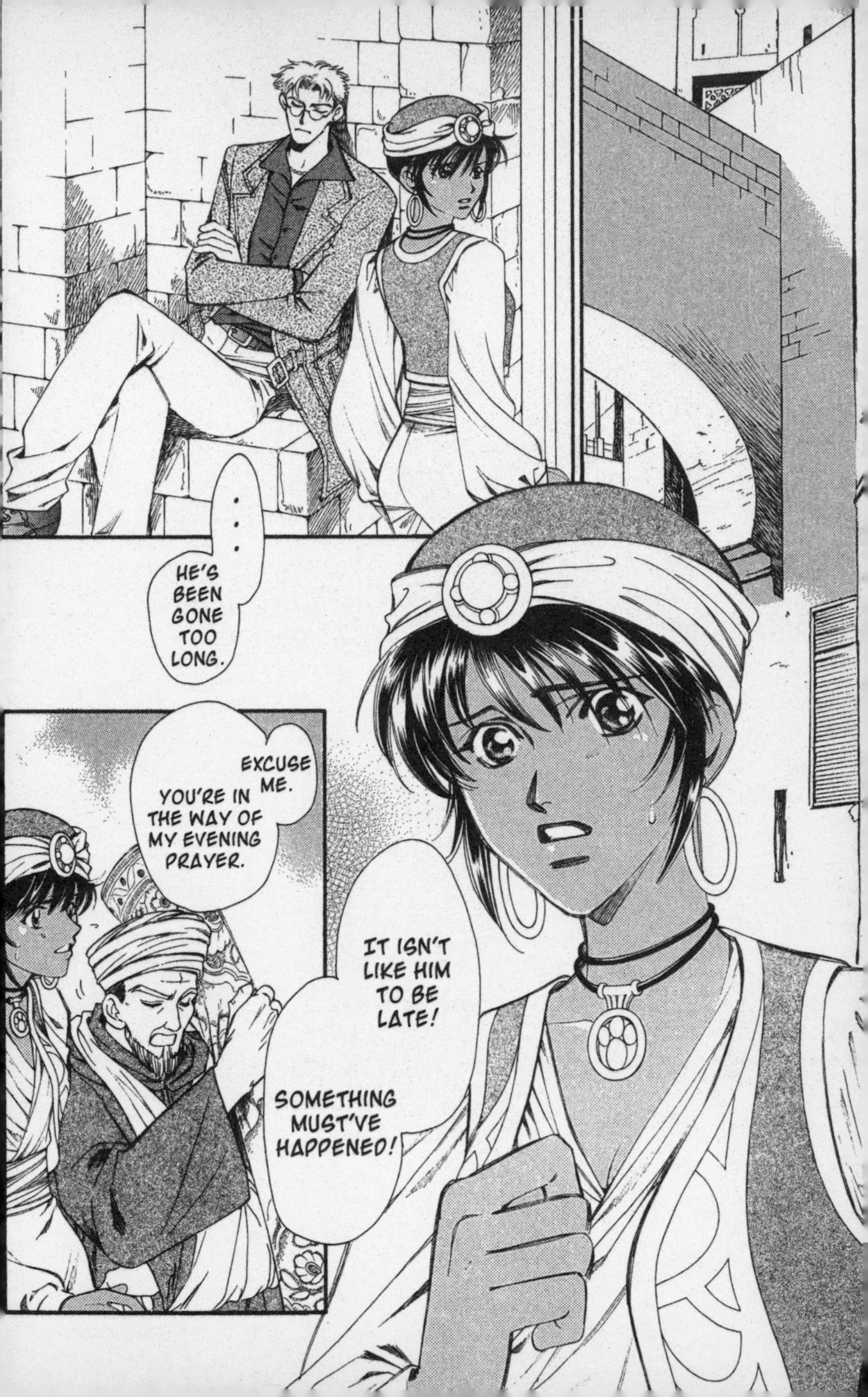

. . .
HE'S BEEN GONE TOO LONG.
IT ISN'T LIKE HIM TO BE LATE!
SOMETHING MUST'VE HAPPENED!
EXCUSE ME.
YOU'RE IN THE WAY OF MY EVENING PRAYER.

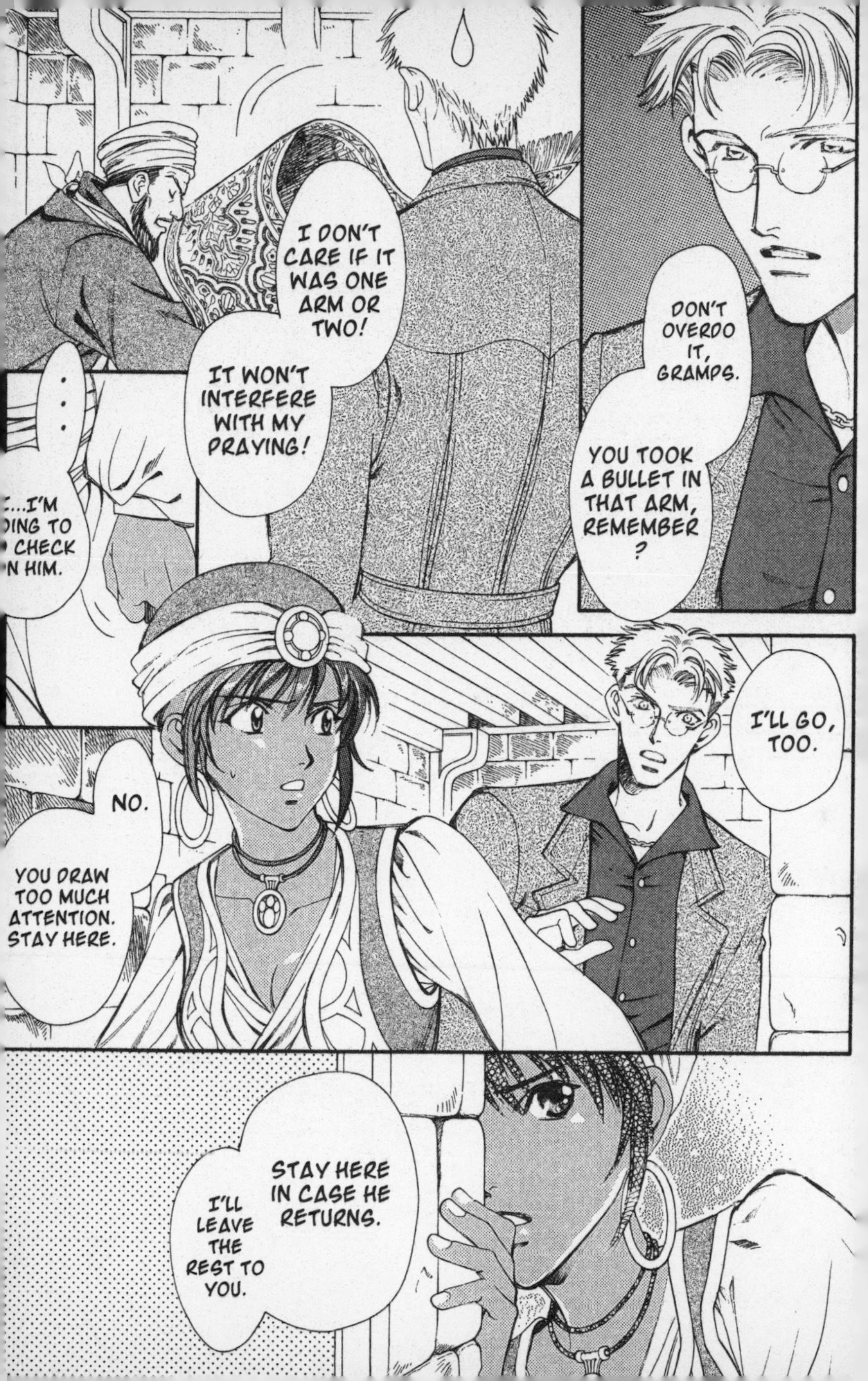
DON'T OVERDO IT, GRAMPS.
YOU TOOK A BULLET IN THAT ARM, REMEMBER?
I DON'T CARE IF IT WAS ONE ARM OR TWO!
IT WON'T INTERFERE WITH MY PRAYING!
...
...I'M OING TO CHECK N HIM.
I'LL GO, TOO.
NO.
YOU DRAW TOO MUCH ATTENTION. STAY HERE.
STAY HERE IN CASE HE RETURNS.
I'LL LEAVE THE REST TO YOU.

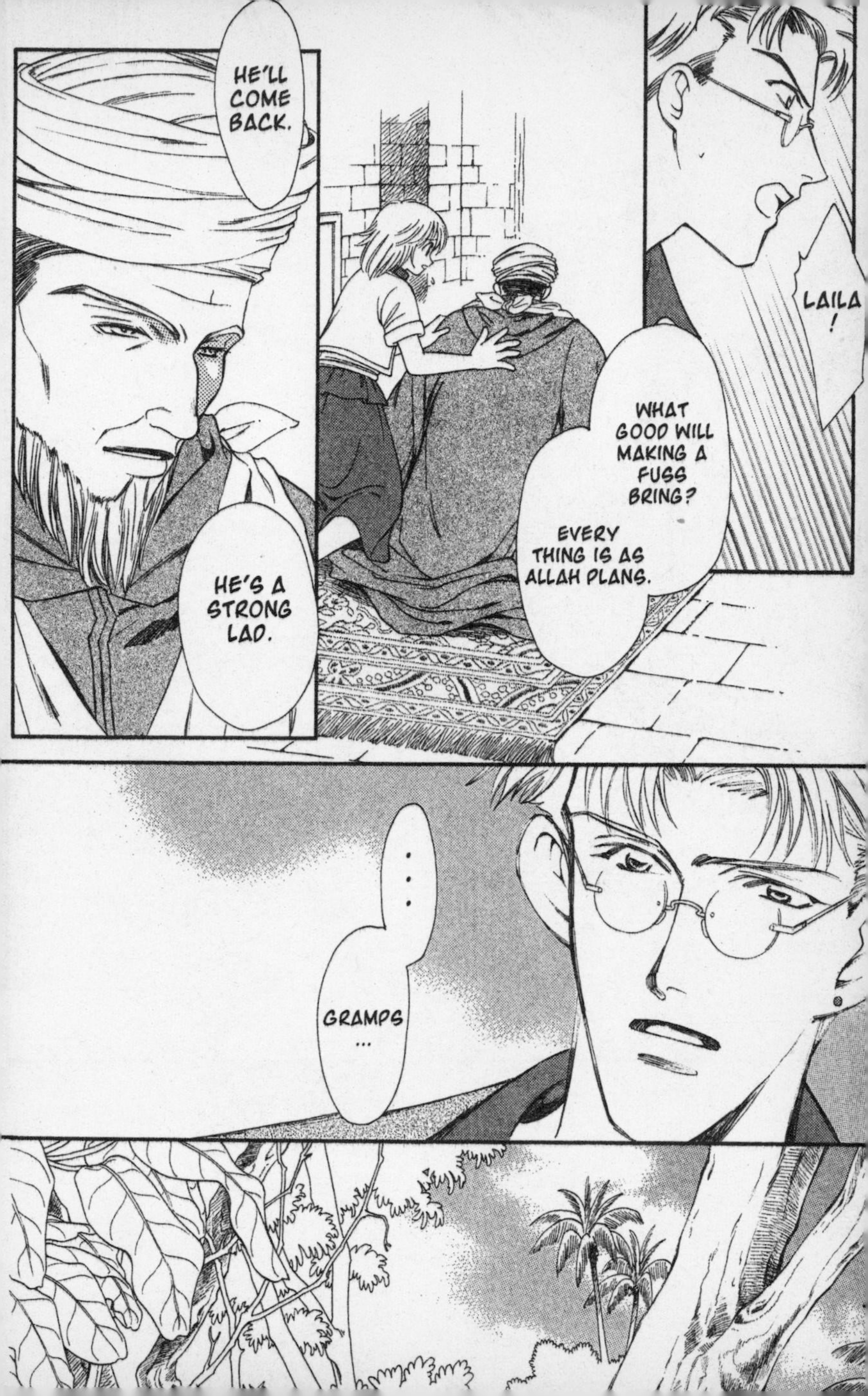
LAILA!
WHAT GOOD WILL MAKING A FUSS BRING?
EVERY THING IS AS ALLAH PLANS.
HE'LL COME BACK.
HE'S A STRONG LAD.
...
GRAMPS ...

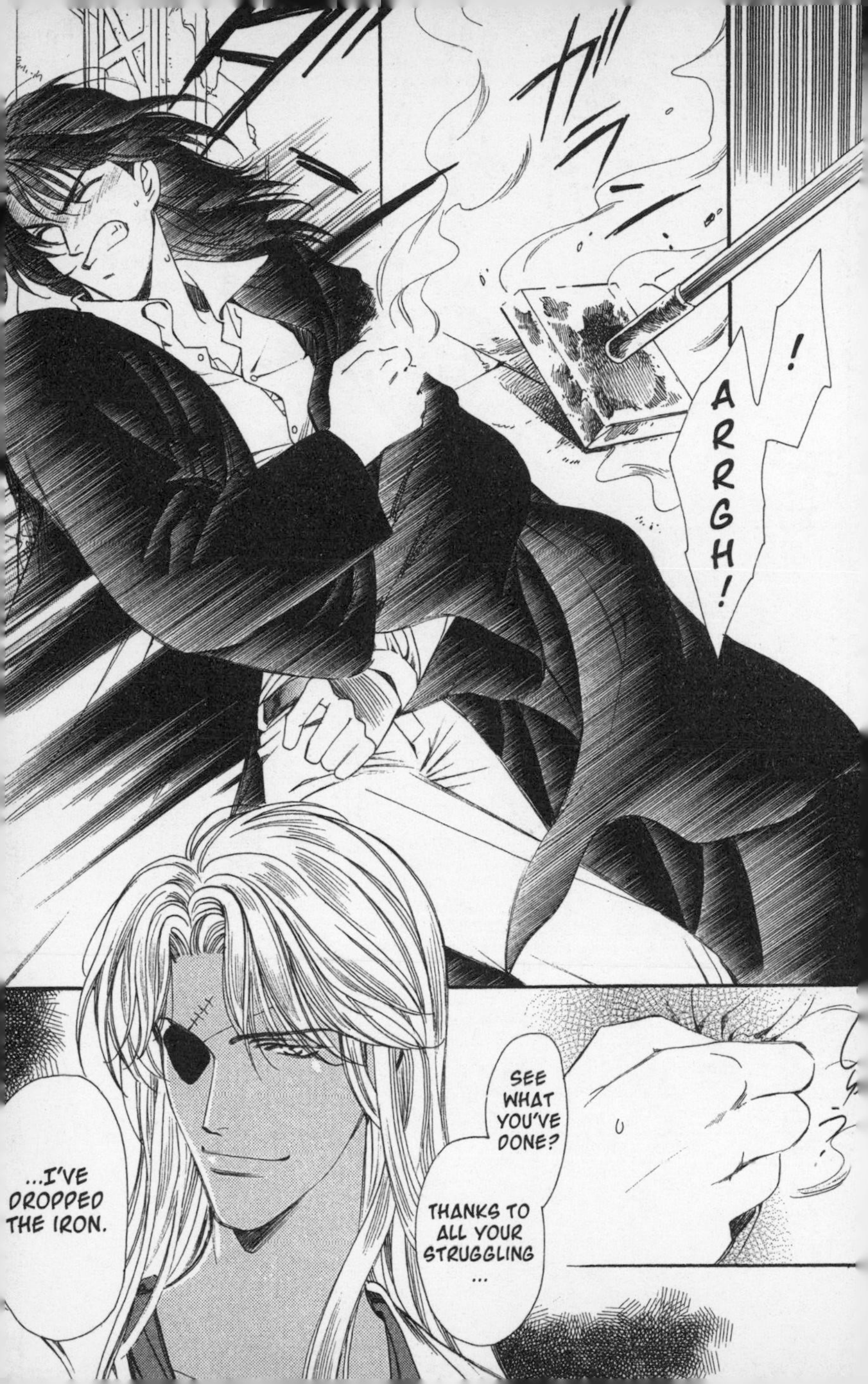
ARRGH!
!
SEE WHAT YOU'VE DONE?
THANKS TO ALL YOUR STRUGGLING ...
...I'VE DROPPED THE IRON.

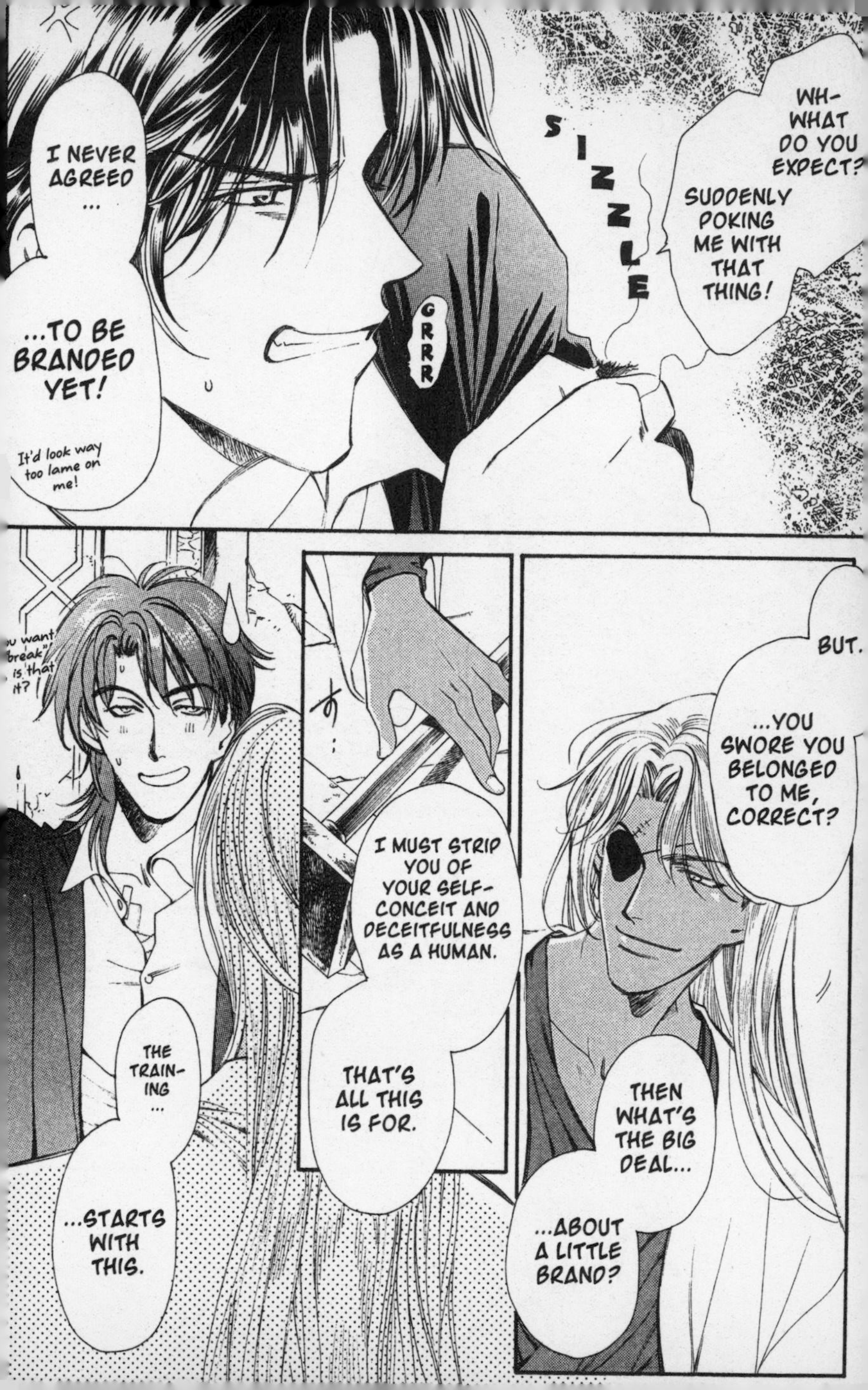
WH- WHAT DO YOU EXPECT?
SUDDENLY POKING ME WITH THAT THING!
SIZZLE
GRRR
I NEVER AGREED ...
...TO BE BRANDED YET!
It'd look way too lame on me!
BUT.
...YOU SWORE YOU BELONGED TO ME, CORRECT?
THEN WHAT'S THE BIG DEAL...
...ABOUT A LITTLE BRAND?
I MUST STRIP YOU OF YOUR SELF-CONCEIT AND DECEITFULNESS AS A HUMAN.
THAT'S ALL THIS IS FOR.
THE TRAIN-ING ...
...STARTS WITH THIS.

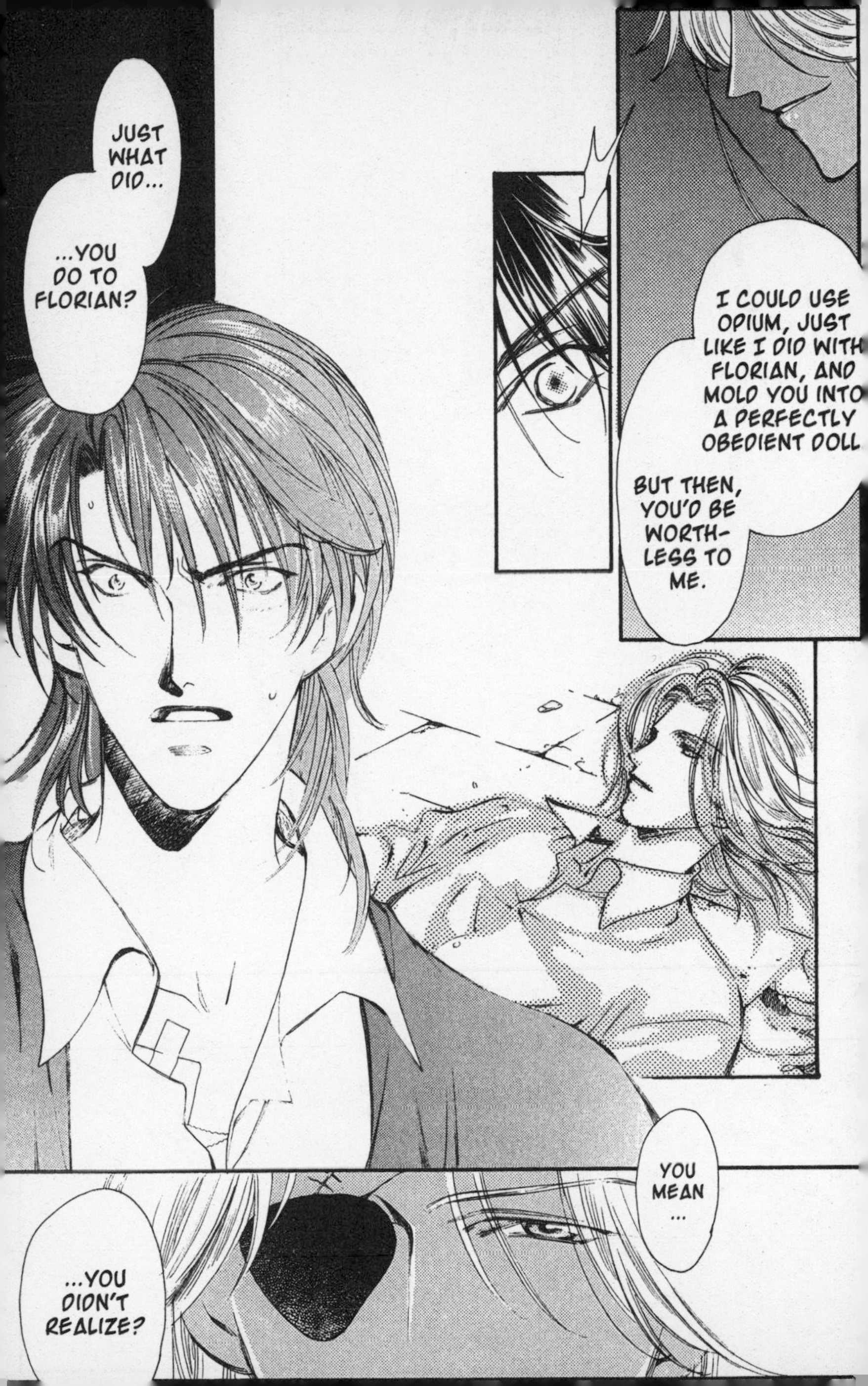
I COULD USE OPIUM, JUST LIKE I DID WITH FLORIAN, AND MOLD YOU INTO A PERFECTLY OBEDIENT DOLL
BUT THEN, YOU'D BE WORTH-LESS TO ME.
JUST WHAT DID...
...YOU DO TO FLORIAN?
YOU MEAN ...
...YOU DIDN'T REALIZE?

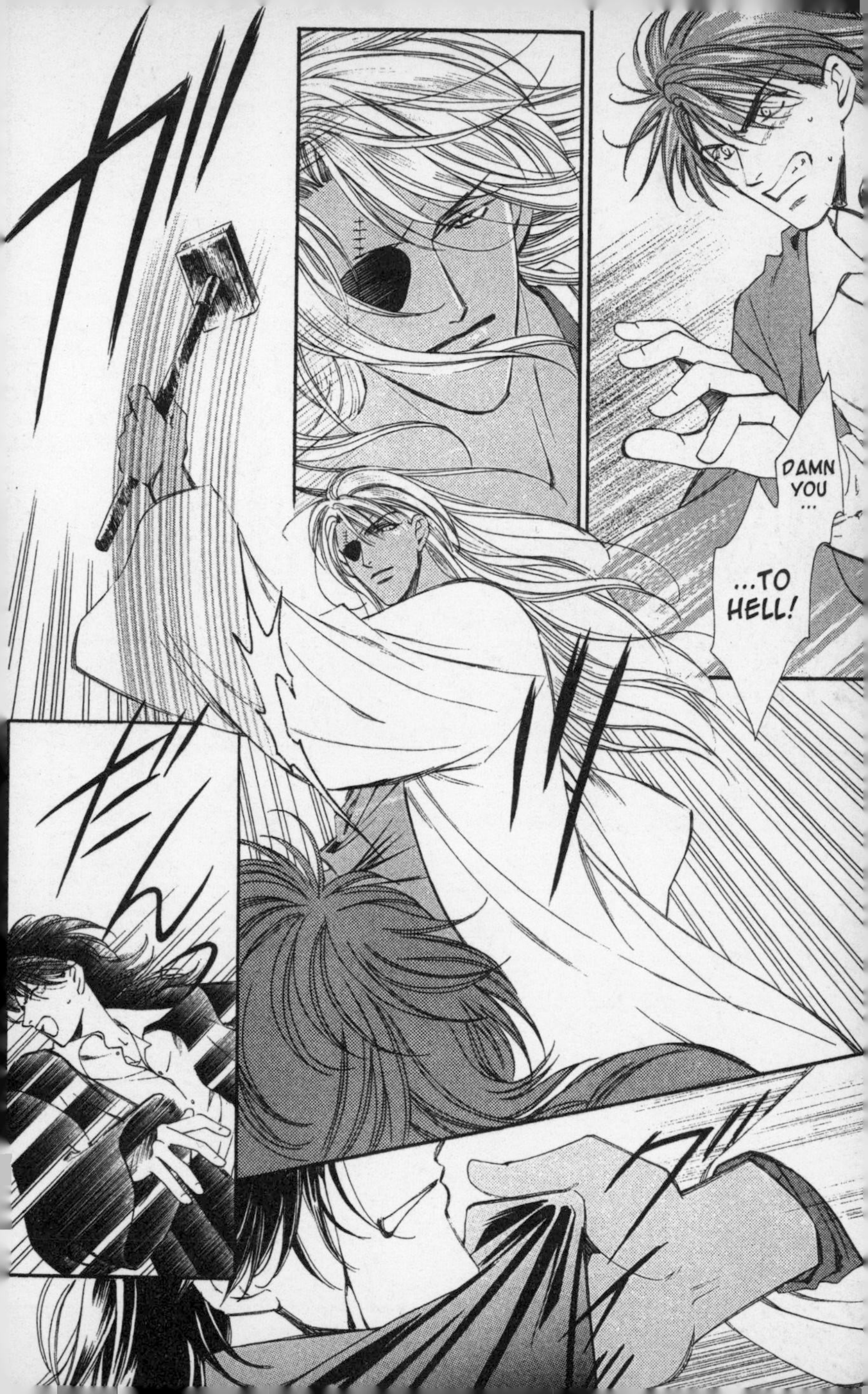
DAMN YOU ...
...TO HELL!

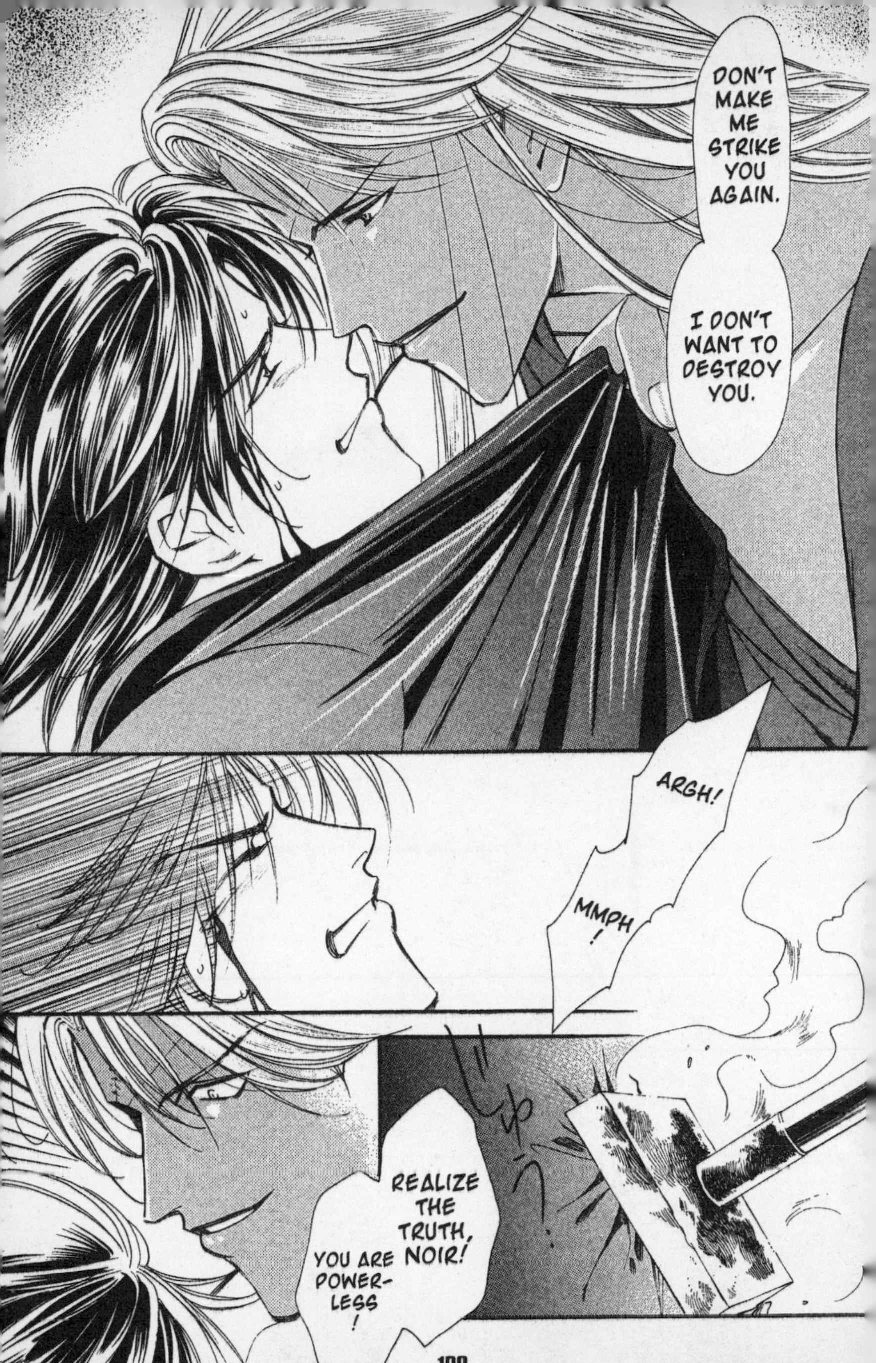
DON'T MAKE ME STRIKE YOU AGAIN.
I DON'T WANT TO DESTROY YOU.
ARGH!
MMPH!
REALIZE THE TRUTH, NOIR!
YOU ARE POWER-LESS!

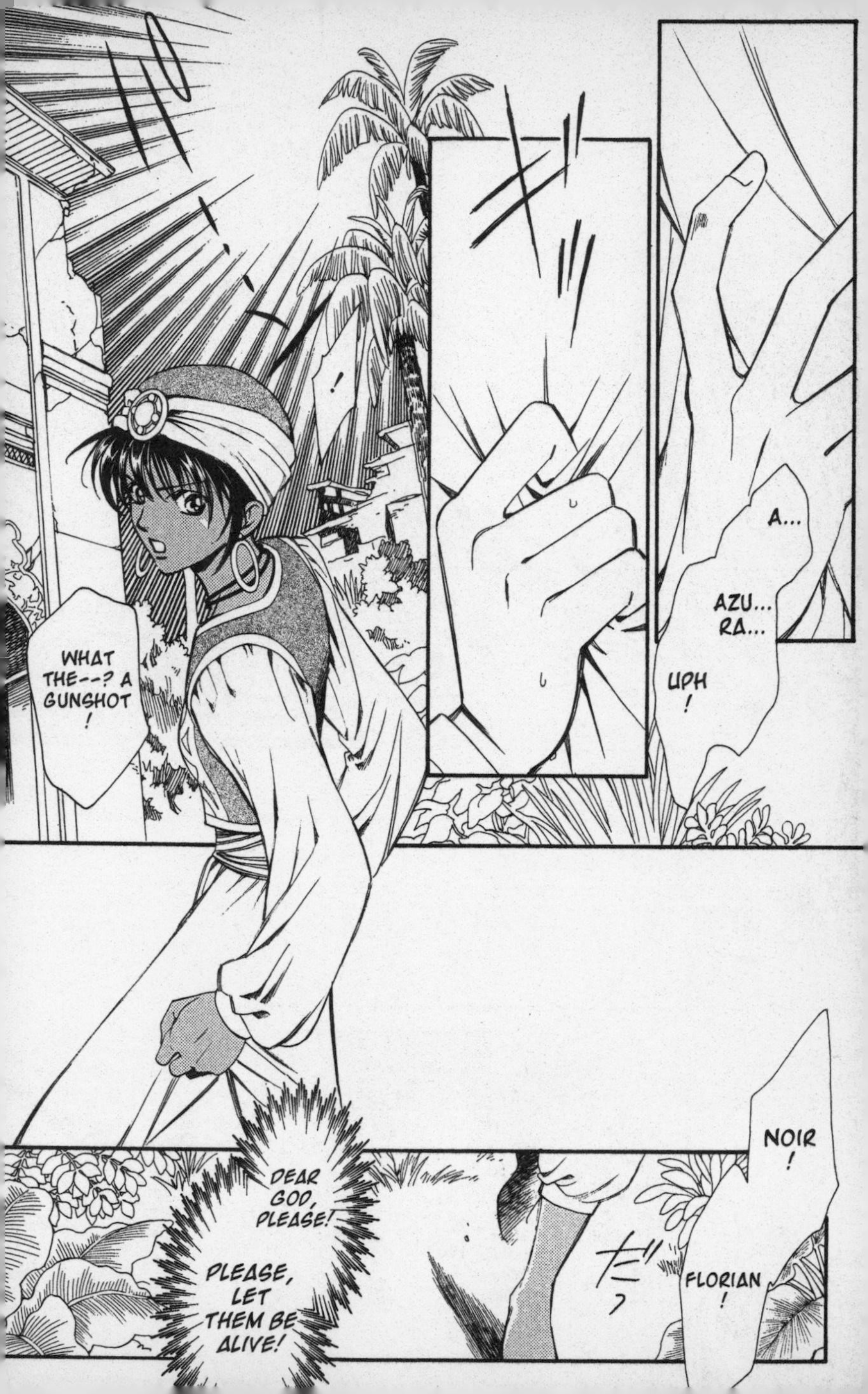
A...
AZU... RA...
UPH!
!
WHAT THE--? A GUNSHOT!
NOIR!
FLORIAN!
DEAR GOD, PLEASE!
PLEASE, LET THEM BE ALIVE!

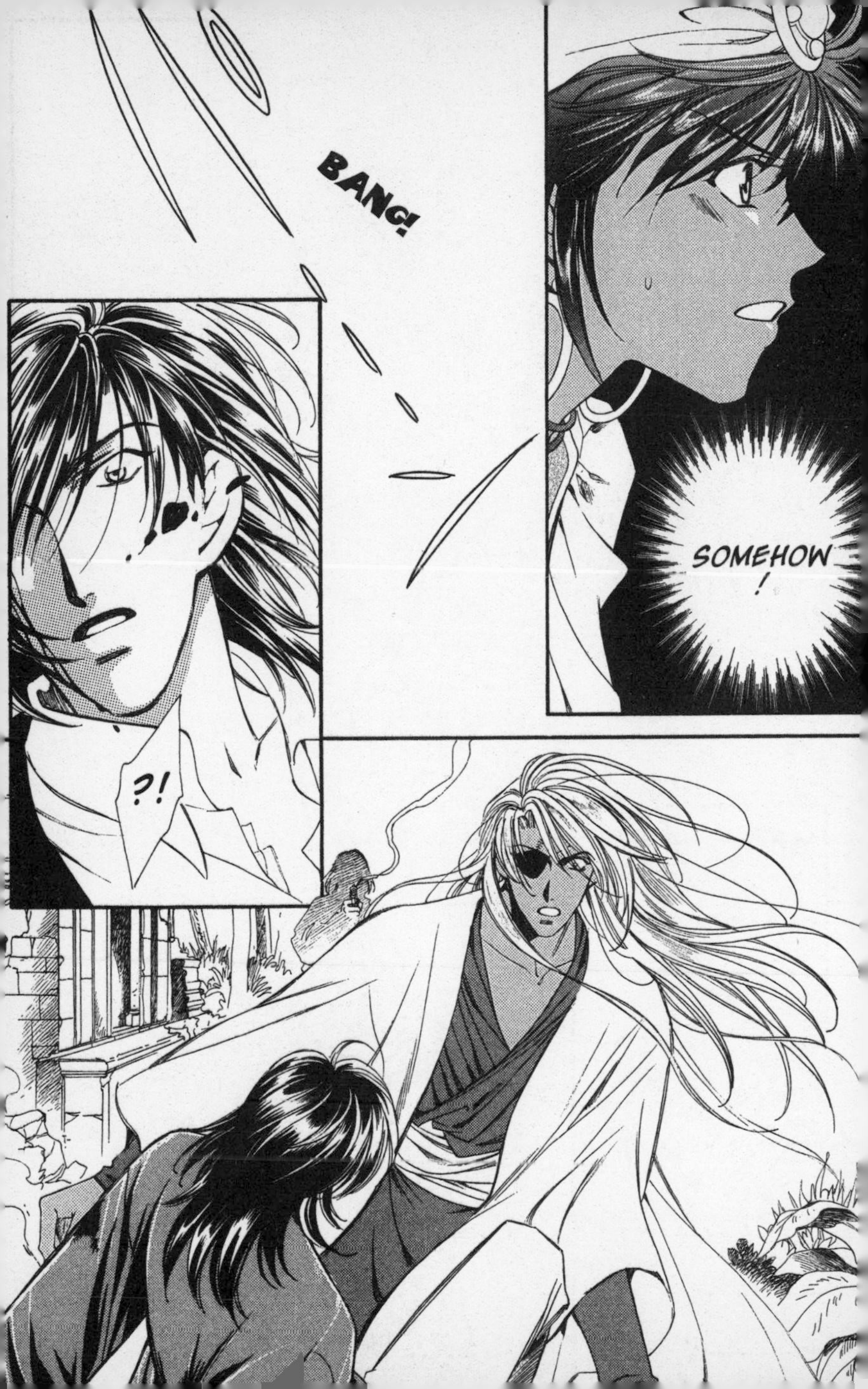
SOMEHOW!
BANG!
?!

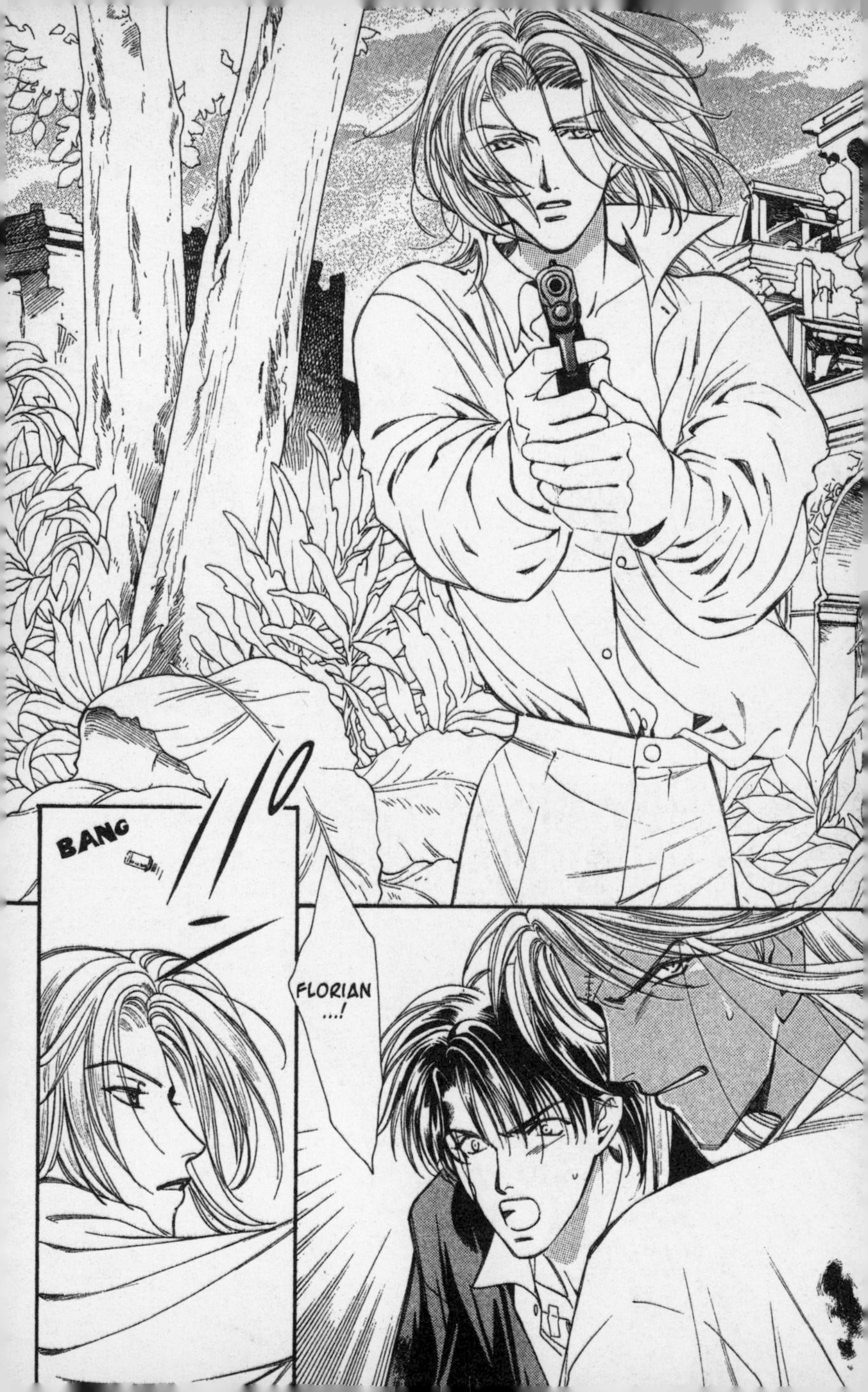
BANG
FLORIAN ...!

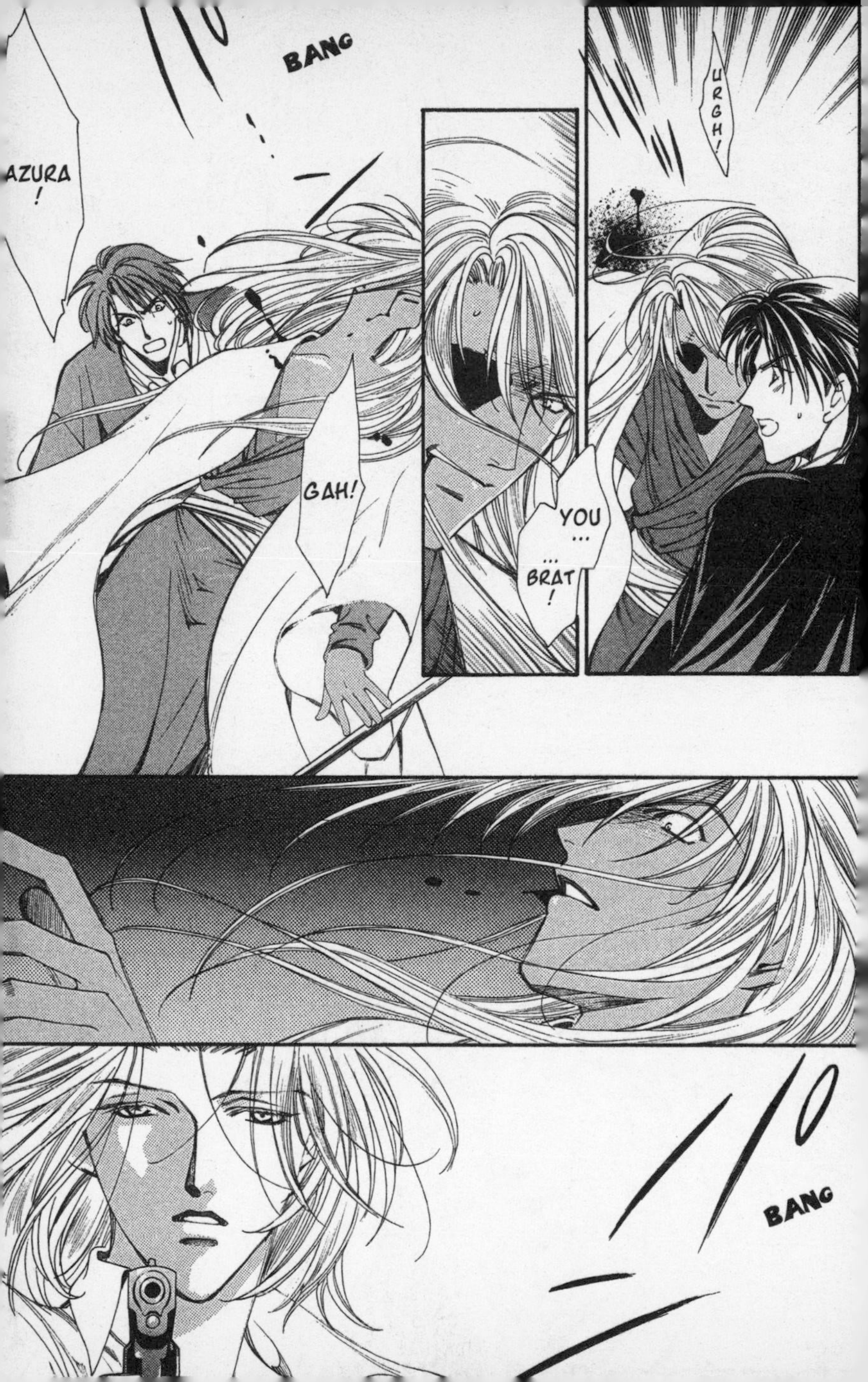
URGH!
YOU... ...BRAT!
BANG
AZURA!
GAH!
BANG

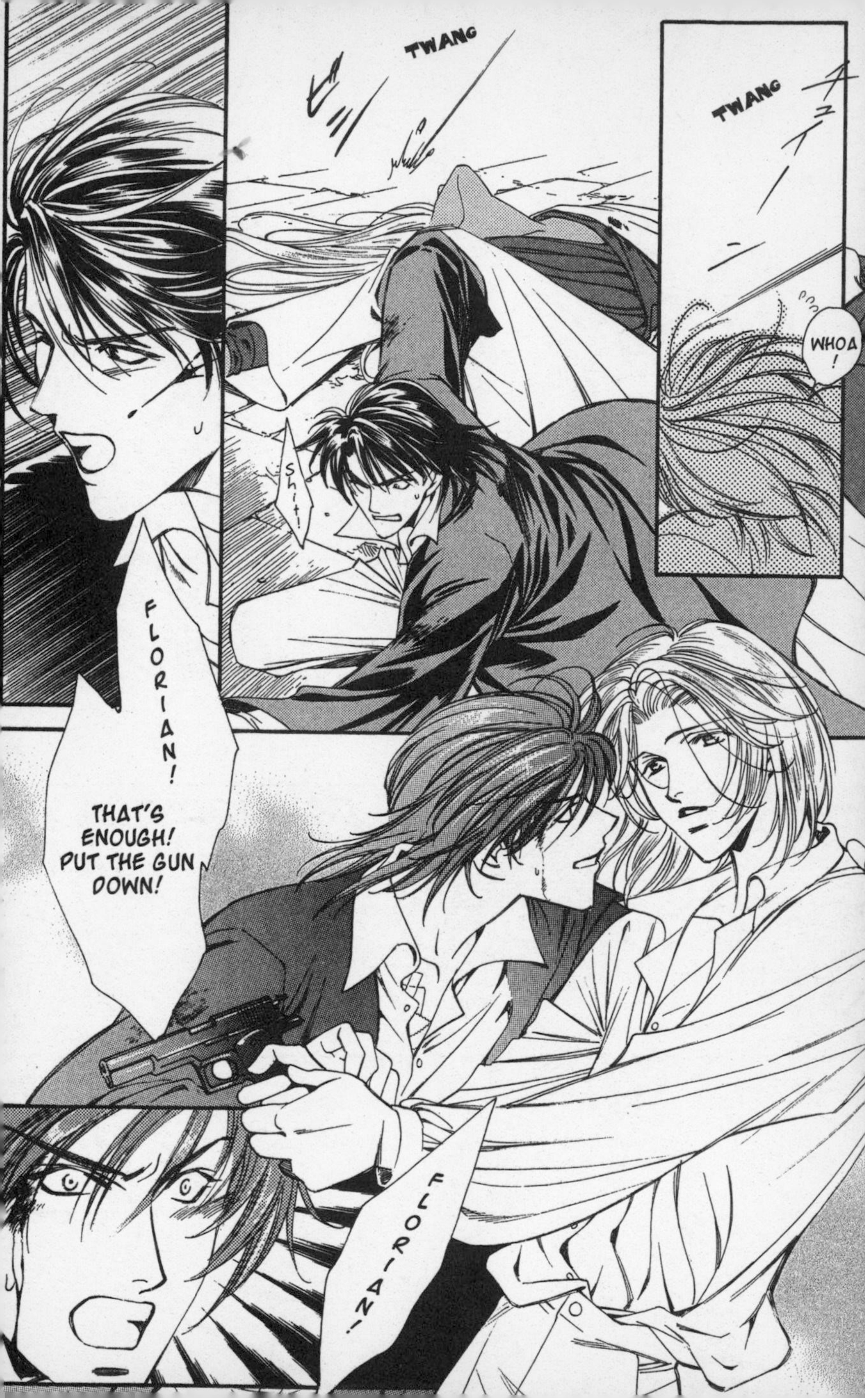

TWANG
WHOA!
TWANG
Shit!
FLORIAN!
THAT'S ENOUGH! PUT THE GUN DOWN!
FLORIAN!

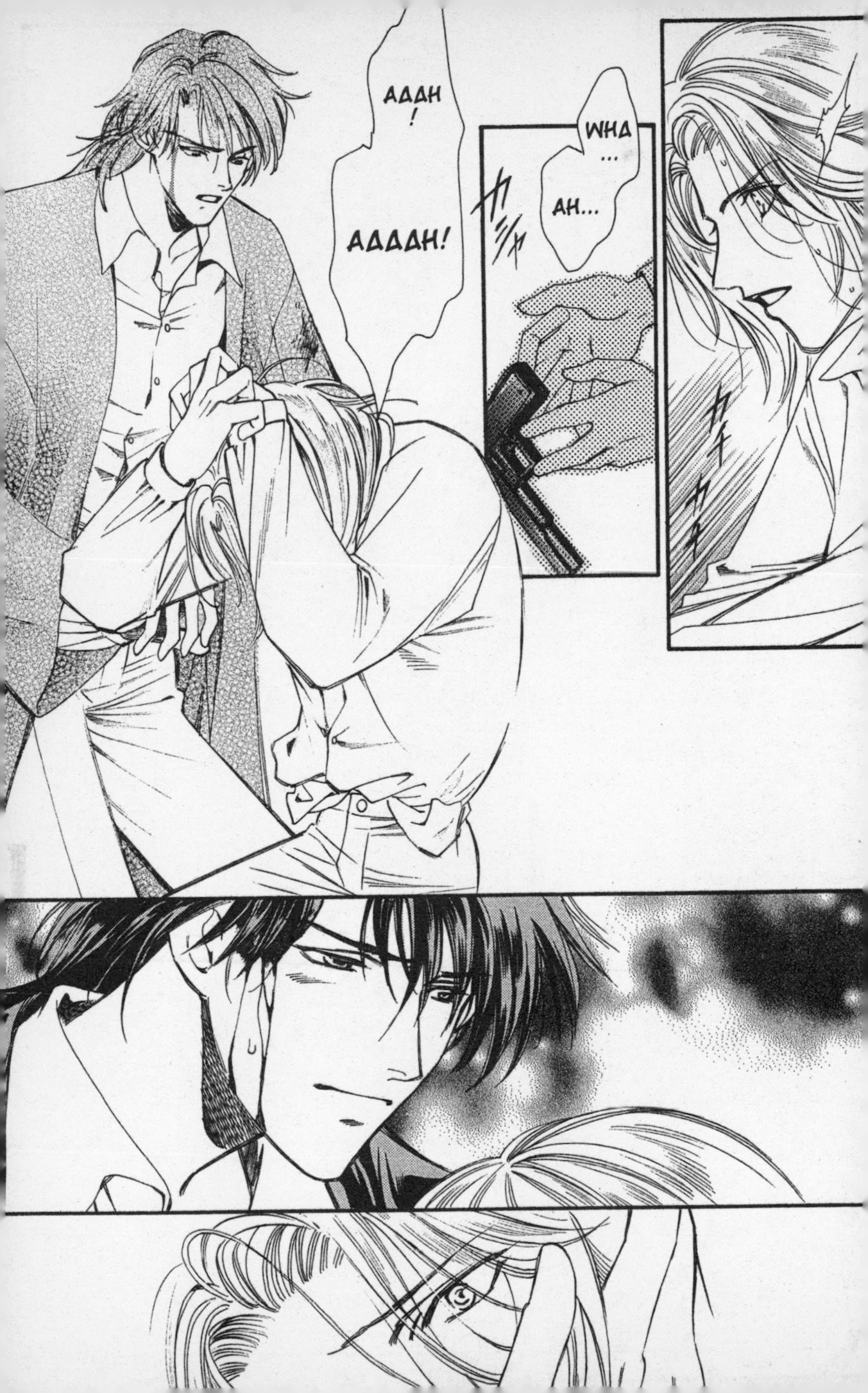
WHA
...
AH...
AAAH
!
AAAAH!

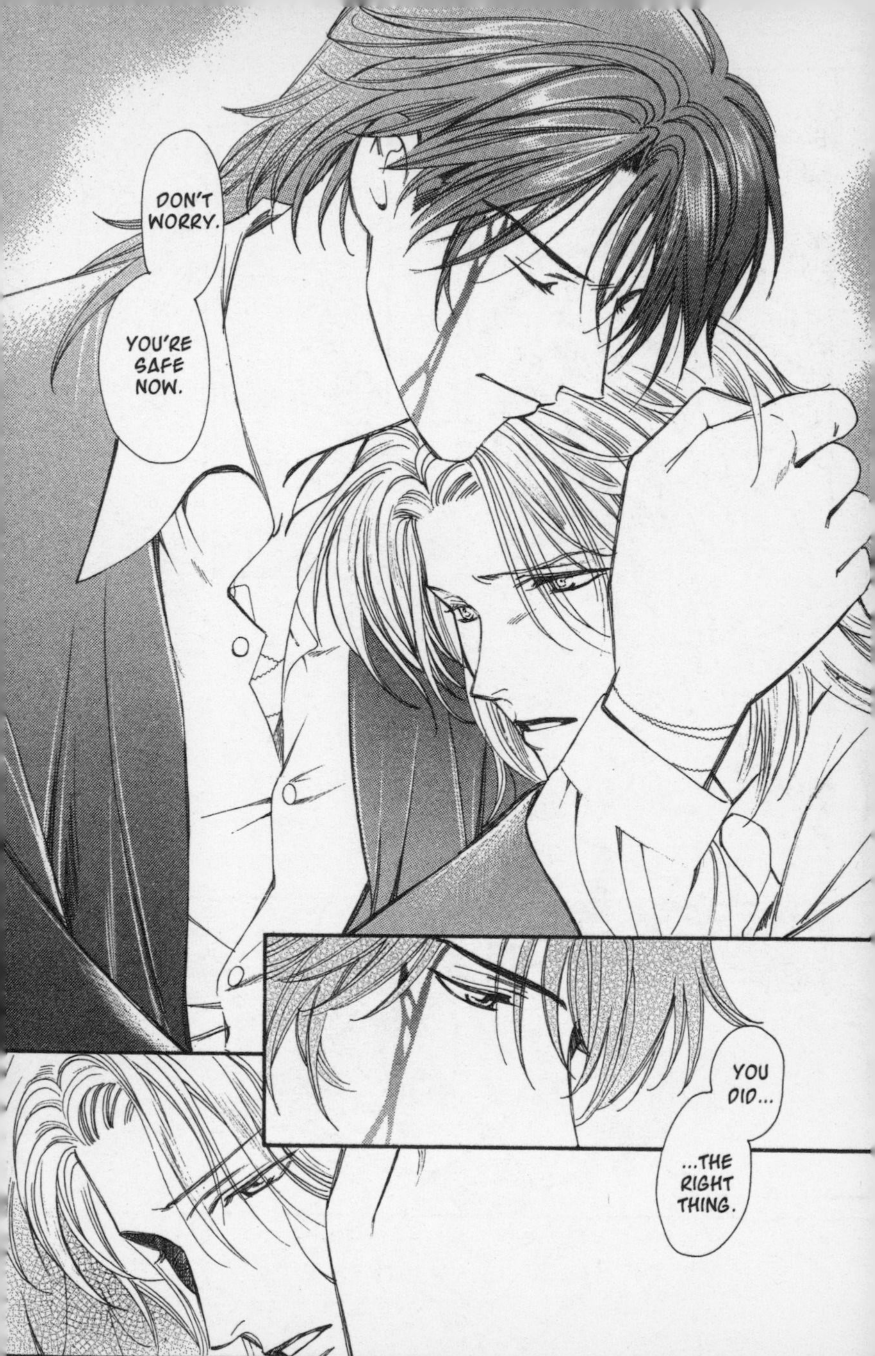
DON'T WORRY.
YOU'RE SAFE NOW.
YOU DID...
...THE RIGHT THING.

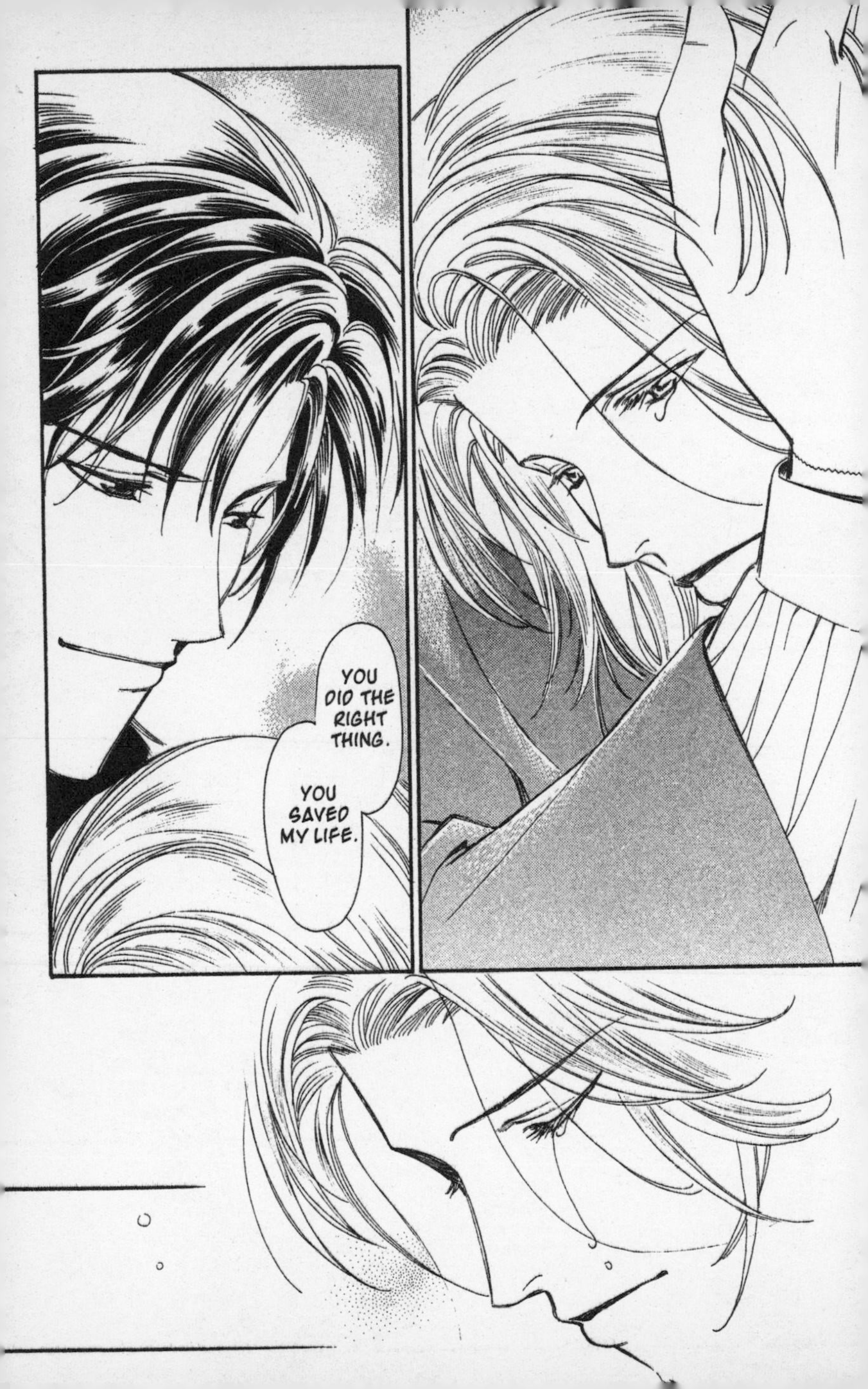
YOU DID THE RIGHT THING.
YOU SAVED MY LIFE.

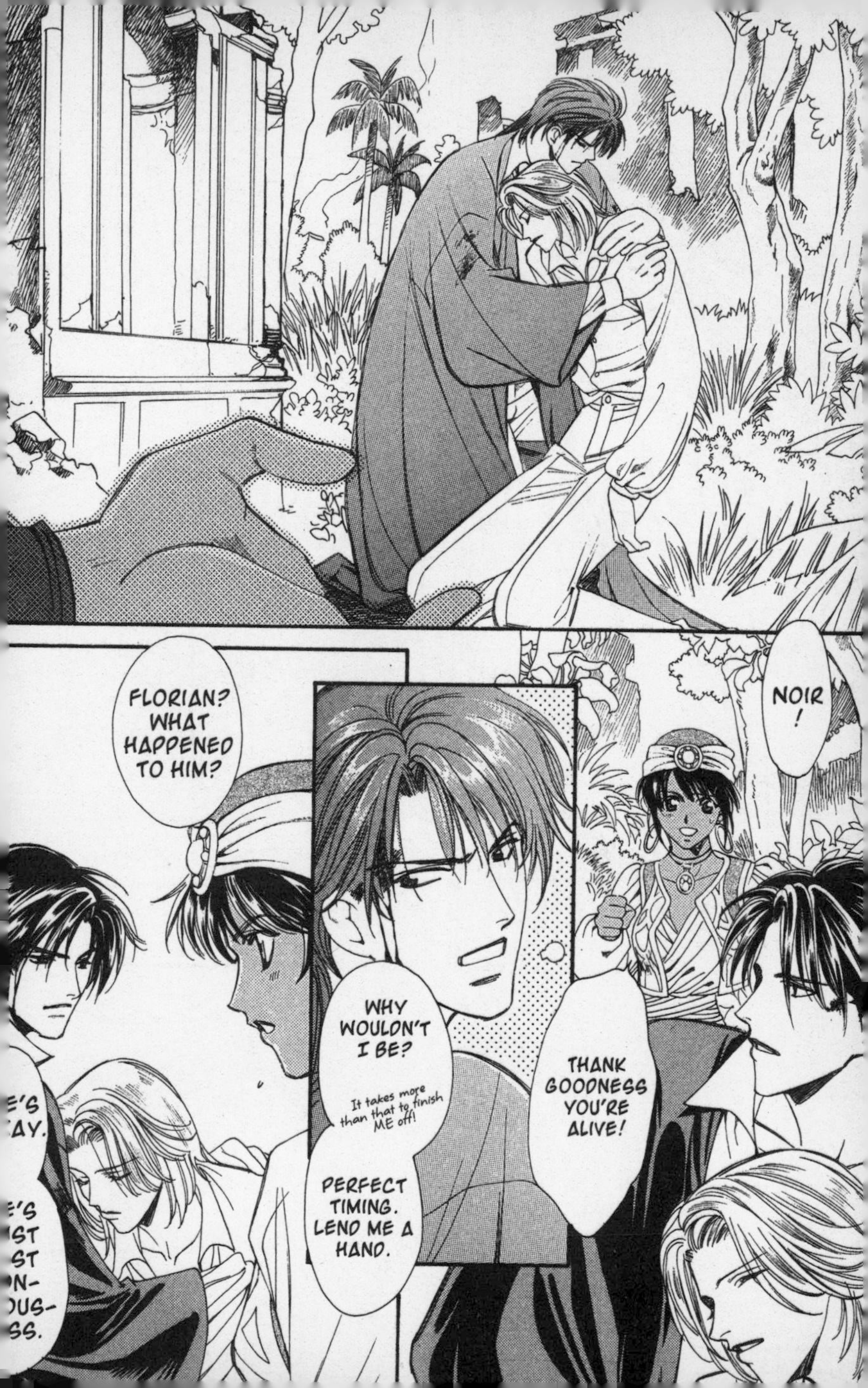
NOIR!
THANK GOODNESS YOU'RE ALIVE!
WHY WOULDN'T I BE?
It takes more than that to finish ME off!
PERFECT TIMING. LEND ME A HAND.
FLORIAN? WHAT HAPPENED TO HIM?

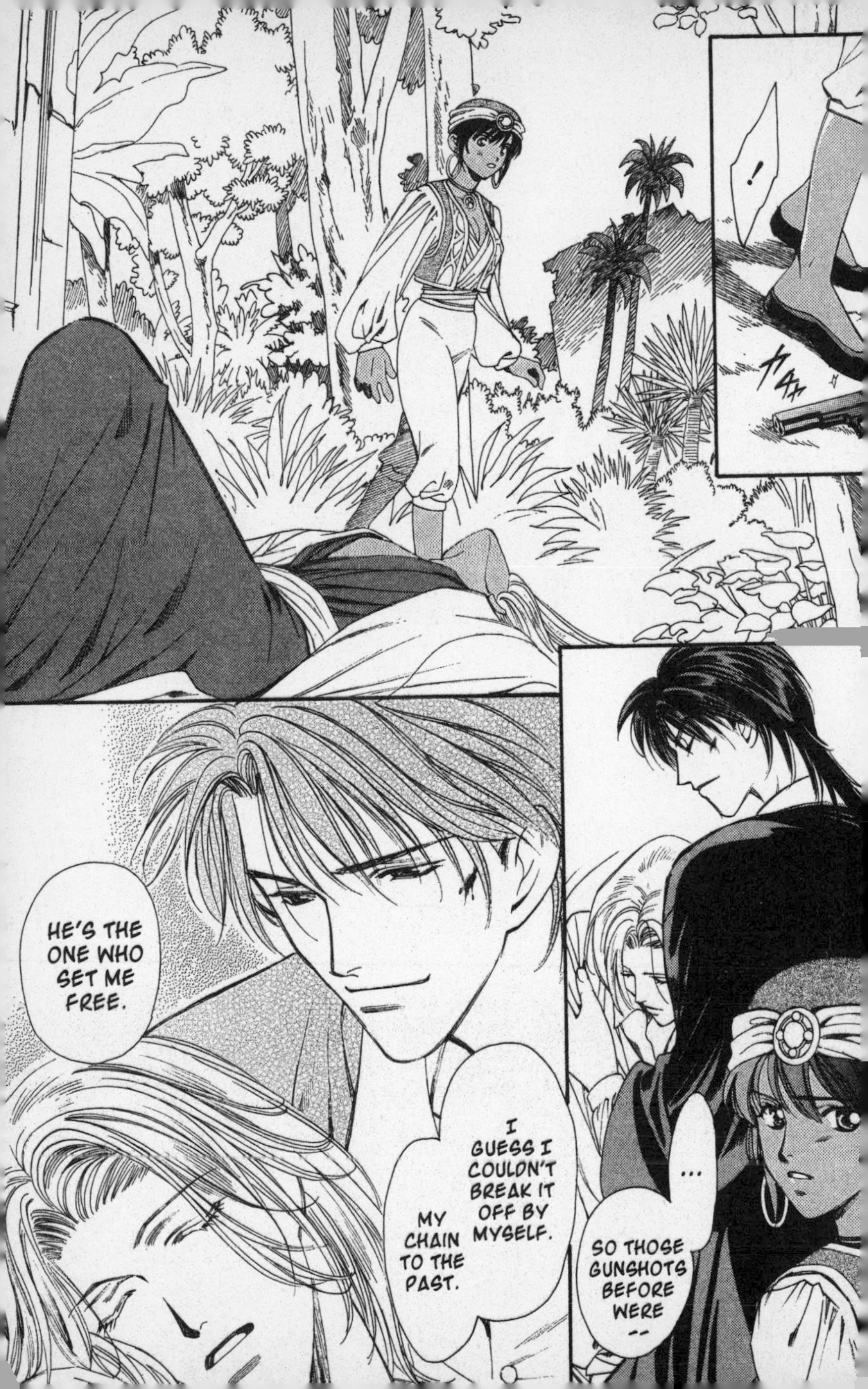
!
...
SO THOSE GUNSHOTS BEFORE WERE --
I GUESS I COULDN'T BREAK IT OFF BY MYSELF.
MY CHAIN TO THE PAST.
HE'S THE ONE WHO SET ME FREE.

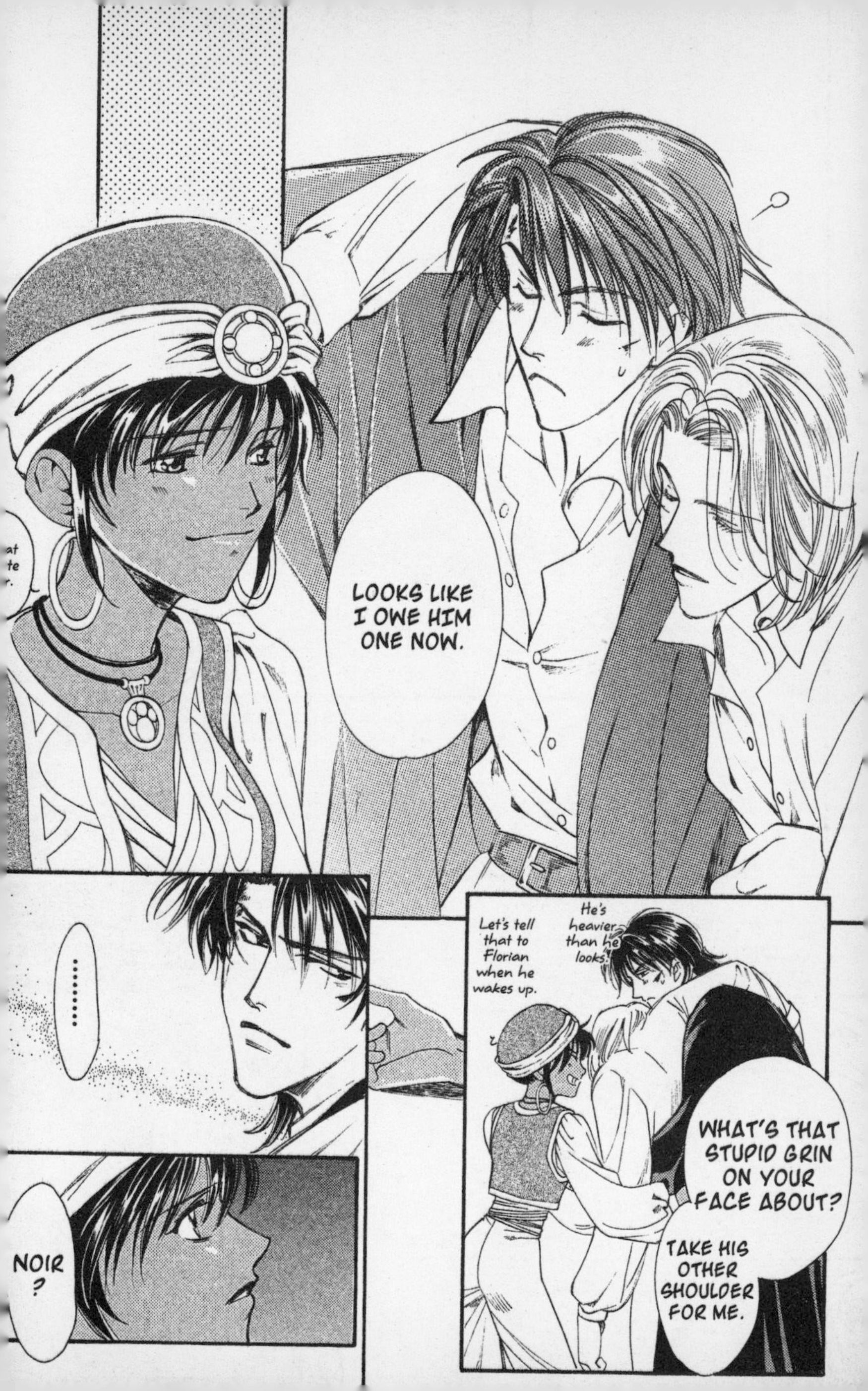

LOOKS LIKE I OWE HIM ONE NOW.
He's heavier than he looks.
Let's tell that to Florian when he wakes up.
WHAT'S THAT STUPID GRIN ON YOUR FACE ABOUT?
TAKE HIS OTHER SHOULDER FOR ME.
......
NOIR ?

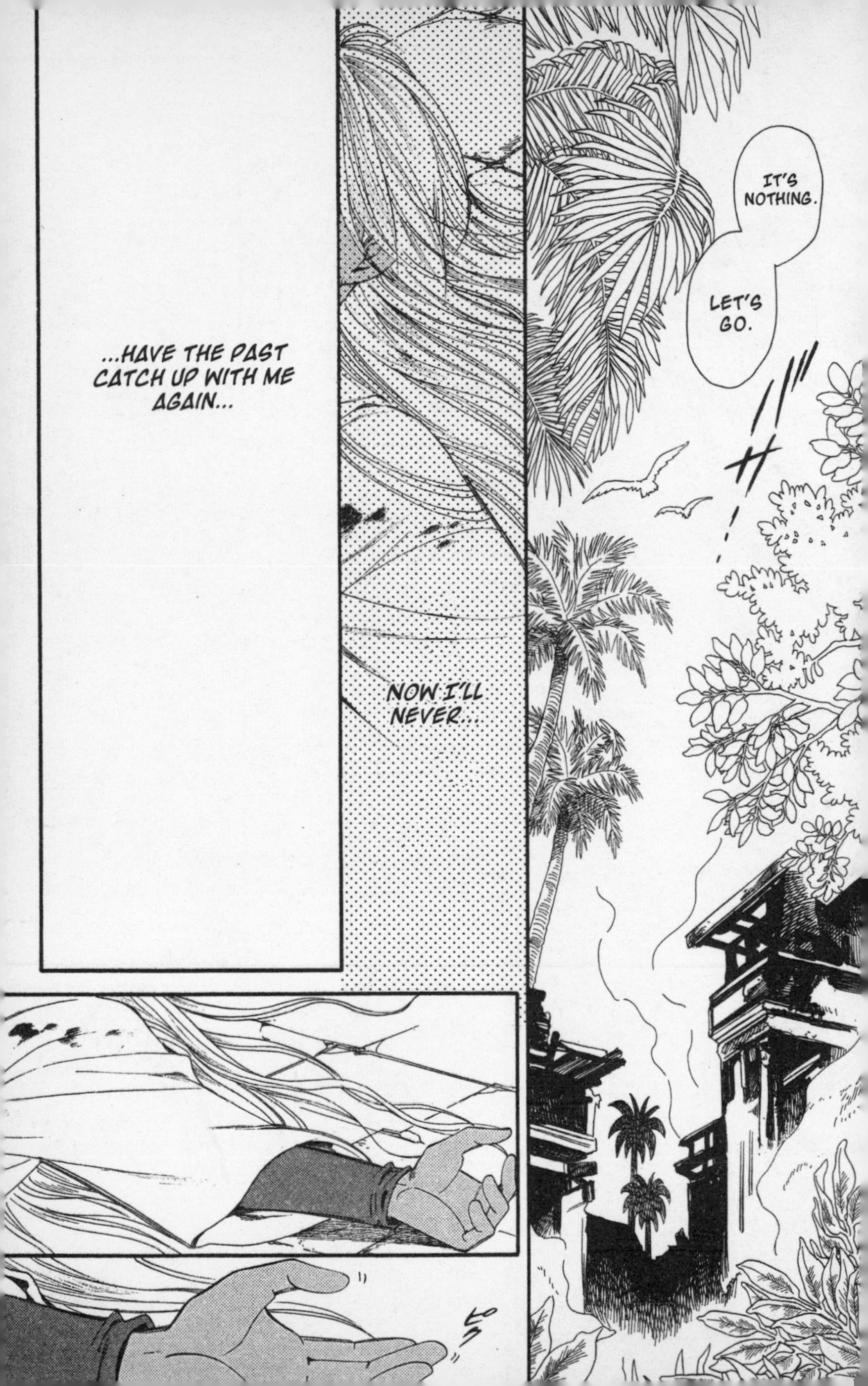
IT'S NOTHING.
LET'S GO.
NOW I'LL NEVER...
...HAVE THE PAST CATCH UP WITH ME AGAIN...

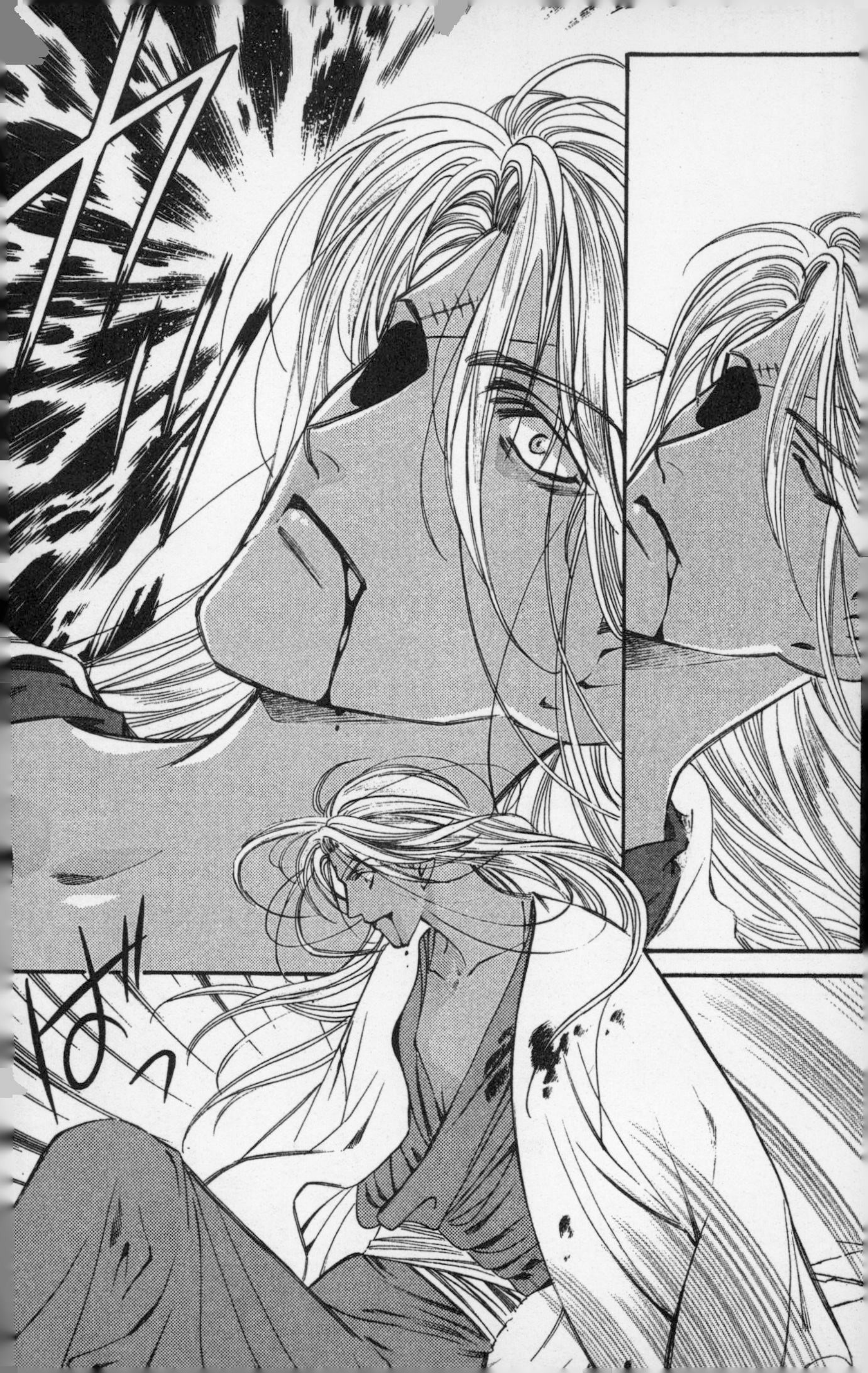

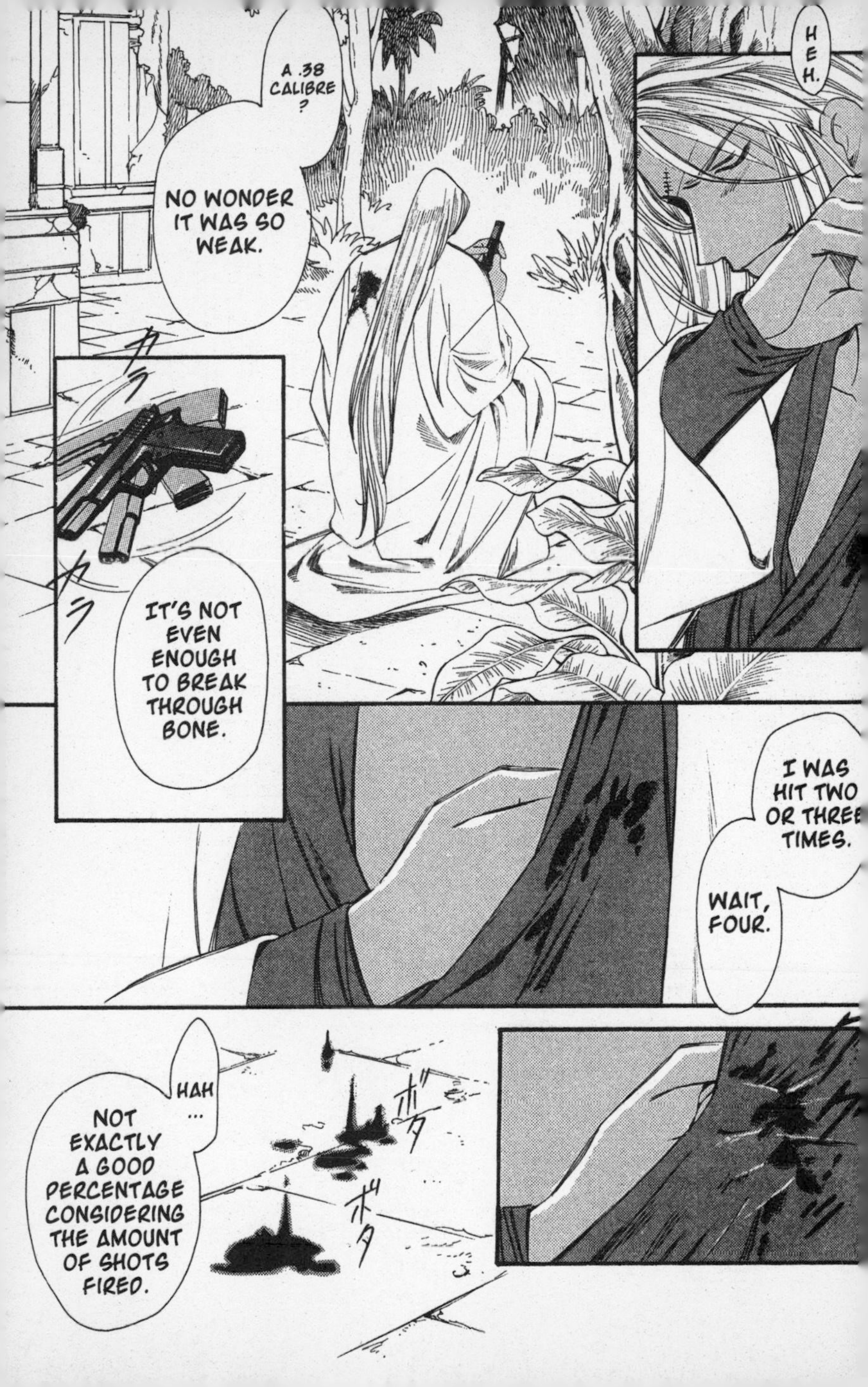
HEH.
A .38 CALIBRE?
NO WONDER IT WAS SO WEAK.
カラ
カラ
IT'S NOT EVEN ENOUGH TO BREAK THROUGH BONE.
I WAS HIT TWO OR THREE TIMES.
WAIT, FOUR.
ボタ
ボタ
HAH...
NOT EXACTLY A GOOD PERCENTAGE CONSIDERING THE AMOUNT OF SHOTS FIRED.

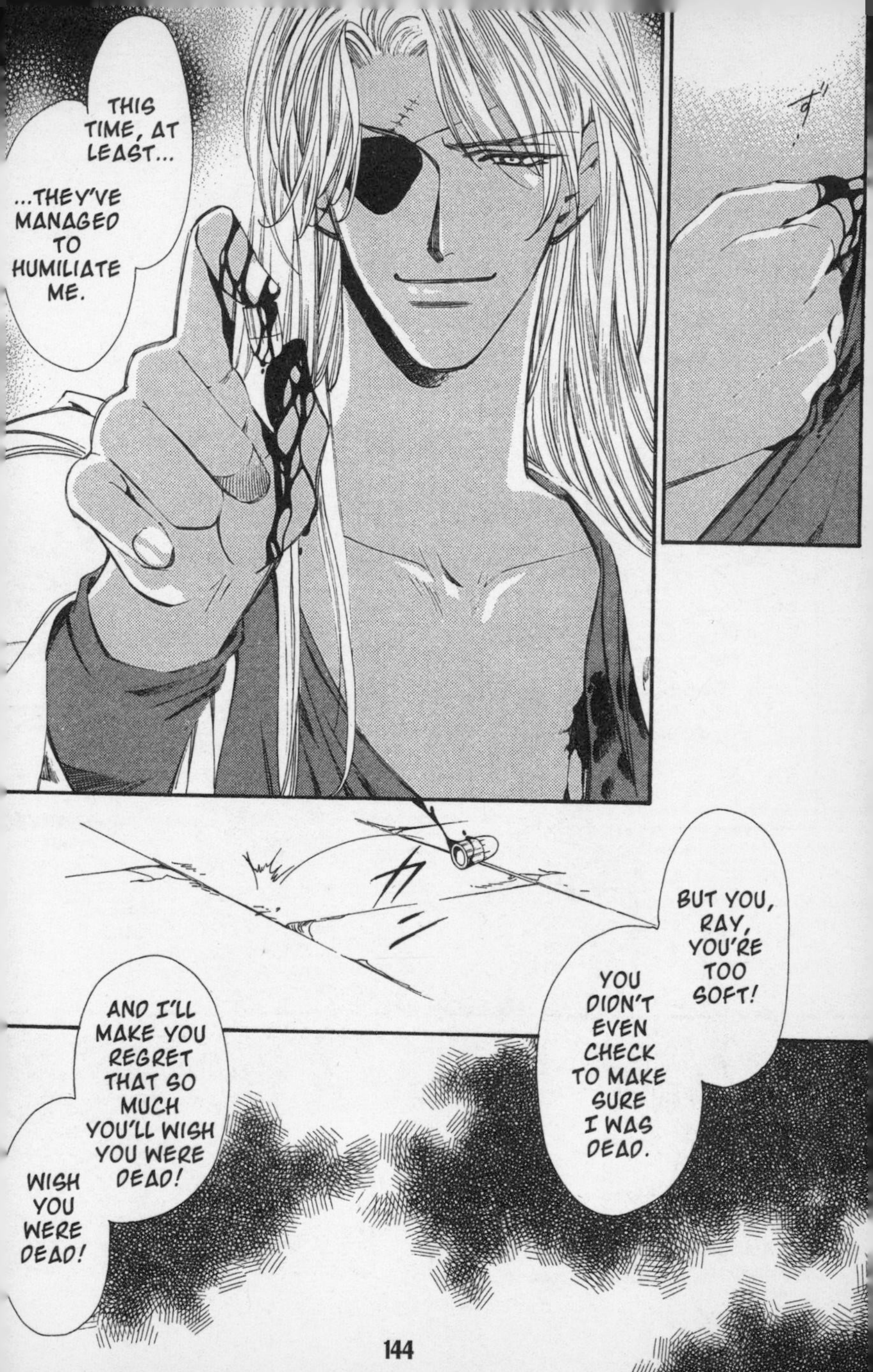
ず
THIS TIME, AT LEAST...
...THEY'VE MANAGED TO HUMILIATE ME.
BUT YOU, RAY, YOU'RE TOO SOFT!
YOU DIDN'T EVEN CHECK TO MAKE SURE I WAS DEAD.
AND I'LL MAKE YOU REGRET THAT SO MUCH YOU'LL WISH YOU WERE DEAD!
WISH YOU WERE DEAD!

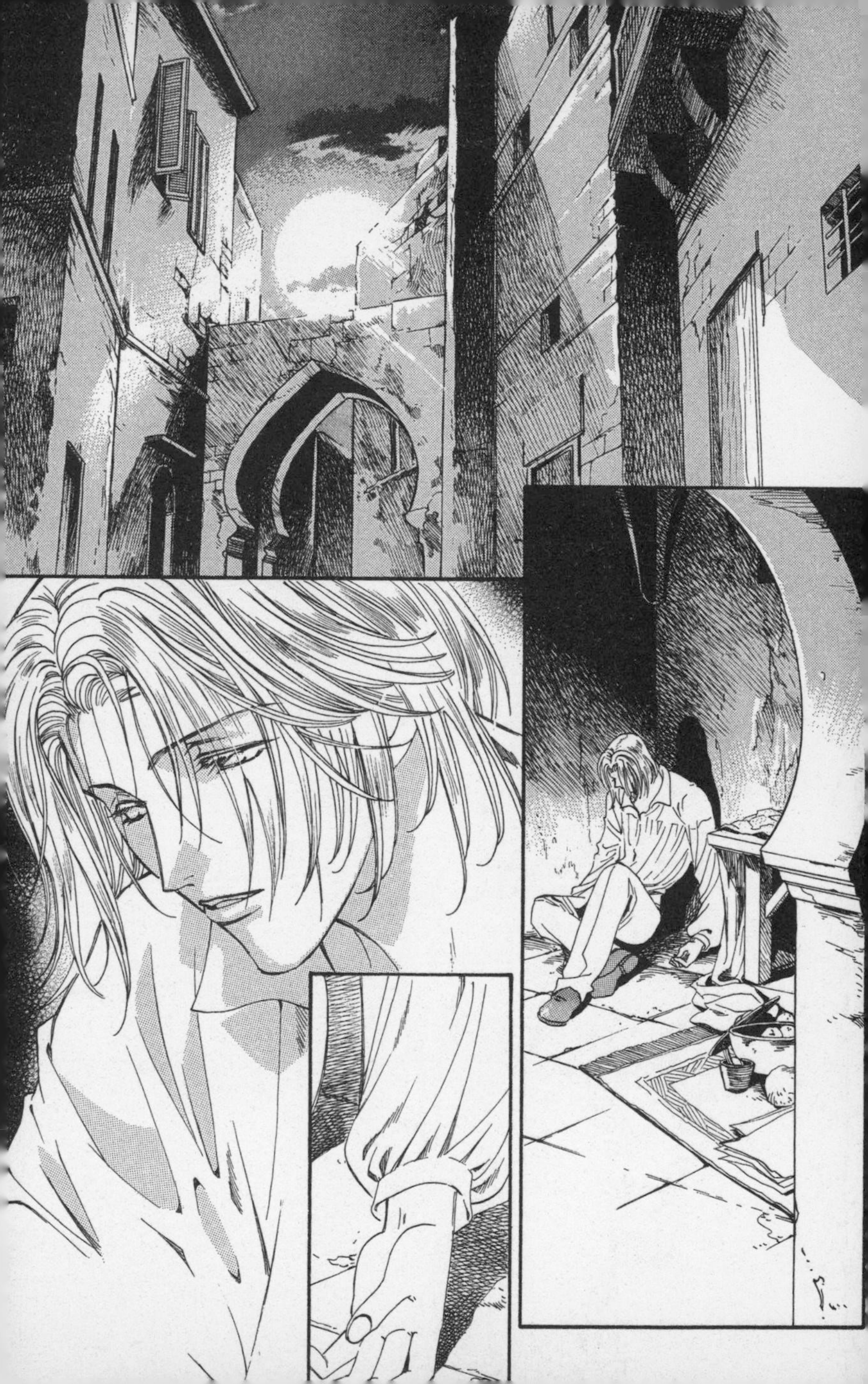

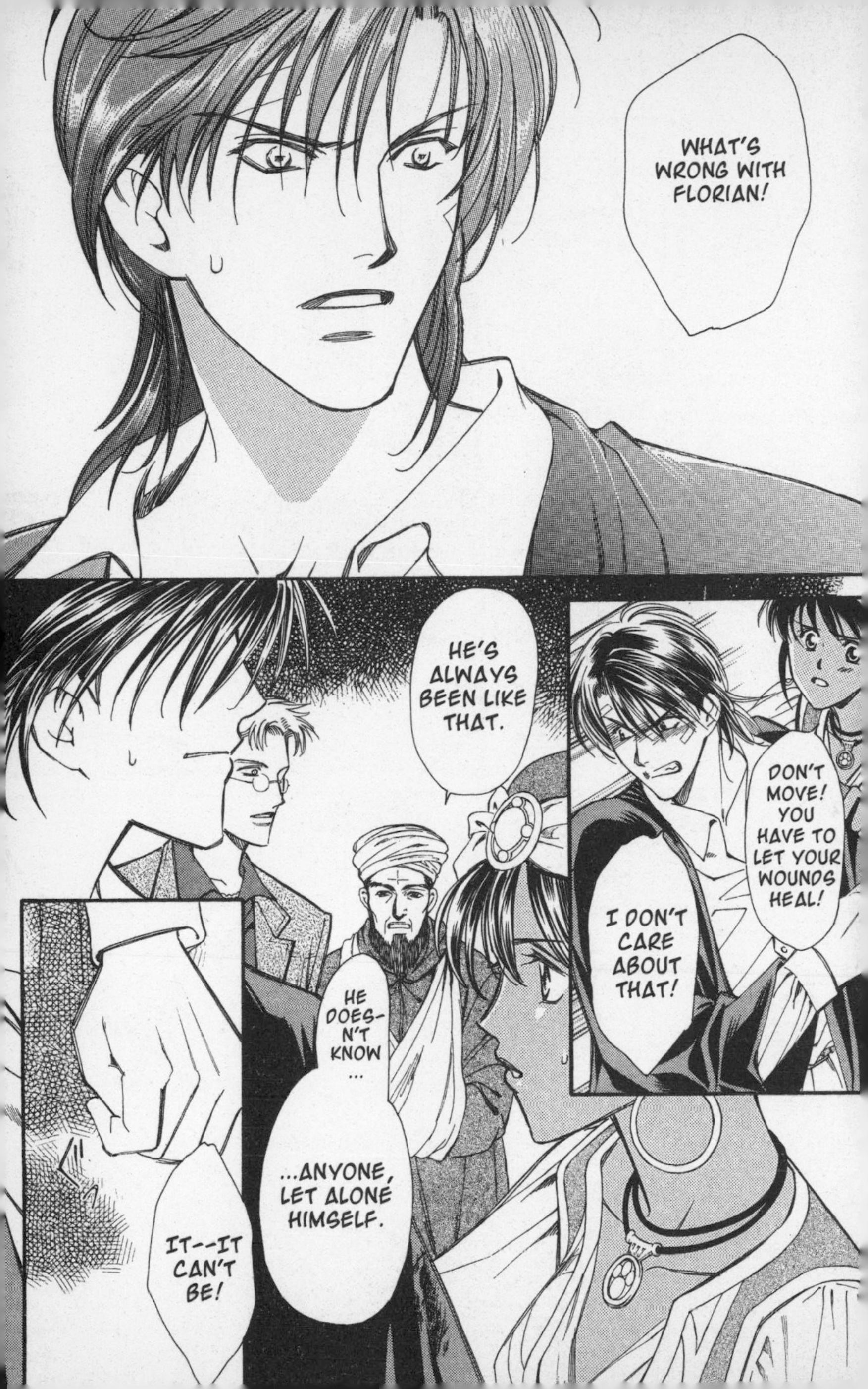
WHAT'S WRONG WITH FLORIAN!
DON'T MOVE! YOU HAVE TO LET YOUR WOUNDS HEAL!
I DON'T CARE ABOUT THAT!
HE'S ALWAYS BEEN LIKE THAT.
HE DOES-N'T KNOW ...
...ANYONE, LET ALONE HIMSELF.
IT--IT CAN'T BE!

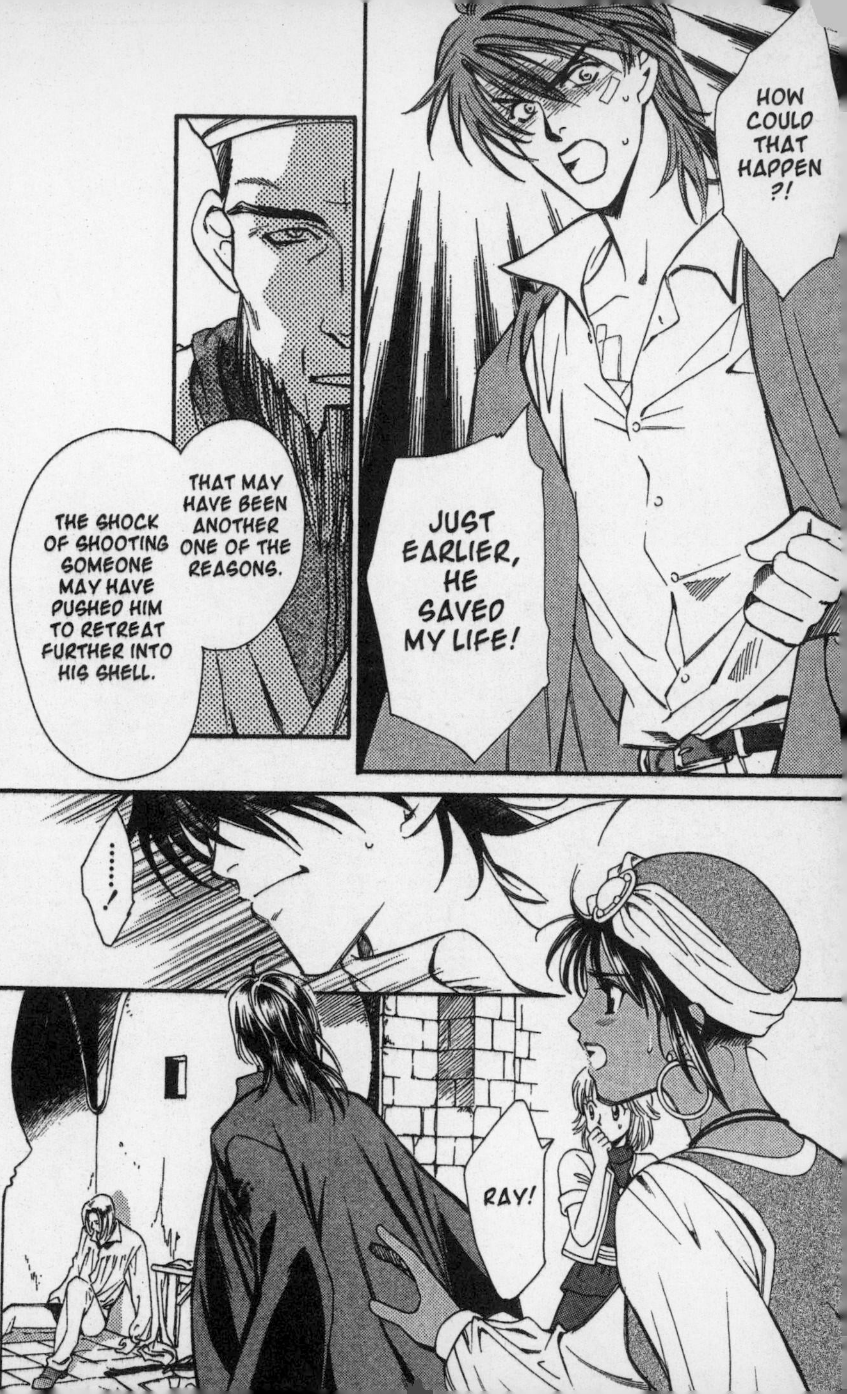
HOW COULD THAT HAPPEN?!
JUST EARLIER, HE SAVED MY LIFE!
THAT MAY HAVE BEEN ANOTHER ONE OF THE REASONS.
THE SHOCK OF SHOOTING SOMEONE MAY HAVE PUSHED HIM TO RETREAT FURTHER INTO HIS SHELL.
......!
RAY!

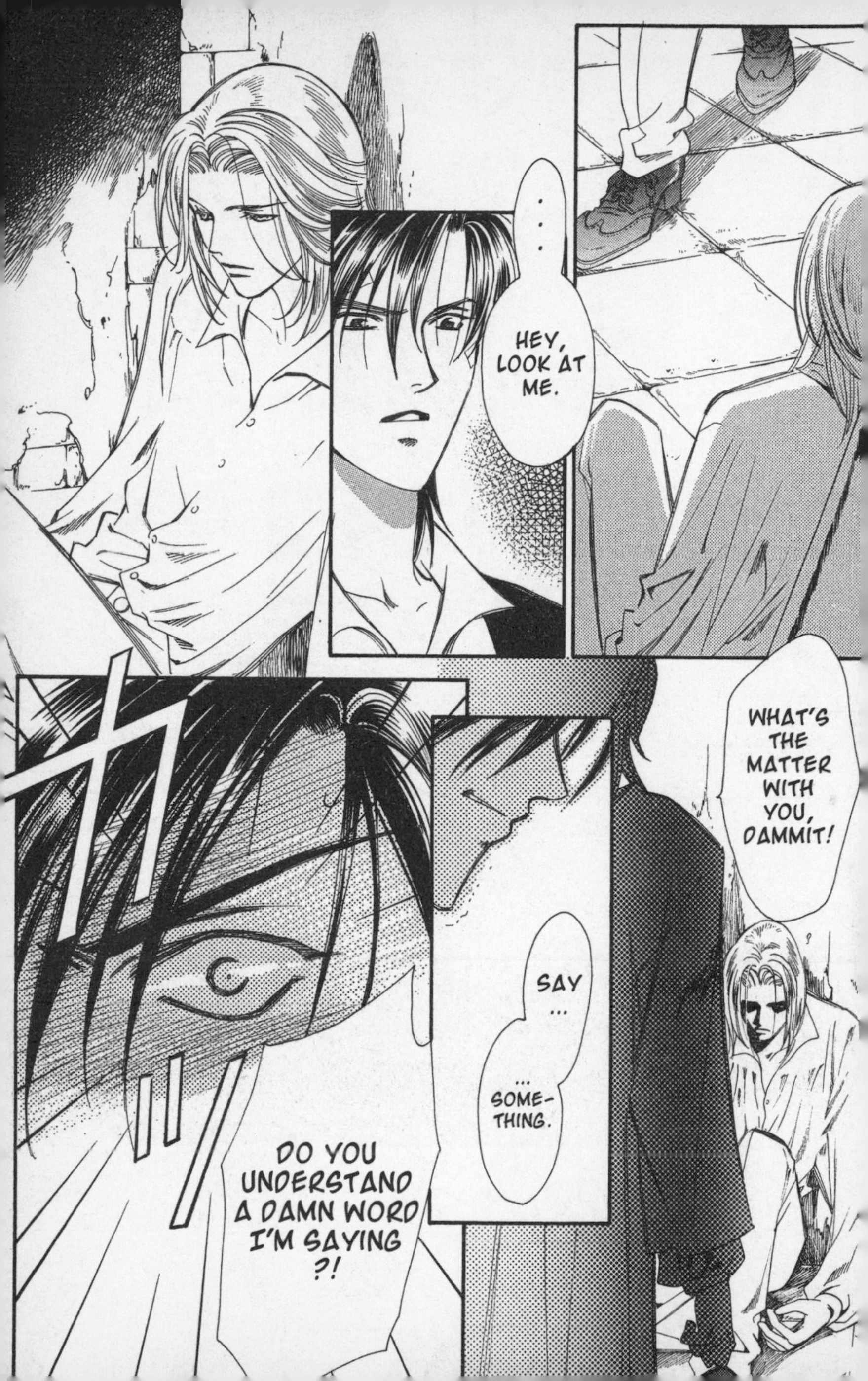
...
HEY, LOOK AT ME.
WHAT'S THE MATTER WITH YOU, DAMMIT!
SAY ...
... SOME-THING.
DO YOU UNDERSTAND A DAMN WORD I'M SAYING ?!

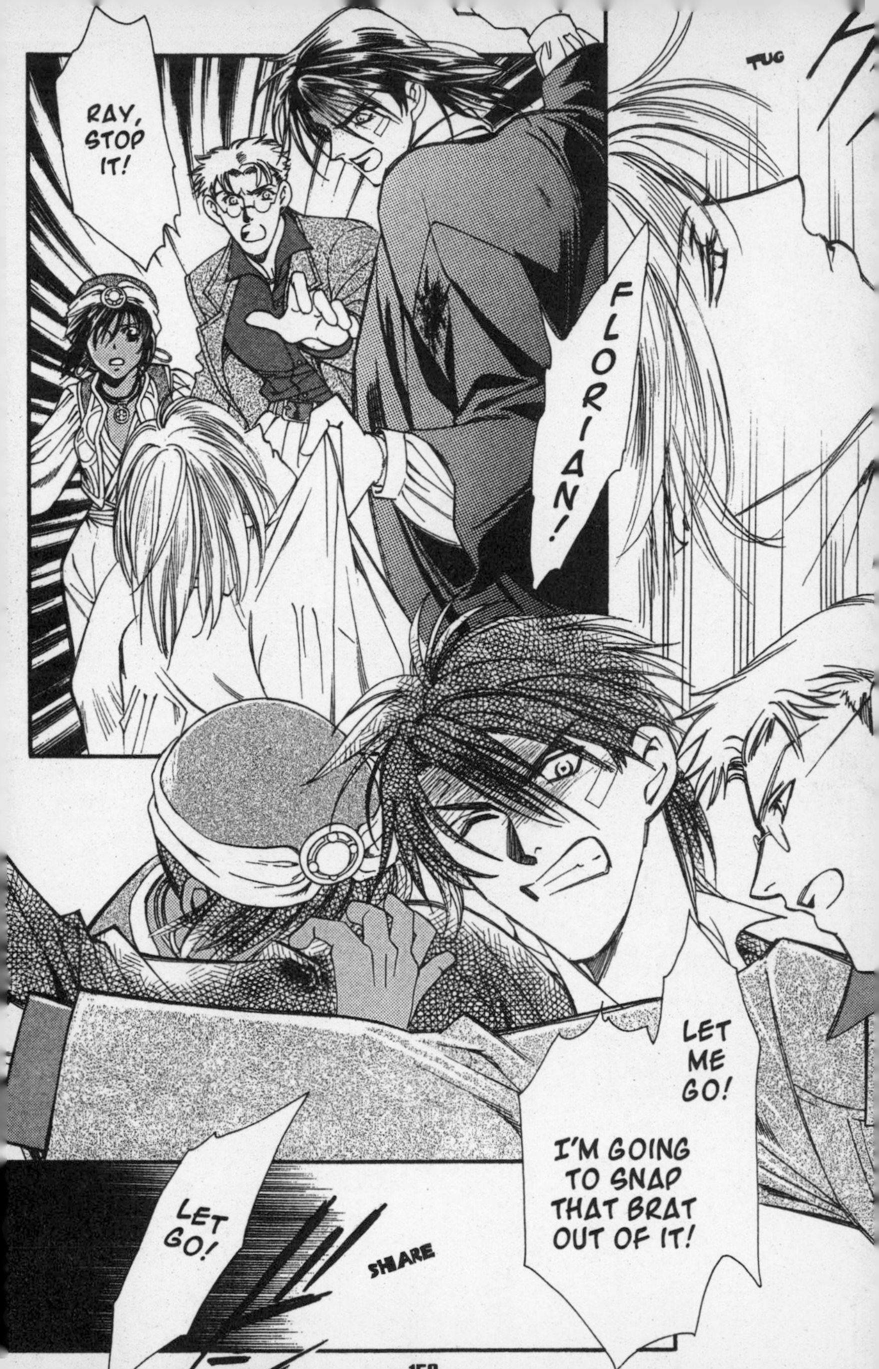
TUG
FLORIAN!
RAY, STOP IT!
LET ME GO!
I'M GOING TO SNAP THAT BRAT OUT OF IT!
SHARE
LET GO!

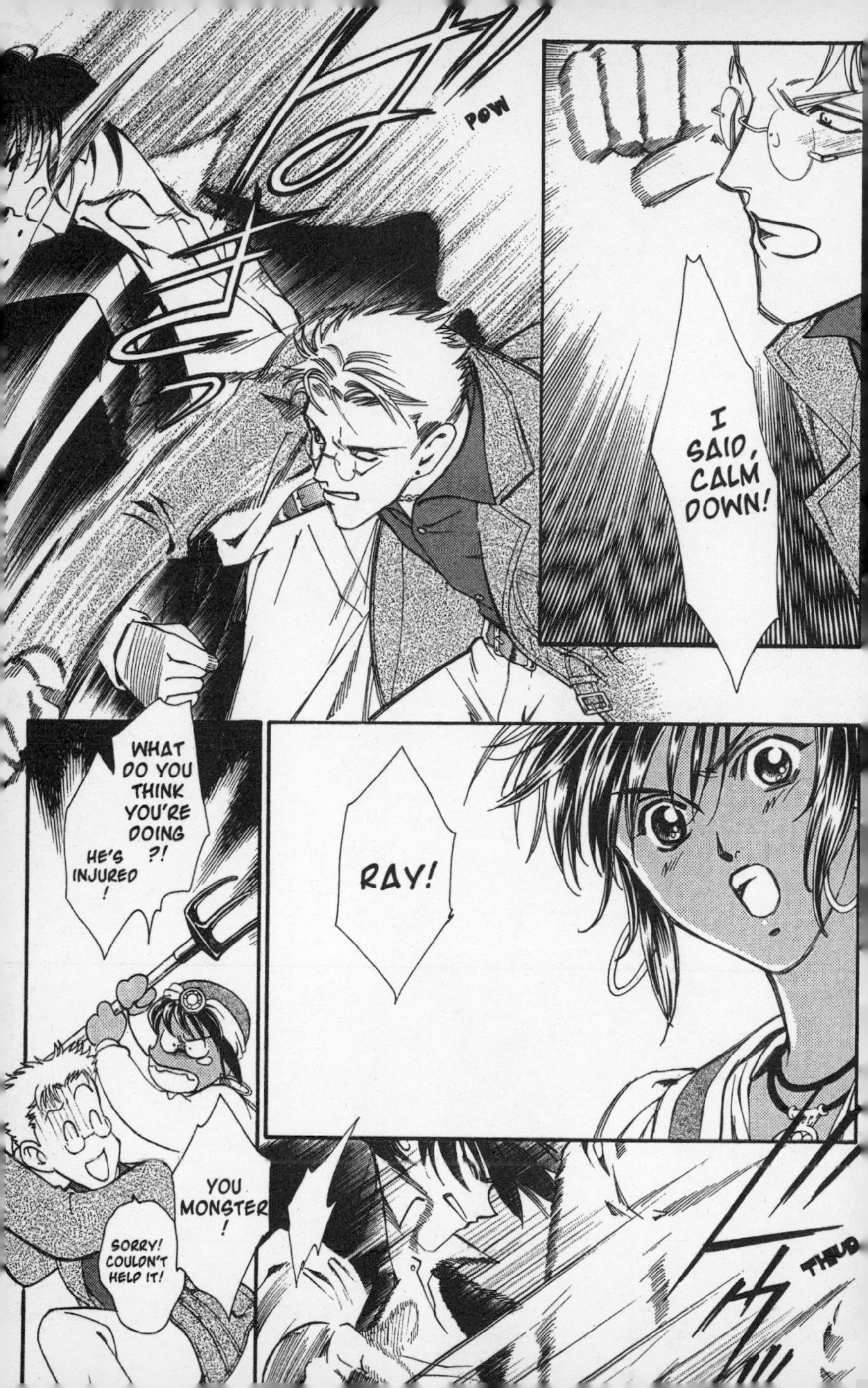
I SAID, CALM DOWN!
POW
RAY!
WHAT DO YOU THINK YOU'RE DOING?!
HE'S INJURED!
THUD
YOU MONSTER!
SORRY! COULDN'T HELP IT!

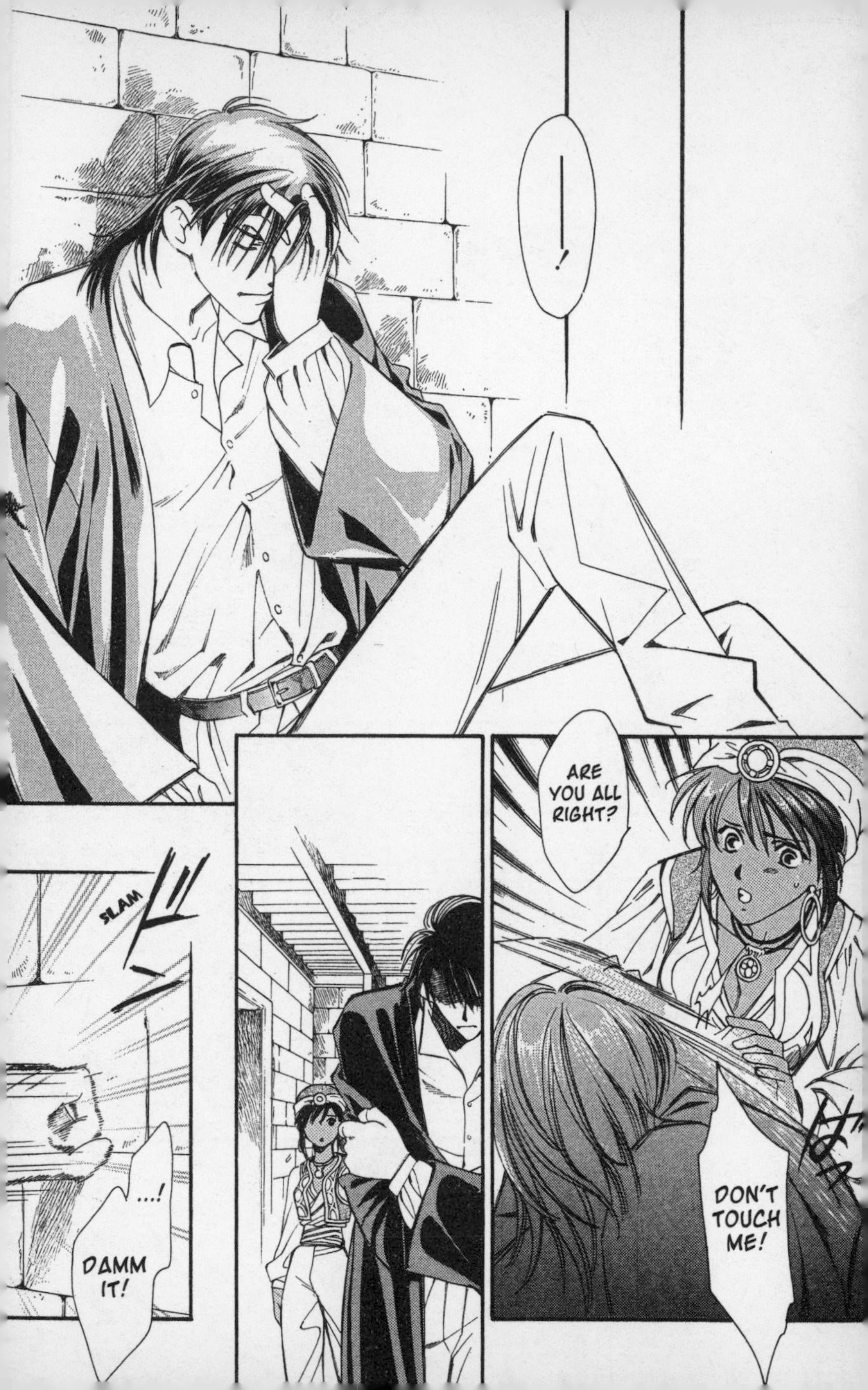
!
ARE YOU ALL RIGHT?
DON'T TOUCH ME!
SLAM
...!
DAMM IT!

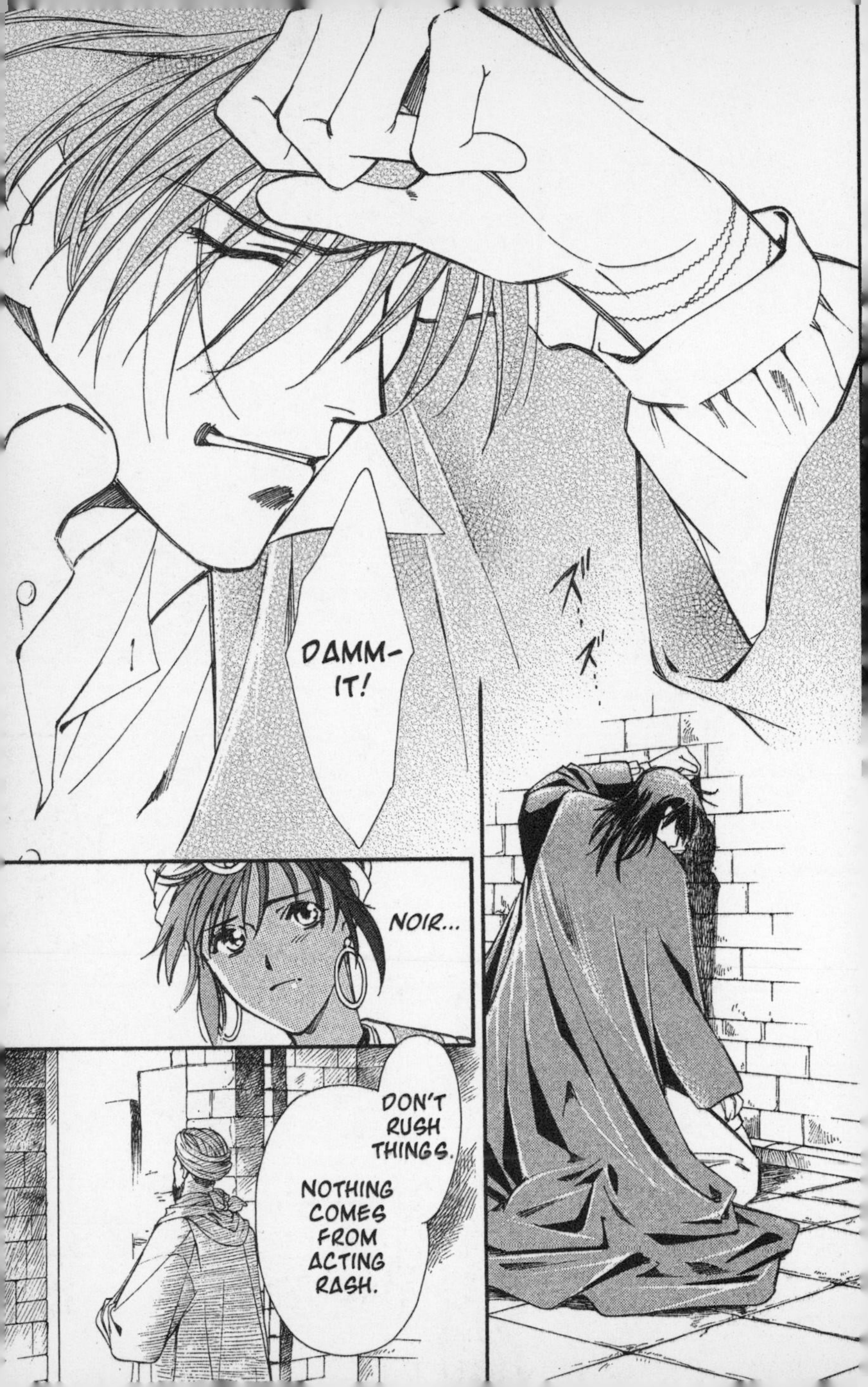
DAMM-IT!
NOIR...
DON'T RUSH THINGS.
NOTHING COMES FROM ACTING RASH.

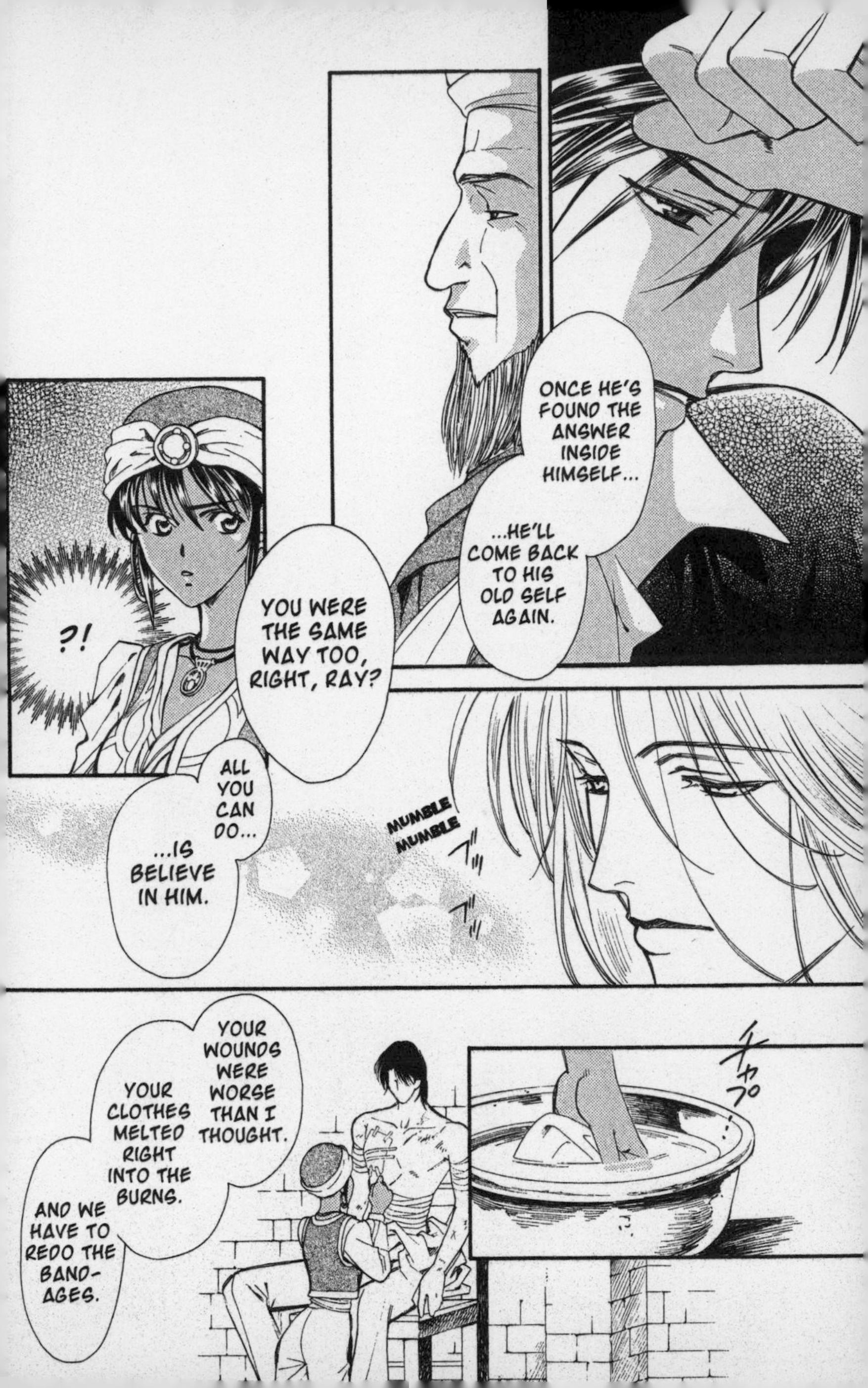
ONCE HE'S FOUND THE ANSWER INSIDE HIMSELF...
...HE'LL COME BACK TO HIS OLD SELF AGAIN.
YOU WERE THE SAME WAY TOO, RIGHT, RAY?
?!
MUMBLE MUMBLE
ALL YOU CAN DO...
...IS BELIEVE IN HIM.
YOUR WOUNDS WERE WORSE THAN I THOUGHT.
YOUR CLOTHES MELTED RIGHT INTO THE BURNS.
AND WE HAVE TO REDO THE BANDAGES.

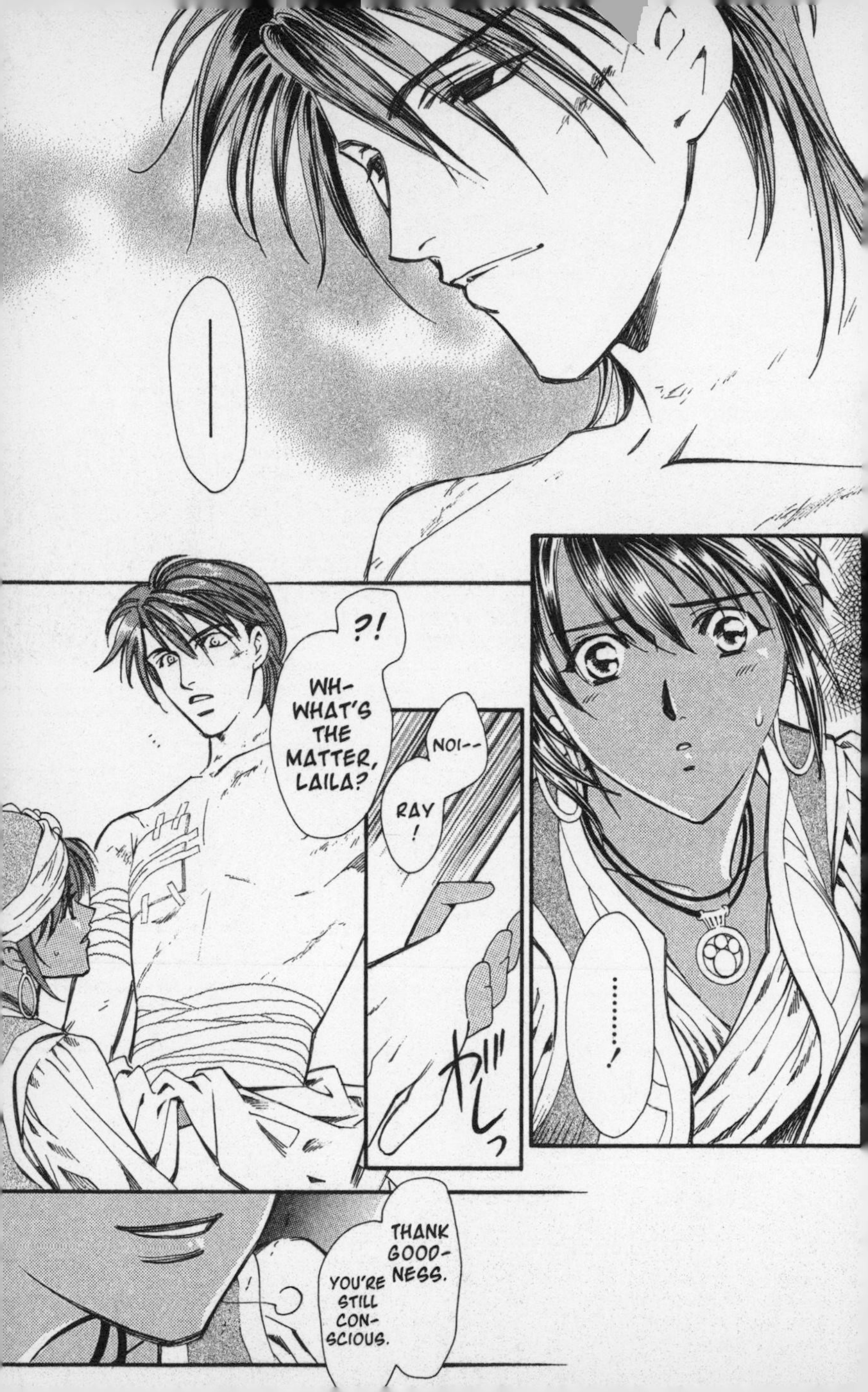

......!
NOI--
RAY!
ガしっ
?!
WH-WHAT'S THE MATTER, LAILA?
THANK GOODNESS.
YOU'RE STILL CONSCIOUS.

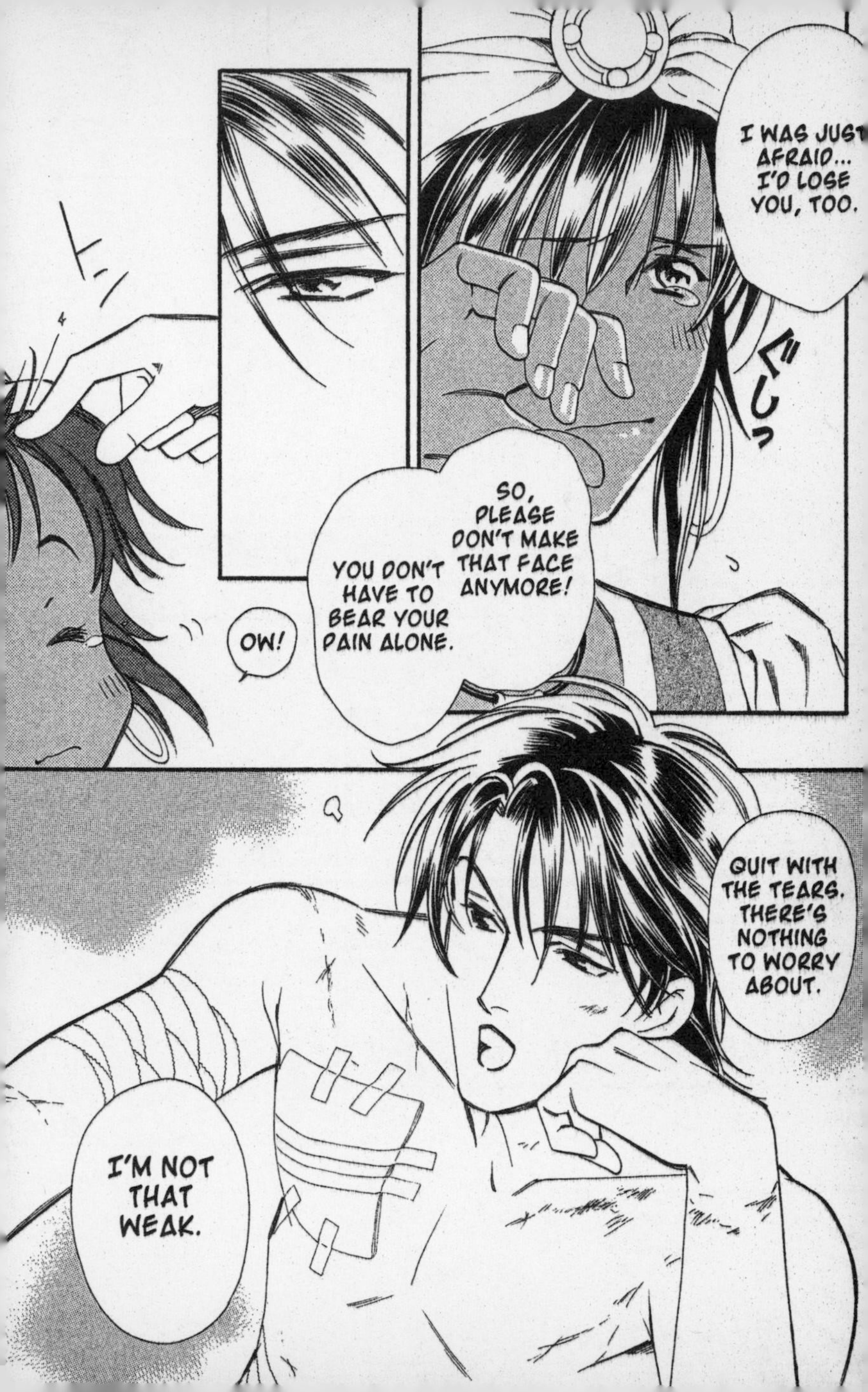

I WAS JUST AFRAID... I'D LOSE YOU, TOO.
YOU DON'T HAVE TO BEAR YOUR PAIN ALONE.
SO, PLEASE DON'T MAKE THAT FACE ANYMORE!
OW!
QUIT WITH THE TEARS. THERE'S NOTHING TO WORRY ABOUT.
I'M NOT THAT WEAK.

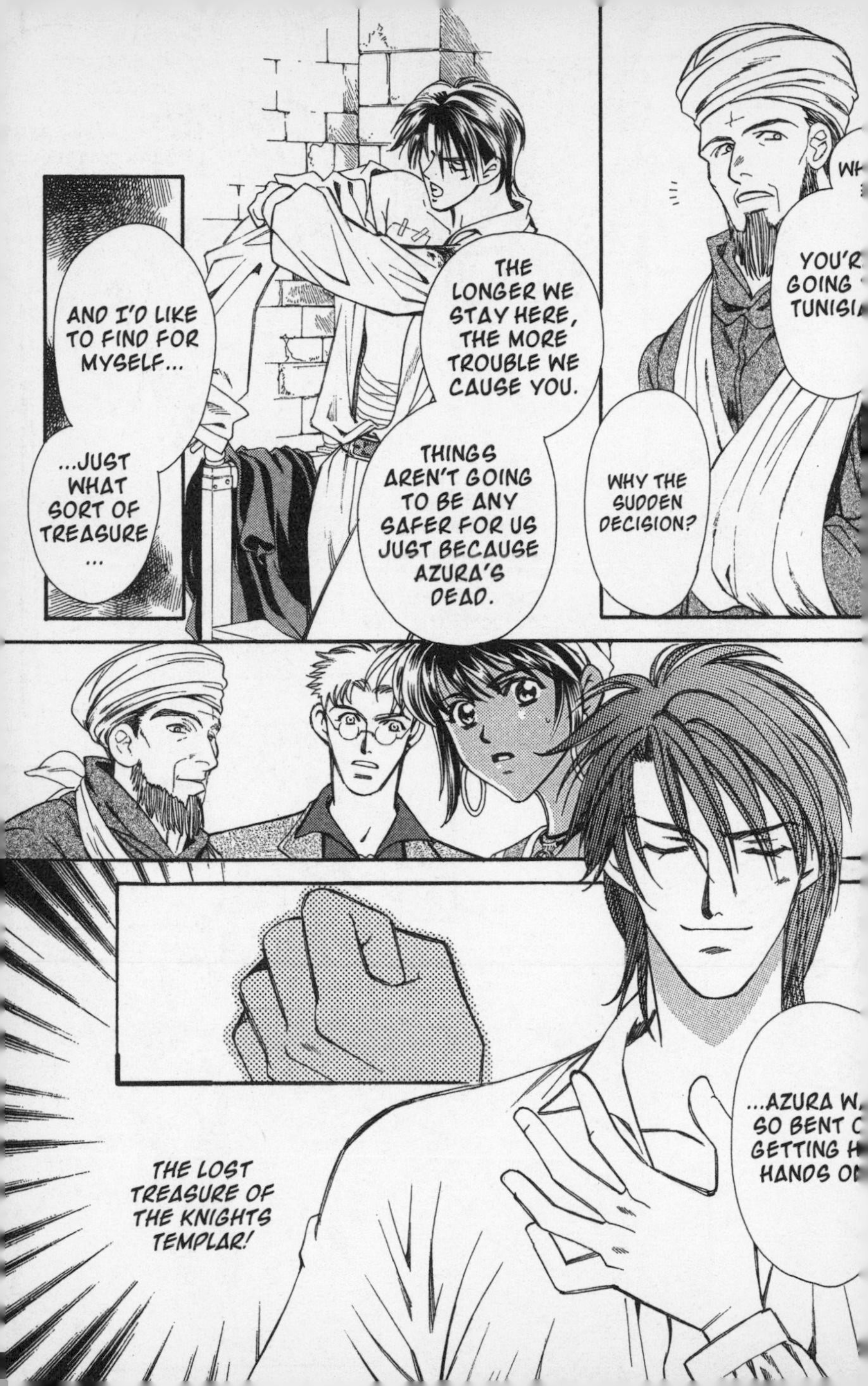
YOU'R GOING TUNISIA
WHY THE SUDDEN DECISION?
THE LONGER WE STAY HERE, THE MORE TROUBLE WE CAUSE YOU.
THINGS AREN'T GOING TO BE ANY SAFER FOR US JUST BECAUSE AZURA'S DEAD.
AND I'D LIKE TO FIND FOR MYSELF...
...JUST WHAT SORT OF TREASURE ...
...AZURA W SO BENT GETTING H HANDS O
THE LOST TREASURE OF THE KNIGHTS TEMPLAR!

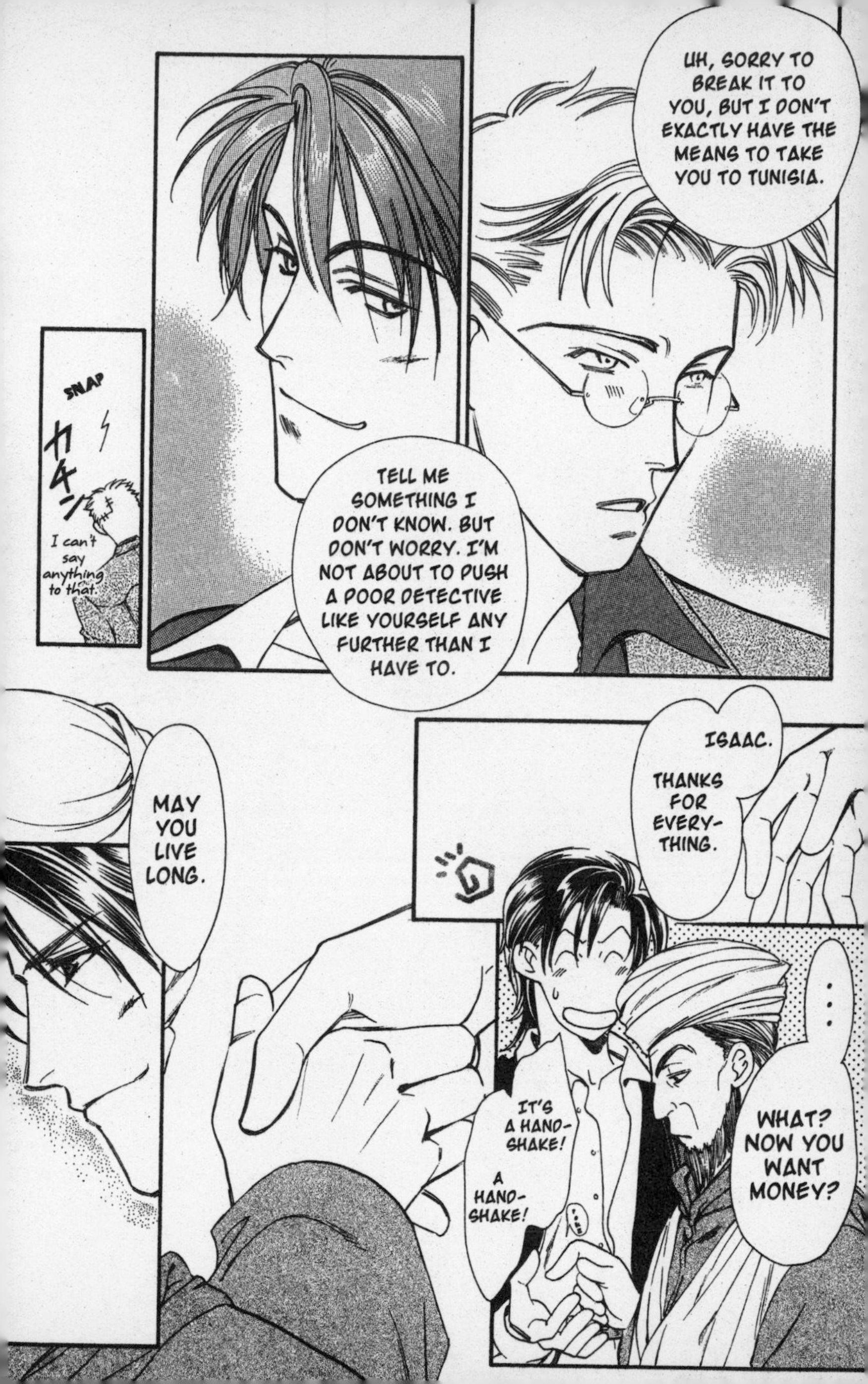
UH, SORRY TO BREAK IT TO YOU, BUT I DON'T EXACTLY HAVE THE MEANS TO TAKE YOU TO TUNISIA.
TELL ME SOMETHING I DON'T KNOW. BUT DON'T WORRY. I'M NOT ABOUT TO PUSH A POOR DETECTIVE LIKE YOURSELF ANY FURTHER THAN I HAVE TO.
SNAP
カチン
I can't say anything to that.
ISAAC.
THANKS FOR EVERYTHING.
...
WHAT? NOW YOU WANT MONEY?
IT'S A HAND-SHAKE!
A HAND-SHAKE!
MAY YOU LIVE LONG.

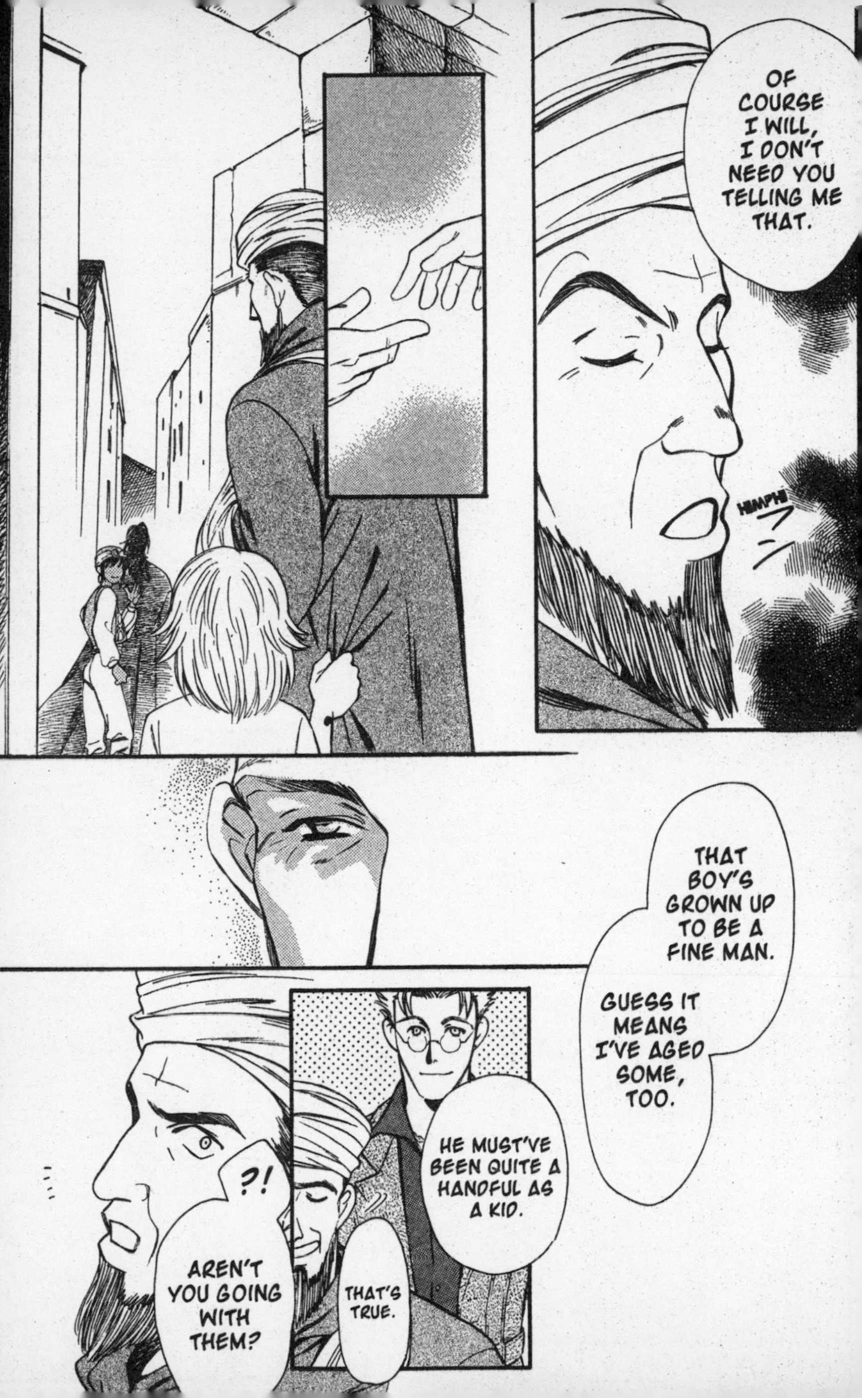
OF COURSE I WILL, I DON'T NEED YOU TELLING ME THAT.
HMPH!
THAT BOY'S GROWN UP TO BE A FINE MAN.
GUESS IT MEANS I'VE AGED SOME, TOO.
HE MUST'VE BEEN QUITE A HANDFUL AS A KID.
THAT'S TRUE.
?!
AREN'T YOU GOING WITH THEM?

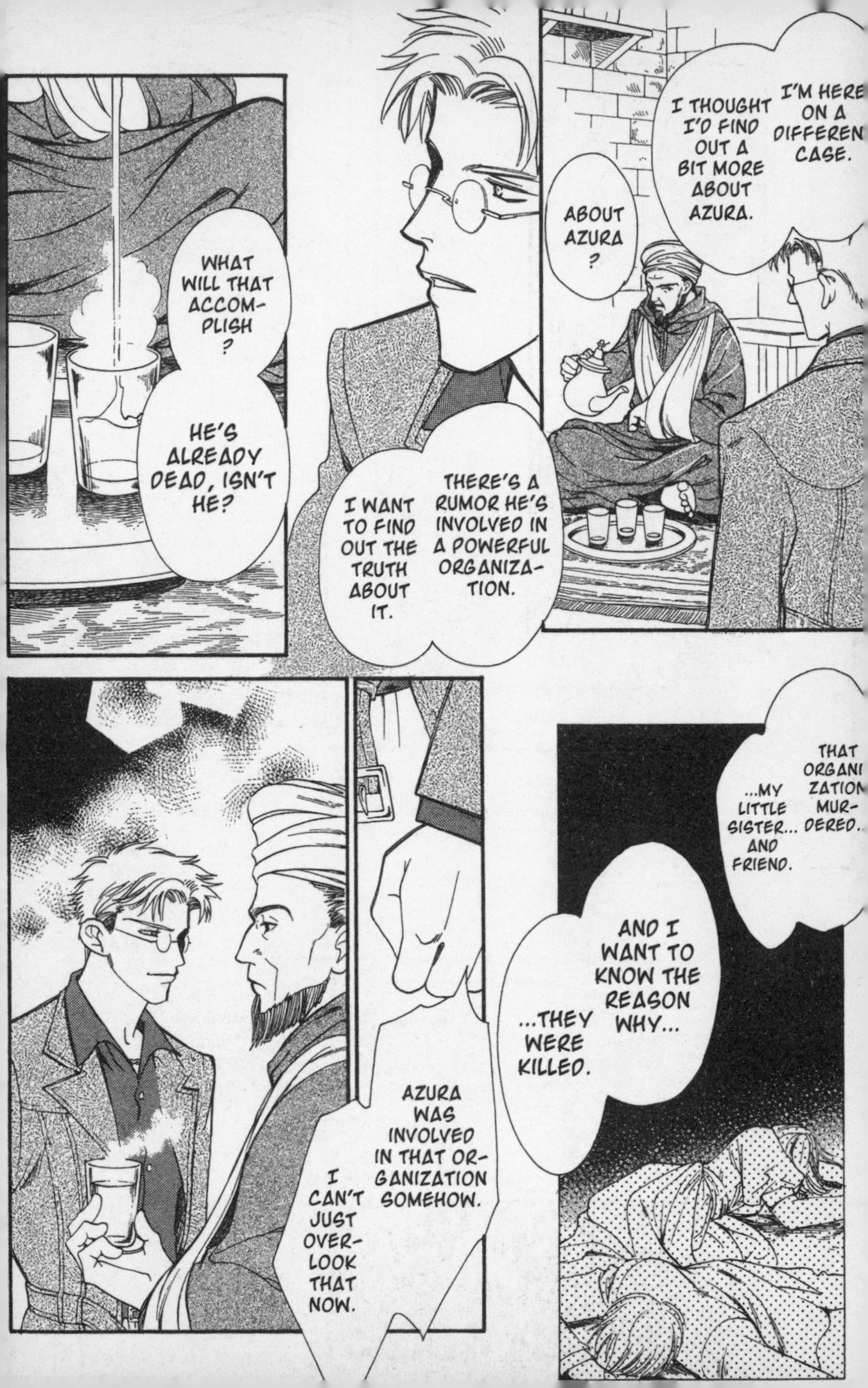
I'M HERE ON A DIFFEREN CASE.
I THOUGHT I'D FIND OUT A BIT MORE ABOUT AZURA.
ABOUT AZURA?
THERE'S A RUMOR HE'S INVOLVED IN A POWERFUL ORGANIZATION.
I WANT TO FIND OUT THE TRUTH ABOUT IT.
WHAT WILL THAT ACCOMPLISH?
HE'S ALREADY DEAD, ISN'T HE?
THAT ORGANIZATION MURDERED...
...MY LITTLE SISTER... AND FRIEND.
AND I WANT TO KNOW THE REASON WHY...
...THEY WERE KILLED.
AZURA WAS INVOLVED IN THAT ORGANIZATION SOMEHOW.
I CAN'T JUST OVERLOOK THAT NOW.

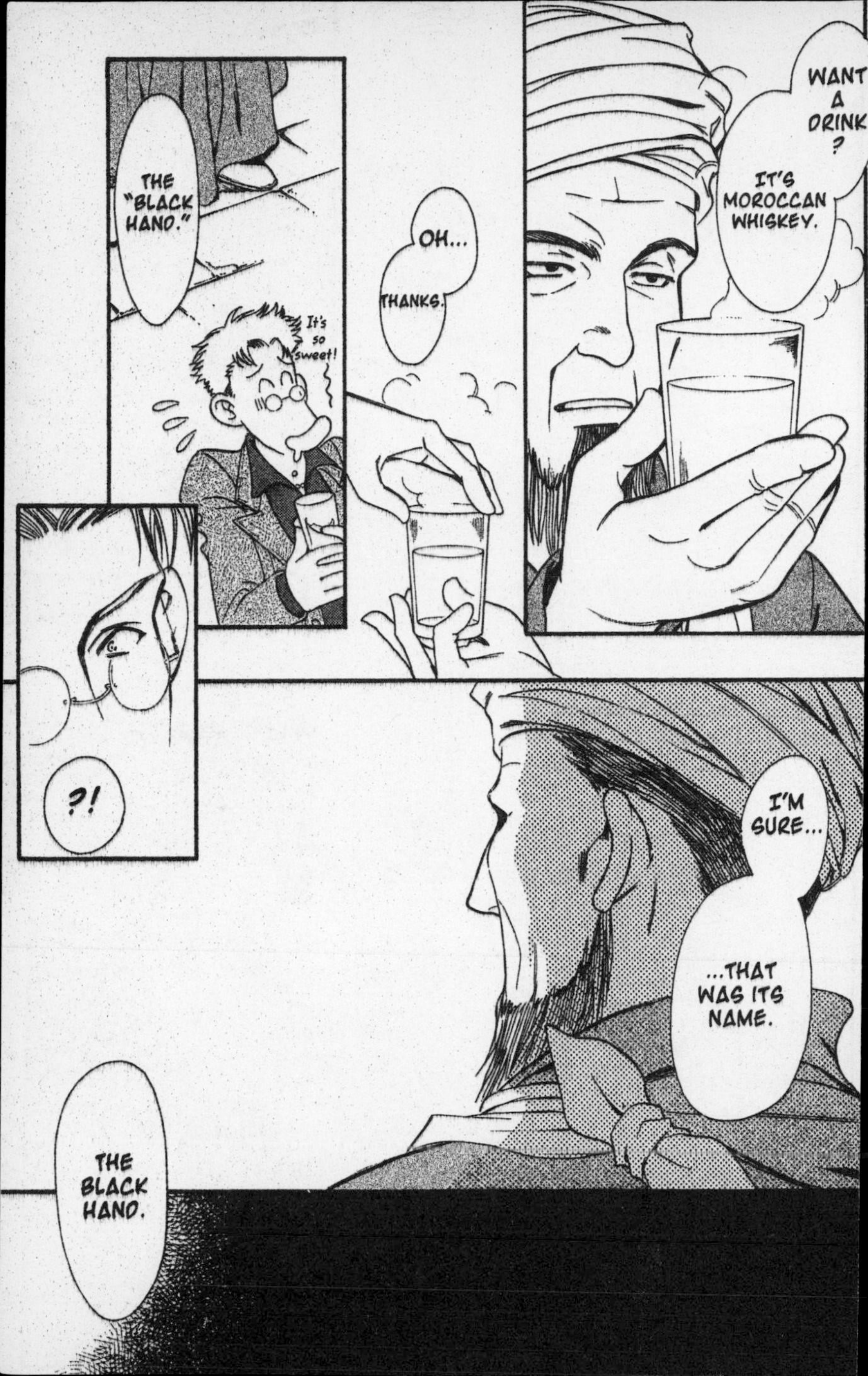
WANT A DRINK?
IT'S MOROCCAN WHISKEY.
OH...
THANKS.
THE "BLACK HAND."
It's so sweet!
?!
I'M SURE...
...THAT WAS ITS NAME.
THE BLACK HAND.

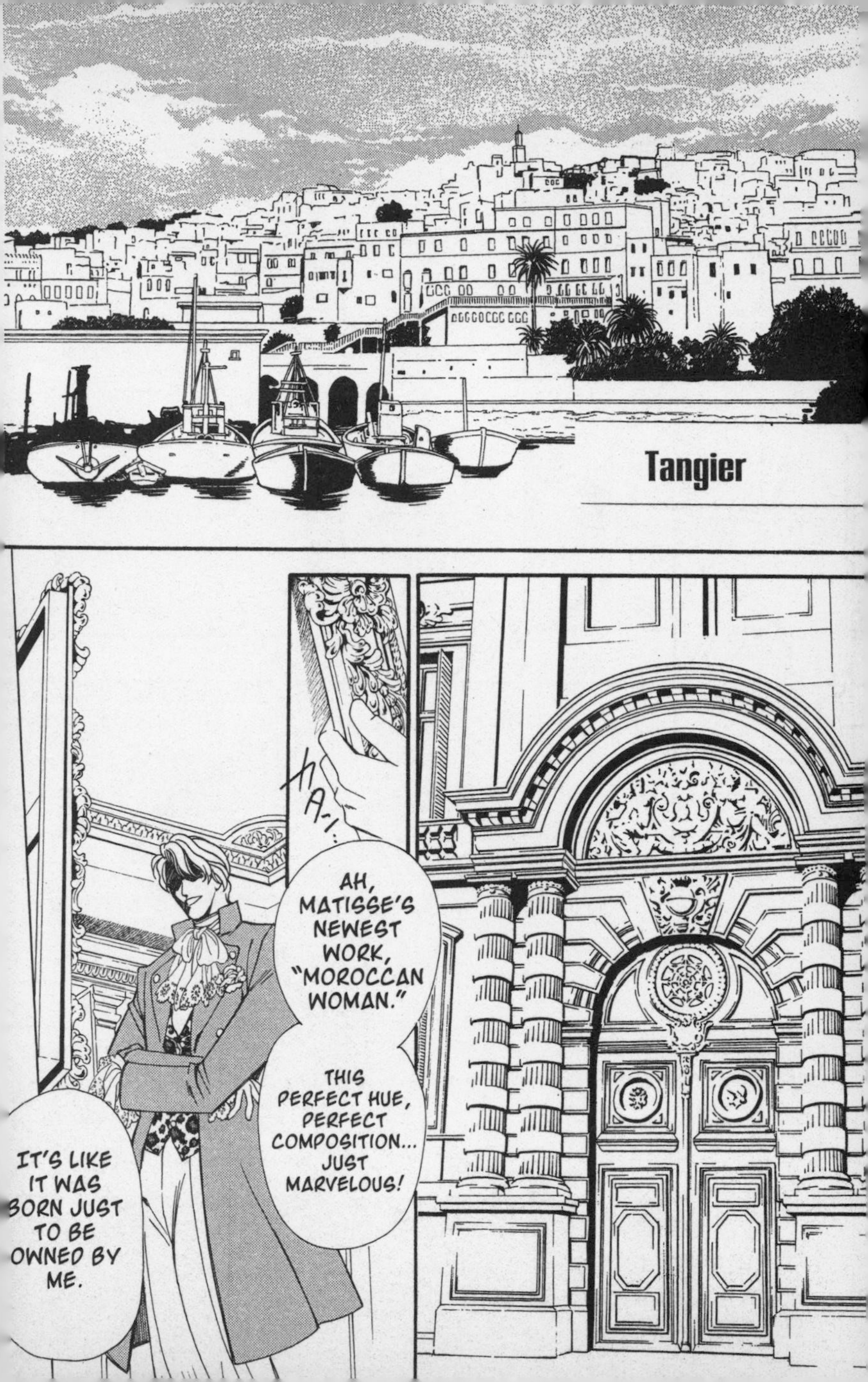
Tangier
KA-I...
AH, MATISSE'S NEWEST WORK, "MOROCCAN WOMAN."
THIS PERFECT HUE, PERFECT COMPOSITION... JUST MARVELOUS!
IT'S LIKE IT WAS BORN JUST TO BE OWNED BY ME.

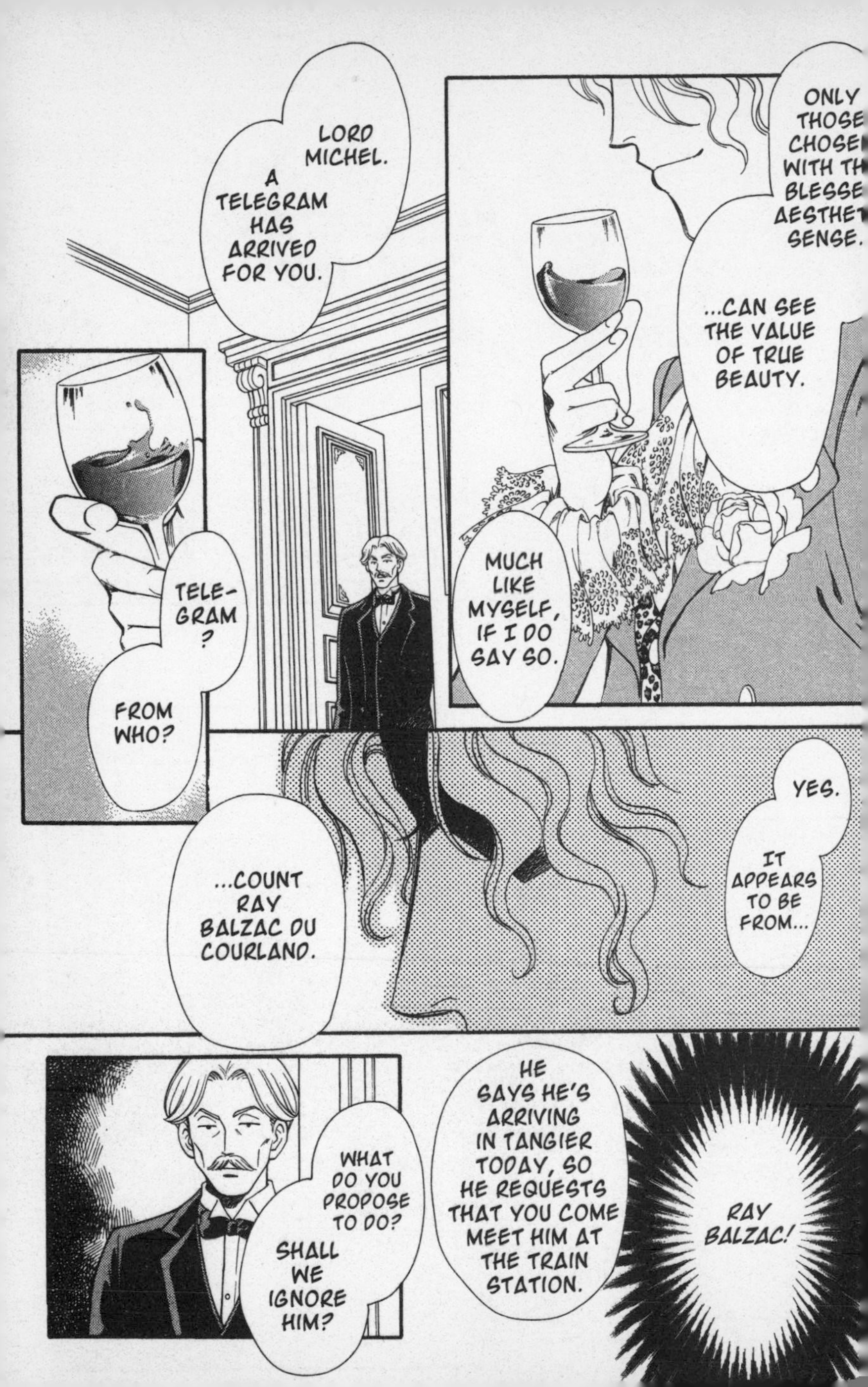
ONLY THOSE CHOSE WITH TH BLESSE AESTHET SENSE.
...CAN SEE THE VALUE OF TRUE BEAUTY.
MUCH LIKE MYSELF, IF I DO SAY SO.
LORD MICHEL.
A TELEGRAM HAS ARRIVED FOR YOU.
TELE-GRAM?
FROM WHO?
YES.
IT APPEARS TO BE FROM...
...COUNT RAY BALZAC DU COURLAND.
RAY BALZAC!
HE SAYS HE'S ARRIVING IN TANGIER TODAY, SO HE REQUESTS THAT YOU COME MEET HIM AT THE TRAIN STATION.
WHAT DO YOU PROPOSE TO DO?
SHALL WE IGNORE HIM?

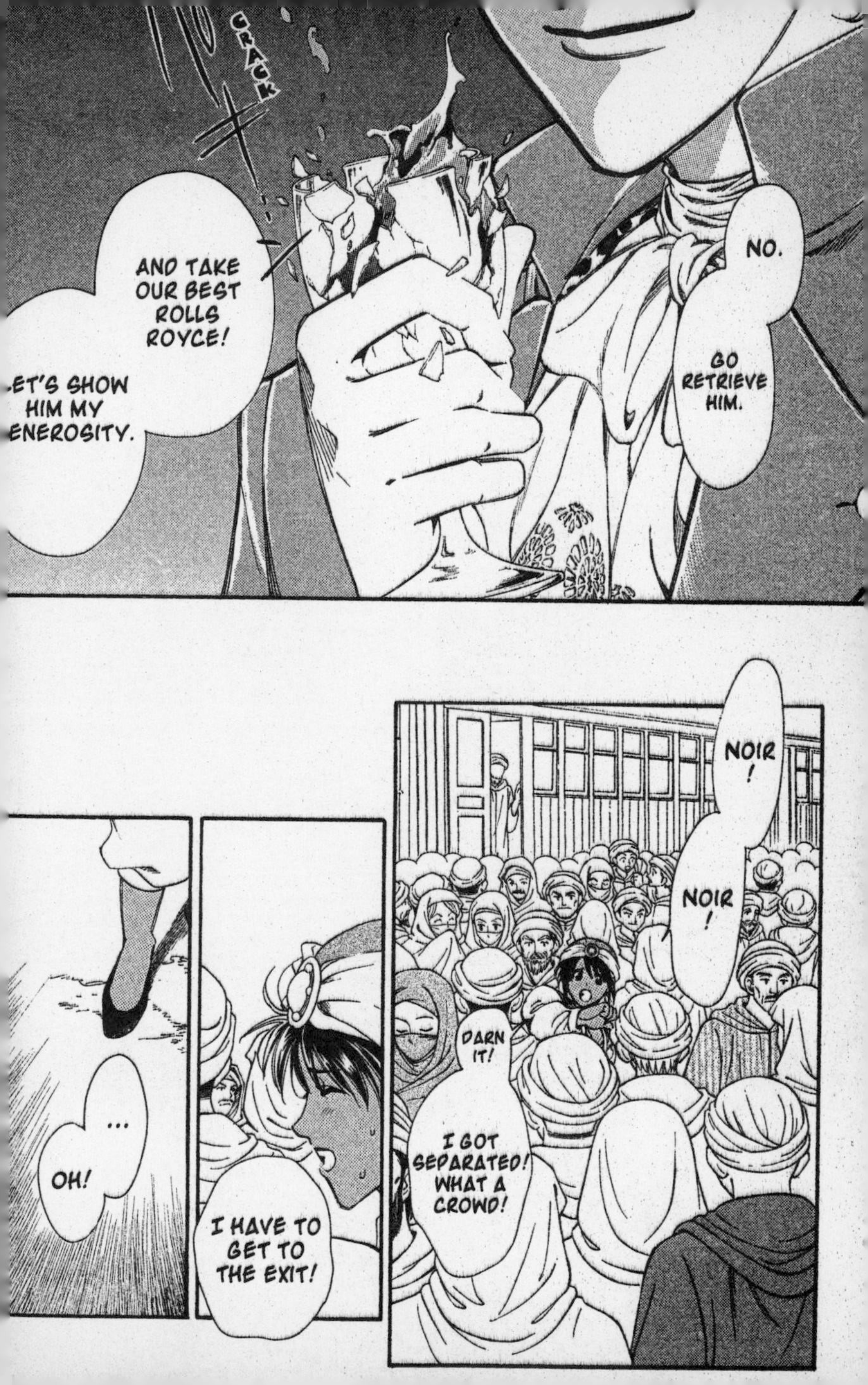
CRACK
NO.
GO RETRIEVE HIM.
AND TAKE OUR BEST ROLLS ROYCE!
-ET'S SHOW HIM MY ENEROSITY.
NOIR!
NOIR!
DARN IT!
I GOT SEPARATED! WHAT A CROWD!
I HAVE TO GET TO THE EXIT!
...
OH!

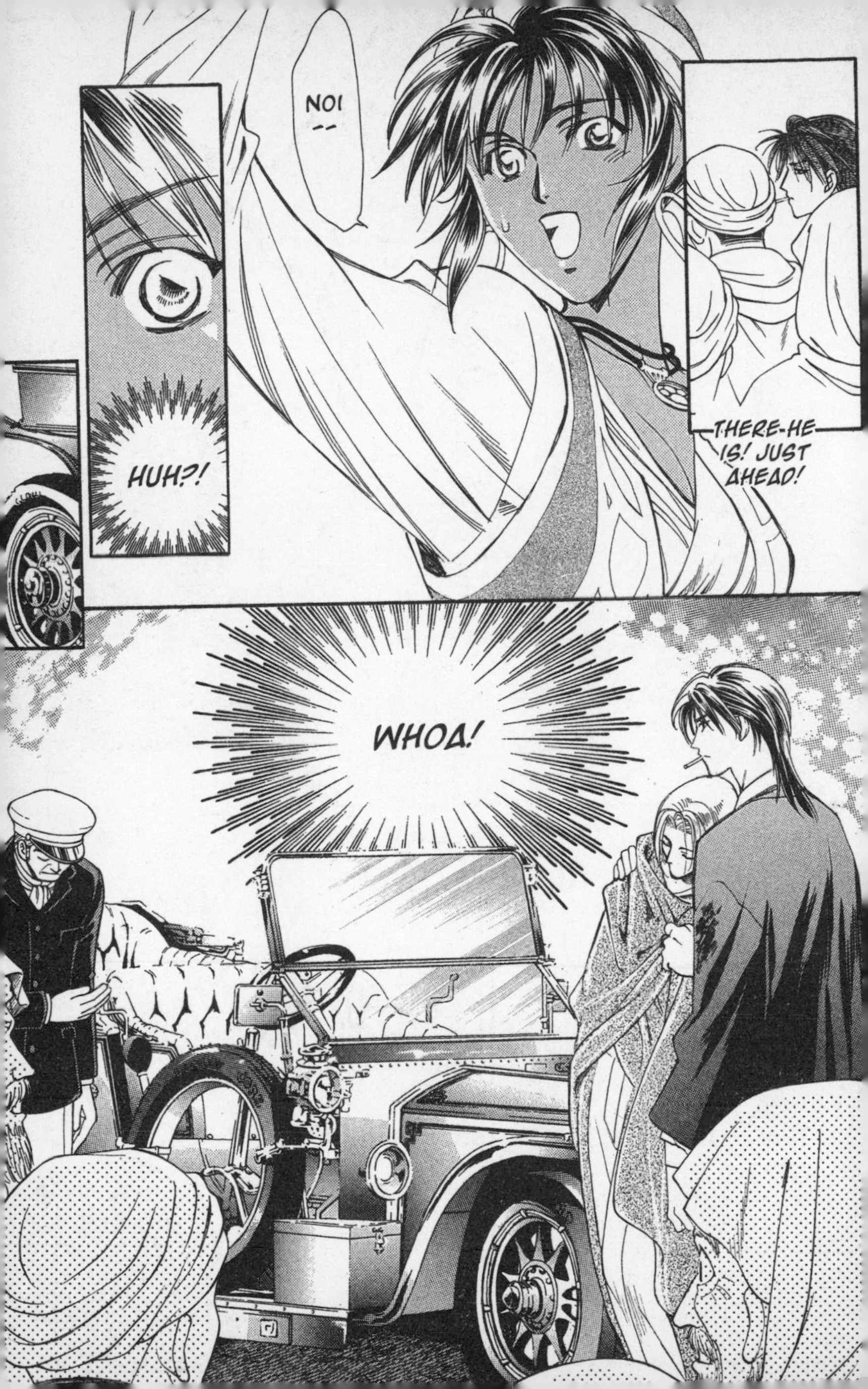
THERE-HE IS! JUST AHEAD!
NO! --
HUH?!
WHOA!

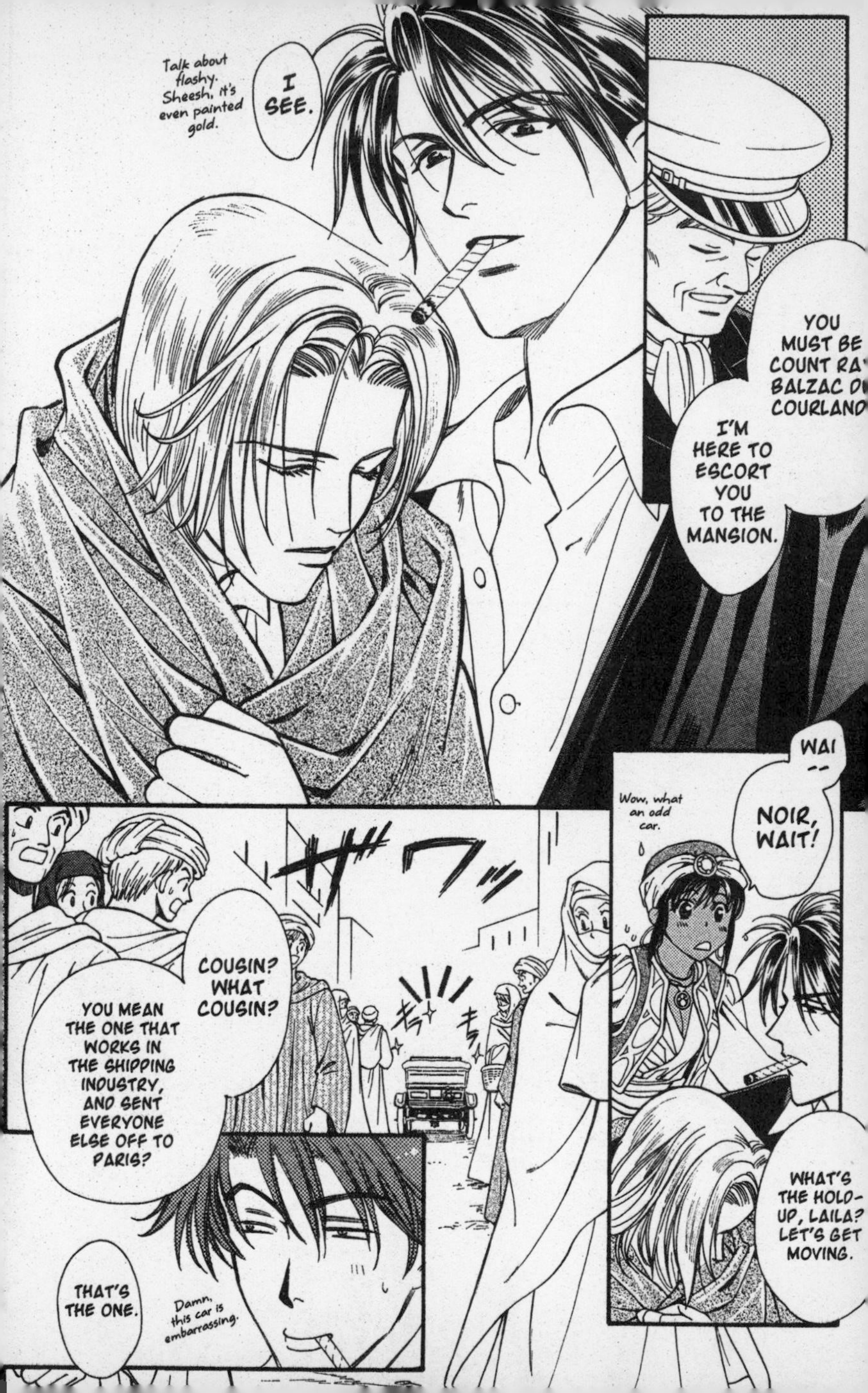
YOU MUST BE COUNT RA
BALZAC D
COURLAND
I'M HERE TO ESCORT YOU TO THE MANSION.
I SEE.
Talk about flashy. Sheesh, it's even painted gold.
WAI --
NOIR, WAIT!
Wow, what an odd car.
WHAT'S THE HOLD-UP, LAILA? LET'S GET MOVING.
ザワッ
COUSIN? WHAT COUSIN?
YOU MEAN THE ONE THAT WORKS IN THE SHIPPING INDUSTRY, AND SENT EVERYONE ELSE OFF TO PARIS?
THAT'S THE ONE.
Damn, this car is embarrassing.

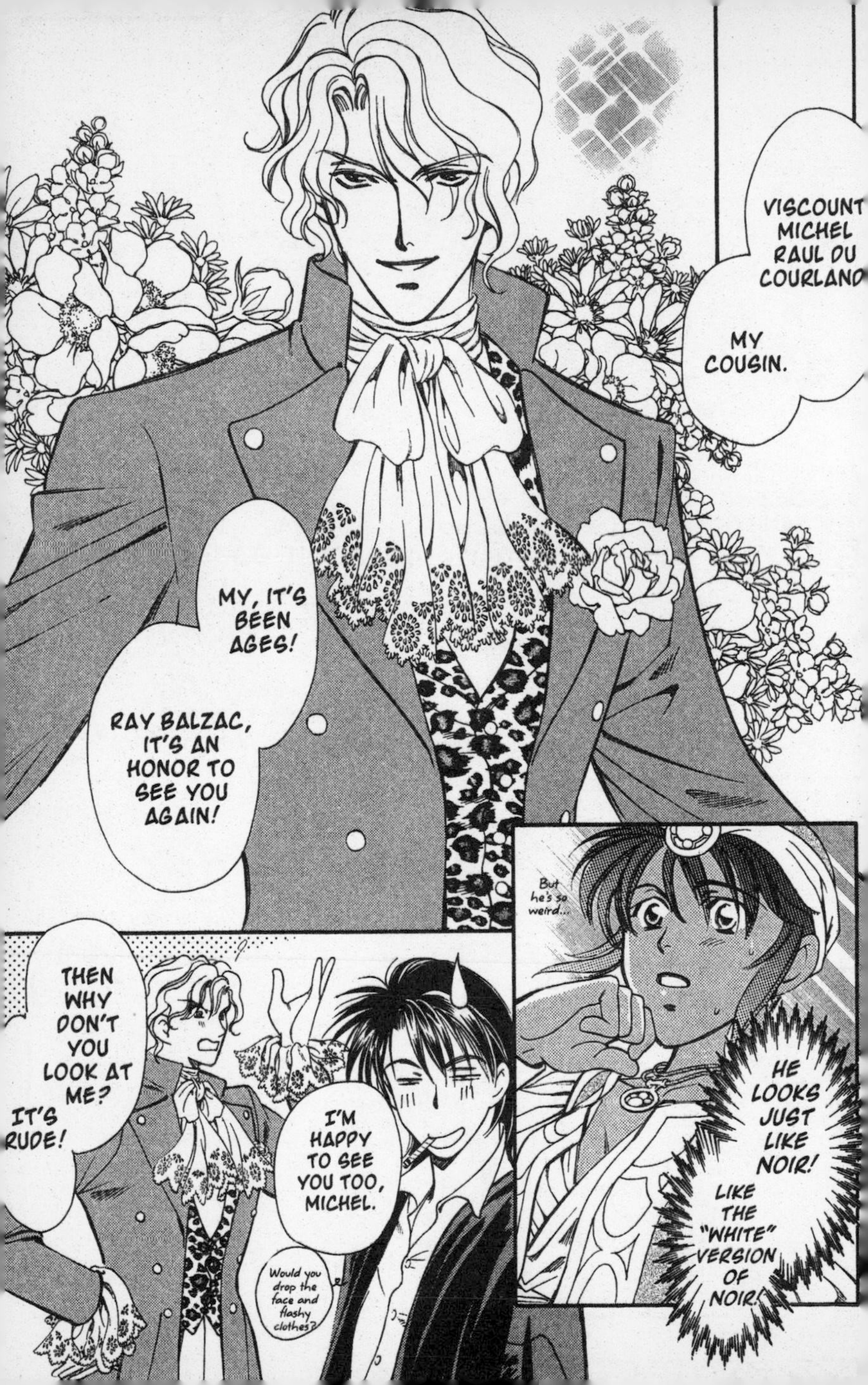

VISCOUNT MICHEL RAUL DU COURLAND
MY COUSIN.
MY, IT'S BEEN AGES!
RAY BALZAC, IT'S AN HONOR TO SEE YOU AGAIN!
But he's so weird...
HE LOOKS JUST LIKE NOIR!
LIKE THE "WHITE" VERSION OF NOIR!
I'M HAPPY TO SEE YOU TOO, MICHEL.
THEN WHY DON'T YOU LOOK AT ME? IT'S RUDE!
Would you drop the face and flashy clothes?

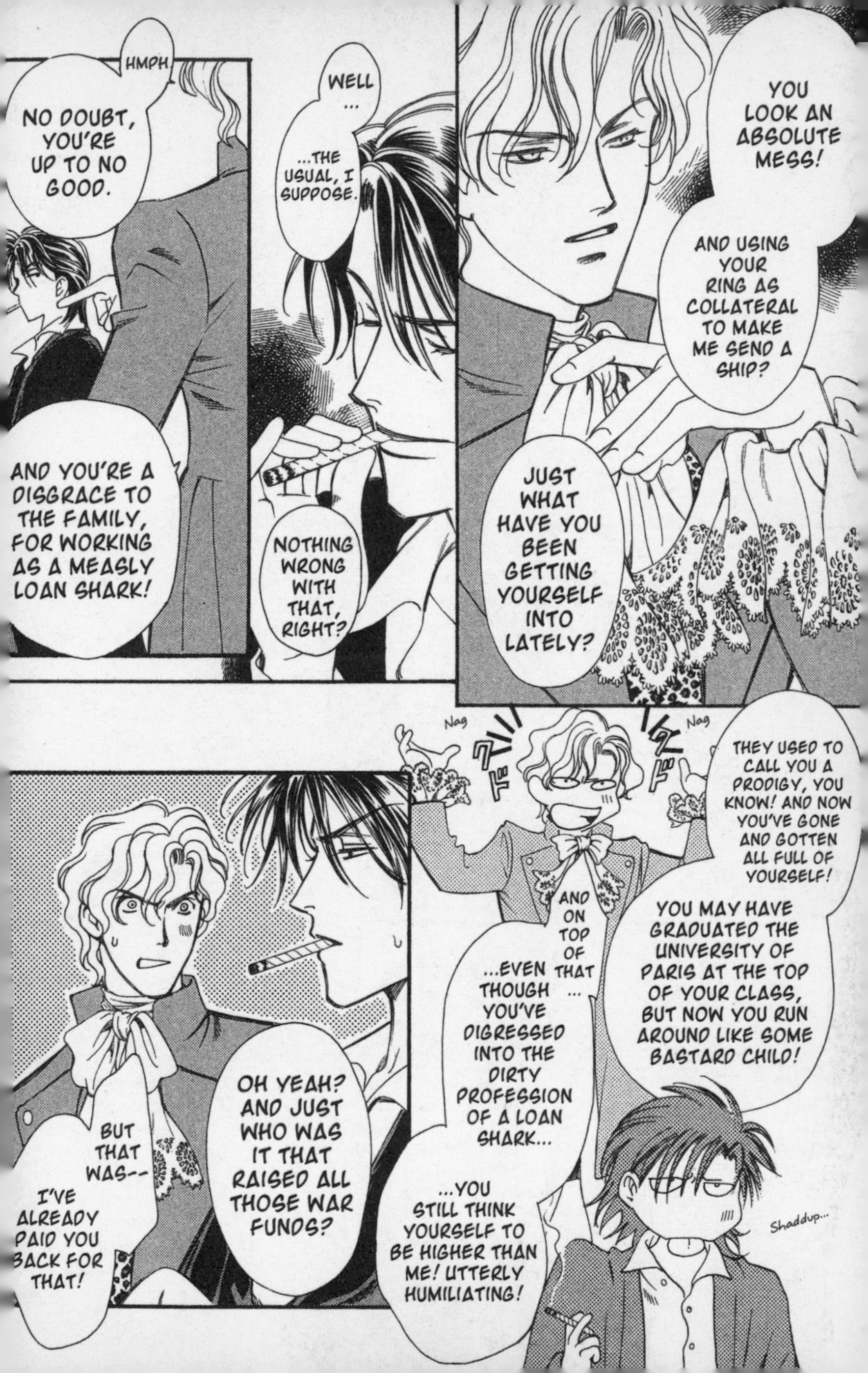
YOU LOOK AN ABSOLUTE MESS!
AND USING YOUR RING AS COLLATERAL TO MAKE ME SEND A SHIP?
JUST WHAT HAVE YOU BEEN GETTING YOURSELF INTO LATELY?
WELL ...
...THE USUAL, I SUPPOSE.
NOTHING WRONG WITH THAT, RIGHT?
HMPH.
NO DOUBT, YOU'RE UP TO NO GOOD.
AND YOU'RE A DISGRACE TO THE FAMILY, FOR WORKING AS A MEASLY LOAN SHARK!
Nag
Nag
THEY USED TO CALL YOU A PRODIGY, YOU KNOW! AND NOW YOU'VE GONE AND GOTTEN ALL FULL OF YOURSELF!
YOU MAY HAVE GRADUATED THE UNIVERSITY OF PARIS AT THE TOP OF YOUR CLASS, BUT NOW YOU RUN AROUND LIKE SOME BASTARD CHILD!
AND ON TOP OF THAT ...
...EVEN THOUGH YOU'VE DIGRESSED INTO THE DIRTY PROFESSION OF A LOAN SHARK...
...YOU STILL THINK YOURSELF TO BE HIGHER THAN ME! UTTERLY HUMILIATING!
Shaddup...
OH YEAH? AND JUST WHO WAS IT THAT RAISED ALL THOSE WAR FUNDS?
BUT THAT WAS--
I'VE ALREADY PAID YOU BACK FOR THAT!

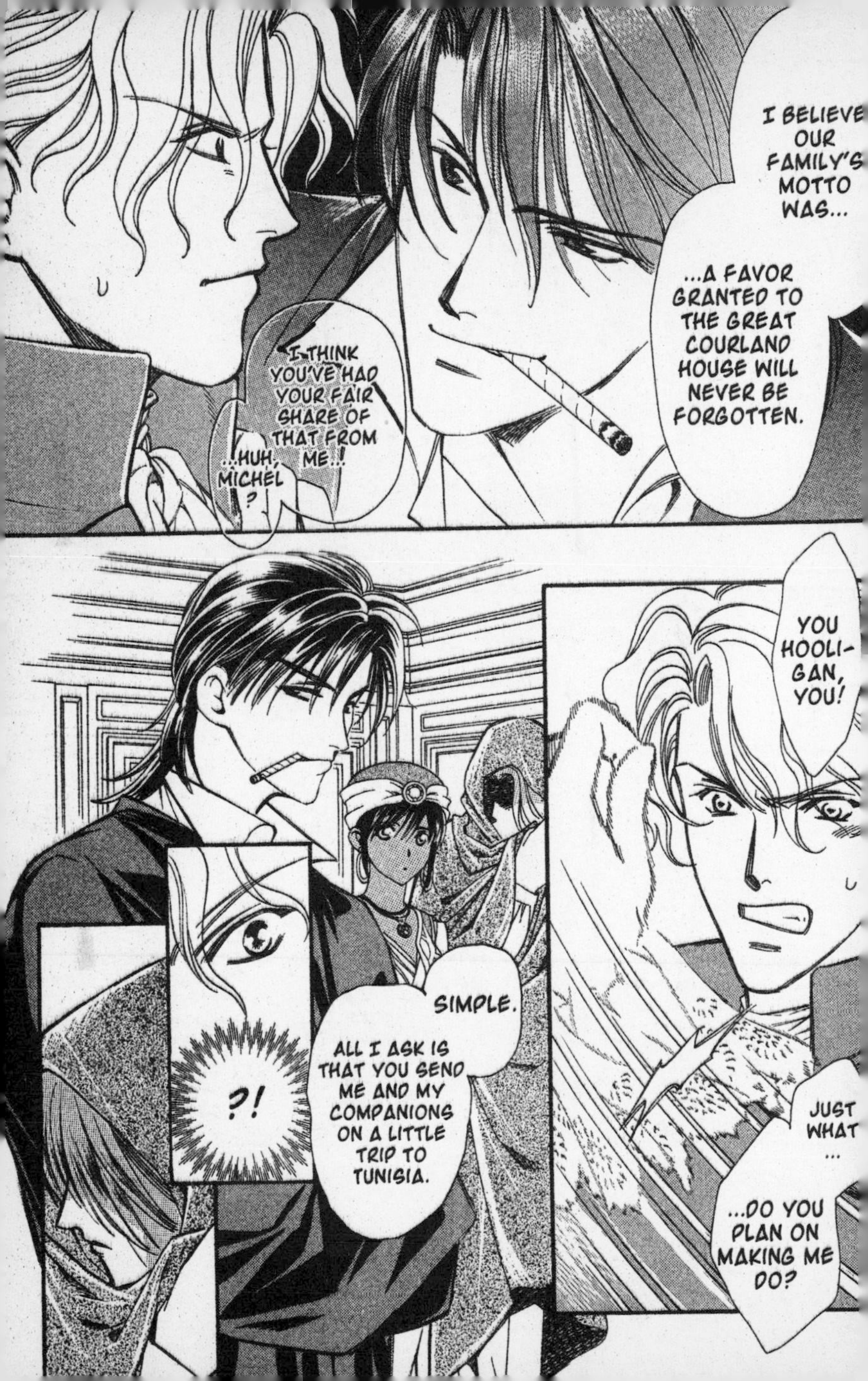
I BELIEVE OUR FAMILY'S MOTTO WAS...
...A FAVOR GRANTED TO THE GREAT COURLAND HOUSE WILL NEVER BE FORGOTTEN.
I THINK YOU'VE HAD YOUR FAIR SHARE OF THAT FROM ME...!
...HUH, MICHEL ?
YOU HOOLI-GAN, YOU!
JUST WHAT ...
...DO YOU PLAN ON MAKING ME DO?
SIMPLE.
ALL I ASK IS THAT YOU SEND ME AND MY COMPANIONS ON A LITTLE TRIP TO TUNISIA.
?!

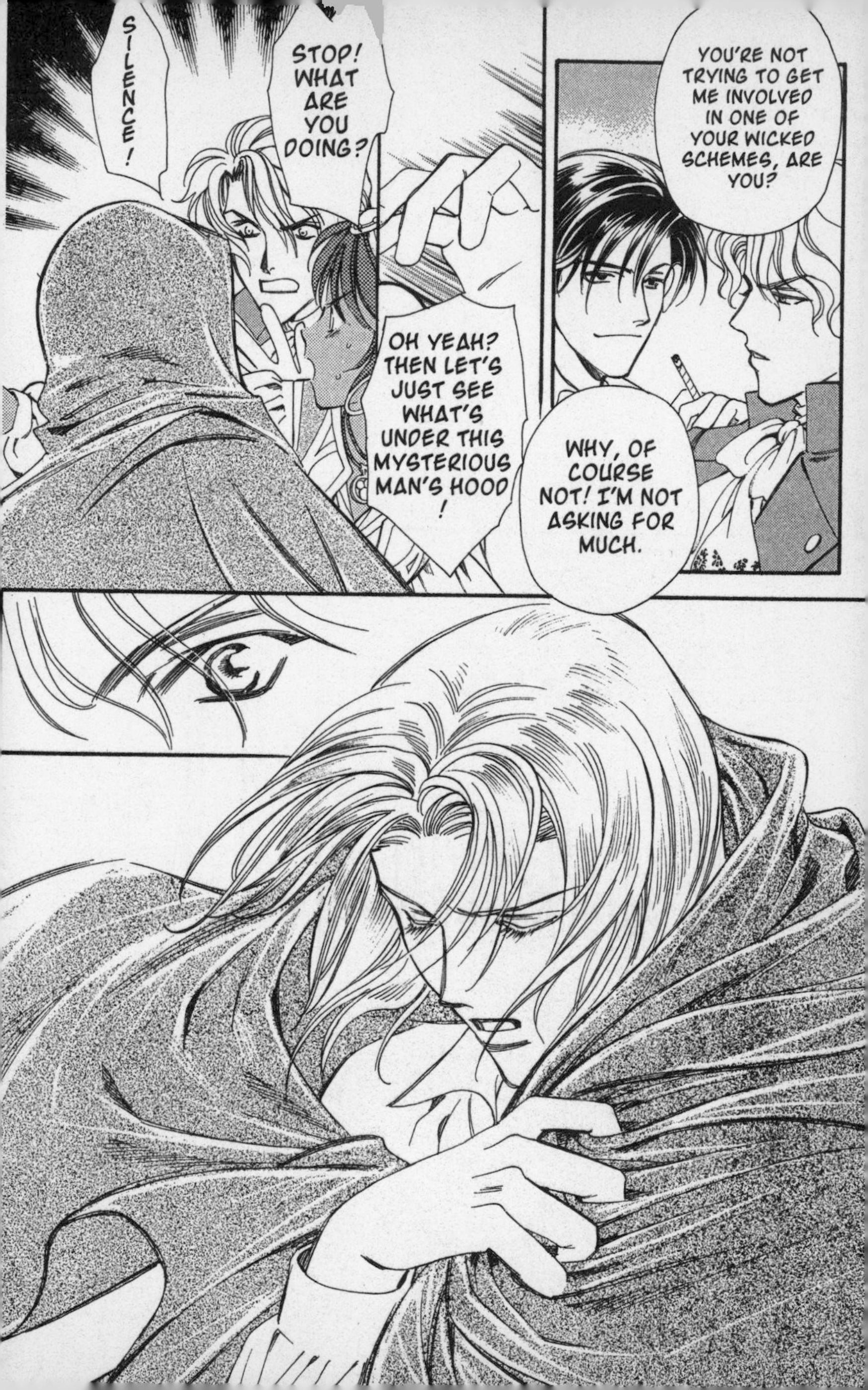

YOU'RE NOT TRYING TO GET ME INVOLVED IN ONE OF YOUR WICKED SCHEMES, ARE YOU?
WHY, OF COURSE NOT! I'M NOT ASKING FOR MUCH.
STOP! WHAT ARE YOU DOING?
SILENCE!
OH YEAH? THEN LET'S JUST SEE WHAT'S UNDER THIS MYSTERIOUS MAN'S HOOD!

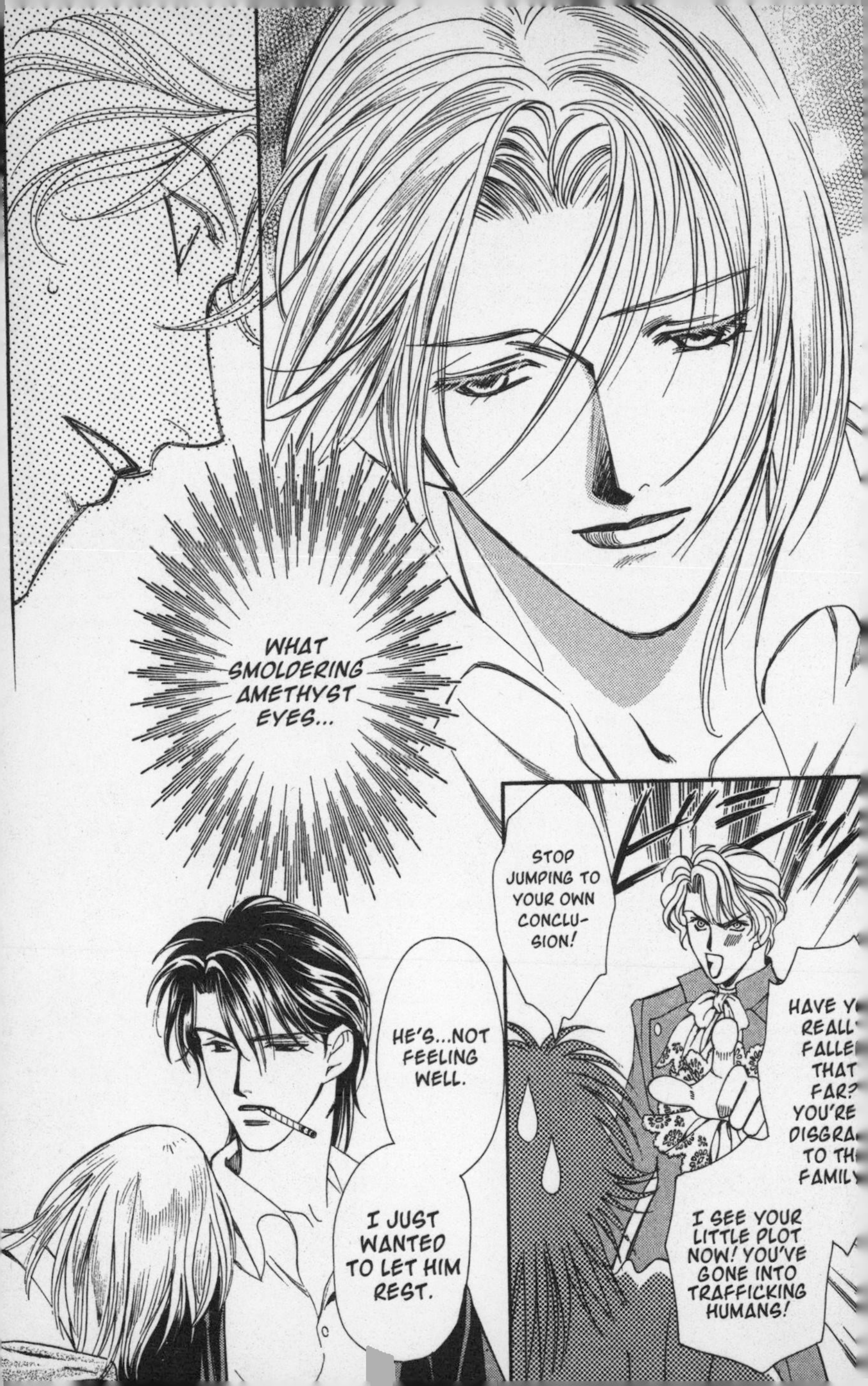
WHAT SMOLDERING AMETHYST EYES...
HAVE Y REALL FALLE THAT FAR? YOU'RE DISGRA TO TH FAMILY
I SEE YOUR LITTLE PLOT NOW! YOU'VE GONE INTO TRAFFICKING HUMANS!
STOP JUMPING TO YOUR OWN CONCLUSION!
HE'S...NOT FEELING WELL.
I JUST WANTED TO LET HIM REST.

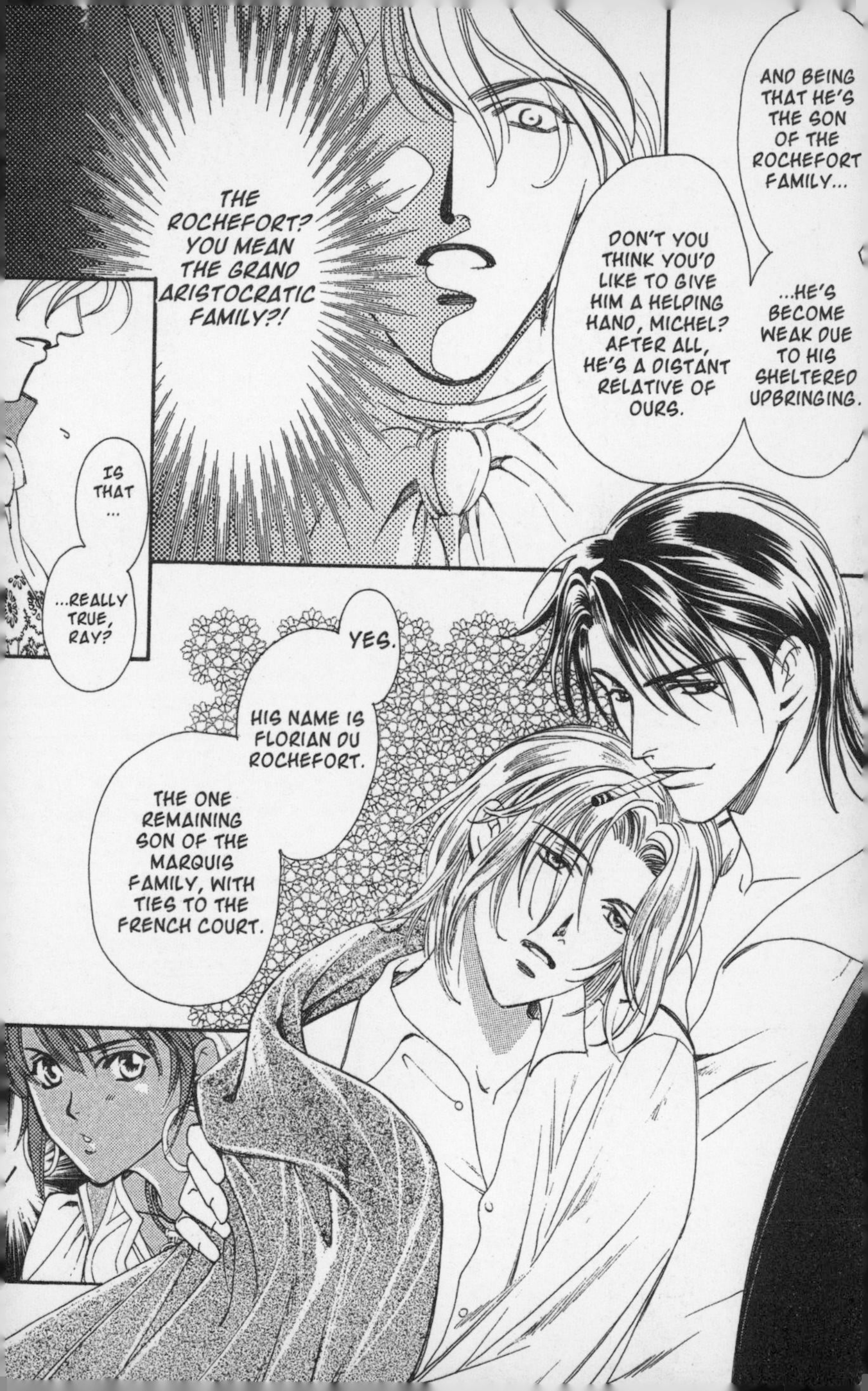
AND BEING THAT HE'S THE SON OF THE ROCHEFORT FAMILY...
...HE'S BECOME WEAK DUE TO HIS SHELTERED UPBRINGING.
DON'T YOU THINK YOU'D LIKE TO GIVE HIM A HELPING HAND, MICHEL? AFTER ALL, HE'S A DISTANT RELATIVE OF OURS.
THE ROCHEFORT? YOU MEAN THE GRAND ARISTOCRATIC FAMILY?!
IS THAT ...
...REALLY TRUE, RAY?
YES.
HIS NAME IS FLORIAN DU ROCHEFORT.
THE ONE REMAINING SON OF THE MARQUIS FAMILY, WITH TIES TO THE FRENCH COURT.

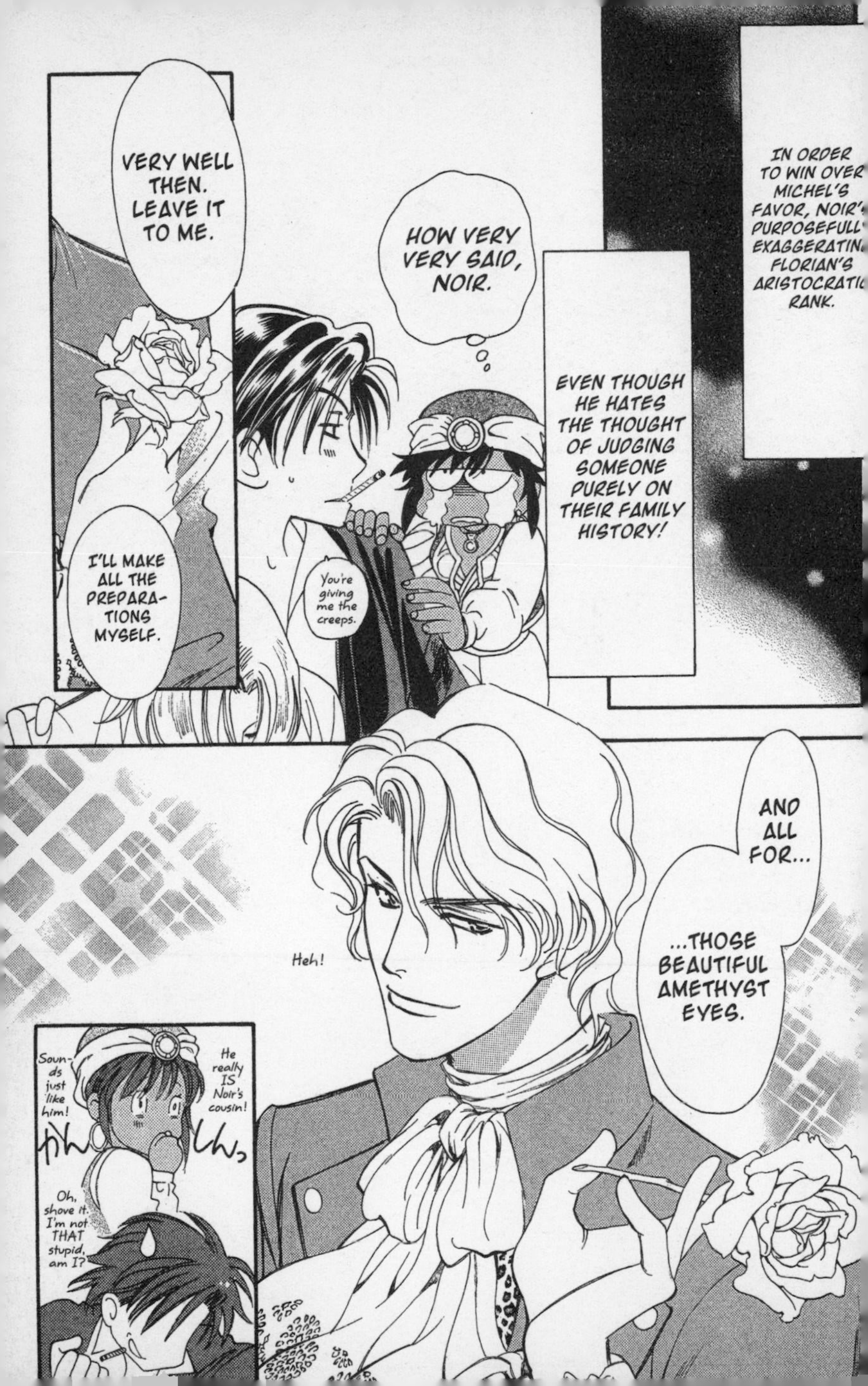
IN ORDER TO WIN OVER MICHEL'S FAVOR, NOIR'S PURPOSEFULL EXAGGERATIN FLORIAN'S ARISTOCRATI RANK.
EVEN THOUGH HE HATES THE THOUGHT OF JUDGING SOMEONE PURELY ON THEIR FAMILY HISTORY!
HOW VERY VERY SAID, NOIR.
You're giving me the creeps.
VERY WELL THEN. LEAVE IT TO ME.
I'LL MAKE ALL THE PREPARA-TIONS MYSELF.
AND ALL FOR...
...THOSE BEAUTIFUL AMETHYST EYES.
Heh!
He really IS Noir's cousin!
Soun-ds just like him!
Oh, shove it. I'm not THAT stupid, am I?

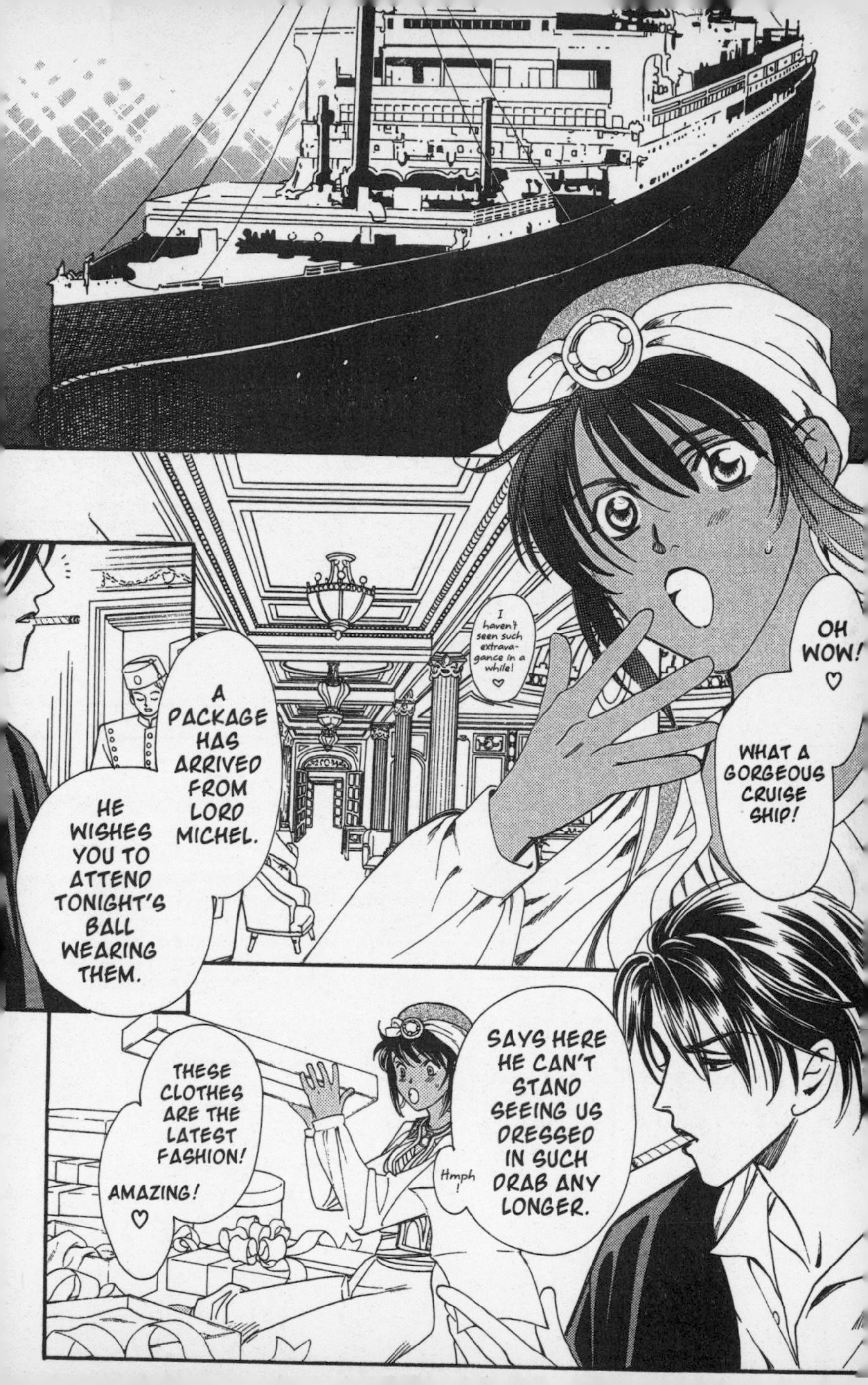
OH WOW! ♡
WHAT A GORGEOUS CRUISE SHIP!
I haven't seen such extrava-gance in a while! ♡
A PACKAGE HAS ARRIVED FROM LORD MICHEL.
HE WISHES YOU TO ATTEND TONIGHT'S BALL WEARING THEM.
SAYS HERE HE CAN'T STAND SEEING US DRESSED IN SUCH DRAB ANY LONGER.
Hmph!
THESE CLOTHES ARE THE LATEST FASHION!
AMAZING! ♡

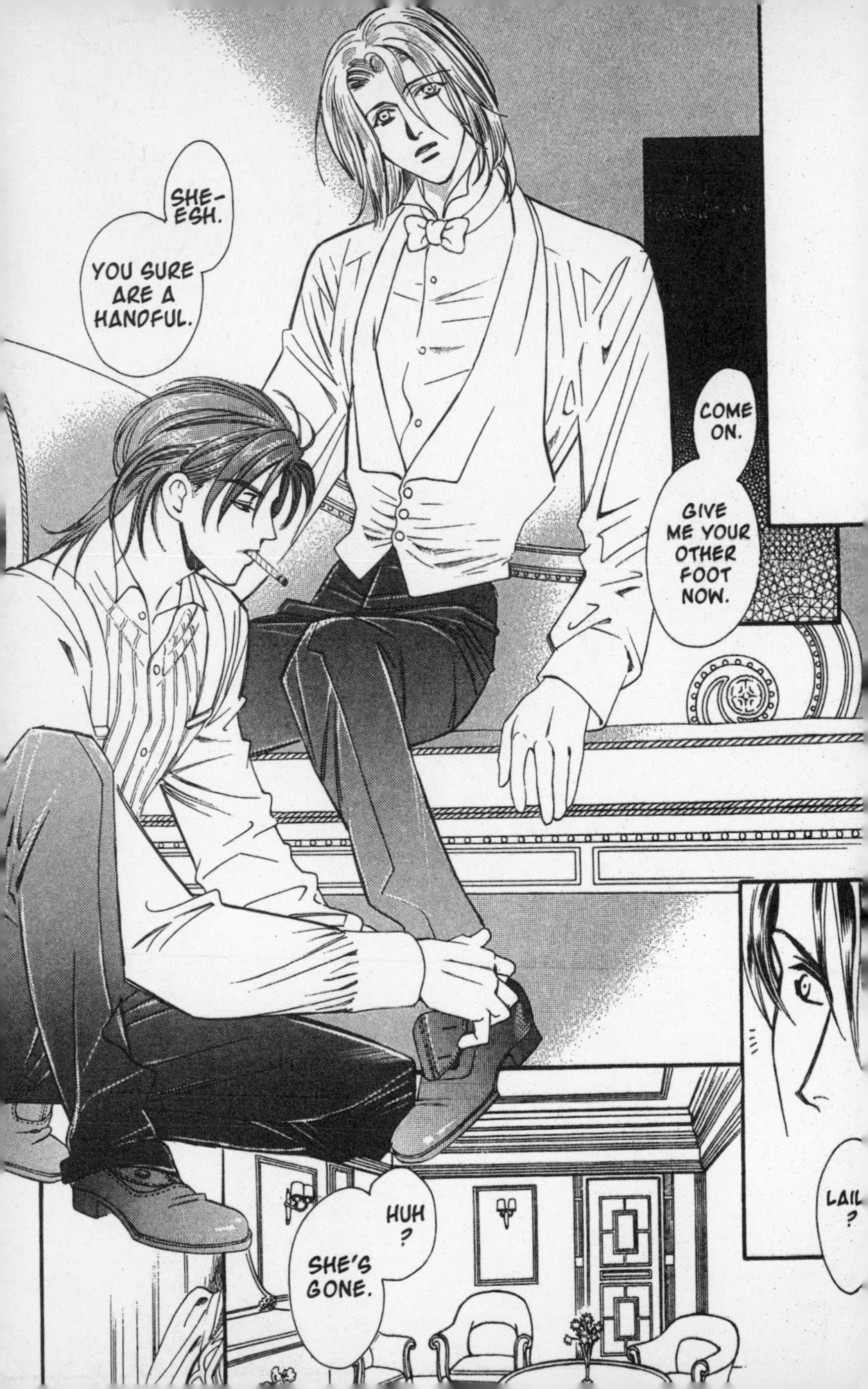
SHE-ESH.
YOU SURE ARE A HANDFUL.
COME ON.
GIVE ME YOUR OTHER FOOT NOW.
LAIL?
HUH?
SHE'S GONE.

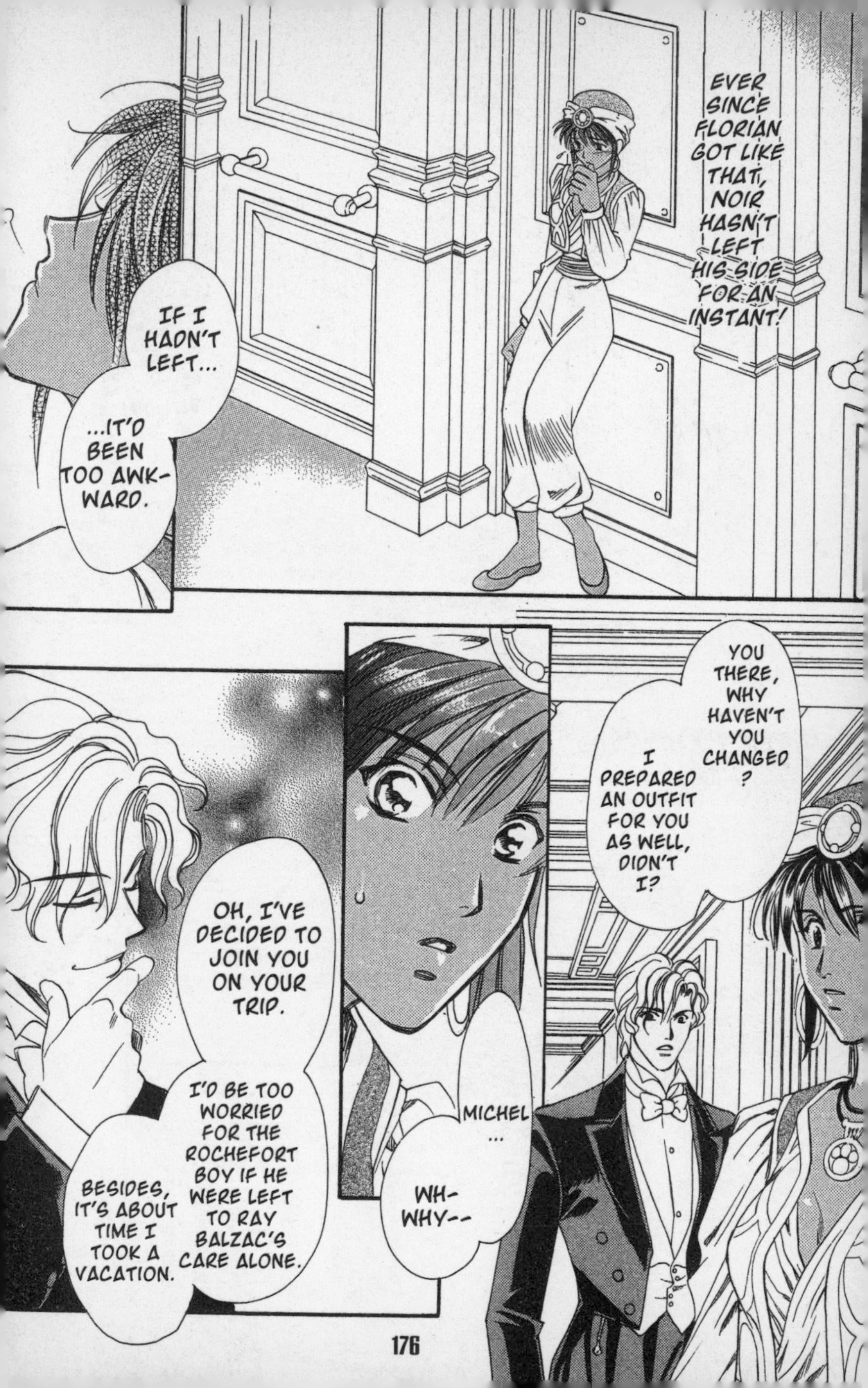
EVER SINCE FLORIAN GOT LIKE THAT, NOIR HASN'T LEFT HIS SIDE FOR AN INSTANT!
IF I HADN'T LEFT...
...IT'D BEEN TOO AWK-WARD.
YOU THERE, WHY HAVEN'T YOU CHANGED?
I PREPARED AN OUTFIT FOR YOU AS WELL, DIDN'T I?
MICHEL...
WH-WHY--
OH, I'VE DECIDED TO JOIN YOU ON YOUR TRIP.
I'D BE TOO WORRIED FOR THE ROCHEFORT BOY IF HE WERE LEFT TO RAY BALZAC'S CARE ALONE.
BESIDES, IT'S ABOUT TIME I TOOK A VACATION.

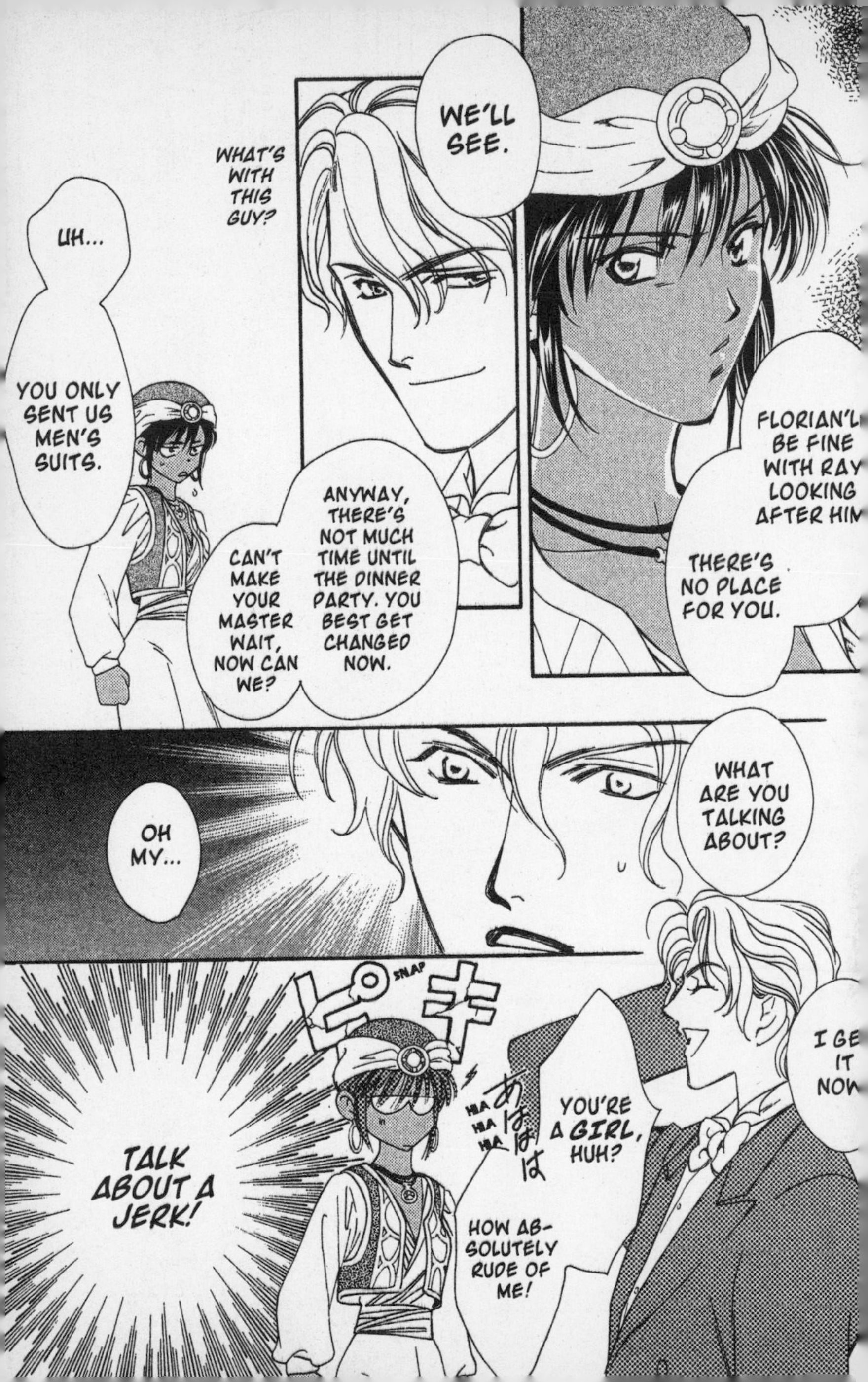
FLORIAN'L BE FINE WITH RAY LOOKING AFTER HIM
THERE'S NO PLACE FOR YOU.
WE'LL SEE.
WHAT'S WITH THIS GUY?
ANYWAY, THERE'S NOT MUCH TIME UNTIL THE DINNER PARTY. YOU BEST GET CHANGED NOW.
CAN'T MAKE YOUR MASTER WAIT, NOW CAN WE?
UH...
YOU ONLY SENT US MEN'S SUITS.
WHAT ARE YOU TALKING ABOUT?
OH MY...
I GE IT NOW
YOU'RE A GIRL, HUH?
あははは
HA HA HA
HOW AB-SOLUTELY RUDE OF ME!
SNAP
TALK ABOUT A JERK!

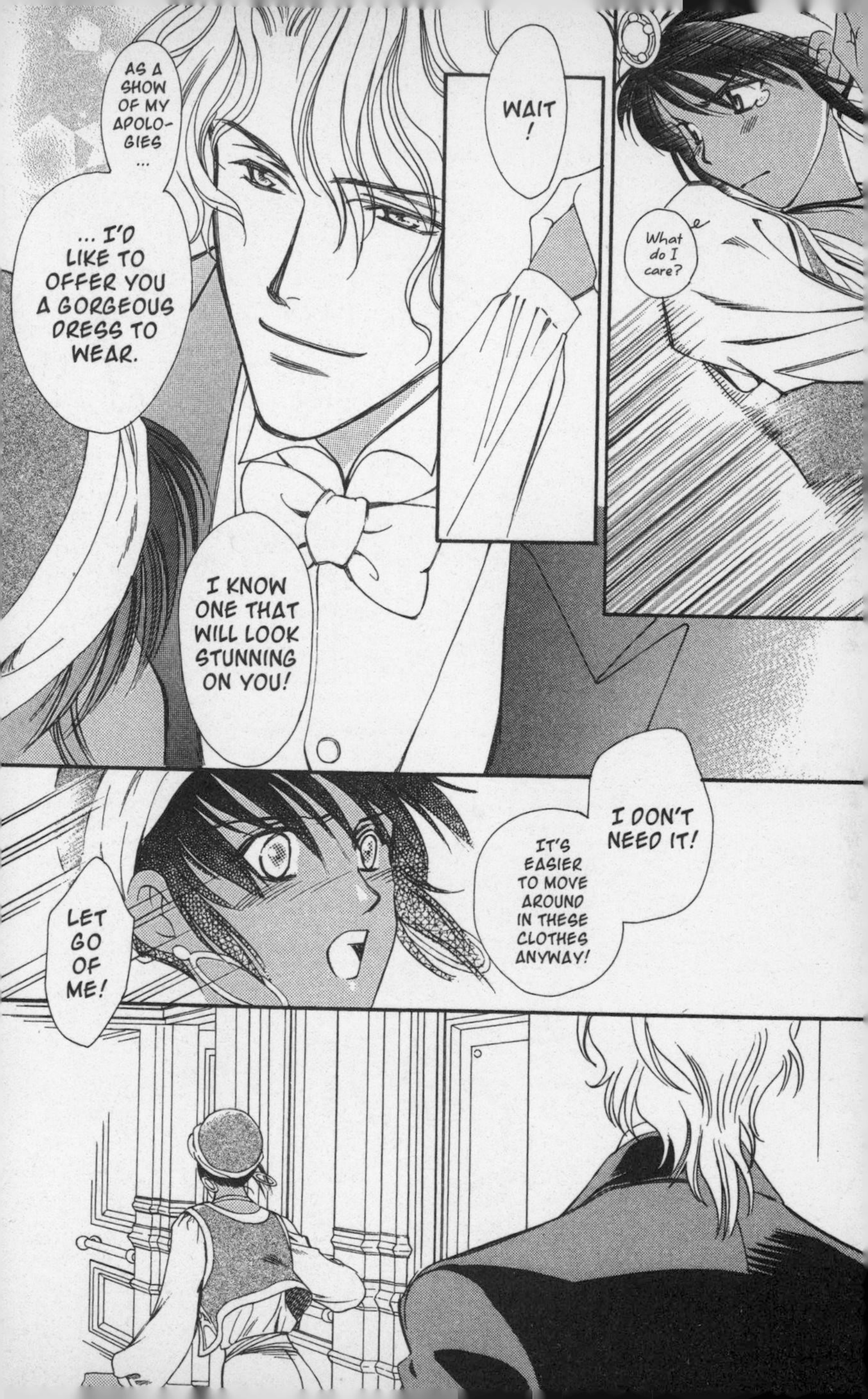
What do I care?
WAIT!
AS A SHOW OF MY APOLOGIES ...
... I'D LIKE TO OFFER YOU A GORGEOUS DRESS TO WEAR.
I KNOW ONE THAT WILL LOOK STUNNING ON YOU!
I DON'T NEED IT!
IT'S EASIER TO MOVE AROUND IN THESE CLOTHES ANYWAY!
LET GO OF ME!

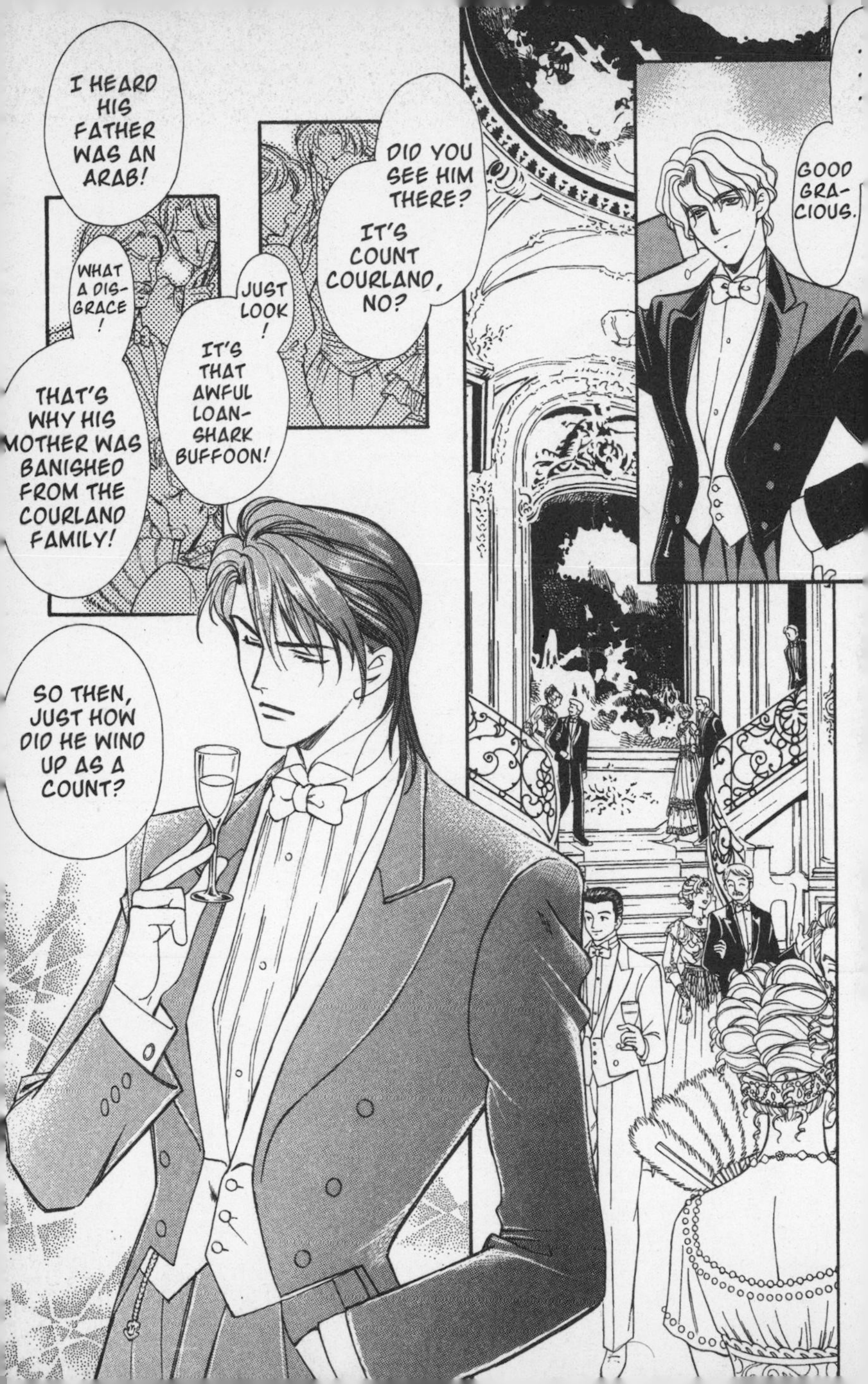
GOOD GRACIOUS.
DID YOU SEE HIM THERE?
IT'S COUNT COURLAND, NO?
JUST LOOK!
IT'S THAT AWFUL LOAN-SHARK BUFFOON!
I HEARD HIS FATHER WAS AN ARAB!
WHAT A DISGRACE!
THAT'S WHY HIS MOTHER WAS BANISHED FROM THE COURLAND FAMILY!
SO THEN, JUST HOW DID HE WIND UP AS A COUNT?

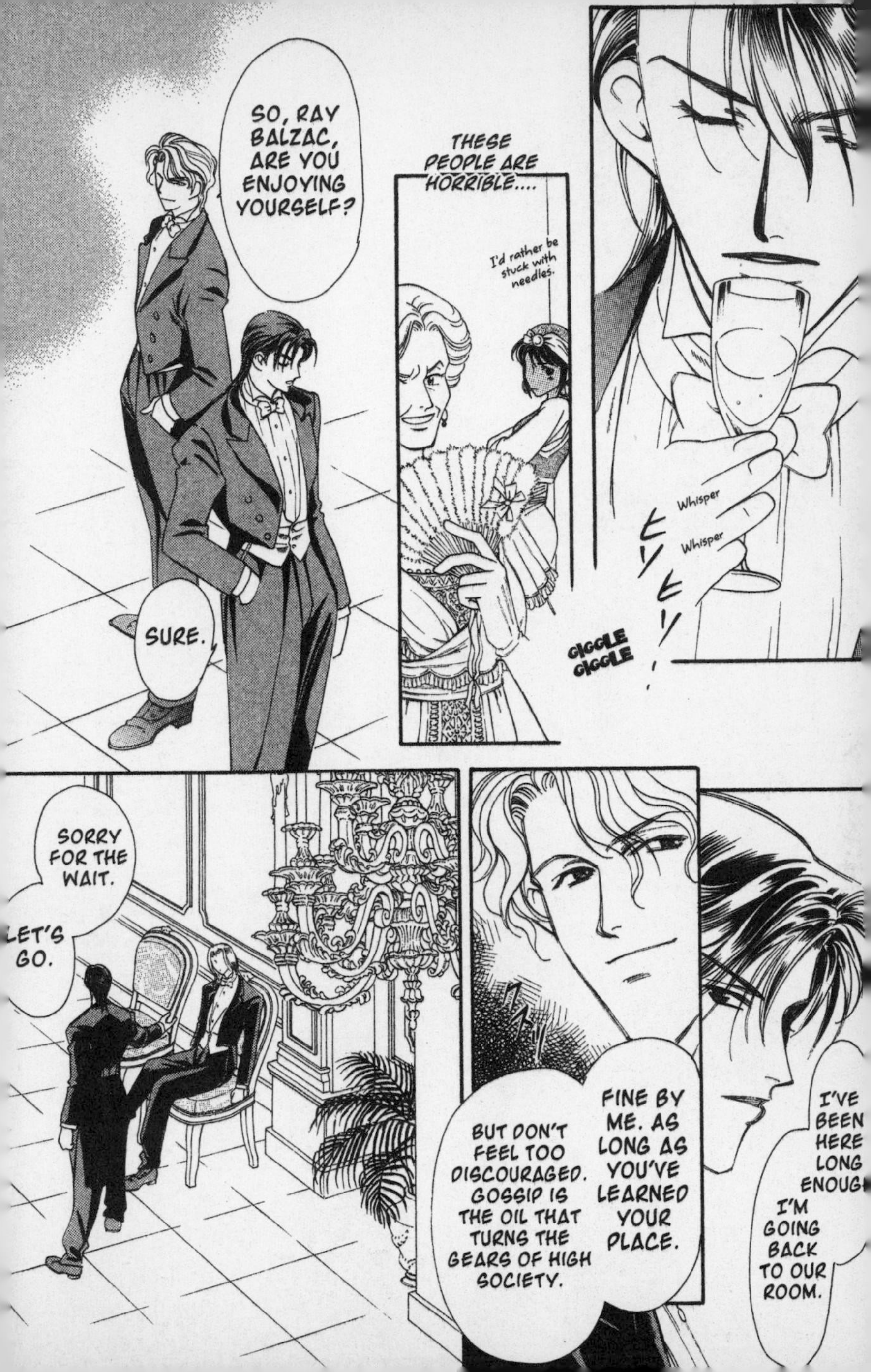
Whisper
Whisper
GIGGLE GIGGLE
THESE PEOPLE ARE HORRIBLE....
I'd rather be stuck with needles.
SO, RAY BALZAC, ARE YOU ENJOYING YOURSELF?
SURE.
I'VE BEEN HERE LONG ENOUGH
I'M GOING BACK TO OUR ROOM.
FINE BY ME. AS LONG AS YOU'VE LEARNED YOUR PLACE.
BUT DON'T FEEL TOO DISCOURAGED. GOSSIP IS THE OIL THAT TURNS THE GEARS OF HIGH SOCIETY.
SORRY FOR THE WAIT.
LET'S GO.

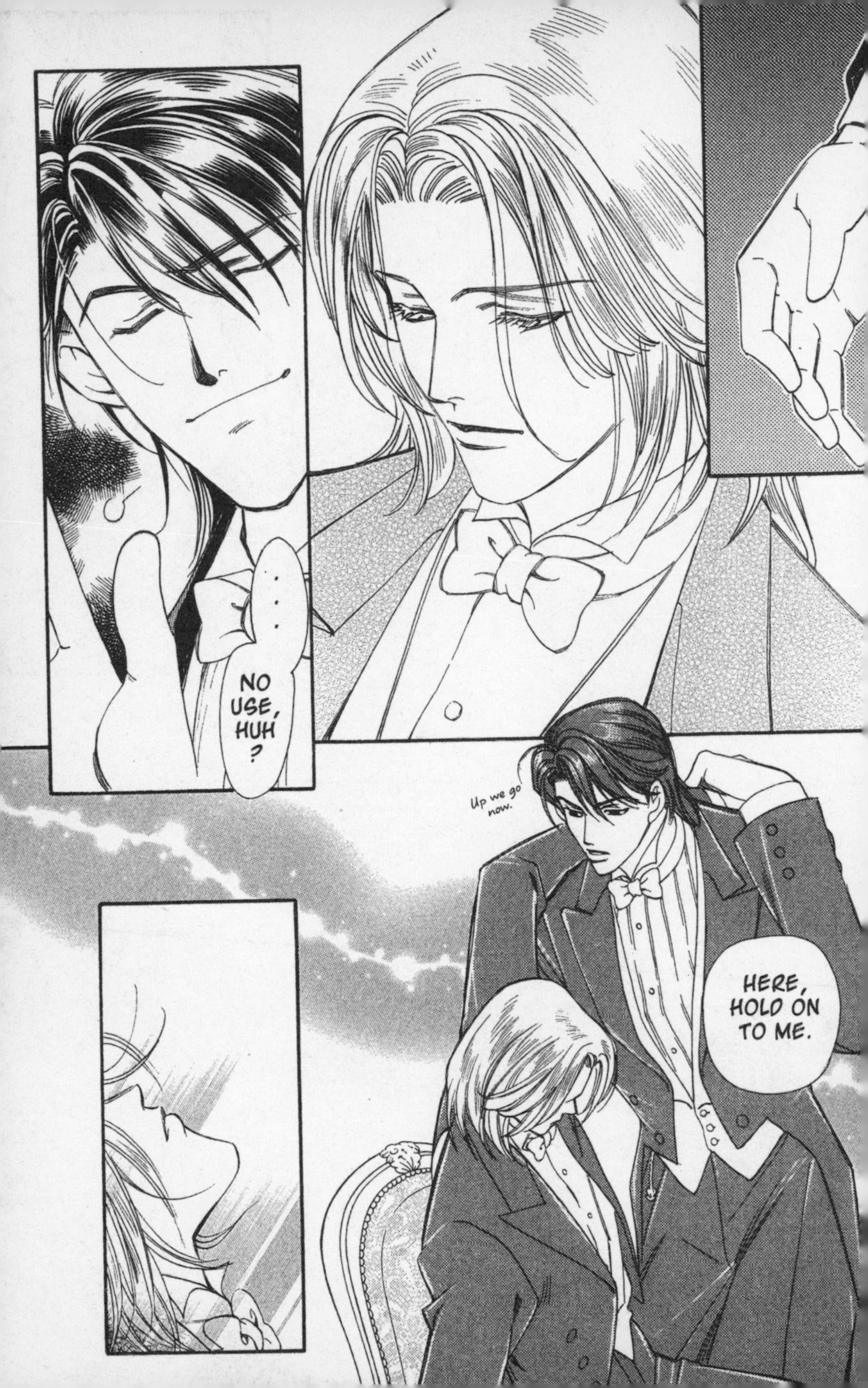
...
NO USE, HUH?
Up we go now.
HERE, HOLD ON TO ME.

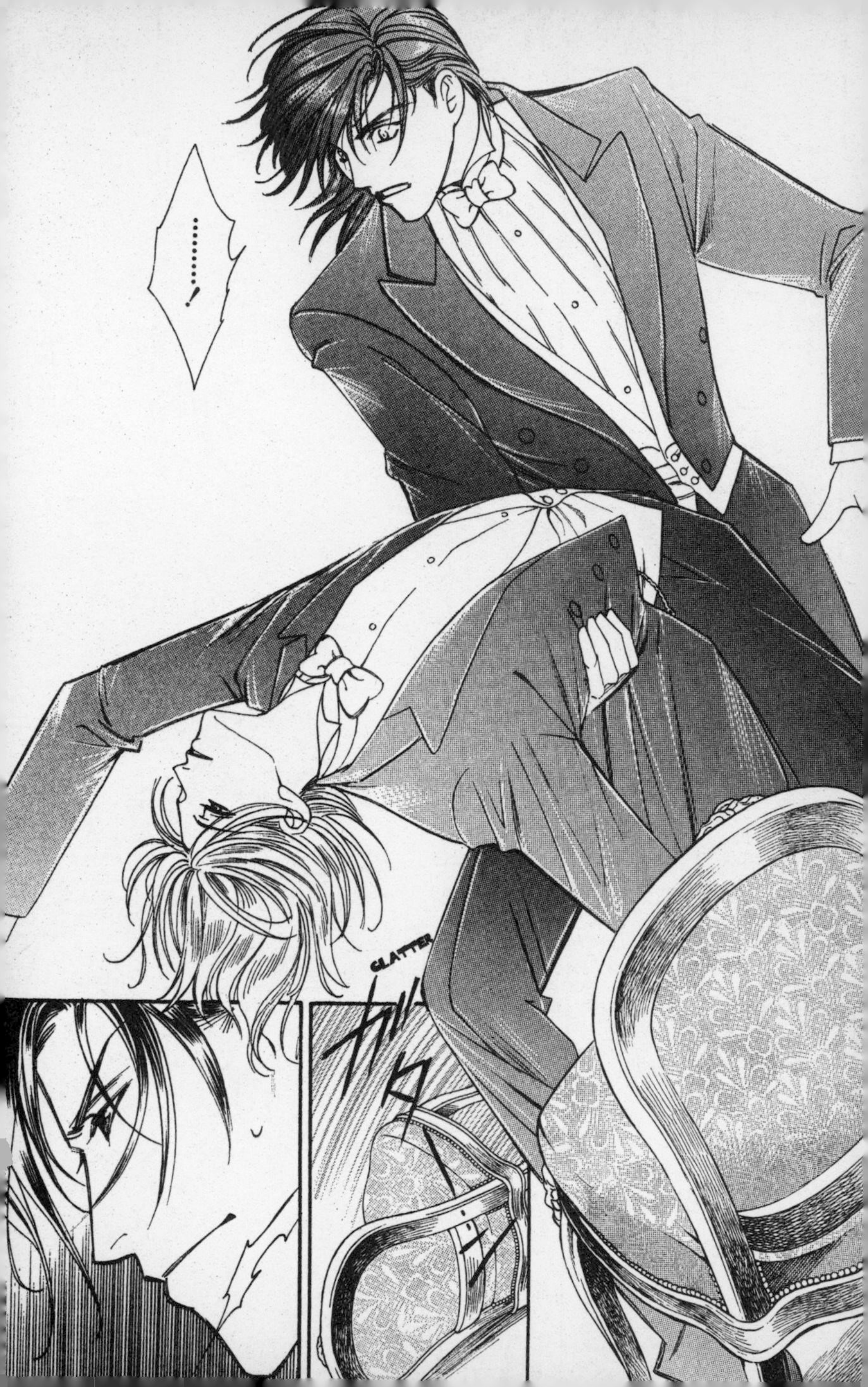
......!
CLATTER

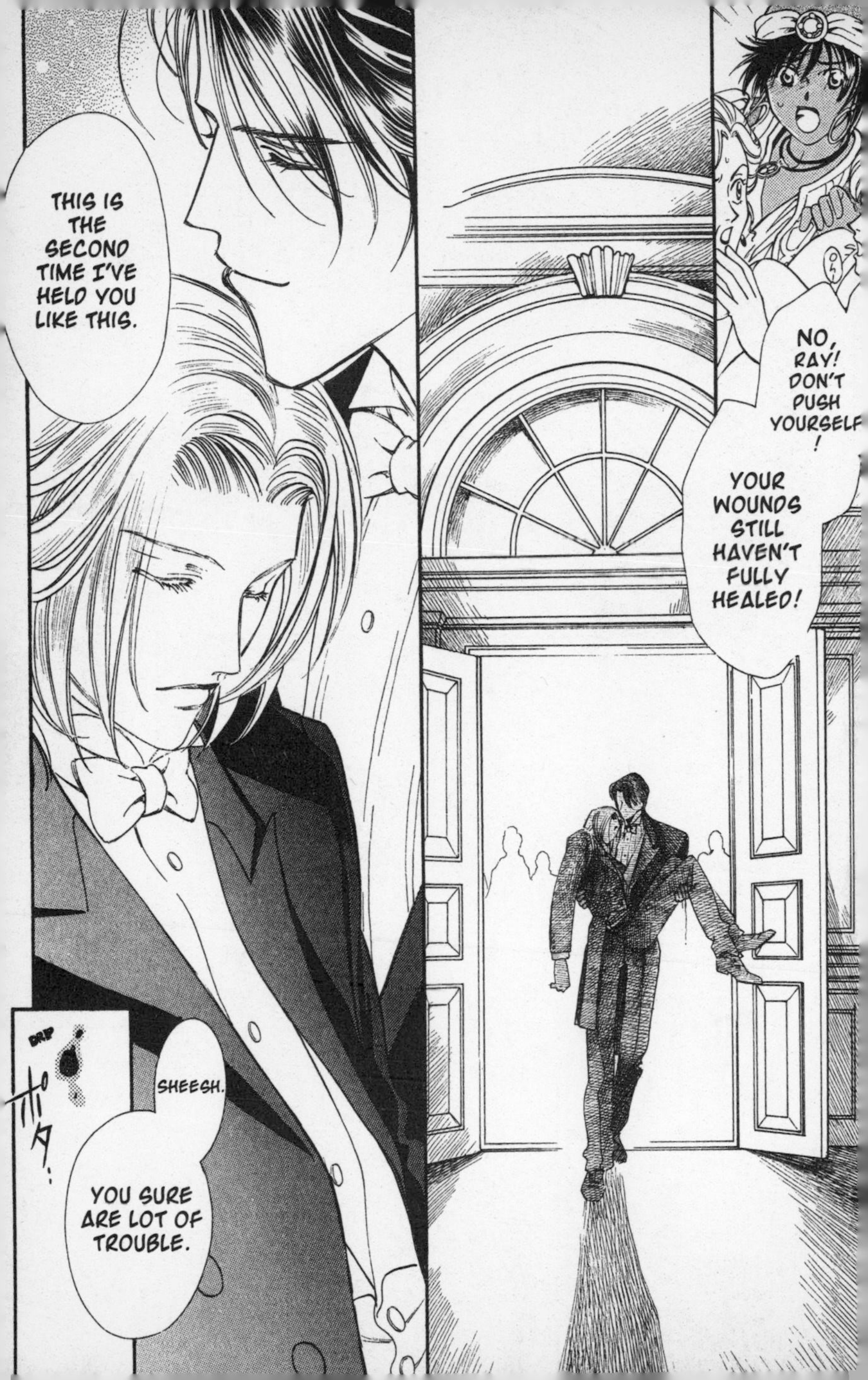
NO, RAY! DON'T PUSH YOURSELF!
YOUR WOUNDS STILL HAVEN'T FULLY HEALED!
THIS IS THE SECOND TIME I'VE HELD YOU LIKE THIS.
DRIP
SHEESH.
YOU SURE ARE LOT OF TROUBLE.

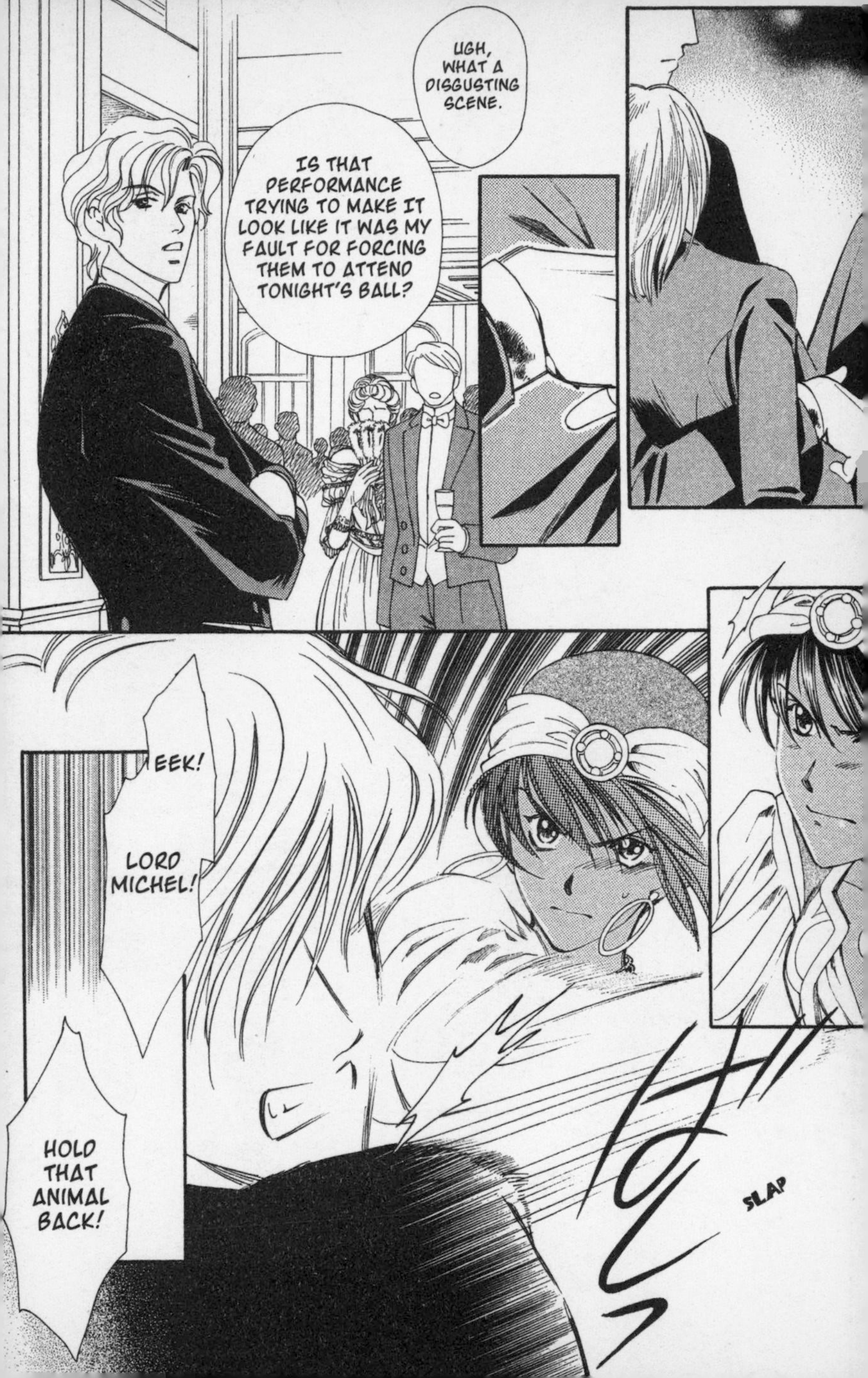
UGH, WHAT A DISGUSTING SCENE.
IS THAT PERFORMANCE TRYING TO MAKE IT LOOK LIKE IT WAS MY FAULT FOR FORCING THEM TO ATTEND TONIGHT'S BALL?
SLAP
EEK!
LORD MICHEL!
HOLD THAT ANIMAL BACK!

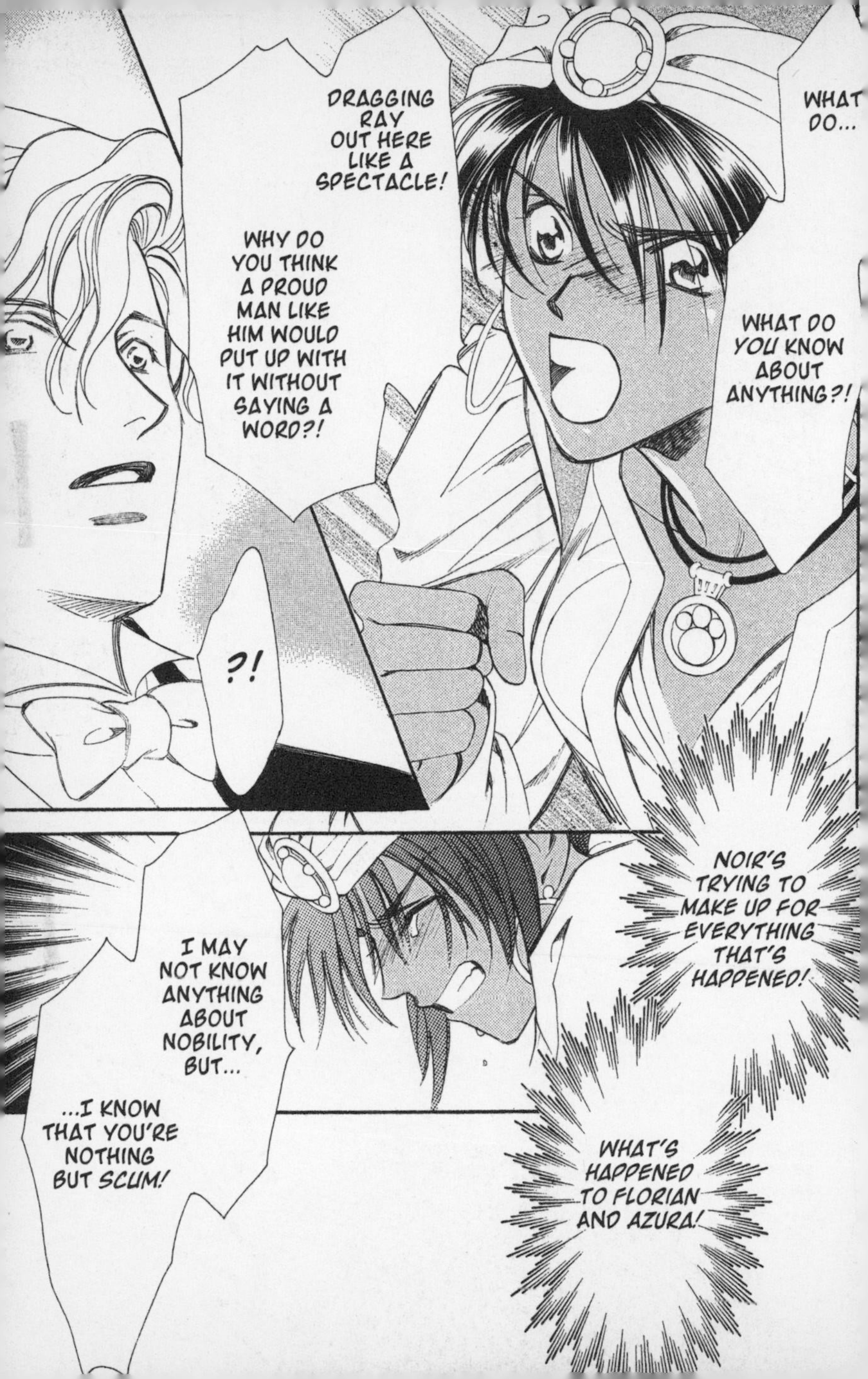

WHAT DO...
WHAT DO YOU KNOW ABOUT ANYTHING?!
DRAGGING RAY OUT HERE LIKE A SPECTACLE!
WHY DO YOU THINK A PROUD MAN LIKE HIM WOULD PUT UP WITH IT WITHOUT SAYING A WORD?!
?!
NOIR'S TRYING TO MAKE UP FOR EVERYTHING THAT'S HAPPENED!
WHAT'S HAPPENED TO FLORIAN AND AZURA!
I MAY NOT KNOW ANYTHING ABOUT NOBILITY, BUT...
...I KNOW THAT YOU'RE NOTHING BUT SCUM!

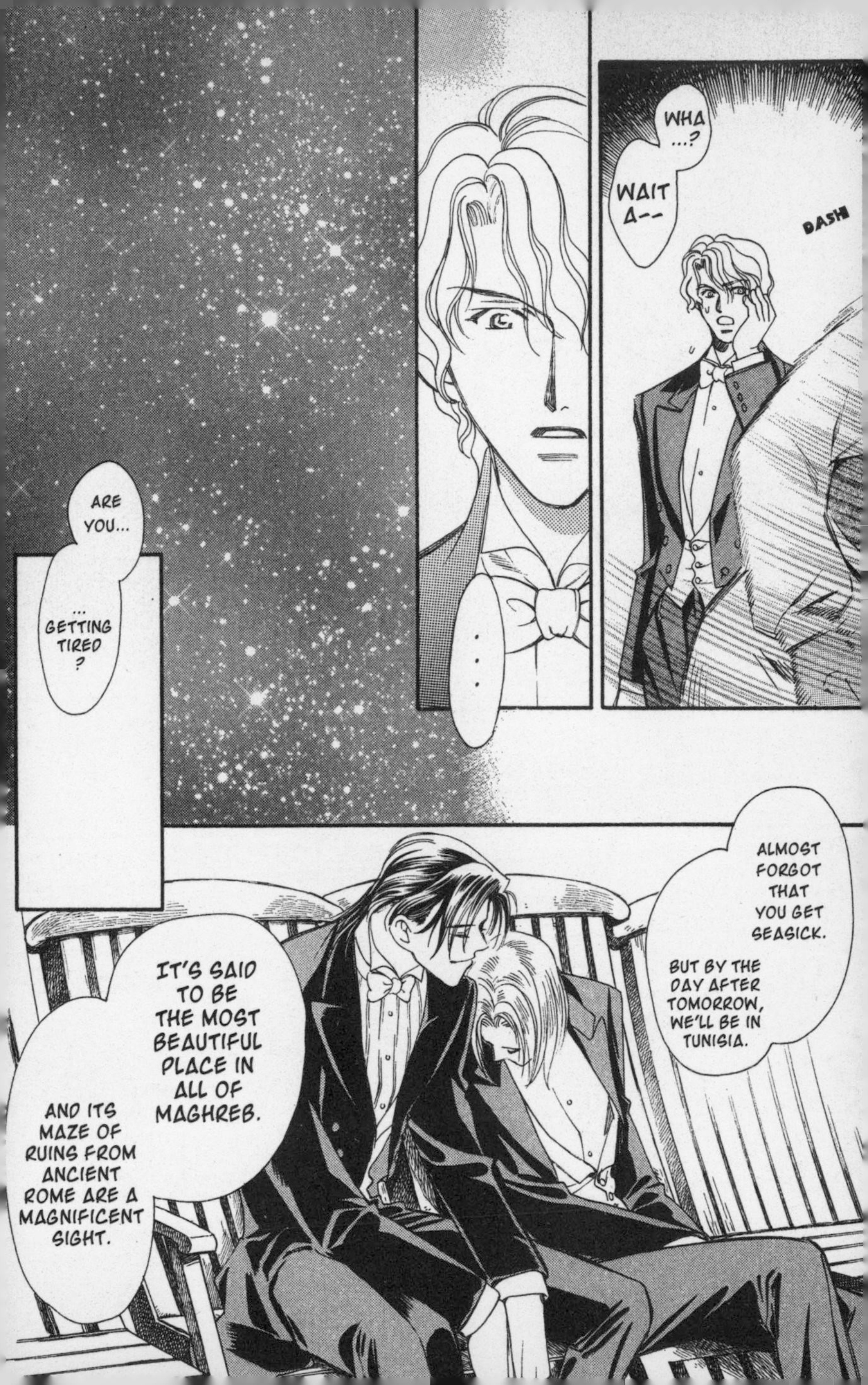

WHA ...?
WAIT A--
DASH
...
ARE YOU...
...GETTING TIRED?
ALMOST FORGOT THAT YOU GET SEASICK.
BUT BY THE DAY AFTER TOMORROW, WE'LL BE IN TUNISIA.
IT'S SAID TO BE THE MOST BEAUTIFUL PLACE IN ALL OF MAGHREB.
AND ITS MAZE OF RUINS FROM ANCIENT ROME ARE A MAGNIFICENT SIGHT.

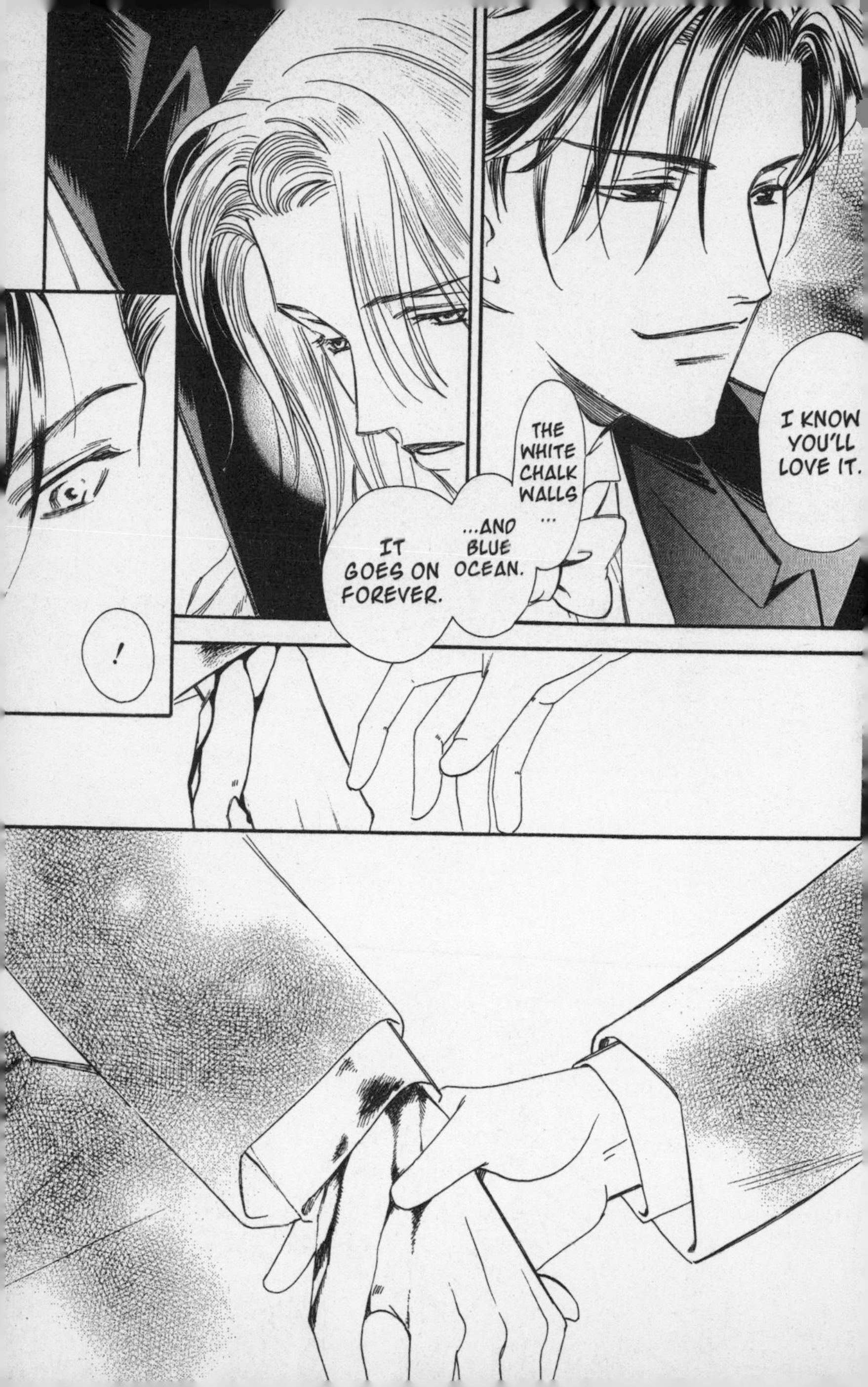
I KNOW YOU'LL LOVE IT.
THE WHITE CHALK WALLS ...
...AND BLUE OCEAN.
IT GOES ON FOREVER.
!

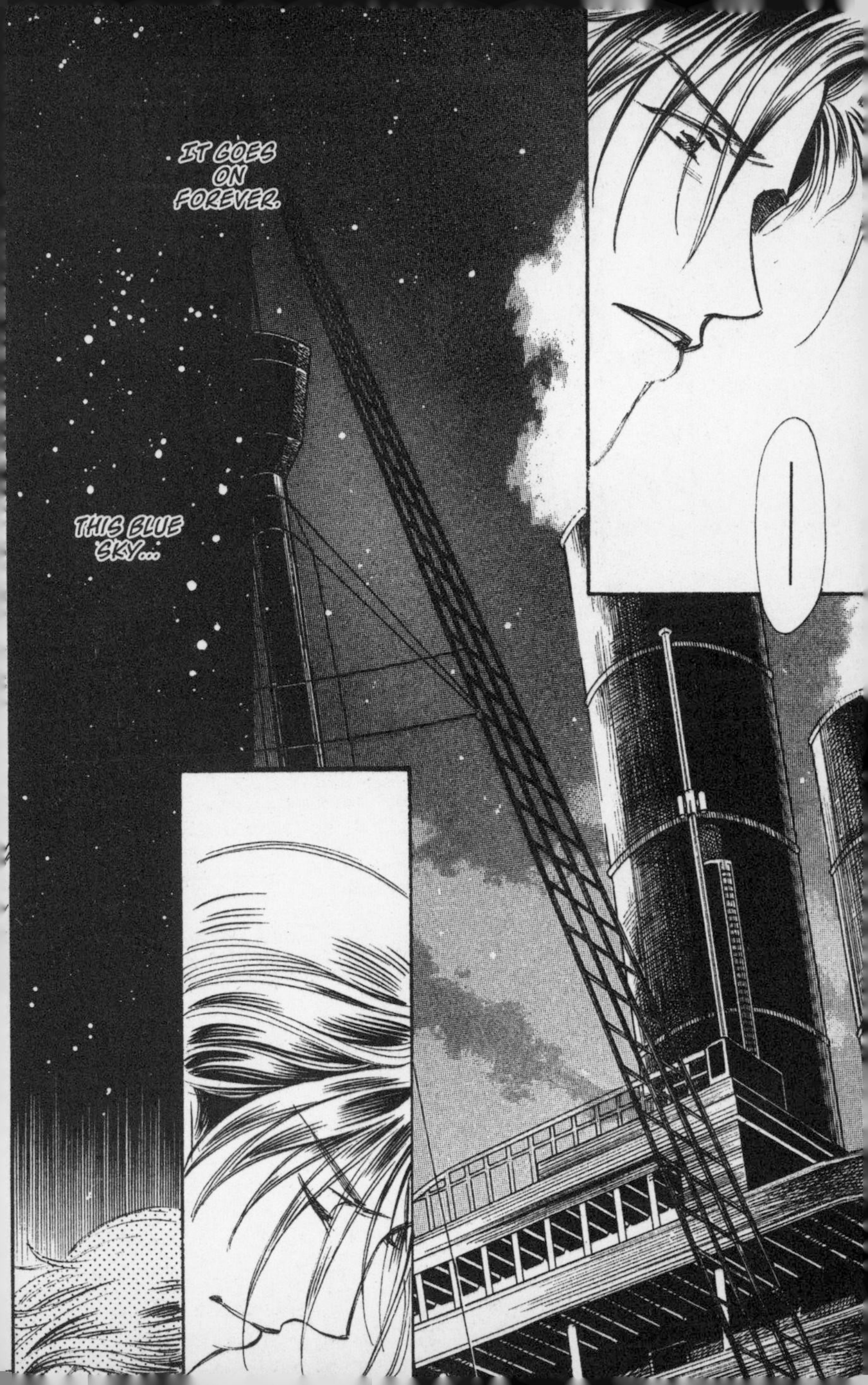
IT GOES ON FOREVER.
THIS BLUE SKY...

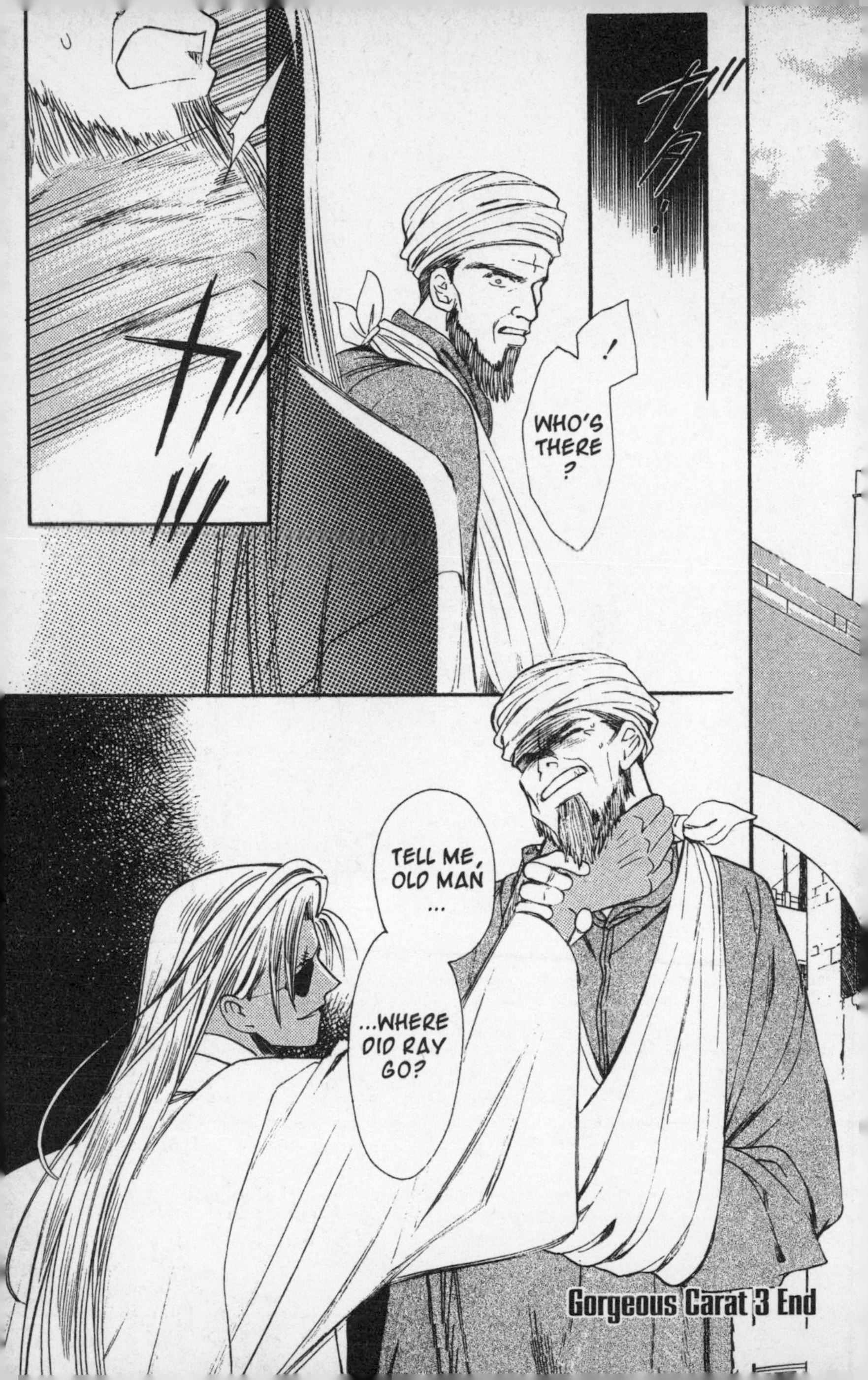
!
WHO'S THERE?
TELL ME, OLD MAN ...
...WHERE DID RAY GO?
Gorgeous Carat 3 End

Post script

Thank you very much for picking up this book.

I've really stretched out the Maghreb arc, but thanks for staying with us until the end.

I feel it's obvious how my passion for the characters is showing more and more, but when it comes to the story's main character, Noir, it's more of an extension of myself in a way. (I don't smoke cigars, though...) He's sort of like the ideal man I imagine with all the good points.

It's actually quite rare for me to come up with a character that makes me happy just drawing him.

I wasn't being sadistic or anything, but...this volume's story was certainly cruel to Noir-kun. But because he's such a strong and positive character, all the dark and gloomy atmosphere doesn't seem to crush him.

I feel like the story is flowing on without any of my intentions in mind, so as to where this story is going to go, I plan on just continuing to ride the wave and enjoy it.

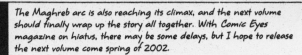

The Maghreb arc is also reaching its climax, and the next volume should finally wrap up the story all together. With *Comic Eyes* magazine on hiatus, there may be some delays, but I hope to release the next volume come spring of 2002.

I hope everything works out well with that.
Things haven't been going as well as they could be but I can't just pity myself all day. I'm always finding some way to escape, and end up doing just whatever I want, rather than NEED to do.

If you work hard enough, what you want will come true someday. The only hard part is trying to figure out how to maintain that mindset.

Sometimes, in order to keep my aspirations strong, I try working hard while munching on my favorite food, beef fillet.

Should I be worried about Mad Cow disease?

And now I'd like to take the time to acknowledge my great assistants that help me through the creation of this book: Naoko Nakatsuji-san, Izumi Hijiri-san, Miyakoshi Wagusa-san, Hondou Makoto-san, Kazuki Mari-san, Fuyutsuki Mitsuru-san, Iwahashi Mikiko-san, Wakimura Yasuko-san, Mizutani Fuka-san, and my chief assistant, Oda Ryoka. I'm so sorry for making you endure the many trials I put you through. Thank you once again. Seriously!

Also, my manager, Ohara-sama. Thank you so much for all the wonderful catch copies. Even now, I can't express my gratitude.

And of course, thank you, all of my wonderful readers who are now reading this book! I hope I didn't let any of you down! And please feel free to send me any feedback you have.

I hope to see you all again in the next volume.

2001.11 Higuri You

FOR MORE INFO ON BLU BOOKS, CHECK:
HTTP://WWW.BLUMANGA.COM

IN THE NEXT VOLUME

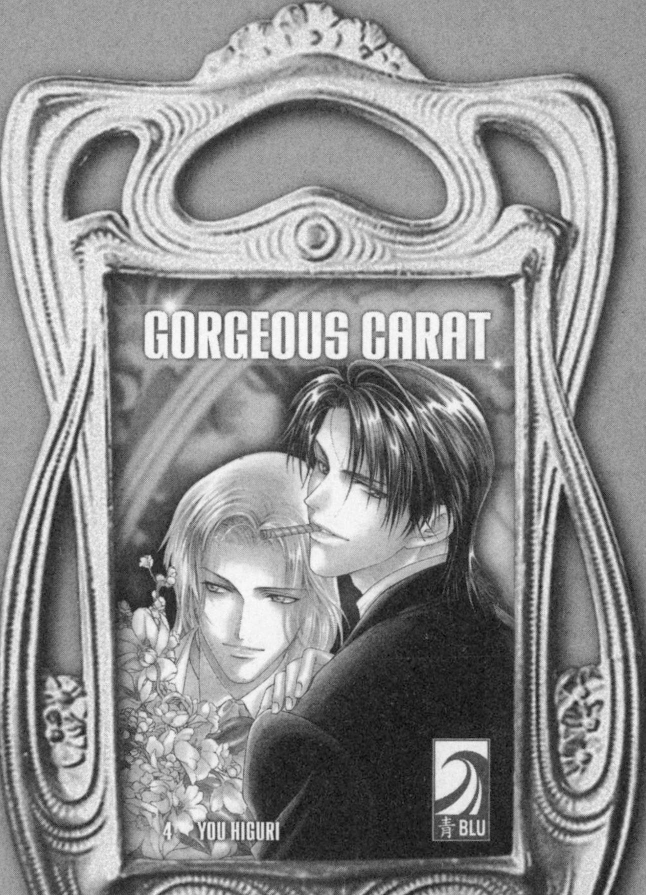
GORGEOUS CARAT
4 YOU HIGURI
青 BLU

As Florian struggles to recover his sanity, Noir and the gang head to Tunisia to locate the lost treasure of the Knights Templar. Meanwhile, an angry Azura is hot on their heels with revenge on his mind. Secrets and mysteries are finally revealed in the fourth and final volume of Gorgeous Carat.

GORGEOUS CARAT VOL. 3
Created by You Higuri

Translation by Katherine Schilling

© 2001 You Higuri. All Rights Reserved.
First published in Japan by HOME-SHA INC., Tokyo, Japan.

English text copyright ©2006 BLU

ISBN: 1-59816-104-0

First Printing: October 2006
10 9 8 7 6 5 4 3 2
Printed in the USA

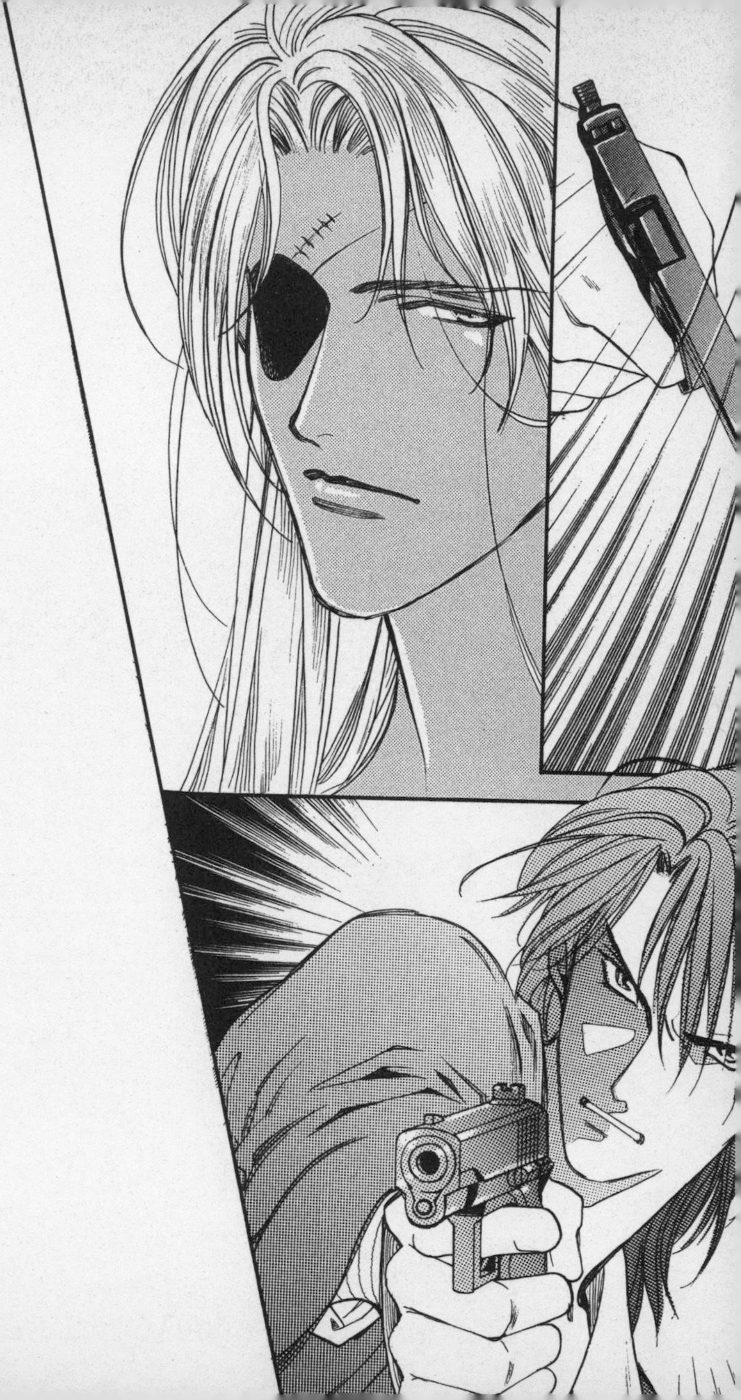

Where schoolwork is the last thing you need to worry about.

When Keita is suddenly admitted to the prestigous all-boys school, Bell Liberty Academy, his life is about to get turned upside down! Filled with the hottest cast of male students ever put together, this highly anticipated boys' love series drawn by You Higuri (*Gorgeous Carat*) is finally here!

GAKUEN HEAVEN

青 BLU

YOU HIGURI   SPRAY

Hisae Shino is an unemployed anime voice actor who also has to support his son Nakaya, a sophomore in high school. The sweet and naive Shino will take any job he can get—even if it means boys' love radio dramas! When he gets paired up with the supercool Tenryuu, the two bond...to a degree that Shino never intended!

A Young Prince Trains For Battle But Instead Learns To Love!

WHEN CHRIS AND ZEKE MEET IN MILITARY SCHOOL, THEY EMBARK ON A LIFE-LONG RELATIONSHIP FRAUGHT WITH DANGER, TREACHERY, AND ABOVE ALL, LOVE.

BLACK KNIGHT IS A SWEEPING ROMANTIC FANTASY EPIC ABOUT THE RELATIONSHIP BETWEEN A DASHING PRINCE AND HIS GUARDSMAN, WITH PLENTY OF SWORD ACTION TO KEEP BOYS' LOVE FANS ENTICED AND ENTHRALLED!

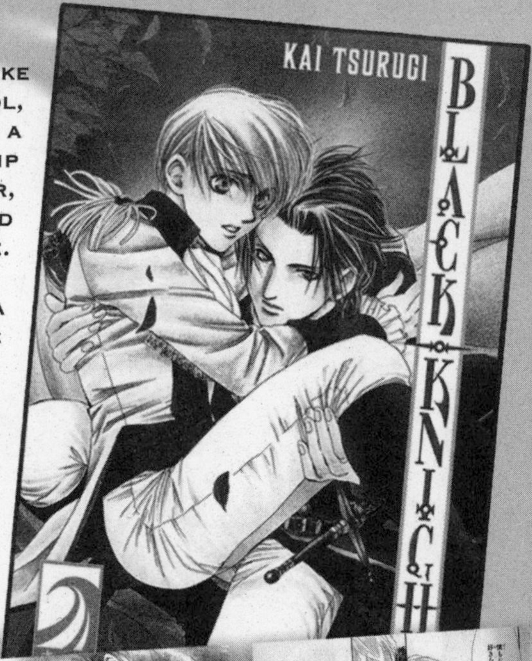
KAI TSURUGI
BLACK KNIGHT

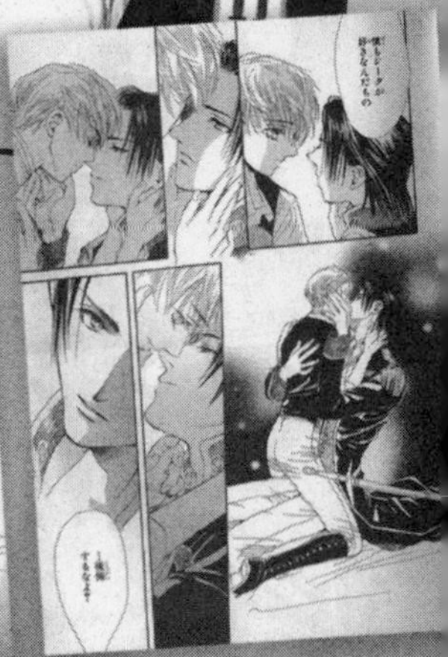

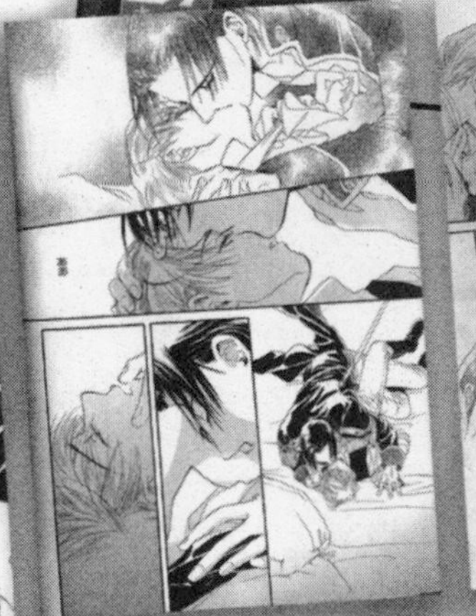

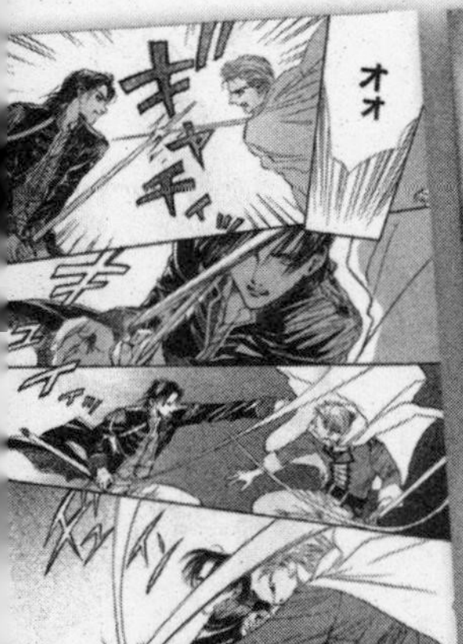
オオ

OR MATURE AUDIENCES ONLY

Price: $9.99

vailable in stores July 2006

or information about where to buy BLU MANGA titles, visit www.BLUMANGA.com

M MATURE

青 BLU

Follow the love lives of Izumi, Takamiya and others as they are brought together at a host club called "Blue Boy" that specializes in high-class male escorts. Love lines cross, chances are lost and found, and hearts are broken in this fan favorite boys' love classic.

LOVE MODE 1

BLU

In stores now! $9.99

Liberté! Égalité! Fraternité!...and Love!

Become enraptured by a thrilling and erotic tale of an unlikely pair of lovers during the tumultuous times of the French Revolution. Freed from a high-class brothel, noble-born Jacques becomes a servant in Gerard's house. First seduced by his new master's library, Jacques begins to find himself falling for the man as well...but can their love last in the face of the chaos around them?

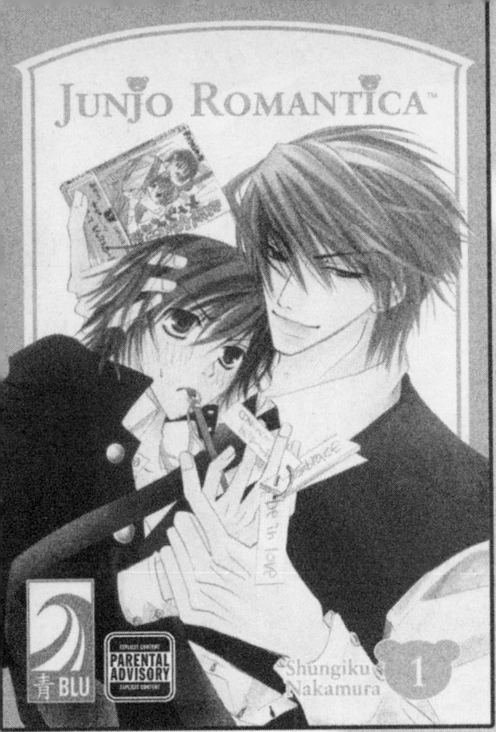

JUNJO ROMANTICA™
PARENTAL ADVISORY
青 BLU
Shungiku Nakamura
1

This "Pure Romance" is anything but pure...

Passing his college entrance exams isn't the only thing Misaki has to worry about! Being romanced by a suave and older tutor is the concern considering his tutor is his brother's best friend and a famous porn novelist who has a habit of throwing Misaki into his latest books. Suddenly Misaki's "normal" life transforms into an odd journey filled with unfamiliar feelings and non-stop insanity.

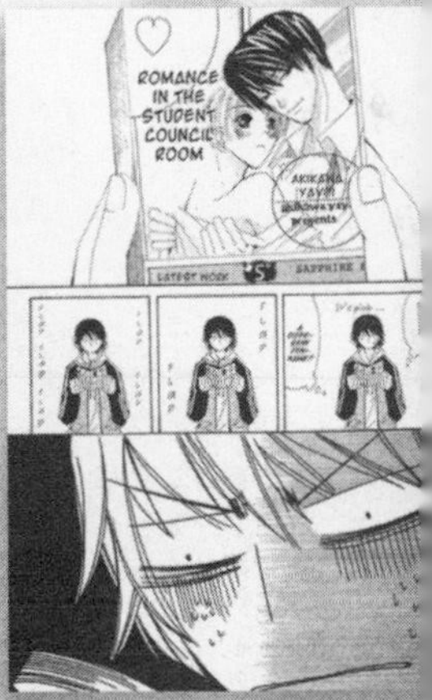

ROMANCE IN THE STUDENT COUNCIL ROOM

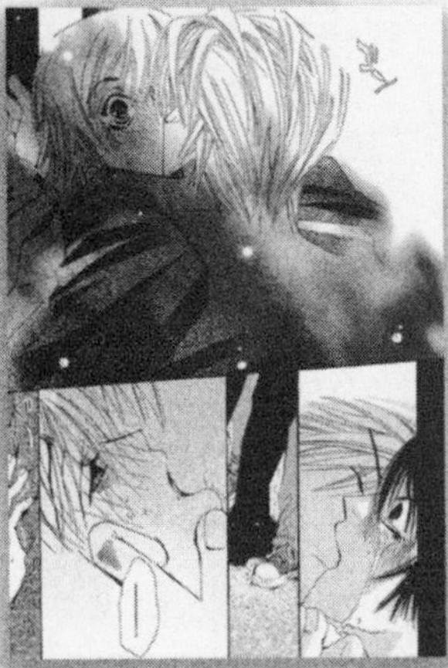

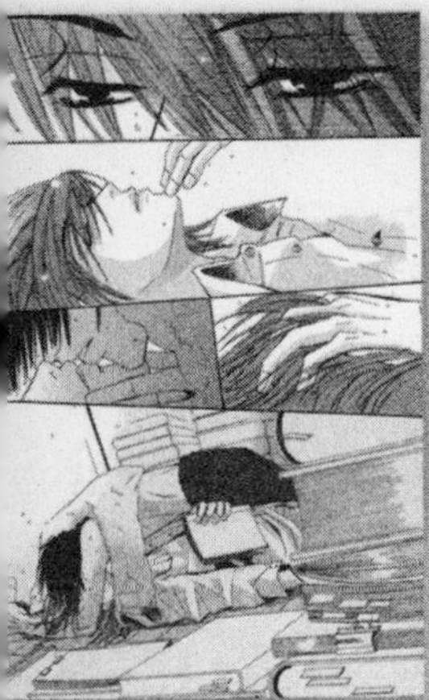

FOR MATURE AUDIENCES ONLY

Price: $9.99
Available Now!

For information about where to buy BLU MANGA titles, visit www.BLUMANGA.com

M MATURE

青 BLU

stop

blu manga are published in the original japanese format

go to the other side and begin reading